THE WARRIOR TRADITION
IN MODERN AFRICA

INTERNATIONAL STUDIES
IN
SOCIOLOGY AND SOCIAL ANTHROPOLOGY

General Editor
K. ISHWARAN

VOLUME XXIII

THE WARRIOR TRADITION
IN MODERN AFRICA

LEIDEN
E. J. BRILL
1977

THE WARRIOR TRADITION
IN MODERN AFRICA

EDITED BY

ALI A. MAZRUI

LEIDEN
E. J. BRILL
1977

ISBN 90 04 05646 7

CONTENTS

ACKNOWLEDGEMENTS

ALTHOUGH I have been thinking about the warrior tradition for a number of years now, and have published a book about Uganda which touches upon that subject, it required an invitation from Professor K. Ishwaran to awaken me to the need for a collection of essays by different authors on that subject. Dr. Ishwaran invited me to edit a special issue of the *Journal of Asian and African Studies*, and I chose for my theme "The Warrior Tradition in Modern Africa." I am indebted to him for serving as a catalyst, and I remain gratified by the positive response I received from a number of distinguished scholars who agreed to contribute to the collection. Those contributions are now herewith presented between these covers.

My own work on the subject has benefitted from a wider project on social and political violence in Africa, which has received generous support from the International Development Research Centre in Canada, the Institute of Development Studies at the University of Sussex, and the Rackham School of Graduate Studies at the University of Michigan.

For editorial and secretarial assistance this collection of essays has also benefitted from support given by the Center for Afro-American and African Studies at the University of Michigan and from the Department of Political Science of the same university.

With characteristic good humour my Secretary, Mrs. Valerie Ward, coped not only with preparing for publication some of the essays in this collection but also with the considerable body of correspondence connected with the enterprise. In these tasks she was often assisted by my wife, Molly. The collection as a whole has profited from this administrative and secretarial partnership.

ALI A. MAZRUI
Editor

Introduction

ALI A. MAZRUI

The University of Michigan, Ann Arbor, U.S.A.

ONE OLD DEBATE—emanating from European cultural arrogance —has now subsided. This is the debate concerning the issue of whether Africa has a history at all. Even the Regius Professor of Modern History at Oxford University may now wish to re-examine his notorious assertion:

> "Perhaps in the future, there will be some African history... But at present there is none; there is only the history of Europeans in Africa. The rest is darkness... and darkness is not a subject of history."[1]

But the argument that African history is only a "history of Europeans in Africa" can take a more subtle and dangerous form. In this latter form an analyst could indeed concede that Africa has a history independently of the Europeans—and go on to assert that the impact of Europe on Africa in a few decades has virtually obliterated almost all traces of that history in the lives and customs of the people. By this argument less than a century of European influence was enough to put an end to two or more millenia of African tradition and experience.

This blindness to the *continuities* of African history is more characteristic of political scientists and economists than of social anthropologists and historians. Among political scientists the study of "modernization" until recently was characterized by a belief that the changes inaugurated by the colonial experience had their own momentum, were desirable and were almost irreversible. Political scientists were so preoccupied with studying political change that they virtually forgot how to study political continuity.

Economists have similarly been relatively indifferent to the continuities of traditional economic behaviour in Africa. One five-year plan after another has floundered on this insensitivity to sociological and historical realities. And one economic projection after another has revealed that the study of development requires more than an expertise in the process of change; it also needs an understanding of the nature of resilience. Future targets can only be approximated after adequate allowance has been made for past origins.

The warrior tradition is of course only one aspect of African historical tradition. Even in its purely historical context in African societies of the past

---

1   Hugh Trevor-Roper, "The Rise of Christian Europe" *Listener* (London), November 28, 1933, p. 871.

this tradition is only just beginning to be studied in depth. African military history—how traditional African states fought their wars and with what forms of organization—is still an underdeveloped field of study. But there is a growing interest in military history among West African historians, and increasingly among Eastern African scholars as well.

Clearly African societies varied enormously in military organization. Considerable additional work needs to be done if we are to grasp the range fully. *This collection of essays is primarily interested in the meeting point between culture, war and politics. The warrior tradition is precisely that meeting point.*

The warrior tradition is that sub-system of values and institutionalized expectations which define the military role of the individual in the defence of his society, the martial criteria of adulthood, and the symbolic obligations of manhood in time of political and military stress.

At one level the warrior tradition is a major link between the individual and society. It signifies the readiness of the eligible individual to sacrifice his life for his society. At another level the warrior tradition links each household with the wider community. In defending his own cattle or his own women from external raiders, the warrior is often fulfilling a *military* obligation as real as participating in a regular army.

The warrior tradition is also a link between culture and war. In some African societies a young man is not eligible for marriage unless he has risked his life in a martial endeavour. When reduced to precise evidence, the custom could mean that no man is really a man unless he has at least engaged in a mortal duel—and killed his opponent. In conditions of normative fluidity what is murder to, say, the Kenya police may be a prelude to matrimony through the eyes of the Kenya tribesman. Armed struggle, dance, romantic courting, betrothal, the right to sire children, protecting cattle and status in the community can all become one inter-related subsystem of values.

Dent Ocaya-Lakidi's, Judith Lynne Hanna's and Mazrui's essays in this collection have emphasized this cultural context of the warrior tradition. The linkages between culture and the warrior tradition encompass *means of production* (land and animals), *sexuality* (virility and marriage), *religion* (invocation of the supernatural), *aesthetics* (dance and song) and *political culture* (system of authority and allegiance).

The link with political culture in turn raises the whole issue of the origins of the state in Africa and how it relates to military factors in historical evolution. With the coming of statehood the warrior tradition becomes absorbed into a larger complex of military organization. Sometimes the individual warrior becomes no more than a cog in a military machine. But the warrior tradition as a sub-system of norms and perspectives may continue to condition military behaviour inspite of the enlargement of organization scale. G. N. Uzoigwe's, Warren Weinstein's and Mazrui's essays in the first section of this collection, touch upon some of the issues which thus link statehood with military history.

But when all is said and done war is primarily a theatre of *violence*. The warrior tradition has to be seen as in part a tradition for legitimizing certain forms of violence. Claude E. Welch Jr. analyzes in both historical and political perspectives four forms of political violence. He examines these in terms of their association with the warrior, the rebel, the guerrilla and the putchist in Africa's experience. Victor C. Uchendu looks at violence in terms which go beyond politics, the warrior tradition and collective purpose, and raises instead questions about aggressivity in relation to culture. Mazrui's essay on "The Warrior Tradition and the Masculinity of War" asks whether there is a link between the fact that most soldiers are men and the fact that most crimes of physical violence are committed by men. "Is this link between *Warriorhood* and *Mafiahood* accidental? Or are there organic interconnections between them?"

Aidan Southall is dismayed by the warrior tradition. He is not convinced that the warrior tradition served Africa well before colonization, and is not convinced either that it has much relevance to contemporary African realities. Southall's position serves as a useful word of caution against romanticizing the warrior tradition. Southall is also sounding a warning against carrying too far the search for precolonial historical continuities in contemporary African experience.

On the other hand, those who are less sceptical about the warrior tradition may be convinced that even the ordinary, rurally-recruited guerrilla fighter in the remote areas of modern Zimbabwe, Namibia or Angola has probably often perceived combat and war in terms which have been influenced by his ethno-cultural universe. And that universe does bear the imprint of precolonial as well as colonial continuities.

Section IV of this collection deals in part with this issue. Modern liberation struggles have had points of contact with the tradition of African primary resistance going back to the nineteenth century and beyond. Mazrui's essay in this section compares the influence of Mahatma Gandhi and his strategy of *passive resistance*, the impact of the warrior tradition on African *primary resistance*, and the influence of Marxism on *revolutionary resistance*.

M. Louise Pirouet reflects on the specific experiences of the Anya Nya in the Sudan and the Mau Mau war in Kenya. She examines the conditions which give rise to political commitment and armed resistance, and explores some of the experiments in counter-insurgency devised by the governments of the Sudan and of colonial Kenya when faced with armed insurrection.

But war—especially in contemporary Africa—has broad international implications even when it seems to be primarily domestic. The civil wars of Nigeria (1967–1970) and Angola (1975–1976) illustrated this even better than did the civil war in the Sudan (1956–1972). J. Isawa Elaigwu takes on the challenge of examining the linkages between domestic politics and diplomatic intrigues, between internal factors and external repercussions. He examines the civil wars of Nigeria and Angola in this broad perspective, and draws conclusions which may have relevance for other areas of civil strife in Africa in the years ahead. Elaigwu's essay is not explicitly on the warrior tradition but it provides the meeting point between war, politics and modern diplomacy.

All collections of essays are exposed to the charge that they have not covered enough of the field they ostensibly sought to examine.

Secondly, all collections of essays are inevitably guilty of imbalance. Even the areas which are covered are not necessarily dealt with in correct proportion.

This collection has not been able to escape these two pitfalls. In a work of multiple authors, with different research interests and different intellectual perspectives, imbalance is natural. What ought to be remembered is that the same imbalance can sometimes be academically rewarding. No art critic today is likely to affirm that symmetry is the be-all and end-all of aesthetic excellence. Similarly, evaluators of works of scholarship may sometimes have to moderate their own preoccupation with symmetry. In trying to promote further understanding of the nature of the warrior tradition in modern Africa this editor has sought to bring together not only perspectives explicitly on the warrior, but also intimately related perspectives on violence, aggression, sexual division of labour, guerrilla struggle, revolution, manhood, and the diplomacy of warfare.

In this collection the warrior is in one sense overshadowed by some of the bigger issues examined by the authors. But in another sense the warrior tradition underlies all those other issues, linking precolonial combat to modern warfare, mediating between culture and politics, affirming the individual's obligations to society, defining the functions of men and women in the social order, and constantly drawing and redrawing the boundaries between war and peace in human experience.

This is a large claim to make for the warrior tradition. But then, the warrior is a large subject in Africa's history.

SECTION I:
THE WARRIOR AND THE STATE

Armed Kinsmen and the Origins of the State

An Essay in Philosophical Anthropology

ALI A. MAZRUI

The University of Michigan, Ann Arbor, U.S.A.

I N A BOOK about the role of political violence in some traditional African communities, Eugene Victor Walter adapted in a new way the categories suggested by E. R. Service to illustrate the nature of fundamental social organization. A "*band*" is regarded as the most rudimentary political community, involving literal face to face relationships. A band may have a leader, but there are no specialized political roles. A piece of land may be jointly exploited, or hunting may be jointly organized, but collective life is based on collective decisions and not on formal roles and carefully differentiated functions.

A "*tribe*" is a larger political community involving more than one residential unit. Walter limits the use of the term "tribe" strictly to what others have regarded as only one kind of tribal society—the stateless tribal society.

> "Lacking officers and specialized political roles, it is integrated by segmentary lineages, clans, age grades, religious associations, or other corporate sodalities, which dramatize relationships that extend beyond the local units occupied with herding or agriculture, and they live in neolithic style... Bands and tribes are egalitarian societies, which shun formal distinctions of rank, but all the others are organized hierarchically."[1]

Walter's third type of political community is a "*chiefdom*", where the notion of a central focus of authority is finally institutionalized. The chief's functions, rights, privileges, and obligations are carefully defined and often limited. A chief organizes the labour of his people for public tasks, and is in charge of collecting revenue and distributing the wealth of his society, as well as of organizing and co-ordinating the functions of arbitration, collaboration, and conflict-resolution in that society.

Walter then passes on to a "*state*", an entity more complex than a chiefdom. The state has a greater degree of centralization, role specialization, and an emergent professionalization of certain services. But even more fundamental

---

1 Eugene Victor Walter, *Terror and Resistance: A Study of Political Violence, with Case Studies of Some Primitive African Communities* (London and New York: Oxford University Press, 1969) pp. 57–58. Walter was adapting E.R. Service, *Primitive Social Organization* (New York, 1962).

than the difference in scale and complexity between a chiefdom and a state is
the difference in the organization of purposeful social coercion.

> "What distinguishes a state from a chiefdom is the nature and means of coercion author-
> ized and exercised in the political community. In contrast to a chief, who can mobilize
> an armed force if necessary, the head of the state claims the legitimate monopoly of force
> and commands a special body of men organized to use it."[2]

Walter's categories, though open to challenge in some important respects,
have decisive advantages in trying to understand the nature of political organization *in Africa*. But that may also be the disadvantage of the categories.
Bands, tribes, and chiefdoms are less fundamental to political organization in
Europe, North America, and Latin America than they are to Africa and to
island societies in different parts of the world. Asia still has bands, tribes, and
chiefdoms, but even in Asia these are less basic to the lives of the great majority
of people than they are in the African continent.

In modern terms, Walter's category of "the state" is the most universal.
We shall have to return to this as a special kind of polity, and estimate in what
way the kinship factor remains pertinent to this level of political organization.

Nevertheless, in their very primordial implications, the other three categories put forward by Walter and Service do provide us with indicators about
the origins of human organization, and the degree to which the political functions of man might have emerged out of roles which were originally those of an
extended family.

What may be illuminating here is to relate Walter's four categories of
band, tribe, chiefdom, and state to another set of categories—society, nation,
and state. Again the state provides the element of overlapping universality in
modern terms between these two categories. The state is the most governmen-
tally oriented of all forms of political organization. At least to that extent, the
state may also be the most political of all forms of human communities.

The question which arises is whether the state is also the least kinship
oriented of all the categories we have mentioned. When the polity becomes the
state, has it ceased to be an extended family? And how does all this development
relate to the phenomenon of division of labour, both inter-sexual and intra-
sexual?

Two forms of survival have been at stake in the history of human collec-
tivization—economic survival and military survival. We use economic here in
the most basic sense—the organization of resources of livelihood and their
exploitation for human purposes. The quest for economic survival was a major
aspect behind the origins of society; the quest for military survival constituted
part of the origins of the state. It is too often assumed that politics and economics have a special intimacy, that man is a political animal mainly because he
has economic needs.

In fact, man was an economic agent before the polity as a distinctive organization came into being. Families had to cultivate land and bands had to

---

2   Walter, *Ibid.*, p. 59.

organize for hunting animals, even in situations where no political organizations or distinct political processes were discernible. Even the pre-political man was at the same time an economic agent. The real push towards the politicization of man lay not in economic but in military considerations. The processes of politicization and militarization were often intimately and mutually reinforcing. One of the great paradoxes of the growth of statehood in Europe was the emergence of the doctrine that the military must be apolitical. It may indeed be true that the culmination of statehood must ultimately lie in a viable divorce between politics and militarism; but this is compatible with the proposition that the very origins of political organization lay in military consideration. Perhaps the basic transition is from the warfare polity to the welfare polity— and underlying that transition is the current of kinship as a system of political symbols.

Kinship and Society

We might ask ourselves which of Walter's four categories of human organization are in fact prepolitical, in spite of Walter's own assumptions that they are all different types of political organization. It is certainly arguable that the "band" is a prepolitical society, organized primarily for economic survival. In the history of political theory there has been a debate as to whether such bands were units of convenience or units of consanguinity. In a way it was the debate which John Locke had with Filmer. Did society originate in the free consent of individuals previously independent, as Locke maintained, or in the natural authority of a father over his children and children's children, as Filmer claimed? Filmer's position was in fact better anthropology, even if poorer philosophy, than that of Locke. There is far more concrete evidence in favour of the family, rather than the individual, as the basis of primordial society.

Filmer's own version of the family may have been excessively oriented towards a patriarchal organization. One does not have to believe in patriarchal authority in order to see kinship as part of the original basis of society. The organization of that kinship need not have involved an omnipotent father figure, exercising dictatorial authority over younger males, women and children. What is basic here is simply the distinction between society as an aggregation of families and society as a collection of individuals. Filmer was nearer to the former familial interpretation of the origins of society; Locke was nearer the latter individualist version. And it was Filmer, rather than Locke, who had anthropologists on his side, at least to some extent.

An additional advantage in the familial approach to the origins of society is the simple fact that it allows for a prepolitical society, before the birth of concepts such as "public purposes" and "public processes". Within relatively small scale extended families, the concept of "public" is not as yet meaningful. And we define the polity as a form of human organization large enough to allow for public functions in pursuit of collective goals. Politics is not merely the process of determining *who* gets what, when and where—but also *how*. The "how" includes the issue scale, and the extent to which collective life requires more than literal familial authority.

By the time we get to Walter's concept of the tribe, the politicization of kinship is already underway. The tribe in this sense is a stateless society, but it is not a pre-political society. On the contrary, the tribe in this sense is a social unit in which kinship ties play a particularly pronounced role in political organization.

But by this time the concept of the *warrior* has entered the scene. Politicization on this scale includes militarization. Initiation into adulthood for every young male often includes initiation into martial virtues. The organization of the functions, rights, and privileges of the warriors becomes an essential aspect of the polity. In some societies age grades come into play. Division of labour then involves not merely issues of economic survival but also issues of real or presumed military survival. There are occasions when the two are intimately intertwined. Raids for economic goods are themselves categories of military behaviour. Counter raids for cattle and sometimes women demand their own forms of military preparedness. Hobbes was right in linking the origins of political organization not only to economic competition but also to military glory. Hobbes saw in the nature of man three main causes of quarrel—"first, competition; secondly, diffidence; thirdly, glory". By diffidence, Hobbes meant the need for security. The pursuit of competitive advantage, security, and glory became central to the phenomenon of conflict itself.

> "The first maketh man invade for Gain; the second, for Safety; and the third for Reputation. The first use violence to make themselves masters of other men's persons, wives, children and cattle; the second to defend them; the third, for trifles, as a word, a smile, a different opinion, and any other sign of undervalue, either direct in their persons or by reflection in their kindred, their friends, their nation, their profession or their name."[3]

The triple quest, for competitive advantage, general security and glory, was to Hobbes a basic aspect of human nature. For us, all we claim for that triple quest is that it provides the main area of interaction between the politicization and the militarization of human society.

A long term consequence of this equation between politics and militarism was the de-politicization of the female. The exclusion of women from the commanding heights of political decisions has its origins in this equation between politics and militarism.

Culture often changes in response to technological innovations. There is one aspect of culture which has resisted the cumulative technological revolutions—the simple cultural fact that it is men who go to the battlefield to fight wars. In the days when fighting involved fact-to-face confrontations, this sexual division of labour made sense. Primordial warfare with fists, clubs, or spears gave advantage to men as the taller and more muscular members of the species. Because the men fought the wars, it was they who reaffirmed the right to decide between war and peace. Such decisions required high political authority. In a

---

3   Hobbes, *Leviathan*, Part I, Chapter 2.

sense, men became politically preeminent because they were militarily preeminent. And they became militarily preeminent because of an old factor in primordial kinship culture which gave the club or the spear to the spouse with greater muscular throwing power. It was thus that the male of the species was converted into the warrior.

Yet the technology of war has by now changed so fundamentally in technologically advanced societies that this particular division of labour needs no longer to be maintained. Intercontinental ballistic missiles require no male finger to press the button. The technology of B-52's requires no male pilot to drop the bombs. And yet the cultural equation between war and masculinity has persisted in spite of these technological revolutions. And partly because of that, the men have retained ultimate control of the polity as a whole to the present day in societies which are otherwise vastly different from each other. The warrior class remains a male class. Nations continue to send their sons to fight their wars, at least in the first instance. Even Israel makes her women equally liable to conscription without making them equally liable to service on the front line. Israel gave herself a woman prime minister—but presiding over a highly masculine cabinet, and certainly a highly masculine military establishment.[4]

Political stratification between the sexes is ultimately based on military considerations, even if political stratification within sexes is based on economic criteria. Men are above women in politics because men are warriors and not because men were in some societies the breadwinners. The role of the male as the warrior is more universal than as the breadwinner. Kinship and the polity have exerted an influence on stratification which bears a military insignia.

Kinship and Nationhood

If the aggregation of families led to the first prepolitical societies, the aggregation of small societies gradually led to the emergence of nations. In 1875 Henry Maine argued that the development of nationhood was in fact a transition from kinship to territoriality. At least in the earlier versions of his theory, Maine saw kinship in patriarchal terms. The bond of union within the group started by being a belief or fiction of common descent, and the myth of origin sacralized a common ancestor. The transition first from family to tribe, and then to nation was, in the words of Maine, "a system of concentric circles which have gradually expanded from the same point."[5]

---

4 Consult also Ali A. Mazrui, "Phallic Symbols in Politics and War: An African Perspective" (Panel on Biology and Politics) and Ali A. Mazrui, "The Militarization of Charisma" (Panel on "Political Elites") 9th World Congress of the International Political Science Association, Montreal, August 20–25, 1973. These issues are discussed in a wider international context in a book by the same author still under preparation, and provisionally entitled *A World Federation of Cultures*, sponsored by the Institute for World Order, New York, and the Carnegie Endowment for International Peace.

5 Maine, *Ancient Law*, Chapters V and VII.

Maine then discussed the transition from bonds of kinship to the boundaries of territory.

"We may bring home to ourselves the transformation of the idea in another way. England was once the country which Englishmen habited. Englishmen are now the people who inhabit England. The descendants of our forefathers keep up the tradition of kinship by calling themselves men of English race, but they tend steadily to become Americans and Australians. I do not say that the notion of consanguinity is absolutely lost; but it is extremely diluted, and quite subordinated to the newer view of the territorial constitution of nations..."[6]

Although Maine's general theory was stimulating and has to a substantial extent been vindicated by history, he grossly underestimated the continuing residual political power of kinship. Territory has not replaced kinship as a basis of allegiance; it has simply introduced a new way of defining kinship. Territoriality is an extension of the old methods by which new members of a society were absorbed by an allocation of artificial kinship roles. Territoriality provides a broader definition of kinship, but by no means supplants it.

In England kinship, real or imaginary, is still a major factor behind attitudes to policies on both immigration and emigration. The Commonwealth Immigration Act of 1968 drew a sharp distinction between citizens who could successfully claim kinship ties with people in England and those who could not. The Act was intended to regulate the flow of British Asians from East Africa, as these individuals sought to claim what would otherwise have been a natural right of access to England as the country of their citizenship. But the British concept of citizenship was pre-modern at least in the sense of clinging substantially to presumed descent as a basis for the right of access to Britain.

Nor is this merely a racial factor, though racism played a large part in the events which led to the Commonwealth Immigration Act of 1968. In 1972, with Britain's impending entry into the European Common Market, a related issue of kinship arose. Would Italians and Germans as citizens of fellow members of the European Economic Community have easier access to Britain than New Zealanders and Australians? An initial draft put before Parliament by Edward Heath's government carried implications which made Australians and New Zealanders less favoured in terms of access to Britain than citizens of the other members of the European Economic Community. The debate culminated in a defeat of the government in Parliament, to the surprise of many observers. Edward Heath's government retreated from the original formulation of the legislation, and proceeded to revise it in a manner which would restore the rights of British "kith and kin" —now citizens of other countries—to have access to Britain on special consideration. The revised Act even made it difficult for the governments of Australia and New Zealand, since it discriminated by implication between Australians and New Zealanders who were of British origin and those who were not. Both governments in the antipodes expressed some anxiety about this differential treatment of their own citizenry in terms of

---

6   Sir Henry Maine, *Lectures on the Early History of Institutions* (New York, 1875).

access to Britain. But for the time being the residual pull of kinship considerations seemed to have triumphed in England. The evidence would seem to
suggest that Sir Henry Maine was a little premature in seeing kinship as an
anachronistic factor in political allegiance. On the contrary, political phenomena which range from racism to regional integration have continued to be influenced by considerations of shared descent. Continental movements like the
European Economic Community, on one side, and the British reluctance to
use arms in overcoming Ian Smith in Rhodesia, on the other side, have all
included various degrees of presumed kinship ties.[7]

When nationality is defined in "racial" terms, the issue of presumed consanguinity asserts its immediacy. Movements in Europe like Pan-Germanism
and Pan-Slavism encompassed theories of nationhood based on shared *blood*.
In Africa, the whole theory of *apartheid* rests partly on considerations of "kith
and kin" and partly on the rationalization of cultural differentiation. In Uganda,
Field Marshal Idi Amin has sought to create a nation of black Ugandans, partly
on the grounds that black peoples are in a sense which is more than metaphorical
what Amin would call "my brothers and sisters". And in the Middle East a
whole new state was created in 1948, on the basis of shared descent from ancient Hebrews. The creation of Israel was once again an event deeply related
to the interaction between kinship and nationhood.[8]

President Idi Amin of Uganda seems to have a general theory to the effect
that people who are not prepared to mingle blood are not prepared to form a
shared political community. The sexual exclusiveness of the Asians in Uganda
prior to their expulsion led Amin to the conclusion that since Asians were not
prepared to mingle blood with black Ugandans, they were by that very reluctance unprepared to share nationhood with Ugandans. There is considerable
evidence to indicate that Amin adheres to this interpretation, and has by his
own example encouraged transethnic marriages within the country. But there
have been occasions when even he has been reported as being suspicious of
Eurafricans and Eurasians. In February 1973 *The Times* of London reported
that there were signs of "a new clampdown beginning on Eurafrican and

---

7 For a recent discussion of the supposed anachronism of kinship in British identity, consult
   Jerome Caminada, "Kith and Kin: A Myth Wearing Thin?" *The Times* (London)
   December 2, 1972.
8 For a more extensive comparison between Israel and Amin's Uganda as racially purist
   states consult Ali A. Mazrui, "Nation-Building and Race-Building: Israel and Amin's
   Uganda as Racially Purist States" (Panel on "Economy and Culture in the politics of
   Nation-Building"), 9th World Congress of the International Political Science Association,
   Montreal, August 20–25, 1973. For issues of nationhood in relation to race in Kenya,
   consult Donald Rothchild, "Kenya's Minorities and the African Crisis over Citizenship,"
   Race (London) Vol. IX, No. 4, April 1968, pp. 421–437. See also the companion piece
   by Rothchild, "Citizenship and National Integration: The Non-African Crisis in Kenya,"
   Studies in Race and Nations, Center on International Race Relations, Graduate School
   of International Studies, University of Denver, Vol. 1, Study 3, (1969–1970), 1970.

Eurasian Ugandans, whom General Amin recently described as even bigger crooks than the Asians."[9]

The link between citizenship and readiness to engage in joint military self-defence has certainly continued into the national scale of the growth of the polity. There was a time when citizenship itself could never be described as complete unless it included eligibility for military service.

> "In the primitive nation as exhibited to us by its earliest records in Greece and Rome, and in the German tribes so far as they have a common permanent head, we find political functions distributed among three differently constituted organs—the king or supreme chief, a council of subordinate chiefs or elders, and the assembly of fully qualified citizens which is ... a martial muster of the freemen in arms."[10]

In the growth of the Islamic Empire, the ultimate differentiating characteristic between fully absorbed citizens and conquered peoples was that the citizens were eligible for military service.

In Israel today the Arabs who are Israeli citizens fall short of being full citizens again by the yardstick of eligibility for military conscription. All Jewish Israelis are liable to military conscription, but not Arab Israelis. In a curious way the Arabs are second class citizens partly because the nature of a racially purist state like Israel is such that the non-Jew cannot be called upon for that ultimate sacrifice in war. Some countries have second class citizens by reducing the rights of the less privileged group; but both Israel today and Islamic states in the past had second class citizens by reducing the *obligations* of the less privileged groups.

Of all the countries in the world, perhaps the United States comes nearest to fulfilling Sir Henry Maine's criteria of territoriality as against kinship as the basis of nationhood. The mixture of nationalities and races in the composition of the population of the United States has certainly transformed the concept of "American" into a territorial concept *par excellence*. Territoriality as a basis of nationhood is even stronger in America than it is in those other immigrant countries like Australia and New Zealand. The greater mixture in the United States has oriented the history of the country precisely towards illustrating Sir Henry Maine's precept.

Even the duty to do military service in the American situation has been distinctive in being distributed not only among first class citizens, nor indeed only among citizens in lower classes, but also among resident aliens. The laws of the United States until recently allowed for the conscription of those who were territorially located in the United States, even if they had not as yet been granted citizenship, nor indeed applied for it. Even foreign students studying in

---

9   *The Times* (London) February 2, 1973. The General had presumably just been irritated by particular individuals, conceivably of mixed racial extraction, and was responding to the mood of the moment rather than to his interest in seeing black men mingle their blood with others as a form of black assertiveness.

10 Henry Sedgwick, *The Development of European Polity* (London: Macmillan and Company, 1920) p. 57.

the United States at the peak of the Vietnam War were sometimes threatened with conscription by American authorities on the basis of the laws as they then existed.

But although the United States has perhaps gone furthest in the move from kinship to territoriality, it has still retained kinship factors as a force within its political system. Again issues of race and ethnicity, taboos of intermarriage and principles governing racial descent, have all had their ultimate roots in the dominant kinship culture of white Anglo-Saxon Protestants. The impact of Anglo-Saxon kinship on other groups has ranged from a desire by Italians or Jews to shed their names in preference for Anglo-Saxon names to the whole problem of racial disparities between black and white within the American society. Sir Henry Maine has not had it all his way in the United States.

Kinship and Statehood

There is a good deal of overlap between the evolution of the polity as nation and the polity as state. And both do link up with Eugene Victor Walter's concept of the chiefdom. In some parts of the world the principle of primogeniture in the family did help to consolidate the principle of hereditary succession in the chieftainship or kingship. Primogeniture sometimes implied the right of the eldest son to inherit *the family*. Primogeniture in Japanese society certainly tended in this direction, thought the system in England narrowed itself more to the right of the eldest son to inherit the title and the lands of his father. The question of how far Japanese and British principles of monarchical succession were conditioned by the broader doctrine of primogeniture in the wider society has remained one of the more intriguing issues in the political anthropology of monarchical institutions.

But apart from the impact of the wider kinship system on monarchical principles, there was also the political role of the monarch's relatives and the role of leading aristocratic families in societies like Japan and England. The polity in Japan and England has at times been indeed a family affair at least to the extent that elite recruitment has drawn so disproportionately from a number of distinguished upper class and upper middle class families. The polity as an extended family in such situations is almost literal, in spite of the enlarged scale of political organization in a nation of fifty million and more.

The behaviour of the monarch's relatives and the leading families in Japan and England bears a strong resemblance to the style of politics in chiefdoms in traditional Africa. Certainly the history of the British monarchy until this century when the monarchy became powerless was the history of an institution subject to the pulls of relatives and distinguished families within the realm, and therefore similar in important respects to experience in chiefly polities in Africa. In the words of Schapera:

"Tribal politics is in fact made up to a considerable extent of quarrels between the chief and his near relatives, and of their intrigues against one another to command his favour...."

They are entitled by custom to advise and assist him in his conduct of public affairs, and they actively resent any failure on his part to give them what they regard as their due."[11]

The interplay between politics and militarism continues both at the level of chiefly polities and on the larger scale of imperial monarchical systems like those of Japan and Great Britain before World War II. Sons from distinguished families entered the military profession, thus partly consolidating the hold which their families already had over the political sector of the power structure in the land. The officer corps in such armies drew disproportionately from the illustrious kinship systems.

When statehood included imperial ambitions the interplay between politics and militarism was particularly strong. Again both Britain and Japan qualify in this regard. But so does Ashanti in Ghana's history. Fortes comments:

"The Ashanti state was created and maintained by war, and a military ideology remained a central feature of its structure to the end. Guns and gold were its training foundations. As imported firearms spread among the populace, the chiefdom which could muster the largest supplies of guns and ammunition had every chance, if ably led, to triumph in the intertribal wars."[12]

That old link between economic survival and military survival had become in Ashanti a link between gold and guns by the 19th century. Statehood and imperial ambitions reinforced the military factor in the foundations of the Ashanti polity. It is here that we come back to the centrality of the concept of *force* in the very definition of statehood.

Statehood which is so defined has important points of contact with Max Weber's classic definition. Weber asserted that, sociologically, the state could not be defined in terms of its ends. Maintenance of law and order, preservation of society, promotion of the well-being of the community, control or suppression of deviant behaviour, may all be central to the purposes of the state. And yet Weber's point was that there is scarcely any task performed by the state that some political association has not taken in hand, and there is no task that one could say has always been exclusive and peculiar to those associations which are designated as political ones. To Weber, the modern state could be defined sociologically only in terms of the specific means peculiar to it, namely, the use of physical force.

Weber went on to quote Trotsky's belief that "every state is founded on force". Weber conceded that force is not the normal nor the only means of the state, but he regarded it as a means specific to the state.

"Today the relation between the state and violence is an especially intimate one. In the past, the most varied institutions—beginning with the sib—had known the use of physical force as quite normal. Today, however, we have to say that a state is a human com-

11   I. Schapera, "The Political Organization of the Ngwato of Bechuanaland Protectorate" in *African Political Systems* eds. M. Fortes and E. E. Evans-Pritchard (London and New York: Oxford University Press on behalf of the International African Institute, 1940, 1950 edition) p. 79.
12   M. Fortes, *Kinship and the Social Order* (Chicago: Aldine Publishing Company, 1963) p. 140.

munity that 'successfully' claims the monopoly of the *legitimate use of physical force* within a given territory. Specifically, at the present time, the right to use force is ascribed to other institutions or to individuals only to the extent to which a state permits it. The state is considered the sole source of the 'right' to use violence."[13]

Eugene Walter's own definition of the state mentioned earlier is Weberian – since Walter sees the chief difference between a state and a chiefdom as lying in the nature and means of coercion authorized within the system and exercised in the political community. To Walter the head of state does claim "the legitimate monopoly of force and commands a special body of men organized to use it."[14]

Radcliffe-Brown, M. Fortes, and Evans-Pritchard take the link even further, and assert that the control and manipulation of force is what all political organization is about, and not just what statehood is about.

"The political organization of a society is that aspect of the total organization which is concerned with the control and regulation of the use of physical force."[15]

British social anthropologists, by venturing into political anthropology, have helped political scientists to refine some of their concepts. And yet this should not blind us to the fact that the social anthropologists themselves betray a residual difficulty in distinguishing between statehood and a political system. Radcliffe-Brown invoked the principle of territoriality not only as part of a definition of a state but as part of a definition of political authority. To Radcliffe-Brown political authority is concerned with "the maintenance or establishment of social order, within a territorial framework, by the organized exercise of coercive authority through the use, or the possibility of use, of physical force."[16]

Another major British anthropologist, John Beattie, has also embraced the principle of territoriality as part of the definition of "political authority". But Beattie goes on further and uses territoriality as a way of distinguishing political authority from authority in the family.

"I take authority to be 'political' only when its applicability depends upon, among other things, the occupation of a certain territory by the persons who acknowledge and are subject to it ...This is not the case with the, for example, domestic authority; a man's acknowledgement of his father's authority over him depends not, or not primarily, on where he is, but on what he is, that is, a son."[17]

---

13 Max Weber, "Politics as a Vocation", in H. H. Gerth and C. Wright-Mills, *From Max Weber: Essays in Sociology* (Routledge and Kegan Paul, 1957) p. 78. For the application of Weber's definition to the situation in Uganda consult Ali A. Mazrui, "The Lumpen Proletariat and the Lumpen Militariat: African Soldiers as a New Political Class," *Political Studies* (Oxford) Vol. XXI, No. 1, March 1973 and Mazrui, *Cultural Engineering and Nation-Building in East Africa* (Evanston, Illinois: Northwestern University Press, 1972) pp. 247–275.

14 Walter, *Terror and Resistance, op cit.*, p. 59.

15 Fortes and Evans-Pritchard, *African Political Systems, op. cit.*, pp. xxiii, 14.

16 A. R. Radcliffe-Brown, Preface to Fortes and Evans-Pritchard, *African Political Systems*, *ibid.*, pp. xi–xxi.

17 John Beattie, *The Nyoro State* (Oxford: The Clarendon Press, 1971) pp. 4–5.

Beattie is awakening us to the limits of regarding the polity as an extended family. While important kinship factors were still at play for a monarch like the Mukama of the Nyoro state, the nature of the Mukama's authority went beyond mere kinship. What Beattie does not fully grasp is that this is because the Mukama's authority was the authority of a head of state, and not merely because it was political authority. While territoriality remains pertinent to the very concept of statehood, it is not necessary as a basis for certain levels of political authority, nor does it necessarily replace the principle of kinship.

The issue of organization of physical force is more difficult to handle if we are to regard the state also as an extended family. Are the bonds which keep a family together ultimately definable in terms of the organization of physical force? We quote Weber again, "the most varied institutions – beginning with the sib – had known the use of physical force as quite normal." But although coercion is a factor which can condition the sib as a system of relationships, it is not a factor important for the sib's definition.

We are back now to the distinction between economic survival and military survival. The sib or family cooperates primarily for economic survival, at least in the sense of eking out a living and having bread to share. Statehood, on the other hand, has so far been the final consummation of that marriage between politicization and militarization. Is the state an extended family? The answer must be negative for as long as the ultimate impulse behind the state is the manipulation of force for public ends. The instincts of companionship and economic solidarity so basic to the survival of a primordial family are not the same as the impulses of organized coercion within a state as a militarized polity.

And yet the twentieth century has seen a closing of the gap between the ethos of an extended family and the ethos of modern statehood. A gradual transition, still incomplete, has started, from a warfare state to a welfare state. The emergence of the welfare state indicates a return to the principle of responsibility for the aged, the economically unproductive, and the infirm.

For the time being the welfare state coexists with the warfare state. Indeed, they are often fused in one. Principles of shared economic survival and policies of presumed military survival are conducted simultaneously. But the very emergence of the welfare state in the twentieth century signifies a reinforcement of the ethos of kinship in this particular kind of polity.

Conclusion

In his book, *Primitive Society*, Robert H. Lowie emphasized the role of *associations* as "potential agencies for the creation of a state by uniting the population within a circumscribed area into an aggregate that functions as a definite unit irrespective of any other social affiliations of the inhabitants."[18]

In a later article on the origin of the state Lowie went on to say that "associations invariably weaken the prepotency of blood ties by establishing novel

---

18   Robert H. Lowie, *Primitive Society* (1920) pp. 394–396.

ties regardless of kinship; and they may indirectly establish a positive union of all the occupants of a given area."[19]

But Lowie came to have second thoughts before long on the issue of the autonomy of associations in relation to kinship within political processes.

"Further study leads to serious modification of this view. Undoubtedly the claims set forth for the destructive efficacy of associations hold: by the very fact of their existence they have created novel bonds bound to encroach upon the omnipotence of kinship ties. But their positive achievement is more doubtful: it is only when supplementary factors of unification supervene that they achieve the solidarity of the entire local group. In itself, in other words, associational activity is not less separatistic than the segmentation of society into groups of kindred."[20]

Lowie sees the need for supplementary factors to give associational activity the driving integrative force. What he does not adequately work out is the impact of kinship itself as a factor behind the integrative functions of association. When political integration is an aggregation of subsocieties, it is quite often also an aggregation of kinship fields, real or fictitious.

The politicization of society had its origins less in economics than in combat. We have sought to illustrate in this paper that the growth of the polity in the direction of statehood was in part a process of militarization. The emergence of political authority was linked more to the dictates of military survival than the impulse of economic self-sufficiency. If Caesar's observations are to be relied upon, the German tribes in his time had chiefs in common only in wartime; as soon as peace was restored, the small clans had separate chiefs who administered justice and reconciled differences. The principle of expanding authority was closely tied to questions of military security rather than economic well-being.[21]

We have sought also to demonstrate how the kinship factor has played a part not only in the origins of human society but also in the system of symbols for races and nations in more recent times. The principle of territoriality behind the emergence of nations has simply transformed the mythology of kinship; it has not obliterated such mythologies. The range of implications in recent international history is from the doctrine of "kith and kin" in British immigration laws to the principle of a Jewish state as a basis for the creation of Israel, and from Field Marshal Idi Amin's expulsion of Asians in Uganda to the nature of interracial marriages in the United States. A particularly obstinate residue of a primordial division of labour is the subordination of woman to man both in politics and in war and the man emerged supreme not because he was supposed to be the bread-winner, but because he was supposed to be the warrior.

---

19   Lowie, "The Origin of the State", *The Freeman* Vol. V, July 19 and 26, 1922, p. 440–442, 465–467.
20   Robert H. Lowie, *The Origin of the State* (New York: Harcourt, Brace and Company, 1927) pp. 107–108.
21   See Sidgwick, *The Development of European Polity, op. cit.*, pp. 44–46.

The Warrior and the State in Precolonial Africa

Comparative Perspectives

G. N. UZOIGWE

The University of Michigan, Ann Arbor, U.S.A.

Introduction

Preparing this chapter was at once intimidating and challenging – intimidating because I have no models to draw from; and challenging because it needed to be done. More significantly, it needed to be done by an Africanist historian. For the days, alas, are gone when such subjects were comfortably left to the nutty anthropologists while historians in their lonely and crusty arrogance, exuded effortless superiority in dusty libraries and archives in a vain attempt to discover the "truth" about the past. "Hard history," difficult enough as it is, is a much more straightforward and simpler affair than the "new history". As our mentors were taught so did they teach us. The result is that most historians of our generation are not properly equipped with the disciplines of anthropology and sociology as well as the other relevant social sciences which are crucial to African historical reconstruction. For a good Africanist, in whatever field, must be a jack-of-all-trades and *master of one*. The truth is perhaps that few of us are really master of anything at all – whatever we may claim. It is possible that I am really describing myself and no one else. Whatever is the case, I must begin this chapter with an apology relative to whatever weaknesses it may have.

At a recent international conference on the military in Africa held in Accra, Ghana,[1] a pet idea of mine received unsolicited support, namely, that a military interpretation of African history ought, at least, to be as rewarding as the economic or any other interpretation for that matter. This idea, however, was clearly implied, but not theoretically focused, in the several papers presented. But it was the general consensus that in precolonial African states, characterized, except in a very few cases, by the lack of visible armies, the distinction between the military, economic, political, social and religious institutions of government were blurred. It follows, therefore, that the historian

---

1 This conference, entitled *African States and the Military: Past and Present*, was held under the joint auspices of the African Studies Centre, U.C.L.A. and the University of Ghana in August, 1975.

who studies the African military as distinct from socio-politico-economic structure does so at his peril. And granted also that there have been discontinuities and continuities in African institutions under both the colonial and post-colonial epochs of African history, it follows, too, that studies of the African military in the twentieth century ought to benefit significantly from its pre-European antecedents. This is a point to which sociologists and political scientists are only now beginning to turn attention. Their predecessors, indeed, were roundly accused in a perceptive, if at times contentious, contribution by René Lemarchand[2] at the Accra conference referred to above of being "unduly selective in their use of history". Their contributions, he suggests, inevitably lack historical depth precisely because "their treatment of the African military shows remarkable regard for historically relevant facts". Such scholars, in short, are wont to react like Johann von Bloch who asked with rhetorical naivery in his *The Future of War* (1898): "What is the use of talking about the past when you are dealing with an altogether new set of circumstances?"[3] Although historians, too, have begun to make a plea for a change in this orientation towards the study of the African military,[4] they are equally accused of preoccupation "with the unique and the specific," of lacking a theoretical framework, and of a tendency to let their imagination run away with them.[5] There is some truth to this accusation. It must be pointed, however, that historians are loath to theorize without empirical data; and given the present rudimentary state of precolonial African military studies,[6] their emphasis has been on the accumulation of the relevant data. This is not to suggest that they are unwilling to profit from any meaningful framework that the social scientists may provide. There is, therefore, no serious conflict – or, at any rate, there ought not to be a serious conflict – between historians and social scientists on this subject. Both approaches should complement each other. This means that a useful study of the African military must, of necessity, be interdisciplinary and comparative. It is, of course, true "that, as a substantive area of study, the military in Africa has been largely preempted by sociologists and political scientists;"[7] the fact remains, nevertheless, that no discipline can effectively dominate the field. Theories without data, and data without theories, if clothed with the garb of academic respectability, will be a very undesirable development in African studies.

And yet the very area of data collection in the precolonial period where, in my opinion, the historian is expected to make an important contribution, has

2 See "African Armies in Historical and Contemporary Perspective: The Search for Connexions (sic)".

3 Cited Lemarchand, "African Armies," loc. cit.

4 See G. N. Uzoigwe, *Revolution and Revolt in Bunyoro Kitara: Two Studies* (Longman: 1970), pp. 1–29; *idem*, "Precolonial Military Studies in Africa", *The Journal of Modern African Studies*, 13, 3 (1975), pp. 469–481; *cf.* B. A. Ogot (ed.), *War and Society in Africa: Ten Studies* (London, 1972).

5 Lemarchand, "African Armies", *loc. cit.*

6 Uzoigwe, "Precolonial Military Studies in Africa", *loc. cit.*

7 Lemarchand, "African Armies", *loc. cit.*

presented him with immense problems. It is, therefore, easy to understand why historians, for so long, have deliberately avoided the study of this sub-field of the historical discipline. To begin with, that the societies with which they are concerned kept no written records of their military establishments or of their military achievements made the task almost an impossible one especially during the era when oral tradition was not taken seriously by classical historians. With the acceptance of oral tradition – scientifically collected and applied – as a legitimate concern of historical writing, the problem has abated somewhat. We know, however, that oral tradition is most unreliable when dealing with the military exploits or martial spirit of a given society. And yet, if the military has been studied as socio-political structure, the problem would have been no more difficult than the general problems of precolonial African history.

In this study of the warrior and the state in Africa, I have relied on first, *oral tradition*. It must be kept constantly in mind that most of these sources are "free texts" with an overlay of nationalistic jingoism and a tintinnabulation of moral righteousness.[8] Second, *travel lore*. These comprise the published works of nineteenth century European travellers, traders, explorers, missionaries and administrators. These sources, too, are based, in large part, on oral testimonies and should, consequently, be used with care. Third, *ethnographic data*. These are also based on oral tradition, oral testimonies, and sometimes on personal observation. They are variably informed but sketchy. And fourth, *published and unpublished materials* on precolonial African military history including my own previous studies. It is hoped that a judicious use of these studies might enable us to gain some insight into the relationship between the warrior and the state in precolonial Africa, and perhaps help to put the "myths" which we love so much and for which we have been for long maligned in historical perspective.

Given these sources, there are, of course, several ways of approaching the relationship between the African warrior and the state as a unit of analysis. I have opted for the structural-functional analysis as the most meaningful approach. This is in keeping with my conviction that the military must be studied and comprehended as socio-political structure. I am not, therefore, concerned with the impressions or images of warriors. Most societies – indeed all societies – have concepts of masculinity, bravery, love of country, love of honour, and martial spirit. But there is no society which is either totally pacifist or totally aggressive. I am suggesting that war, or the use of naked force to achieve desired goals, has proved to be a permanent feature of human society. It is as old as the world and, therefore, older than history. The warrior, the fighting

---

8   The major traditions I consulted include John W. Nyakatura, *Anatomy of an African Kingdom: A History of Bunyoro Kitara* (New York: 1973), ed. G. N. Uzoigwe; Kabalega and Winyi, "The Kings of Bunyoro-Kitara" in three parts, *Uganda Journal*, 3 (1935), pp. 155–160; 4 (1936), pp. 75–83; 5 (1937), pp. 53–68; A. B. (Ruth) Fisher, *Twilight Tales of the Black Baganda* (London: 1911, 2nd ed. 1970), pp. 69–178; Apolo Kaggwa, *The Kings of Buganda* (Nairobi: 1971), ed. M. S. M. Kiwanuka; A. T. Bryant, *Olden Times in Zululand and Natal* (London: 1938); Samuel Johnson, *The History of the Yorubas* (London: 1921; reprinted 1969).

man, the man of action, is always the executor of violence but not necessarily always its originator. He is, in the context of the state, the instrument of political action. Wars are never fought for illusory ends. States fight for a variety of reasons: survival, power, wealth, prestige, sex and so forth. In precolonial African states, therefore, where the state and the military were fused, the study of the warrior is, in essence, the study of the state. But yet not everyone, strictly speaking, was a warrior. This study, therefore, is concerned with the very difficult task of (a) isolating those aspects of precolonial African state organisation that have a discernible military function; (b) of identifying the function of the warrior in that context; and (c) of comparing this structural-functional aspect of the warrior in several African state systems.

The Warrior as a Political Animal

In no state, traditional or modern, is the military totally divorced from the political structure. The degree of integration, however, between the military and politics varies from state to state. It follows, therefore, that the warrior tradition, in the sense I conceive it, cannot be uniform. But this is not to suggest that dramatic differences necessarily existed. The warrior, in a traditional society, was a political animal, more so than the rank and file of the citizenry. He saw politics as state power; he knew that the art of politics concerns how to acquire that power, how to wield it effectively, and how to preserve it. Most importantly, he knew that the surest means of achieving state power is through the agency of the warrior. Since a considerable number of precolonial African states were conquest states, the integration of the military and politics, as well as the invocation of warrior values in these states, was carefully cultivated along with the construction of historic – invariably mythical – charters with an overlay of the divine right of rulers in order to ensure the survival and viability of these states. Even among non-conquest, invariably non-kingdom, states, the function of the warrior was, indeed, assured. We shall examine the theme of the warrior in politics under the following sub-categories: the relationship between the ruler and the warrior class; the function of the warrior in territotial administration; and the impact of the rise of the professional warrior on the primordial state. We shall draw our illustrations primarily from the Zulu, Bunyoro Kitara and Buganda, Oyo and the Yoruba states, and Kikuyu, indicating differences and similarities where appropriate.

The political organisation of the Zulu before 1800 did not differ markedly from those of small scale, precolonial African societies which evolved a chiefly system of government. Warfare appears to have been rare, and when it did occur, it was usually a struggle for power between a chief and his relatives.[9] The

---

9   E. A. Ritter, *Shaka Zulu: The Rise of the Zulu Empire* (London, 1955: reprinted New York 1973), pp. 22–23; Max Gluckman, "The Kingdom of the Zulu of South Africa" in M. Fortes and E. E. Evans-Pritchard (eds.), *African Political Systems* (New York: 1940), p. 25; M. Gluckman, "The Individual in a Social Framework: The Rise of King Shaka of Zululand," *Journal of African Studies*, 1, 2 (1974), pp. 124–125.

civil war in Zululand between 1808 and 1818 significantly changed the situation. For one thing, it brought about enlargement of political scale; for another it began a tradition of militarism among the Zulu which exists to the present day. Shaka's much vaunted revolution is, in fact, not as original as his numerous admirers like to suggest. It has, indeed, been noted that "he duplicated in his great new nation early Nguni tribal organization, though on a much larger scale and with a deeper hierarchy of officials."[10] The political organisation of the pre-Shaka Nguni state, like those of the other southern Bantu states, was headed by a hereditary chief, assisted by sub-chiefs – usually members of the royal family – who administered the districts as well as by other officials called *indunas*. The senior *indunas* had also the rank of deputy chief. The *indunas* were powerful officials and were not chosen from among the ranks of the royal eligibles to the throne. The chief and his officials were commanders of their people in war and political leaders in war and peace. A chief was usually a great warrior, and his officials were appointed, in large measure, as a result of their military valour. In the pre-Mfecane Zulu state, therefore, the military and politics were dangerously fused. The ordinary citizens had no means of removing an unpopular government. Of course, a "palace revolt" sometimes occurred, but the system of government did not change. This is very reminiscent of contemporary military-cum civil dictatorships in Africa.

The interlacustrine states of Bunyoro Kitara (popularly known as Bunyoro) and Buganda have also a long tradition of the warrior in politics. In the first instance, both are, according to their traditions, conquest states. In the process of consolidating their hold on the newly acquired territories, the Omukama of Bunyoro and the Kabaka of Buganda had no choice but to invoke warrior values and construct historic charters in the process of legitimacy engineering. As the last Kabaka of Buganda, the late Sir Edward Muteesa, put it with respect to Buganda: "The word Kabaka means "emissary", and some time in the past an overseer sent from Bunyoro had set himself up as an independent ruler. For a long time we struggled for survival, surrounded by larger neighbours, existing like a garrison state; and herein lay our strength."[11] In Bunyoro, too, the word "Kitara means a sword but has historically come to signify an empire worn by the sword by individuals possessed of excessive virtue."[12]

At this early stage, the ideal king was the great warrior, larger than life. The military activities – or supposed military activities – of these kingdoms are eloquently recorded in the traditions. The dominant picture that has emerged from these sources is that the political history of the interlacustrine states of east Africa is, in large measure, a study of the Abachwezi Kitara empire and the struggle for mastery following its collapse between Bunyoro and Buganda. It is understandable, therefore, why in states such as these the military was

10   Gluckman, "Individual in a Social Framework," p. 134.
11   Sir Edward Muteesa, *Desecration of My Kingdom* (London: 1967), p. 30.
12   G. N. Uzoigwe, "Bunyoro Kitara in the North Interlacustrine Region," in S. Kiwanuka and A. Temu (eds.), *East African Kingdoms* (forthcoming).

destined to play a crucial role. But like the Nguni state, too, the military was not distinct from the political structure: it followed closely the organisation of the state. There was, constitutionally (in either kingdom), a monocephalous kingship which, as both a centrifugal and centripetal force, was at the apex of the political order. Authority flowed from the king to the abakungu (territorial administrators). These abakungu were assisted by a hierarchy of deputies who, together with their immediate overlords, were expected to provide warriors for their king's wars. Traditionally, the abakunguship was not necessarily hereditary. Such an appointment was usually a reward for military valour. Bunyoro tradition, indeed, maintains that originally only outstanding warriors were made *abakunga*.[13] Neither in Bunyoro nor in Buganda was a cowardly chief likely to retain his position for long. Although in Buganda the danger of a successful *omukungu* (singular of *abakungu*)-cum-general overthrowing the Kabaka was unthinkable since he was neither a prince nor a royal eligible, yet the possibility remained that he could be wooed by a royal pretender to the throne to help him overthrow the incumbent Kabaka. Therefore, before a commanding general left for the battlefield, he was expected to leave behind with the Kabaka a precious hostage.[14] In Bunyoro, on the other hand, where the danger of secession was ever present especially as a considerable number of the most important abakungu belonged to the royal family, the Omukama took steps to ensure that his omukungu-cum-general would not be contumacious, or more seriously, seditious.[15] The history of Bunyoro is full of examples which illustrate that he did not always succeed. It was, however, during succession and civil wars[16] that these civil-military administrators exerted the decisive political impact.

In a general sense, the political organisation of the Yoruba state systems resembled that of the Kitara empire. There is the Alafin of Oyo who was regarded as "the supreme head of all the kings and princes of the Yoruba nation"[17] who traces his descent to Oranyan, the supposed founder of the old Oyo empire. At the height of Oyo power these kings and princes are estimated to have numbered 1060. But according to Johnson, however, "The word 'king'" included "all more or less distinguished chiefs, who stand at the head of a clan, or one who is the ruler of an important district or province, especially those who can trace their descent from the founder, or from one of the great

13 Uzoigwe, *Revolution and Revolt*, p. 1.

14 John Roscoe, *The Baganda* (London: 1911; 2nd ed., 1965), p. 350.

15 John Roscoe, *The Banyoro or Bakitara* (Cambridge: 1923), p. 52; John Beattie, *The Nyoro State* (Oxford: 1971), pp. 137–138; 4. idem, *Bunyoro: An African Kingdom* (New York: 1960), p. 36.

16 For succession and civil wars in Bunyoro and Buganda see G. N. Uzoigwe, "Succession and Civil War in Bunyoro Kitara," *The International Journal of African Historical Studies*, VI, 1 (1973), pp. 49–71; Martin Southwald, "The History of a History: Royal Succession in Buganda," in I. M. Lewis (ed.), *History and Social Anthropology* (London and New York: 1968), pp. 127–151.

17 Johnson, *History of the Yoruba*, p. 41.

leaders or hereos who settled with him in this country." They all owed allegiance "to the Alafin or king of the Yorubas."[18] In the context of the Kitara empire, therefore, most of the *abakunga* would qualify as kings in the Yoruba usage; and the position of the Alafin resembles that of the Omukama of Bunyoro.

Apparently, before Oranyan who has been described as "primarily a political adventurer,"[19] the Yoruba had no common political head. It was Oranyan, also reputed as "a very brave and warlike prince" who, after the foundation of Oyo, had set in motion the political federation of a congeries of chiefdoms and principalities which appear to have exhibited a remarkable cultural homogeneity. He is said to have started his campaign with a bodyguard of "150 well-trained soldiers."[20] The Oyo empire, therefore, like those of Bunyoro, Buganda, and Zulu was also a conquest state from whose inception the military played a crucial role. The warrior ideal was relentlessly cultivated. The Alafins, like the earlier Abakama of Bunyoro, were required to be great warriors and to exhibit militant leadership as well. Alafin Ajaka, for example, was deposed by the Oyo Mesi (Council of State) for his lack of militarism and replaced by Sango, Oranyan's son, who was known to have demonstrated warlike characteristics. It is interesting to note that when Sango died prematurely and Ajaka was given a second chance, he proved to be more warlike than his predecessors. Oyo became the terror of its neighbours as it established overlordship over the other Yoruba state systems. The relaxation of the warrior tradition in subsequent reigns led to the defeat of Oyo by Nupe. The reigning Alafin, Onigbogi, fled to exile. The exile of the Alafins lasted for 75 years. While in exile, the Alafins of Oyo revived their warrior tradition, restoring eventually the military might of Oyo and reoccupying Old Oyo around A.D. 1610.[21]

To ensure that the disaster which occurred in the reign of Onigbogi was not repeated, the Alafins of Oyo began a policy of military reorganisation and militant expansion of Oyo influence. Conquered areas were placed under the effective administration of the *Ajele* (political residents). It was during this period that Alafin Ajagbo created the position of Are Ona Kakanfo (Generalissimo of Oyo's army). The Kakanfo (as he is popularly known) was expected to wage war regularly, to win each war "within three months or be brought home dead."[22] By mid-eighteenth century Oyo had become the largest state system in Yorubaland. It had also become a military machine which, if not properly controlled, could prove dangerous for political stability.

Constitutionally, Oyo was a semi-divine monarchy ruled by an Alafin whose

---

18 *Idem.*
19 See J. A. Atanda, "The Military in the Politics of the Old Oyo Empire," paper presented at the Accra Conference, August 1975; *cf.* Johnson, *History of the Yorubas*, pp. 143–148 for Oranyan's career.
20 *Ibid.*
21 R. S. Smith, "The Alafin in Exile: A Study of the Igboho Period in Oyo History," *Journal of African History*, VI ,1 (1965), pp. 57–77.
22 Atanda, "The Military in Politics," *loc. cit.*

power, in theory, was absolute; in practice, however, his authority was subject to checks and balances by the Oyo Mesi. Unlike his eastern and southern African counterparts, the Alafin was obliged to carry out the decisions of the Oyo Mesi or commit suicide. The Bashorun, as leader of the Oyo Mesi, was a very powerful person but he did not exercise absolute power either. Nor did the great Ogboni chiefs whose head was called Oluwo. The Oluwo checked the ambitions of the Bashorun who, in turn, checked the ambitions of the Alafin. And none of these three powerful leaders had individual control over the Kakanfo and his corps of 70 standing army officers called the Esos. But the Kakanfo, too, was forbidden to live within the capital. The idea was to cut him off from possible dangerous influence over the Esos who lived there. The Esos were distributed equally (ten each) among the seven members of the Oyo Mesi and put under their control. No single individual, therefore, could use the army to achieve his objectives. The Oyo Mesi, by having corporate control of the army, could also check the ambitions of the Oluwo and his Ogboni.

This complex and delicate political balance was upset when a change in the succession to the throne increased the powers of the Bashorun at the expense of those in charge of the other arms of government. It is said that during the third quarter of the eighteenth century Bashorun Gaha, using his new powers, was able to set up five Alafins, four of whom he destroyed. Having subverted the constitution, he ruled despotically for 20 years but somehow he could not gain exclusive control of the military. His power collapsed when an apparently puppet Alafin called Abiodun secretly plotted with the Kakanfo and the provincial chiefs to bring about his overthrow. The constitution was, therefore, restored by military intervention and Gaha was burnt at the stake. Coup d'etats always tend to be a way of life once introduced into the political system. Oyo was no exception. It was the coup led by Kakanfo Afonja which set in motion the trend of events which eventually led to the total destruction of the Oyo empire in 1837.[23] It is ironic that the political system which took very carefully calculated measures to avoid a coup eventually fell by it.

The army, then, was a very important instrument in the rise and fall of the Oyo empire. But Oyo was not a military state. The 70 Esos divided into seven equal parts did not constitute much of an army. The military and politics were still dangerously fused and the ordinary citizens were ready pawns in whatever power politics their leaders might choose to initiate. Little is known about the military in the other Yoruba states which numbered 39 by the nineteenth century. We know, however, that the Elegbe (military chiefs) of eastern Yoruba formed a distinct category from the civilian chiefs, that their influence was minimal during peacetime, and that they posed no threat to constitutional, political authority.[24]

---

23 *Ibid*; Johnson, *History of the Yorubas*; J. B. Webster and A. A. Boahen, *The Revolutionary Years: West Africa Since 1800* (London: 1967), pp. 92–95.

24 S. A. Akitoye, "The Military Among the Yoruba of South-Western Nigeria in the Nineteenth Century," paper presented at the Accra Conference, 5 August, 1975.

According to the mythical constitution of the Kikuyu – which abolished "the status of a king or nobleman" – government was the responsibility of the *Kiama* (councils of elders). The *Kiama* were all retired warriors. The military, then, was a training ground for political office. The *Anake* or warrior class consisted of young men between the ages of eighteen and forty. This very important class formed the *njama ya ita* (council of war) which, in addition to "its military activities, represented the interests of the young people in the government."[25] The Kikuyu system of government as well as its military organisation was more democratic than the others we have discussed so far. Kikuyuland was a non-kingdom state in which the warrior was a political animal *par excellence*. From his early years, a youth knew that to reach the coveted position of membership of the *Kiama* – and more importantly to be able to influence its deliberations – he must strive to achieve reputation as a great warrior. The warrior tradition, therefore, as a way of life, was institutionalized. In such a system, the military overthrow of the government did not make sense and apparently was never attempted. The *Kiama* was continuously changing as a result of new additions through the age-grade system or as a result of the death of some of the existing members.

The African warriors were, therefore, from the examples we have seen, an indivisible element of the central government. But since they were also military leaders as well as administrators, they played crucial roles in territorial administration. In the kingdom states, it was the duty of the civil-military administrators of provinces to provide soldiers for their king's wars while the king undertook to protect them and their provinces from both internal and external attack. The king was their commander-in-chief; they were the king's generals; and their deputies could be ranked in descending order from what might be the equivalent today of brigadiers to lieutenants. The rest of the population comprised the citizen militia; the so-called invisible armies. Failure to support their king during a military emergency constituted a rebellion. Such a rebellion might succeed or collapse depending on the alignment of political forces in the country. Sometimes a successful rebellion resulted in secession and the foundation of a new kingdom especially if the rebellions commander was a prince and a royal eligible.

This was particularly true of Bunyoro where the defence of the kingdom was the responsibility of the *obwesengeze*[26] (territorial armies) which were under the direct command of their civil-military administrators. They were, in essence, private companies who owed nominal allegiance to the Omukama through these territorial administrators. The Omukama, too, had his own private companies, or palace guards, but they were not strong enough to determine the outcome even of internal conflicts. In such a situation his terri-

---

25 Jomo Kenyatta, *Facing Mount Kenya* (London: 1938; N. York: 1965), p. 187.
26 *Obwesengenze* is a Luganda word. The Banyoro used it to denote personal possession with all rights of disposal. The Runyoro equivalent is *abahinya*. My Banyoro informants, however, seem to prefer the Luganda variety. In the context in which it is used in this essay, the territorial armies were considered to be the personal possession of the military chiefs.

torial administrators, who behaved as kings, except in name, were potentially dangerous. In any political structure, then, where the civil-military administrators of provinces form the basis of military organisation, the position of the central government was bound to be weak. This was the dilemma of the Bunyoro kingdom prior to the rise of Kabalega.[27] In Buganda, too, the territorial administrators, like their compatriots in Bunyoro, by being civil-military leaders, exercised tremendous impact on historical movements in their kingdom. Admittedly, they were not royal eligibles but they could combine, under the umbrella of a royal eligible, to depose a ruling Kabaka; admittedly, too, the position of the later Kabakas was, at any rate, in practical terms, stronger than that of the later Abakama of Bunyoro with the exception of Kabalega. Nevertheless, the Buganda territorial rulers were also the accredited defenders of their kingdom and literally owned all the individuals living within their territorial limits.[28] In either kingdom it was the mystique of kingship and the monarch's ability to manipulate different interest groups – and not the actual military force wielded by him – which ensured stability. The source of military strength of a civil-military administrator was ultimately all the able-bodied citizens who constituted the fighting force. In wartime, they fought under his banner; in peacetime, they belonged to him, although, in theory, everybody belonged to the king. They were by no means serfs since they did not cultivate the fields for their lords. Cultivation, generally, was done by women. The male citizens constituted, rather, a militia who served directly the ambitions of their civil-military overlord. The function of the warrior in territorial governance in Zululand and Yorubaland prior to the nineteenth century did not differ dramatically from that obtained in Bunyoro and Buganda and should not, therefore, detain us.[29] Among the Kikuyu, on the other hand, the variation is worth emphasizing. The *anake* (warrior class) was divided into senior warriors and junior warriors. Kenyatta describes their governmental function thus:

> Each group had its village, district and national leaders (*athamaki a riika*), who acted as spokesmen in all matters concerning the welfare of the groups and the tribe. These leaders were chosen by their particular groups at general or public assembly. They were men who had proved by their own actions, their capability of leadership; had shown bravery in wars, impartiality in justice, self-sacrifice, and above all, discipline in the group. A man with these qualities was able to attain a high position and esteem in the community, especially when he had retired from the activities of a warrior. Judges and responsible elders... were chosen from such men.[30]

27 See G. N. Uzoigwe, "Kabalega and the Making of a New Kitara," *Tarikh*, 3, 2 (1970), pp. 5–20; *cf.* reprint of same in Obaro Ikime (ed.), *Leadership in 19th Century Africa* (London: 1974) pp. 000.

28 C. C. Wrigley, "The Changing Economic Structure of Buganda," in L. A. Fallers (ed.), *The King's Men* (London: 1964), pp. 21–22.

29 Those interested in pursuing the subject further should consult for Zululand Gluckman, "The Kingdom of the Zulu," *loc. cit.*; idem, "The Individual in a Social Framework," *loc. cit.*; Ritter, *Shaka Zulu, op. cit.*; Bryant, *Olden Times in Zululand, op. cit.* And for Yorubaland, Johnson, *History of the Yoruba, op. cit.*; Atanda, "The Military in Politics," *loc. cit.*; R. S. Smith, *Kingdoms of the Yoruba* (London: 1969).

30 Kenyatta, *Facing Mount Kenya*, p. 192.

What emerges from the Kikuyu system as described by Kenyatta is a government founded on the principle of division of functions with harmony, stability, respect, age, and lack of individualism as its most cherished characteristics. Underspinning all these characteristics was the ideology of the warrior as the bedrock of statehood.

The Kikuyu system did not change until the advent of British rule. Within the kingdom states we have discussed so far, however, tremendous changes occurred during the nineteenth century, a century characterized by revolutions, transition, and change. One of the revolutions pertained to the military; and the basic military revolution was the rise of professional and standing armies. Hitherto, such armies were rare in Africa. The new armies challenged established authority or restored it as the case might be, subverted the constitution or ignored it, enlarged the political scale or decreased it, and brought about stability or created instability. And to add to the revolutionary situations that existed, the new-style warriors came increasingly to employ the use of firearms.

Among these developments the bantu revolution in southern Africa is the most celebrated by historians. The Zulu empire of Shaka which his successors – Dingaane, Mpande, Cetewayo, and Dinuzulu – somehow managed to lose, is a good example of a conquest state in which this new-style warrior was dominant and which institutionalized and invoked both the reality and myth of warrior values. We have already noted that Shaka improved and enlarged what he inherited without necessarily destroying the basic organisation of society. "Dingiswayo", indeed, "played Philip to Shaka's Alexander" as Ritter suggests,[31] but Shaka militarized the politics of the state more than any leader in Africa before him. The Zulu state was now organised along military lines; the king depended almost entirely on the military *indunas* who, in turn, depended on their *impis*. Those warriors, together with their commanders, were grouped by age, quartered in barracks, and forbidden to marry before they retired from the military. Their influence was such that the old aristocracy of chiefly *indunas*, by now means abolished, quickly became a cypher in politics. It is doubtful, however, that in the post-Shaka era there was a chiefly induna who was not a retired warrior, very much in the Kikuyu tradition. The Zulu king, himself a respectable military leader, remained, nevertheless – much in the tradition of contemporary military dictatorships in Africa – both a centrifugal and a centripetal force in the state. In legal theory he owned all the land and exercised unrestrained sovereignty over all his people. His official title of Nkosi was also the official name of the National Parliament or the Royal Assembly just as in Bunyoro the name Obukama means kingship or the state and the name Omukama means the king. In practice, however, this sovereignty was subjected to various and subtle checks and balances prescribed by custom and dictated by political realities. Not even the great Shaka – before he became practically insane with power or grief or both – could afford to act outside of the law. And when he did so, he paid with his life.

31   Ritter, *Shaka Zulu*, p. 41.

The survival of the Zulu state therefore as well as the survival of the king himself depended on the alliance between the king, the standing army of warriors, and the chiefly indunas. In this alliance the warrior was dominant. Shaka knew, in his years of sobriety, that without his warriors he was nothing. That was why he spared no efforts to please them. And to ensure that the elite among his warriors did not become overmighty subjects – as Mzilikazi Kumalo attempted to be afterwards – he militarized the entire population including all traditional ceremonies. The idea of individuals living in military barracks, built like ordinary Zulu homesteads but containing thousands of men under arms was mind-boggling at the time. These barracks were, in addition, regarded as royal homesteads. The age-regimental system, introduced by Dingiswayo, but perfected by Shaka, was used to ensure the total submission of the people to military authority.[32] A new regiment was created each year as the occasion arose until Zululand became a military camp; and politics became, not the art of the possible, but the art of the strongest.

The strongest was the warrior; and the king and commander-in-chief was the strongest and bravest warrior of them all. He punished and pampered his warriors – as the occasion demanded – with equal exuberance. "The secret of Shaka's "popularity", Ritter has noted, "was his great liberality to his soldiers at the expense of his tributary chiefs and the personal attention he gave to the needs of his warriors." And "like his contemporary, Napoleon, who told his soldiers that they each carried a Field Marshall's baton in their knapsacks, Shaka let his warriors know that there was no limit to their promotion, irrespective of their clan or social status, provided only that they had proved their merit."[33] Shaka, however, did not tolerate civil jurisdiction over the army; the responsibility of dealing with his warriors was his alone.[34] The Zulu state resembled the timarchic state of Sparta although Spartan warriors were allowed to marry. "A man," writes Gluckman, "was called *isihlangu senkesi* (war-shield of the king). The dominant values of Zulu life were those of the warrior and they were satisfied in service at the king's barracks and his wars."[35] Nothing else, apparently, seems to have mattered.

The repercussions of Zulu militarism in Bantu Africa were enormous. Warrior institutions and values *a la* Shaka spread like wildfire throughout south

---

32 Perhaps it is worth pointing out at this point that at the Accra Conference referred to above, one of the suggestions (relative to the best means of putting a stop to the epidemic of military coups in Africa) which produced the most hilarious reception was the abolition of the present structure of the African military and the compulsory arming of every citizen. It was felt that Africans everywhere are being totally submitted to military authority.

33 Ritter, *Shaka Zulu*, pp. 99–100.

34 *Ibid.*, p. 270.

35 Gluckman, "The Kingdom of the Zulu," p. 31. It is interesting to note that as early as 1918 W. S. Fergusson compared the Zulu and Spartan military system. See Fergusson, *The Zulus and the Spartans: A Comparison of Their Military Systems* (Cambridge, Mass.: 1918).

central and east central Africa. These institutions and values were modified to suit differing situational factors. And warrior values, at any rate, persist to the present day within, of course, the limitations imposed by harsh, European minority overlordship. It has also been pointed out that during the "early colonial period the tradition of the Mfecane ... played an important part in determining psychological attitudes to white rule."[36] For example, the Ndebele revolts in Southern Rhodesia (1896–1897), the revolt of the Zulu against white rule (1906), the Maji Maji revolt against the Germans in which the Ngoni (who inrupted into East Africa under the leadership of Zwangendaba during the Mfecane) played an active part, were all influenced, in large part, by the traditions of the Mfecane. So also were the millenarian and nationalist liberation movements in southern Africa.[37] The Ndebele and the Ngoni regard the nineteenth century as a golden age in their history destroyed by the imposition of European rule.

The rise of a professional warrior class in Bunyoro and Buganda during the second half of the nineteenth century proved momentous in the history of both kingdoms. The creation of the *abarusura* (national standing army) by Omukama Chwa II Kabalega of Bunyoro was a direct challenge to the military power of the civil-military administrators. It denuded the territorial *obwesengeze* of able and ambitious young men, anxious to improve their lot, who enlisted in the national army to serve their king, enrich themselves, and help to defend their country. Whether Kabalega knew it or not, and whether the civil-military administrators realized it or not, the creation of the *abarusura* was constitutionally fundamental for it amounted to a drastic change in power relations in Bunyoro. The professional warrior, not the good old warrior-politician, had now become the backbone of the new power in the land. And he was used by Kabalega to ensure the ascendancy of royal, over aristocratic, power. The territorial administrators remained, nevertheless, a relic of the old political order, performing now the dreary functions of collecting the king's taxes and settling disputes. They also still retained their military *obwesengeze* who acted as reserve warriors to be called up by the king during an emergency. The *abarusura*, on the other hand, were precluded from exercising, at any rate, direct political power. Nevertheless, under Kabalega, Bunyoro was an armed camp. The military, without having a clear political role, was nevertheless dominant in politics.[38] The soldiers threw their weight about and quickly gained a bad reputation.[39] Gaetano Casati, who was a prisoner of the *abarusura* recorded: ". . . the power of the *banassura* (sic) in the government was assured. The owners of the land were deprived of every customary right . . . the military party became preponderant in Unyoro . . . (and even) the supervision of government councils

---

36   J. D. Omer-Cooper, *The Zulu Aftermath: A Nineteenth-Century Revolution in Bantu Africa* (London: 1966), p. 181.

37   *Ibid.*, p. 181; *cf.* B. G. M. Sundkler, *Bantu Prophets in South Africa* (London: 1961); E. Roux, *Time Longer than Rope* (London: 1964).

38   Uzoigwe, *Revolution and Revolt*, pt. 1.

39   *Ibid.*, pp. 13–16.

and administration of justice were given up to military influence."[40] Kabalega had deliberately set his territorial administrators and his new style generals against themselves. But he balanced the forces in such a way that the administrators still exercised considerable authority, if not effective power, since real power was bound to lie with the sword. And the sword, at this time, was strengthened by the addition of firearms.

In Buganda, Kabaka Mwanga created his version of the *abarusura* which has been described as "a new *corps d'elite* of fusiliers, who decided the issue of battles."[41] They differed from the *abarusura* in the sense that they combined the functions of the old provincial administrators as well as those of professional warriors. The difference, really, between the old and the new was not only in the *locus* of power but also in the class of the "new men" who led these forces and who by the last two decades of the nineteenth century wielded enormous influence in Kiganda politics even at the expense of the Kabaka himself. They began their career as young men most of whom had been educated as pages in the Kabaka's court where they had adhered to either Islam or Christianity depending on the predilection of the Kabaka at that time. It was Kabaka Mwanga who formed them into new regiments after the persecution of the Christians in 1886 as a counterweight to what he considered to be the reactionary forces of the old territorial rulers. Without destroying the ancient and well-tested mechanism of territorial administration, Mwanga simply removed from the old civil-military barons of the kingdom the military power which was the source of their enormous influence. Unlike Kabalega, however, Mwanga was unable to manage the monster he had created and quickly fell prey to it.[42]

As a result of the nineteenth century civil war in Yorubaland, the military assumed unbridled influence in politics. The new warlords who rose to influence in this period used their private armies to reduce the traditional rulers as their puppets. The new-style warlords, quite different from the traditional *Elegbe* (warrior-chiefs), were usually young and ambitious men anxious to make a name for themselves in what they perceived to have been a new heroic age in Yoruba history in which heroism and military adventurism assured not only survival but also glory, honour, and wealth. They still recognised, however, the nominal sovereignty of their respective Obas; sometimes they gave them part of their booty; and in many cases their armies were used to defend or expand their Obas' territories.[43] But yet, like the *abarusura* of Bunyoro, the "new men" — the warlords — constituted a departure from customary practice as well as a

40 Gaetano Casati, *Ten Years in Equatoria* (London: 1898), pp. 272–274.
41 Wrigley, "Changing Economic Structure of Buganda," p. 25.
42 This episode of Buganda's history ought to be well known by now. The most relevant works for our purposes, however, include J. A. Rowe, "The Baganda Revolutionaries," *Tarikh* 3, 2 (1970), pp. 34–35; D. A. Low, *Buganda in Modern History* (London: 1971), pp. 13–54; Michael Wright, *Buganda in the Heroic Age* (New York: 1971).
43 Akintoye, "Military Among the Yoruba," *loc. cit.*; idem, *Revolution and Power Politics in Yorubaland* (London: 1971); Smith, *Kingdoms of the Yoruba*, pp. 120–129, 155–174; J. F. A. Ajayi and R. S. Smith, *Yoruba Warfare in the 19th Century* (Cambridge: 1964).

challenge to the leadership role of the territorial administrators. But, unlike the *abarusura*, they were not a creation of the Obas. Their success in this confrontation was due to their possession of personal standing armies armed with fire-arms as well as with traditional weapons. The rise of the warlords, it has been argued, resulted in the loss of personal freedoms among ordinary citizens who, in search of security following the breakdown of law and order, sought the protection of powerful leaders who maintained their positions by force.[44] With the advent of British rule ended the era of the great warlords in Yoruba history.

To summarize our sampling so far: the African warrior was a political animal more than the rest of the citizenry especially as the military and the state were dangerously fused; that the study of the warrior is tantamount, in fact, to the study of the state; that in the study of the state, the political function of the warrior was dominant in both national and territorial administrations; and that the rise of standing armies or professional warriors tended to upset the political balance. In the case of the Yoruba and Buganda, both the king and the old civil-military administrators became subjected to domination by their warriors; in Bunyoro and Zulu, on the other hand, only the old civil-military administrators of territories were reduced to a political cypher. There was an alliance between the military and the monarchy which gave rise to centralisation and stability. In all these developments, politics was so structured that the people could not change an oppressive government. Governments were of course overthrown, but these were usually "palace revolts" in which the position of the ordinary citizens did not change markedly. Politics among the Kikuyu was apparently more democratic than in the other samples. There was no king; there was no nobleman; there was neither a standing army nor professional warriors as such; and the individual citizen was an indivisible element of the government. Although our samples are understandably limited – but nevertheless carefully chosen – we may hazard the conclusion that the function of the warrior in precolonial Africa exhibited more similarities than dissimilarities.

The Warrior in a Socio-cultural Framework

The warrior tradition manifested itself also in a variety of interlocking socio-cultural and economic relationships within the social organisation of the state. The individual warrior, it must be understood, was, first and last, a citizen. He was therefore only significant in the context of the larger society. In short, he was subject to social manipulation by the state in the interests of statal stability and survival. This manipulation attempted to achieve several ends, the most important of which, at any rate, for our immediate purposes, included (a) the inculcation of the idea of a joint identity, common heritage, and common future (nationalism, patriotism); (b) the achievement of corporate alliances and other social arrangements (social transformation); and (c) educa-

---

44   Akintoye, "Military Among the Yoruba," *cf.* also Smith and Alayi in f.n. 43.

tion with respect to guides and sanctions of a nationally or culturally accepted moral order (social therapy). The ultimate end of all these devices is to ensure social control. The warrior, then, must also be studied as social structure.

The extended family is the starting point of our analysis. It is not only the beginning of the political community but also the foundation of society. The African state is an organism growing out of the family; and the warrior, as we saw, is part of that organism. Among the Kikuyu, for example, the individual warrior is responsible to his *Mbari* or *Nyomba* (family group) through which he is responsible to his *Moherega* (clan) as well as to his *riika* (age-set). The activities of the warrior, his successes and failures, reflect on his *Mbari* and *Moherega*. Since the Kikuyu practice is almost universal throughout Africa, it will be superfluous to burden ourselves with further samples. It is the starting point of the education of the warrior. Notions of nationalism and patriotism are learned within the family group and extended to the wide society as we shall see. The state, then, is the extended family writ large.

The age-set and the circumcision guild constitute another form of social control which is crucial to our understanding of the African warrior especially in his relationships with the state. It is a widely adopted method of unifying the community and of determining status and behaviour patterns. It is a means for organising corporate alliances with the aim in view of not only achieving social transformation but also of organising the state for offence and defence. Kikuyu, once more, provides us with a good sample. Kenyatta writes: "the *Mbari* and the *Moherega* system help to form several groups of kinsfolk within the tribe, acting independently; but the system of the age-grading unites and solidifies the whole tribe in all its activities."[45] Kikuyu warriors were grouped according to their *riika*. Boys and girls became members of a *riika* by passing through the rite known as *gotonya ndogera na mato* (piercing of the ears). This was done between the ages of four and five. Then, between the ages of eighteen and twenty they undergo circumcision ceremonies. To become a warrior one must have performed these rites. The *Kehee* (uncircumcised person) was regarded as a coward, a social undesirable. According to Kenyatta:

> He cannot build a homestead of his own. In the days of tribal war he could not go to the battlefield; he could only stay at home with the women and defend the homestead. He cannot boast or brag or even appear to do so. He is not allowed to wear the long hair of the *mwanake*, circumcised youth; it is taboo for him to have sexual intercourse with circumcised girls. In meat feasts, he is not allowed to eat certain joints; he cannot have a circumcised man as an intimate friend. In contrast with all this, the circumcised youth is a warrior, a dandy, a dancer, an eater of good food. He is full-grown, a proper man, a full member of the tribe.[46]

In short, a coward in a society such as this is, for all practical purposes, a non-person beneath the law. A circumcised Kikuyu, on the other hand, was regarded as a brave man and was called a *mondomorome* (a he-man); he was ad-

45   Kenyatta, *Facing Mount Kenya*, p. 4.
46   *Ibid.*, p. 104.

mitted to the *njama ya anake a mumo* (the national council of junior warriors) and introduced "into the general activities and etiquette of the warrior class". After this introduction, the leading warrior utters the *rohio* (a war cry) and the young warrior joins his companies in making the following *mwehetwa wa anake* (warriors' resolution):

> We brandish our spears, which is the symbol of our courageous and fighting spirit, never to retreat or abandon our hope, or run away from our comrades. If ever we shall make a decision, nothing will change us; and even if the heaven should hold over us a threat to fall and crush us, we shall take our spears and prop it. And if there seems to be a unity between the heaven and the earth to destroy us, we shall sink the bottom part of our spear on the earth, preventing them from uniting; thus keeping the two entities, the earth and the sky, though together, apart. Our faith and our decision never changing shall act as balance.[47]

The young warrior then is allowed to demonstrate his skill in a mock battle. He has to wait, however, for "about eighty-two moons or twelve rainy seasons following the circumcision ceremony" for promotion to the rank of *njama ya ita* (council of senior warriors).[48] At this point his formal education is over and he assumes the political and social positions for which he has been training since the age of four or five.

The social philosophy behind age-sets and circumcision rites is fascinating. A few more samples, therefore, will be worthwhile. The Tiriki of Kenya, too, had, for the sake of corporate unity, defence and offence, divided their male population into seven age-sets. They also practised circumcision which gave a ritual embodiment to the passage from boyhood to manhood. During the period of seclusion, lasting some six months, period the youth went through a carefully laid out programme to bring about social transformation. Communal undertakings were encouraged; individualism was discouraged. It took the young Tiriki some fifteen years, however, after the initiation ceremony before he was admitted to the rank of the warriors, the most admired honour for men in that society. Before attaining this honour, he must have demonstrated qualities of leadership, charisma, and prowess in conflict. By the age of forty he would be elevated to the status of elder warriors. At this point his formal education would be completed. It was these elder warriors, we are told, who actually ruled Tirikiland.[49] Among the Tiriki, therefore, the warriors formed an elite set, a sort of military aristocracy, the elderly among whom controlled political power. As in Kikuyu, Tirikiland institutionalized and vigorously cultivated the warrior tradition. The warrior-politician manipulated Tiriki society to ensure its survival and thereby protected their position.

In Uganda the Bagisu are well known for the organisation of their society by age-sets through a ritual circumcision of boys and girls, very much in the

---

47   *Ibid.*, p. 191.
48   *Ibid.*, p. 192.
49   Basil Davidson, *The African Genius: An Introduction to African Social and Cultural History* (Boston: 1969), pp. 84–86.

tradition of the Kikuyu, unlike whom, however, such a practice did not appear to have had much military significance. Of course, the Bagisu fought wars – or more likely battles – when the occasion demanded such a solution. But such occasions appear to have been very rare, and when they did occur, the wars or battles were of short duration.[50] The warrior tradition among the Bagisu was therefore weak. For the interlacustrine Bantu, on the other hand, where ritual circumcision was not practised and where variations of a centralized form of government were operated, the warrior tradition had more social significance. The ruling aristocracy of the conquest state of Banyankore, for example – the Bahima – dominated the more numerous Bairu until the colonial period, due, in part, to greater military cohesion and prowess in war. Through the existence of warrior bands, led by certain military chiefs who recognised the Omugabe (king) of Nkore as their sovereign, the Bahima aristocracy perpetuated the social domination of the Bairu. Marriage between a Mwiru and a Mukima was strictly prohibited, and the illegitimate offsprings between Bahima men and Bairu girls were legally classed as Bairu although they were called Abambari (half-castes). Their lot, however, as was usual in similar cases in other parts of the world, was better than that of the Bairu. A Mwiru was forbidden to kill a Muhima for any reason whatsoever while the same rule did not apply to a Muhima. The Bairu were forbidden to own "productive cows"; but they were ruthlessly exploited through the imposition of food and labour tribute.[51] The military in Nkore was an instrument of class and social domination in pre-colonial Uganda.

Before the Mfecane, the Nguni regarded the age-set rite and ritual circumcision as a sacred institution. The Nguni age-set organisation or circumcision guild differed, however, from the others we have discussed so far in one important respect: each age-set was associated with a royal age-mate who led his peers in war and peace. But the principles of the institution as well as the concomitant rite of circumsision was similar.[52] During the Mfecane, as we shall see, the age-regiment replaced the age-set; circumcision was abandoned, and society took a more military character.

The age-set organisation appears to have been better developed – in terms of its structural-functional significance – in eastern African and Bantu southern African societies than in those of West-Africa. Circumcision, for example, among the Igbo or among West African Muslim communities has no discernible military or age-set connotation since it was carried out within the first two weeks of a child's birth. The age-set organization existed to perform several social functions, the military aspects of which, though important, were not particularly pronounced. Among the Yoruba, on the other hand, the lineage and age-set systems did provide, to some degree, the social machinery for defence and

---

50   John Roscoe, *The Northern Bantu* (London: 1915 and 1966), p. 190.
51   K. Oberg, "The Kingdom of Ankole in Uganda," in Fortes and Evans-Pritchard, *African Political Systems*, pp. 121–136.
52   Omer-Cooper, *Zulu Aftermath*, pp. 27–28.

offence within the various state systems. Members of a lineage lived in an Agbo-Ile (compound) under the leadership of a lineage head, usually the eldest member of the lineage. The age-sets were formed from several lineages to perform social functions similar to those performed by Kikuyu age-sets. In wartime, the age-sets were led by the Elegbe chiefs. As a result of the nineteenth century civil wars, the warriors came to assume greater social significance. The age-set, as a machinery for achieving social cohesion, joint identity, common heritage and common future, broke down. Ibadan led the way in this transformation. Here, the civil war had given rise to prominent warriors who headed their own armies. It is true that the nucleus of each war leader's army still came from his own lineage or village, but as the civil war progressed, the ranks of this army were swollen by the process of accretion. The new additions included war captives as well as free men from various parts of Yorubaland (especially refugees), "who, eager to share in the greatness [of the warlord]" as well as in his successes and in his protection, "willingly attached themselves to him." They were settled in an Agbo-Ile belonging to the warlord. In a sense, then, an Ibadan army did not exist; there existed only a band of warriors "each owned, led, and provided for by its chief."[53] It would appear that a client – captive or free – after making a name for himself in this sort of military activity, would return to his own home and raise his own personal army in the tradition of his former Ibadan overlord. In this way, what has been described as the "Ibadan System" gradually spread throughout Yorubaland during the nineteenth century. These warlords forced their followers to cultivate large farms for the purpose of producing food for sale, to engage in trade in order to raise revenue, including the distribution of imported goods. Nineteenth century Yoruba history is full of examples of outstanding warlords whose versatility, ambition, greed and restlessness made war a permanent necessity. War became a necessity for a warlord not only for the purpose of keeping his warriors constantly occupied but also for increasing his following (since a large, well trained and well led following ensured survival in this dangerous and highly competitive age); it was essential for the purchase of arms and ammunition to be used in the execution of further wars. Success bred success; failure meant death or enslavement. The rise of the warlords altered social relationships in Yoruba country by successfully challenging the social and political dominance of the traditional rulers who were now their puppets. But it also resulted in the loss of personal freedoms among ordinary citizens who, in search of security and livelihood following the breakdown of law and order, sought the protection of powerful individuals. It was the British conquest of Yorubaland which brought to an end the era of the great warlords in Yoruba history.[54]

The age-set organisation does not appear to have existed among the Akan of Ghana. However, the *asafo* (military organisation of the towns) and the *abusua* (clan system) seem to have performed a similar function. "Every Agona

---

53   Akintoye, "Military Among the Yoruba," *loc. cit.*
54   *Ibid.*

(and for that matter every Akan)", writes Maxwell Owusu, "belongs to some asafo on the father's side (patrilineally) as he or she belongs to an abusua on the mother's side (matrilineally)."[55] The asafo, nevertheless, seems to have been most developed among the Fante. It comprised both men and women but only the men engaged in its military activities. The asafo is a social and military institution through which individuals who proved themselves in battle were rewarded with honours including chieftainships.[56] It was aimed not only at demonstrating common identity but also at ensuring the stability, survival, and power of the Akan states, thereby promising a common and bright future. We shall return to the asafo presently.

Suffice it to say, in summary, that the asafo, as a social control system, performed similar functions as the age-set, the age-regiment, and the circumcision guild. All these systems are significant as instruments of primodial nationalism and patriotism, social transformation, and social therapy. In short, we are dealing with social manipulation at its best. And, in the final analysis, society is broadly manipulated for offence and defence.

The Organisational Dimension

Most studies of the precolonial African military are concerned with the military organisation of individual state systems. These studies, provided mainly by anthropologists, are usually sketchy and largely descriptive. Few comparisons are attempted. In a recent sampling of precolonial African military systems, however, Claude Welch, noted in an otherwise useful study, what he saw as "the extraordinary variations in African military organisation."[57] I think this is a gross exaggeration. Varieties certainly there were; but there was nothing extraordinary or dramatic about them. If our contention is correct, namely, that African military organisation followed closely the organisation of the state, and if this state organisation can be broadly classified – as is usually the case – into centralised, semi-centralised (semi-segmentary), and non-centralised (segmentary), military organisation ought therefore to reflect these three broad distinctions. And even if we added to these three categories Aidan Southall's intriguing as well as baffling notion of "segmentary kingdoms", we can hardly assert that precolonial African military organisations are myriad. On the contrary, similarities in organisation are more common than dissimilarities. In this section our sampling will be more extensive than hitherto and, inevitably, less detailed. The organisational dimension of the African military may be studied under the following aspects: Leadership and Command Hierarchy; Recruitment and Mobilisation; Technology, Training and Tactics.

---

55   M. Owusu, *Uses and Abuses of Political Power: A Case Study of Continuity and Change in the Politics of Ghana* (Chicago: 1970), p. 41.
56   For a study of the Asafo system see Ansu K. Datta and R. Potter, "The Asafo System in Historical Perspective," *J.A.H.*, XII, 2 (1971).
57   C. Welch, "Continuity and Discontinuity in African Military Organisation," *J.M.A.S.*, 13, 2 (1975), p. 235.

Leadership and Command Hierarchy. Leadership in war, even when it resided in the dominant group within the state system, on heredity, or is clan based, was generally entrusted to the most capable hand among the privileged. It is, indeed, part of the command hierarchy which follows closely the state organisation. Among the so-called egalitarian Igbo, for example, leadership in war was not hereditary. It was earned on merit, that is, proven ability in battles, including demonstrable excellence in the mastery of the martial arts.[58] I have no information, however, to suggest that an Osu (untouchable?) or Ohu (slave?) was ever made the generalissimo. They did fight with the rank and file citizens and were rewarded according to their merit. The essential point here is that leadership in war is a function of the Igbo political organisation. But the issue of ability and excellence among the privileged as the prerequisite for leadership is also true of the Kikuyu Acholi, Bunyoro Kitara, Buganda, Nkore, Zulu, Ndebele, Rwanda, Akan, Oyo, Tukulor and so many others. The morality of dividing society between privileged and unprivileged classes is not here my concern. The point I wish to stress, however, is the similarity of the leadership ideology within states of differing political organisation.

In Bunyoro Kitara, the Omukama was the commander-in-chief of his warriors, and the territorial administrators, as we saw, comprised what might be called the officer class. Together they led the citizen militia in war and ruled them in peace. When, as a result of widening responsibilities and internal problems he was forced to surrender field command to his military chiefs, his political effectiveness declined; and by the middle of the nineteenth century, the great Kitara empire had become a shadow of its former self. Kabalega's creation of the abarusura, as we also saw, was intended to check the dominant influence of these military chiefs. This policy naturally involved a change in command hierarchy. All the commanders, for example – with the exception of three[59] (whose loyalty was not in doubt) – were no longer territorial rulers; equally importantly, *every commander* could be transferred from one command to another which meant that the command was no longer, as in the past, a sort of territorial fief. The generalissimo, too, was no longer necessarily the most important and able territorial ruler. Military command and territorial rulership, in short, had become separable. In Bunyoro, at any rate, change in military organisation affected decisively power relationships within the state.[60]

This is also true of the Zulu and the Ndebele. The barrack system which Kabalega developed in the second half of the nineteenth century, had earlier been developed by Shaka. I have no reason to believe that Kabalega copied

---

58   S. C. Ukpabi, "The Military in Pre-Colonial Igboland," The Accra Conference, August, 1975.

59   These were Nyakatura Nyakamatura, Ireeta Byangombe, and Kikukuule Runego. These important personalities had helped put Kabalega on the throne during the succession war of 1869–1871. He therefore rewarded them by appointing them abarusura generals while allowing them to retain their chiefly responsibilities as well.

60   Uzoigwe, *Revolution and Revolt*, pp. 1–29; *idem*, "Kabalega and the Making of a New Kitara," pp. 5–20.

this system from Shaka. But the introduction of the barrack system in Zululand also changed power relationships, especially command hierarchy. During the Mfecane, and as a result of increasing military insecurity, the Mthethwa (under Dingiswayo), the Ndwandwe (under Zwide), the Ngwane (under Sobhuza), and the Pondo were forced to abandon the sacred rite of circumcision whose ritual seclusion tied up a significant flighting force in times of crises, and changed the age-sets into age-regiments. It was Shaka, however, who perfected the age-regimental organisation. The regiments, unlike those we have studied so far, were not grouped according to clan ties. They were, on the contrary, trans-ethnic and "national" in composition. They were forbidden to marry until they reached the age of between thirty-five and forty years at which period they were permitted to marry from a regiment of girls of between twenty-three and twenty-five years of age. Both the regiment of boys and the regiment of girls as well as royal Zulu women were housed in barracks. These innovations, in addition to the military tactics developed by Shaka, were the most important contributions he made to the social history of the southern Bantu. The great Mzilikazi Kumalo, king of the Ndebele, conqueror of the Shona, and founder of what later came to be called Rhodesia instead of *Mzilikazia* (Zimbabwe), did not establish the barrack system (within which he was schooled) in his new kingdom. Nor, indeed, did he enforce celibacy for himself or his warriors. But, then, his problems were different from Shaka's; on the contrary, he used his regiments as an army of occupation.[61] Barrack existence and celibacy were seen by Shaka as a *conditio sine qua non* for military discipline. It is remarkable that these soldiers did not practise homosexuality. Everyone, except the diviners or the infirm, belonged to a regiment.[62] The Zulu were definitely a "nation in arms". The Zulu state was a timarchy, the like of which Africa had not seen before and probably would not see again. The territorial chiefs of earlier days were no longer significant in the new scheme of things. By the second half of the nineteenth century when the Zulu military machine reached its perfection, it seems reasonable to assume that the territorial chiefships were occupied by retired warriors.

Command hierarchy among the Ndebele was an elaborate administrative system. Matabeleland consisted of four *imikhono* (saza in Runyoro; provinces or countries in English) which also coincided with the four divisions of Mzilikazi's army. Each imikhono was administered by an *induna Nkulu* (senior chief); it was also divided into districts which, except for those under the control of the chiefs of the conquered and assimilated Shona, coincided with the *impi* (regiments) of the army. There was also the *buto* (military regimental town) which was under the control of the *induna yabuto* (commanding general). But there were usually also, in each buto, an *induna Umuzi* who was in charge of civilian

---

61   Gluckman, "The Individual in a Social Framework," *loc. cit.*, p. 139.
62   E. J. Krige, "The Military Organisation of the Zulus," in Elliot P. Skinner (ed.), *Peoples and Cultures of Africa* (New York: 1973), p. 484; *cf.* James Stuart, *History of the Zulu Rebellion 1906* (London: 1913), esp. p. 72.

as opposed to military matters. Below both indunas were the *abalisa* (battalion commanders); and above the indunas was the Nkosi (king) himself.[63] The structure of Matabeleland was, like that of Zululand out of which it grew, simply the structure of an army. In war and peace, the Nkosi, like the Omukama of Bunyoro or the Kabaka of Buganda, was a centrifugal as well as a centripetal force in the kingdom. But neither Bunyoro nor Buganda was militarized to the extent that Matabeleland was.

Among the Akans command hierarchy also followed the state administrative pattern. Maxwell Owusu, writing about Agona states: "The organisation of stools and swords in Agona is nothing but military formation based on the logistics of war developed by the people. Political organization is ipso facto military organization."[64] This statement may well apply to all the Akan states generally. Among the Asante, for example, the members of the *oman nhyiama* (ruling state council), for example, also headed the military divisions of the state. The Asantehene (king) held the position of supreme commander of the army; two of his deputies who administered the state in his absence, the Kontihene and the Akwamuhene, were also the first and second war chiefs respectively. Below them were the Adontenhene (commander of the main force – "the carrier of the foot of the Omanhene"); Nifahene (right wing); Benkumehene (left wing); Kyidomhene (rearguard); and Gyaesehene (Omanhene's bodyguard as well as the head of the domestic bureaucracy). Here, once again, is a dangerous fusion of military and political functions. These leaders, too, except in a few cases, were also either lineage heads or chiefs of provinces. In peacetime, they managed the state apparata; in wartime, they took all decisions including the prosecution of the war itself as well as the making of peace.[65] These samples will suffice to show that the command hierarchy in the kingdom states of Africa reflected the political organisation of the states. Minor variations occurred here and there, but there was really nothing dramatic about these variations.

Igboland, on the other hand, which included both the characteristics of the semi-kingdom and non-kingdom state systems, does vary from the classic kingdom states but only because of the varying political structure. Among those uninfluenced by kingdom characteristics, the war commander was usually appointed by the consensus of the warriors prior to their departure for the battlefield. The commander, called Ochiagha (leader in war), was always someone whose warrior reputation was already secure; but during his tenure he must continuously live up to that reputation or yield his place to a more deserving comrade. The Ochiagha commanded the centre in battle. He was assisted by two other commanders, also appointed by consensus because of proven ability,

---

63   David Chanaiwa, "The Army and Politics in Pre-Industrial Africa: Ndebele Nation 1822–1893," Accra Conference, August, 1975.
64   Owusu, *Uses and Abuses of Political Power*, p. 39.
65   Agnes A. Aidoo, "The Role of the Military in Politics and Society in 19th Century Asante," Accra Conference, August, 1975; Kwame Arhim, "Asante Militarism: A Preliminary Note," Accra Conference, August, 1975; cf. Owusu, *op. cit.*, pp. 39–40.

who commanded the right and left flanks respectively.[66] The Ochiagha was responsible to no one but to his village or town. Among Onitsha, Oguta and Aboh Igbo – areas influenced by kingdom characteristics – there was also always a commander-in-chief called the Iyase. But he wielded no more authority than the Ochiagha.[67] Like the Igbo Council of Elders, the Acholi *rwot* (lord or clan leader) and his counsellors and other advisers were not military men *per se*. They concerned themselves with civil matters although they decided when to go to war and when to make peace. But the general was chosen in peacetime by censussis. He had a free hand in the prosecution of war. The civilians, however, made decisions regarding the spoils of war.[68] The Acholi, like the Igbo, believed in specialisation and division of labour.

Recruitment and Mobilisation. Except in a few cases, and mostly during the nineteenth century, African warriors were assembled *ad hoc* to deal with specific emergencies or to execute certain state objectives. They were agriculturists, pastoralists, artisans, administrators, etc. who reverted unobtrusively to their occupations as seen as the campaigns were over. In short, every able-bodied male of military age was a soldier in addition to his other occupations. In some societies, Igbo[69] and Dahomey, for example, females participated in the fighting but there was no general mobilisation among them; in most societies, however, women contributed indirectly but significantly to the war effort. There were, of course, certain states – usually conquest states – which adopted the principle of differential recruitment by linking class with military specialisation. This was true of the Mossi where only the noblemen served in the cavalry and commoners served as infantrymen; and in major battles, infantry was only auxiliary to cavalry. But yet all able-bodied males of military age went to war. It has also been noted among the Hausa, slaves dominated the infantry and formed a considerable part of the cavalry as well. Here, therefore, differential recruitment was mitigated somewhat. For the Wolof in the nineteenth century the bulk of the warriors were *thiedos* (unbelievers) who served under the command of village chiefs.[70] The pattern of social dominance was such, however, that the *thiedos* could not overthrow the theocratic state system. In Rwanda, the reverse was the case. The dominant Batutsi (pastoralists) used differential recruitment as one of the means of perpetuating their dominance over the Bahutu (agriculturists). And although by the nineteenth century certain Bahutu such as Bisangwa and Bishingwe rose to be military commanders, the

---

66 Ukpabi, "The Military in Pre-Colonial Igboland", *loc. cit.*

67 *Ibid.*

68 John O. Dwyer, "Acholi Military History", African Studies Association Conference paper, Philadelphia, 10 November 1972.

69 The role of Dahomeian women in war is well known. For Igbo women see Paul Edwards, *Equiano's Travels* (London: 1967), pp. 9–10.

70 Welch, "Continuity and Discontinuity in African Military Organisation", pp. 232–233; *cf.* Elliot P. Skinner, *The Mossi of the Upper Volta: The Political Development of a Sudanese People* (Stanford: 1964), pp. 97–106; M. G. Smith, *The Economy of Hausa Communities of Zaira* (London: 1955), p. 10.

fact remained that the Bahutu did not generally form part of the state *itero* (military units). The Batwa (pigmies), too, could only serve as the Mwami's (king's) personal bodyguards, as bodyguards of important chiefs, and as warriors outside the *itero* organisation.[71] We have also noted that in those societies where military service depended on circumcision and age-sets, individuals who failed to perform these necessary *rites de passage* were also affected by differential recruitment. In terms, however, of the generality of African state systems, recruitment and mobilisation patterns were more simular than dissimilar. Among the states which developed standing armies, ability, loyalty, and bravery rather than class differentiation seems to have determined a warrior's future in the military hierarchy. Indeed, Shaka or Kabalega would go out of his way to hunt down and kill a disloyal warrior or one who was convicted of cowardice; they would also reward generously a loyal and outstanding warrior irrespective of his class.

Technology, Training and Tactics. The impact of technological innovation on the histories of nations cannot be overemphasized; but it is also apt to be misunderstood. Superior military technology is not only an instrument of imperial domination but also one of internal coersion. More importantly, it is an instrument controlled by the ruling elite. Where centralised control is impossible as in the case of the "democratic" bow and arrow, the state manipulates its use through specific acts of social and political engineering. But since the ruling elite of precolonial African states comprised also the warriors, it means that precolonial African history was characterised by a dangerous fusion of politics and violence. In both the colonial and postcolonial periods of African history, such a trend has continued unabated. A colonial situation was created by violence and maintained by violence or the threat of it – whatever the apologists of colonialism may say. Independent African states – and I am really hard put to make an exception here – even where the military is not exercising open power, have tended to show less restraint in the use of violence to ensure individual, particularist, ethnic, or state ends. The warrior, then the soldier, has become more and more, not the instrument of defence and offence, but an instrument of coercion. Indeed, I think it is fair to say that precolonial African states, in spite of their dangerous fusion of politics and the military, in general used less physical coercion than the colonial and postcolonial states; but they were more adept at politico-socio manupilation than their twentieth century successor states.

What is easily noticeable about precolonial African military technology is its simplicity. For our immediate purposes, however, what is intriguing is the similarity of the military technology of these African state systems as shown below:

---

71 Welch, "Continuity and Discontinuity," pp. 233–234; *cf.* J. J. P. Maquet, *The Premise of Inequality in Ruanda: A Study of Political Relations in a Central African Kingdom* (London: 1961), pp. 109–10.

STATE	TECHNOLOGY
Acholi	Shield, spear, knife
Buganda	Shield, throwing spear, stabbing spear, firearms (19th century)
Bugisu	Shield, spear, knife
Bunyoro Kitara	Shield, throwing spear, stabbing spear, bow and arrow (used only by the fishing community of Bugungu), firearms (19th century)
Hausa	Shield, horse, sword, bow and arrow, firearms
Igbo	Shield, spear, bow and arrow, dagger, spiked club, matchets, steel knife, firearms
Ndebele	Shield, throwing assegai (spear), stabbing spear, firearms (19th century)
Tukulor	Shield, horse, sword, firearms
Yoruba	Shield, spear, bow and arrow, sword, horse, firearms
Zulu	Shield, throwing assegai (spear), stabbing assegai, firearms (19th century)

From the above sampling carefully selected to reflect ecological, regional, and constitutional variables, we may arrive at the following conclusions. First, precolonial African military technology was very rudimentary and shows more similarities than dissimilarities. Shields and missiles provide the common denominator. Second, it follows therefore that in either offensive or defensive war, training, tactics, cohesion, leadership, discipline, martial spirit, numbers, and geography, in varying ways, would seem to be more crucial than technology. Hausa horsemen, for example, fighting in the forest areas of Igboland, would not have a ghost of a chance. Nor would Igbo warriors fare any better in the grassland against the Hausa. Third, firearms were fairly well spread, at any rate, by the nineteenth century. But their use by no means discouraged the use of other weapons. Indeed, my studies in East Africa demonstrate that the impact of firearms on the outcome of battles has been exaggerated. Nor did firearms necessarily prove a worse instrument of coercion in the period under survey than the other military technologies. Shaka's Zulu, we know, did not use firearms; and yet his Zulu state was the most coercive state in nineteenth century Africa. And fourth, the crucial point to note in any discussion of the warriors and the state is not only the novelty of the technology available to the state but also – and more importantly – who controlled what technology there was, how effectively it was controlled, and to what end.

In this consideration the nature of the socio-political structure of the states, as we have shown, becomes crucial. Religion, not firearms,[72] led to the rise of bureaucratic states in the central Sudan during the nineteenth century; and it was the quality of Shaka's military leadership and military tactics that proved more crucial as centralising modes than the mere introduction of the assegai. Indeed, the assegai, as a technological innovation, cannot be attributed to Shaka. It was a weapon with which the Zulu were already familiar. Shaka's

---

72 Joseph P. Smaldone seems to argue the contrary. See "Firearms in the Central Sudan: A Revaluation", *J.A.H.*, XIII, 4 (1972); cf. *idem*, "Military Organisation, Warfare, and Sudanic State Structure: Some Sociological Aspects of Technological Change," African Studies Assocation Conference paper, Philadelphia, 10 November 1972.

great military contribution, therefore, was in the areas of tactics and training. Even under Shaka, a warrior carried both his throwing spear and his stabbing spear. The stabbing spear, as we saw, was also familiar to the Baganda and Banyoro. And yet East African historians have not made much noise about its existence. The reason, I suppose, is because the East African warriors were unable to put it into the revolutionary use to the extent that Shaka did. The difference between, say, Zwide's warriors and those of Shaka was that the latter were better trained, better disciplined, and better led. The standing army created by Shaka was also a tactical innovation designed to ensure discipline and the enhancement of his power which were crucial for empire-building. In Bunyoro, Kabalega who bears comparison with Shaka in several respects, was nonetheless not a military genius; but he was a great warrior who realised, as did Shaka, that the army was the instrument to maintain state, and consequently, royal power. His formation of the *abarusura* was a significant military development in the interlacustrine region. It was a tactical contribution designed to subdue overmighty subjects, pick up the pieces of the practically disintegrated Kitara empire, check the prospering ambition of Buganda, and if possible, recreate the old Kitara empire. Finally, it is in the area of systematic, sustained military training that precolonial African warriors were least deficient. Technological innovation, unsupported by adequate training and tactics, loses its effectiveness.

Conclusions

This chapter is a contribution to the study of the precolonial African military as an indispensable aspect of African history. The images of the warrior are not its theme. On the contrary, it is a comparative study of the institutional-functional aspects of defence and offence among carefully selected precolonial African state systems. It aspires, however, to be no more than an introduction – a prospectus, if you will – to a field of research that promises a bright future ahead of it. The information at my disposal, nevertheless, has led to certain conclusions which further, more systematic, researches may well modify or even confirm; first, that the study of the precolonial African military is the study of the structure of African history itself. Therefore, a military interpretation of African history should prove as rewarding – or even more rewarding – than the prevailing interpretations. Second, the African warrior was a political animal *par excellence* particularly because of the fusion of the state and the military. The study of the warrior, then, is tantamount to the study of the state. And since the Africans saw the state as organism, the warrior, too, must be studied as organism. The ambitious youth was well aware that excellence as a warrior was an impeccable passport to important political offices, wealth, glory, honour, themselves part of the equation. The warrior tradition was the bedrock of statehood; and politics, in short, was organised around the warriors. Politics, law, and the instruments of destruction resided in the same hands. *Prima facie*, this was an unhealthy development especially as the warrior was dominant in both national and territorial administration. The ordinary citizens had no means of overthrowing unpopular military-civilian governments in the kingdom states. Palace rebellions, sometimes leading to changes in personnel, did, of course, occur from time to time; but the structure of government hardly changed. The rise of standing armies and professional warriors in the nineteenth century did, indeed, upset the political balance; but politics remained structured in such a way that the people could still not change an oppressive government. Nevertheless, few governments were ever as oppressive as the colonial or the post-colonial governments. Among non-kingdom states such as the Kikuyu and the Igbo, the myth that the ordinary citizen was an indivisible element of government was so astutely cultivated that the overthrow of those who controlled power was considered unnecessary. This brings us to our third conclusion, namely, that the warrior was, first and last, a citizen. His education was a brilliant lesson in social manipulation and social control. The sacred notion of the extended family, the *rites des passage* of age-sets and circumcision guilds, and age-regiments (whether they be of the variety perfected by the Zulu or the *asafo* of the Akans) were all intended to inculcate the idea of nationalism and patriotism, to achieve social transformation, and to act as social therapy. In the final analysis, the philosophy behind these social institutions is a broad manipulation of society for offence and defence in the interests of stability, survival, and prosperity of the state. Fourth, since the organisation of the military followed closely the organisation of the state, and since the organisation of African state systems are reducible to three broad categories, the dramatic variations that are supposed to characterize precolonial African military organisations are fictitious. Within the broad categories differences did exist, but there was nothing extraordinary about them. On the contrary, the precolonial African military organisation – and indeed the military in general – exhibits more similarities than dissimilarities. And fifth, to understand fully the military in contemporary Africa, the character and nature of the military in precolonial Africa must first be comprehended. It is only then that the question of continuities and discontinuities in the African military tradition which is now attracting some attention can be more fruitfully tackled. It is hoped that this study has made a small contribution – in spite of its weaknesses – in that direction.

Military Continuities in the Rwanda State

WARREN WEINSTEIN

Institute of International Law and Economic Development, Washington, D.C. U.S.A.

RWANDA is a small mountainous state in central Africa distinguished by its severe overpopulation and extreme poverty. Its population consists of three ethnic groups: the Hutu majority (89%); the Tutsi (10%); and the pygmoid Twa (1%). For the social scientist Rwanda is an attractive case study because of its social complexities and rich traditions. It is not a new state, although pre-colonial Rwanda was much smaller than the current borders and central control was not uniform in all parts of the country.

At no point in Rwandan history were Tutsi more than 16% of the population of present-day Rwanda, but their regal manners and large herds enabled them to infiltrate Hutu regions and exercize influence among these agriculturalists. Over the centuries the Tutsi imposed their domination. In addition, the superior military organization of the pastoralist Tutsi allowed them to impose their will where they met with opposition.

The traditional military experience in Rwanda dates back several centuries. At first it amounted to little more than sporadic cattle raids against neighboring pastoralists and agriculturalist groups in the vicinity of the original Rwandan kingdom. This was a small state situated in the Mubari region of what is now central Rwanda. Succeeding monarchs improved the state's military potential. Their superior martial abilities enabled them to annex more territory. But they also suffered reverses, and the size of the kingdom varied from king to king.

Luc de Heusch (1966: 113–117) suggests that Rwanda's precolonial military structure and traditions were influenced significantly by the impact of Nyoro superior military organization. Nyoro armies defeated Rwanda as they made incursions southward from present-day Uganda during the 16th century. The Nyoro armies defeated two Rwandan *bami* (sg. *mwami*) or kings: Kigeri Mukobanya (ca. 1506–1528) and Mibambwe Mutabaazi (ca. 1528–1552). Vansina (1962: 84–85) has argued that the Nyoro were able to devastate the Rwandan forces because they had many more warriors and a more unified command structure. The Rwandan mwami, at the time of these defeats, fought alongside his vassals but lacked the power to deploy those forces as he wished. Nor was he able to create new armies of his own. (Vansina, 1962: 65).

Mutabaazi, impressed with Nyoro tradition, reformed Rwanda's army. He imposed a unified command on all armed forces in time of war. An additional change was made either under Mutabaazi or mwami Yuhi Gahima (ca. 1552–1576): entire lineages were assigned to the existing armies of royal pages (*intore*) and these armies became hereditary. The number of pages in each army was increased. As a result of these reforms it became necessary to divide the armies into companies (*itorero*).

An unintended consequence of the establishment of hereditary armies was an added problem over succession to the throne. As a result of this reform each mwami created new armies. This added to the kingdom's overall military might, but when succession struggles occurred they now developed into full civil wars. Prior to these reforms succession struggles could be described as quarrels. However, after the reforms, different hereditary armies were commanded either by the contestants themselves or commanders who owed allegiance to one of the contestants.

The new military structures were perfected by succeeding bami, and the armies were wielded into a formidable force which served Rwanda's expansionist appetite. Mwami Ndoori (ca. 1600–1624) used the armies to extend his borders to those pre-dating the Nyoro invasions and to consolidate the kingdom. Mwami Cyilima Rujugira (ca. 1744–1763) increased the number of companies in each army and the number of armies. In response to a coalition of three bordering states against Rwanda, Rujugira instituted a major innovation. All border regions were placed under the authority of an army chief, and most soldiers were required to live in these frontier provinces. Military camps were created in all strategic points along Rwanda's borders.

The pre-colonial military structure was fashioned on a chiefship command structure. Army chiefs were autonomous of two other chiefships that co-existed in the kingdom: pasture or land chiefs and cattle chiefs. The individual selected to serve as the head of an army was called an *umugabo* or *umutware w'ingabo*. He tended to be an important chief, and disposed of large cattle herds which were obtained either as gifts or as his share of the army's booty. Cattle were the basis of wealth and prestige in pre-colonial society. Through the distribution of his cattle and lands the *umugabo* maintained a close network of personal clients among members of his army (*ingabo*). As a rule these clients were Tutsi.

In addition to Tutsi lineages which were assigned to an *ingabo* created with each new reign, Hutu and Twa lineages were attached to these permanent armies. The Hutu did not function as warriors. They served as herdsmen and provided services to Tutsi warriors while the army was on expeditions. The Twa functioned as the mwami's police and personal spies. They served as the Tutsi army's advance troops.

At the end of the 19th century the role of army chiefs was clearly defined. They commanded an entire province. In frontier provinces the army chiefs exercized full jurisdiction, had responsibility for maintaining army camps, and guarded the kingdom against invasion. Within his province, an army chief appointed all of his subchiefs. He exercized justice over all patrilineages assigned to his *ingabo* whether or not the individuals resided within the confines of his province. Whenever a new mwami ascended the throne, the boundaries of provinces commanded by army chiefs were changed to provide lands to create a new province for the chief of new armies. The army chiefs were required to spend much of the time at the royal court (*ibwami*) (Vansina, 1962: 57).

Each army or *ingabo* was subdivided into the warrior section (Tutsi) and herder section (Hutu). The warrior groups (*intore*, i.e. "chosen ones) "became the highly disciplined and constantly ready nuclei" of the *ingabo* (Des Forges, 1972: 4).

> While the *ntore* of each ngabo were personally selected and trained by the leader of that *ngabo*, the rest of the able-bodied men of the kingdom were assigned to the *ngabo* by lineage. The lineages were distributed by the mwami according to their strength rather than their location, so the members of an *ngabo* might be clustered in one region or distributed throughout the kingdom. Membership in the *ngabo* was ordinarily hereditary, although men were detached from one to constitute another at the will of the court (Des Forges, 1972: 4–5).

The young Tutsi *intore* who formed a company (*itorero*) of 150–200 men resided at the king's court or at the court of a "chief who had been allowed to recruit an army" (Maquet, 1961: 109). Over a period of several years they were trained in the martial arts, to perform warlike dances, and to memorize as well as compose epic poems exalting the deeds of great warriors. The *intore* wore special badges.

Maquet (1961: 118) insists that Hutu did not participate in actual battle. D'Hertefelt (1962: 65) suggests that Hutu acted as porters and auxiliaries while the Rwandan army was still on Rwandan soil, and that they became pillagers once in enemy territory. Accounts provided of military expeditions during the reign of mwami Yuji Musinga (1896–1931) indicate that Tutsi served as the warrior nucleus of the army and officered Hutu troops who also participated in battle.

Army regiments created with each new reign did not cease to exist when a new king came to power. As Rwanda expanded, its armies drew upon the additional manpower of new territories incorporated into the kingdom. This contributed to significant increases in the armies' total size. The newer armies tended to camp in border regions threatened by Rwanda's neighbors. Armies created in previous reigns tended to camp in the interior of the kingdom (Maquet, 1961: 110–111).

Military expeditions were of two kinds: "those planned by the king (*igitero*) and those planned by a military chief" (Maquet, 1961: 111) Maquet continues,

> The latter expeditions were short raids which could not last more than two days (*agatero-shuma*). A very complicated ritual was observed in the choice of the leader of the expedition (*umugabe w'igitero*). ...During the battle the general of the expedition would sit motionless in his headquarters; every move backwards of his would have resulted in his forces' flight.
>
> Some of the warriors (*abakoni*, stick-bearers) had the special charge of capturing cattle. If the expedition was successful, it ended with a celebration lasting several days.

There is little information on the exact size of Rwandan forces when they engaged in battle. Expeditions against other states lasted for several weeks and involved regular combat. Based on information provided by a Burundian chief, Vansina calculated that the armies ranged in size from 1,000–2,000 warriors (i.e. *intore*) (Vansina, 1962: 82). When Mwami Rutarindwa dispatched his armies against a Belgian fort in late 1895, that force numbered several thousand of the king's best warriors (Des Forges, 1972: 19). In 1907, when the German Duke of Mecklenburg arrived at the *ibwami* with more than 600 soldiers and porters, mwami Musinga was able to mobilize between six and eight thousand notables at the royal court to protect himself against the Germans.

During the 19th century Rwanda's armies continued to raid neighboring areas in actions which lasted for one or two days. Such raids were undertaken sporadically at first, and then with some regularity. Once the Tutsi felt they could impose their domination on the region, a full scale expedition was mounted to conquer it. This escalation tactic was used against the Hutu states of western and northern Rwanda.

When it attacked, the Rwandan army sought to inflict a devastating defeat and laid waste those regions or states which were attacked. Mwami Rujugira's sons led expeditions against the states of Ndorwa and Gisaka which they devastated (Vansina, 1962: 88). The Tutsi armies' actions against Hutu states in northern and western Rwanda were so devastating during the 19th century that they sometimes provoked a famine. One expedition is referred to locally by the Hutu as the *inkemba*, the predators. They "pillaged and burned the possessions of all in their path . . . (they) so devastated the region that it suffered a serious famine soon after" (Des Forges, 1972: 27).

A European White Father described the devastation wrought by Rwandan soldiers in the Hutu regions of the north during a campaign in 1912:

> The war continues; the batutsi massacre, are without mercy; half of the population of Bumongo will be destroyed. Groups of women are led away and will become the booty of the great chiefs (Des Forges, 197: 193).

The importance of pillaging cannot be discounted. This provided the chief of each *ingabo* with additional wealth. Part of it was given to the mwami and part was retained by the army chief who then redistributed it to his clients and obtained new ones. The role of the army in the 19th century was to expand the borders of the original kingdom and to loot surrounding peoples. It also engaged in cattle rustling and brought back captives. Maquet downgrade's the defense function, and emphasized that the army of the 19th century was an "organization for conquering and looting rather than defense" (Maquet, 1961: 116). Vansina (1962: 56–94) suggests defense remained an important function. Codere's (1962: 58) analysis points out that, in addition, the army functioned to maximize extortion of agricultural surplus from the subordinate Hutu majority and to guarantee Tutsi domination. An important social consequence of the clientship ties, of the protection of army chiefs provided to members of patrilineages assigned to their *ingabo*, was the promotion of Tutsi national integration.

The Colonial Period

German troops penetrated Rwanda during the 1900s. They annexed it as part of German East Africa. German troops assisted Mwami Musinga (1896–1931) in extending his rule outward over peripheral regions and downward over rebellious chiefs. In 1910 Rwanda achieved its current borders. German rule ended unexpectedly, from the Rwandan viewpoint, in 1916, when a Belgian invasion force captured the territory.

During the initial European penetration, the Rwandan military response was limited to guerrilla attacks. In March, 1876, Stanley sought to penetrate the Gisaka region of Rwanda. He was driven off by armed Rwandans (Chronology, 1954, 12–13). In 1894, Count von Götzen led an exploratory expedition into Rwanda. Despite a cordial reception at the royal capital, his expedition was attacked at night by Tutsi warriors while camping at Bugoyi. The night attack was a traditional Tutsi tactic. At this time, Rwanda's military posture was strong. In 1889 the Mwami had led a campaign against the state of Ankole, a state on Rwanda's northern border in what is today Uganda. In 1892, the umugabe (chief of armies) Nturo, defeated Ankole.

In 1895 the mwami of Rwanda died, and in 1896 the armies of contending chiefs were engaged in a civil war over the succession. At the same time, the Germans established a military station at Ishangi in Western Rwanda. Tutsi warriors attacked, led by Chief Bisangwa. The Germans repulsed them, killing the chief. Anyhow, the Germans decided to withdraw from Ishangi.

A new mwami was installed in 1896, Yuhi Musinga, but many important chiefs considered him to be a usurper. The new mwami found it expedient to accept a treaty with the Germans. He faced opposition from chiefs who were against his enthronement. In addition, Belgian forces were threatening Rwanda to the west. Musinga hoped he could manipulate the Germans. Nevertheless, German missionaries were attacked by Tutsi guerilla bands. The response to Europeans had not changed completely.

The Germans cooperated with Musinga to mount campaigns against recalcitrant chiefs, and to subdue Hutu in peripheral areas where the mwami's authority was not respected. This enhanced Musinga's warrior image although it eroded his real power. In 1906 hereditary armies led by rebellious chiefs were defeated by hereditary armies loyal to the mwami, commanded by loyal chiefs. The last campaign led by the umugabe Nturo was in 1911, when he led the royal armies against rebels led by a former queen. Nturo defeated the rebels and brought the rebellious former queen to Musinga's royal residence, the Ibwami, at Nyanza. The umugabe Nturo was the last Rwandan chief of armies until 1959 who engaged in traditional military operations. In 1917, the new Belgian masters deprived Musinga of his power over life and death, and in 1926 the office of army chief was abolished (Chronology, 1954: 15–24).

During the 1920s the Belgians consolidated their control. The Rwandan military tradition was downgraded because the new European administration opposed an autonomous indigenous military force. In addition, in 1924 Rwanda was joined with Burundi to form a League of Nations mandated territory placed under Belgium's administration. The international status of Rwanda prevented the Belgians by treaty from organizing any local military levees. This restriction continued after the Second World War, when Rwanda and Burundi formed dual United Nations Trusteeship territory.

The legitimacy of Tutsi domination was eroded as a result of the cumulative effects of changes introduced during colonial rule.[1] In 1957 an emerging Hutu elite issued a direct challenge to continued Tutsi supremacy in the form of a political manifesto. They demanded radical social and political reforms. The Hutu organized two major political movements: ARROSOMA, led at first by Joseph Gitera; and PARMEHUTU, led by Grégoire Kayibanda.

In 1958 the Belgian administration espoused the Hutu thesis. In addition, the Belgians promised political reforms for their larger territory, the Congo. This triggered a resurgence of the Tutsi warrior traditions.

In late 1958, at a Kigali bar, Mwami Mutara (1931–1959) stated publicly that he would govern Rwanda, "and compel the Europeans to leave using force if necessary."[2] In early 1959, under the authority of the mwami and his queen-mother, Tutsi from important noble families organized a league to mobilize a defense of Tutsi interests against rising Hutu demands. This league was transformed into a political movement named UNAR. Anti-Belgian pamphlets began to appear signed "Rwanda's Warriors" (Van Hoeck, 1966: 127). Mutara mobilized Twa shock troops. The Belgian administration reported, "[Twa] were paramilitarily organized by Mutara ... [They were] his shock troops, henchmen for underhanded tasks" (Harroy, 1959: 2). In another report, the administration noted, "Mwami Mutara sensed the [Hutu] danger, [he] organized his cadre of chiefs and subchiefs, and his armies (ingabo), including the Twa formations. At his death, Mutara's organization became UNAR" (Quelle Politique ..., 1959).

The warrior epic poety was also revived to call Tutsi to arms. During 1959 a Tutsi leader, Gratien Sendanyoye, authored an incendiary tract entitled *Urwanda Urusasira* and written in the style of the warrior epic poetry:

> Parents of Rwanda
> Children of Rwanda
> Young men of Rwanda
> Let us rise up together.
> Gitera and a small number of his supporters
> Have sold out Rwanda.
> Let us swear as follows
> Rwanda who gave us life we shall die
> For you.[3]

---

1   This process is analyzed in detail by several authors. See Mary Catherine Atterbury, *Revolution in Rwanda* (University of Wisconsin, Wisc. 1968); René Lemarchand, *Rwanda and Burundi*, Praeger Publishers, Inc., New York: 1970.

2   Territoire du Ruanda-Urundi. Administration de la Sûreté. Bureau d'Usumbura. No. 0570/1168/R.P.4. *Rapport Périodique*, 4ème trimestre, 1958, p. 11. (Unpublished).

3   Territoire du Ruanda-Urundi. Administration de la Sûreté. Bureau d'Usumbura. No. 0570/460/R.P. 2. *Rapport Périodique*, 2ème trimestre, 1959, p. 15.

A second tract, "Children of Rwanda, Be Prepared for Battle", included two phrases which were a direct resurrection of the precolonial warrior tradition:

> Let us all swear together...
> Oh Rwanda our mother,
> We shall die for you,
> *I swear total devotion to you* (1)
> —The defender-warriors of Rwanda (2)

Phrase (1) is the fealty oath sworn to the Mwami in precolonial Rwanda. The entire oath is what warriors once swore to their mwami before a military expedition: "An oath intended to mobilize the warriors to a fanatic pitch. This was achieved through a succession of ceremonies and oaths organized during the evenings before the exploit, following the general mobilization" (Nkundabagenzi, 1962: 76). The second phrase, the defender-warriors, is an allusion to the *abatabazi*: a precolonial epithet given to warriors called upon to sacrifice themselves within the boundaries of Rwanda in order to repulse a foreign invasion. Those called upon to die abroad in defense of Rwanda are known as *abacengeri* (Nkundabagenzi, 1962: 76).

On July 24th, 1959 Mwami Mutara died mysteriously at a Bujumbura hospital after a Belgian doctor gave him an injection. The Belgians were blamed, and royalist leaders revived the precolonial tradition which requires a ritual revenge against a member of the group responsible for the mwami's death before the king's body can be enterred. These revivals, even if not all Tutsi leaders believed in them, served to keep alive the kingship mystique and strengthen the appeal of the Tutsi movement (Lemarchand, 1970: 200). This was essential in 1959 because the legitimacy of the kingship was questioned by Hutu leaders.

In the day which followed Mutara's death Europeans were attacked on several occasions, to avenge the mwami's death.[4] Armed bands of Tutsi and Twa roamed the countryside in central Rwanda. A Belgian territorial agent was wounded slightly in the head with a machette when attacked by a group of Hutu officered by Tutsi (Hubert, 1965: 27). Another European territorial agent who identified strongly with the Hutu leadership, Nijs, was hunted down by Twa commandos. He was saved when Belgian reinforcements arrived quite by accident. (Harroy, 1959: 3). At Nyanza, the mwami's capital, a European police commissioner was attacked with stones but escaped. The car of a European social worker was hit with spears, and a Volkswagen minibus belonging to the pro-Hutu *Kinya mateka* (a Catholic newspaper) was attacked (Nkundabagenzi: 1962, 87–92).

Mutara's death was itself a resurrection of a warrior tradition, that of the *umutabaazi*.[5] This name is given to a mwami who martyrs himself to save the nation. By tradition a mwami who carries the dynastic name of Mutara cannot

---

4 Territore du Ruanda-Urundi. Administration de la Sûreté. Bureau d'Usumbura. No. 0570/822/R.P. 3. *Rapport Périodique*, 3ème trimestre, 1959, p. 10.
5 For a discussion of the umutabaazi tradition see Vansina (1962: 11).

make war, but the next dynastic name in the royal cycle is Kigeri which is associated with battle (Bourgeois, 1954: 45–47). Mutara's death was a voluntary act to make way for a Kigeri who would lead Rwanda's armies to victory.

At Mutara's burial, July 28, 1959, indications were clear that a traditional army was being formed. Among the 3,000–4,000 Rwandans attending the ceremonies were "a certain number carrying indigenous weapons (bows, knives, spears and cudgels). Among them were mainly Twa who traditionally constituted the Tutsi's shock troops."[6] Another account described the assembled armies composed of Tutsi warriors and officers drawn from the cadre of Native Authorities (chiefs and subchiefs) and Hutu attendants:

> About half the crowd assembled for the funeral are dignitaries... chiefs, subchiefs, notables, évolués [western-educated Rwandans], from all corners of Rwanda; and half are commoners [Hutu]...most are armed... [W]ell-informed persons indicated that these commoners were exclusively inhabitants of Nyanza's environs, direct subjects of the crown... subject fully to its orders (Nkundabagenzi, 1962: 88–9).

As in precolonial Rwanda, the *ibwami* was transformed into a military headquarters. The chief royalists were able to impose a new mwami on the Belgian administration at the time of Mutara's burial and so Rwanda had its Kigeri (Nkundabagenzi, 1962: 87–180). Following tradition, the new mwami selected a Tutsi of a noble or good family as the *umugabo* of the Tutsi armies being assembled. The man chosen was subchief Nkuranga who "by his noble origin and character, possessed the requisite qualities to become chief of the army" (Hubert, 1965: 69). The choice was also made to reinforce the image of continuity with warrior traditions of the past. Nkuranga was the son of the preceding *umugabo* Nturo (Nkundabagenzi; 1962: 331–32).

The military mobilization was carried out as in precolonial times, despite the Belgian presence. Events were moving very quickly, and the Tutsi plans were executed with amazing speed. The mobilization is described by two sources:

> The drums called people to arms; not only Tutsi and Twa, but hundreds of average Hutu... streamed toward Nyanza [i.e., the Ibwami] in their banana leaf shoulder belt uniforms [i.e., ibilele] and armed with spears, cudgels, knives, and assagais. There they awaited instructions. These were given on November 6: decapitate the APROSOMA leadership (Van Hoeck, 1966: 164).

> Very rapidly... there was a veritable [military] mobilization: drums were beaten resounding the customary call to arms; Twa moved about to direct persons with banana leaf shoulder belts... to Nyanza, where they assembled to await orders (Nkundabagenzi, 1962: 153).

On November 1, 1959, a popular Hutu subchief was maltreated by Tutsi youths. On November 3, 1959, Hutu revolted against Tutsi domination. The revolt spread to most parts of the country. Hutu gangs roamed the hillsides attacking Tutsi, burning and pillaging their homesteads. This Hutu rampage

---

6 Territoire du Ruanda-Urundi. Administration de la Sûreté. Bureau d'Usumbura. No. 0570/822/R.P. 3. *Op. cit.*, p. 10.

was a reaction to an intense Tutsi campaign of intimidation against Hutu political leaders during the early days of the Tutsi military mobilization.

Tutsi and Hutu were operating in a context of almost total chaos because the Belgian administration had not yet organized its response, and opposing parties were able to roam freely engaging in arson and murder. The formal Tutsi armies received their instructions on November 6, 1959. They were told to attack specific individuals collectively called APROSOMA. The Twa commandos, led by chief Harelinka, were instructed to execute particular APRO-SOMA or to bring them back to the *ibwami*. Any who refused to come were to be killed. APROSOMA was the name of one of Rwanda's two Hutu political movements, and the weaker one. It was the most active in central Rwanda, where its leaders insulted the mwamiship. As a result, the royal court applied the name APROSOMA in a general manner to designate "enemies of the king". In precolonial times this had particular meaning, because an "enemy of the king" was considered an outlaw subject to terrible sanctions". This device provided the *ibwami* with a traditionally legitimate mechanism to mobilize even Hutu against the leadership and members of Hutu political parties.

A letter was sent by François Rukeba, one of Kigeli's closest advisors, to all Rwandan Native Authorities denouncing moderate and pro-Belgian Tutsi as "enemies of the king". Posters denouncing these Tutsi were pasted up throughout the territory. This group of Tutsi included chief Prosper Bwanakweli, the son of a chief who belonged to a group of Tutsi notables who had opposed Mwami Musinga and had contrived with the Belgian administration to have him dethroned. This group, the *Inshongore*, continued in opposition to Musinga's son, Mwamu Mutara III (Des Forges, 1972: 252.354). Kigeli's orders to have them killed was another strand of continuity in traditional Tutsi military ways. It was accepted practice for a mwami to have chiefs opposed to him either murdered or brought to the *ibwami* to be punished. Kigeri's action was a response to dissident Tutsi notables that neither Mwami Musinga nor Mwami Mutara had been able to choose because of Belgian policy. Kigeri acted, taking advantage of the breakdown in Belgian control which began with his own enthronement.

A full-scale Tutsi counter-attack against Hutu rebels was launched on November 7, when armies and commando units asembled at the *ibwami* were ordered into action against Hutu leaders and their followers. Several military expeditions reveal the extent to which precolonial warrior traditions were revived. An official Belgian inquiry into the Rwandan civil war concluded that emissaries were sent from Nyanza with verbal orders (this too was traditional, since Rwandans now had a written language, but the Tutsi military headquarters wanted no evidence of their movements) to kill or bring back specific persons. Their orders empowered them to request local Native Autorities to assist by mobilizing local armed troops to seize "APROSOMA". The local chiefs and subchiefs called enough men to arms to prevent resistance or any escape by wanted "enemies of the king". The Belgian inquiry concluded that "these Tutsi operations, executed on a grand scale, mobilized armed forces of,

at times, several hundred persons and resulted in actual military operations."
(Nkundabagenzi, 1962: 153).

Six incidents of Tutsi maneuvers described below, which occurred during November 8–10, 1959, provide an appreciation of the extent to which warrior traditions were used by the Tutsi leadership at the *ibwami*. Several specific aspects of this Tutsi warrior tradition were revived: the office of the *umugabo* (variant, *umugabe*); use of the *ibilele* uniform; the imagery of the *abatabazi*; the role of the *abahevyi* border guards; extensive use of the drum to mobilize armies and to call warriors to arms. As in pre-colonial times Tutsi political authorities in the countryside, the Native Authorities, were transformed automatically into a pool of military commanders available for service. The *ibwami* served as a unified military command, sending emissaries throughout Rwanda to transmit military orders. In part, this traditional response to a political challenge and a Hutu revolt was conditioned by a deliberate desire to manipulate traditional symbols which legitimized the Tutsi campaign to crush Hutu and Tutsi opposition. In part the traditional response was chosen because the Belgians had not trained Rwandans in more modern military strategy and procedure.

Incidents

1. After Nkuranga was appointed *umugabo*, the mwami ordered him to attack members of the Hutu political movements in the Marangara chiefdom (Gitarama territory, central Rwanda). This is the birthplace of Grégoire Kayibanda. The original aim was to kill Kayibanda but he had been placed under Belgian military protection. Therefore, it was decided at the *ibwami* to kill two other Hutu leaders: Sindibona and Munyandekwe.

Nkuranga assembled 1,500 men from two chiefdoms (Busanza and Mayaga) who were officered by their subchiefs. They marched north from Nyanza to Marangara. The troops arrived on November 8th. They split into two columns which simultaneously attacked the homes of the two victims. They killed them and pillaged their homes and business. On the same day, numerous Hutu homesteads in the Marangara chiefdom were burned and pillaged by Tutsi officered troops (Hubert, 1965: 37, 68–70).

2. During the night of November 7–8, 1959, messengers were dispatched from the *ibwami*, as in the past, with orders for chiefs and subchiefs to undertake specific military operations. One chief contacted was Mfizi, chief of Rukoma (Gitarama territory, central Rwanda). He was ordered to kill the Hutu subchief of Ndiza, Mbonyumutwa.

Mfizi rallied troops who wore the banana leaf shoulder belt. Following tradition, the troops were rallied in the morning, and some came by foot from a distance of fifteen kilometers. The army was officered by subchiefs and divided into two columns to attack Hutu in the subchiefdoms of Cyesha and Gaseke. Each column, following pre-colonial military tactics, was divided to achieve a pincer movement against the attacked subchiefdom.

In Cyesha more than 150 Hutu homesteads were burned and pillaged.

Their coffee plantations and banana groves were devastated. In Gaseke sub-chiefdom twenty Hutu homesteads suffered the same fate. A Belgian administrator who arrived in the area during the afternoon reported as many as 6,000 Rwandans in the *ibilele* uniform were returning to their homes carrying off their booty. (Hubert, 1965: 66–67).

3. On November 8, 1959, subchief Benzinge led attacks against Hutu in the Kinihira subchiefdom (Nyanza territory, central Rwanda). Benzinge was seen at the *ibwami* that same morning, where the *umugabo*, Nkuranga, ordered him to undertake an expedition against Hutu in Kinihira. Benzinge convoked the traditional army. His force numbered between 2,000 and 6,000 men, with warriors arriving by car and on foot. The Tutsi subchief of Kinihira had been beating the war drum for two days. The army proceeded to attack, burning and pillaging Hutu homesteads. The army divided into two, each column attacking Hutu in different parts of the subchiefdom (Hubert, 1965: 76–77).

4. On November 8, 1959, in Astrida (Butare) District, in southern Rwanda, an army dispatched from Nyanza came to arrest or kill an important local Hutu leader, Polepole, and to attack suspected APROSOMA Hutu sympathizers (Nkundabagenzi, 1962: 153). The army divided into two columns, each commanded by a Twa. In one case it was possible to distinguish the Twa advance troops from the remainder of the column composed of Tutsi and Hutu (Hubert, 1965: 80–82). Harelinka, the Twa chief of Twa commandos, led a squad to the Cyanka mission church, where they seized Polepole as he left Sunday services. They murdered Polepole and left his body on a road some distance from the mission station, to serve as a warning to other Hutu. This act was reminiscent of traditional Twa terror tactics (Nkundabagenzi, 1962: 153).

5. On November 9, 1959, in the evening, a war drum was beaten to summon a local army "on the pretext that 'APROSOMA' from Save hill were about to attack, and that the people had to arm themselves" (Nkundabagenzi, 1962: 153). Men were called to arms in the name of the mwami, who was rumored to be a prisoner at Save. Several thousand troops were assembled, mainly Hutu officered by Tutsi.

On November 10, the Tutsi officered forces attacked Save, the stronghold of Joseph Gitera who was the first president of the APROSOMA political party. "Several thousand men mobilized by numerous local notables were ordered to storm Save . . . The attack commenced with a late morning assault on the southern slope to the accompaniment of war drums." (Van Hoeck, 1966: 165). Simultaneous assaults were launched against the hills other slopes, although the actual attacks began at different times. This is important, because the delay allowed the Belgian to maneuver against the other columns.

The attack was interrupted by the arrival of a Belgian administrator accompanied by troops armed with rifles and submachine guns. None of the Tutsi assailants had modern arms, placing them at an extreme disadvantage which the traditional armies had met during the original penetration by Europeans. The Belgian officered troops dispersed the Tutsi led assailants with some grenades, using superior modern fire power to repel a traditional army armed with non-modern weapons. In addition, the Belgian administrator used a megaphone to announce that the mwami had not ordered the attack, and that he was not being held prisoner on Save hill. This was another modern intrusion which impaired the traditional Tutsi military response. It impaired the communications network of the traditional armies which depended on verbal orders. For the first time, Tutsi commands were undermined because critical counter information was made available to the Hutu soldiers. Many Hutu refused to fight after they were told the mwami had not ordered the attack, and that he was not being held prisoner. The Tutsi officers could not rally their troops because they had no proof to convince the Hutu that Mwami Kigeri had ordered them to attack Save. The Tutsi were forced to use written communications later in 1960 and in 1961, perhaps as a result of this and their recognition that in a context of modern communications verbal orders were insufficient.

Other Tutsi officered columns attempted to assault the eastern and northern slopes of Save Hill. The Belgian troops were able to move about before the attacks were launched, and, using the same tactics that worked on the south slope, they dispersed the armies. The defeat of the Tutsi war machine at Save hill was the first major defeat since the Tutsi counterattack was launched. It was the last major military operation of a traditional nature, where Tutsi officered Hutu columns mounted the attack. On the same day, another Tutsi attack was launched into Burundi.

6. This last case involved the revival of the *abahevyi*. These are the descendants of "border guard armies" (Hubert, 1965: 84). Chief Mbanda had been ordered to kill an important Hutu leader, Kanyaruka, who had escaped to Burundi. The chief called upon his *abahevyi*. On November 10, about twenty *abahevyi* crossed into Burundi and killed Kanyaruka as well as his relative who had housed him. They then carried off their belongings and took their cattle as war booty. The order to kill Kanyaruka and send his cattle back to Rwanda was the precolonial manner "to punish enemies of the king" (Nkundabagenzi, 1962: 154).

The Belgian Response

The Belgian administration confronted with a resurgence in traditional Tutsi military maneuvers declared "war on UNAR" (Quelle Politique . . ., 1959). On November 5, 1959, the Mwami and UNAR formally requested the right" to reestablish order . . . since the Belgian administration was unable to do it." Vice-Governor General Harroy rejected this request. On November 7, 1959, Mwami Kigeri sent a telegram to the King of Belgium to indicate the *ibwami* felt obliged "to take measures [to establish order] awaiting dispositions [by Belgium] to stop the troubles." On November 8, Vice-Governor General Harroy wired the Mwami to disband the armies being assembled at Nyanza. The Mwami, in a return wire, refused. Vice-Governor General Harroy was powerless to stop the Mwami because his forces in Rwanda were too weak. He ordered reinforcements who arrived during the following days. On November 11, the day after the Tutsi defeat at Save, Harroy declared a state of emergency, placing Rwanda under military rule.

The Tutsi complained about Belgian interference, suggesting the European administration was partial to the Hutu rebels. The Belgians were convinced that strong measures were justified to protect the Hutu:

> The Tutsi leaders acted as if the Belgian administration was inexistent. They reestablished the old right of life and death... (Nkundabagenzi, 1962: 156).

The quote is from an official Belgian report drafted in late 1959. Vice-Governor General Harroy justified the state of emergency as an intervention to allow for peaceful elections for a new African administrative hierarchy as promised in an official Belgian declaration on political reforms which was announced on November 10, 1959. These elections were destined to allow Hutu to gain power by constitutional means, and the Tutsi at the *Ibwami* knew that. Harroy wrote,

> Twa bands roamed the countryside... this situation is being carefully studied... by the territorial and judicial authorities. The ability, with impunity, to deploy killers or shock troops to intimidate the population would be serious when elections will occur (Harroy, 1959: 3).

The conclusion of the Belgian inquiry into the fighting during November 1959 was that,

> Between [the Hutu] revolution and the Tutsi reaction, [the Belgian] administrations' action and military operations were [begun]... The military measures... inhibited and, ultimately, caused the failure of the... UNAR counter-revolution (Nkundabagenzi, 1962: 148).

Under the military emergency and imposed martial law, Colonel B.E.M. Logiest was put in command of Rwanda, and additional troops were brought in from the Congo. Belgium also airlifted in some 1,500 crack Belgian paracommandos. These troops intervened effectively to break the backbone of the Tutsi armies. Military courts were established. They tried Tutsi and Twa military leaders. Between November 12, 1959 and May 11, 1960, these courts judged 1,240 individuals. This drained the Tutsi of the military commanders. Many fled or were arrested.

The Belgian response caused a shift in Tutsi tactics back to guerilla style warfare which was used against Europeans in the early years of their penetration into Rwanda. In addition, Tutsi obtained modern arms to challenge the administration's troops. The Tutsi military response was now a different one, but it continued on an intense scale. The administration, at the end of 1959, reported that the murder of Hutu leaders continued, and that guerilla attacks were even occurring "almost in full daylight to be more impressive" (Quelle Politique . . ., 1959). The traditional guerilla attack was made at night. The Belgian administration forces were still not numerous enough to prevent Tutsi guerilla attacks. "The force Publique [the Belgian colonial army recruited in the Congo], even now, one squad per district, could not prevent secret crimes by two or three [Tutsi] henchmen committed at night on the hills." (Quelle Politique . . ., 1959). The administration reported that a "maquis" had organized in the forest of the Congo-Nile Divide which transverses Rwanda from north to south. They indicated that "Twa attacked cars, isolated colonials and mission stations, in raids after which they disappeared into the forest" (Quelle Politique . . ., 1959).

Colonel Logiest espoused the Hutu cause and helped to ensure a Hutu victory in Rwanda. As a result, Hutu gained political power in 1960. This had a significant effect on the ability of Tutsi to mobilize armed resistance. In early November 1959 Twa continued to serve as the Tutsi's shock troops as they had in the past. In addition, Hutu constituted almost half of the royal armies. However, by late 1960 it was evident the regular Tutsi armies had been defeated. Twa now abandoned them. Hutu participation in Tutsi armies dropped significantly to no more than one third of the forces. At the request of the territory's new Hutu political leadership, the Belgian administration created a new modern styled army called the Garde Territoriale. Recruitment was limited largely to Hutu, to provide a military shield for the new Hutu regime Belgians were helping to put in place.

The abandonment by Twa and Hutu provided additional impetus for the Tutsi decision to shift to guerilla tactics. The Tutsi population of Rwanda were never more than 15–16% of Rwanda's total population. More than 100,000 Tutsi had fled Rwanda to escape the Hutu rebels. The exiles formed armies and commando units. They launched raids into Rwanda from sanctuaries in Uganda, Zaïre and Burundi. These attacks were aimed at creating a sense of insecurity within Rwanda, and the prime targets were Hutu officials and European administrators. The guerrillas hoped to convince Rwanda's Hutu that their new leaders and the Belgians were unable to protect them.

The Shift to Guerrilla Tactics

In part, the shift to guerrilla tactics was a break with the past because it responded to novel conditions. Several Tutsi exile leaders received training in the People's Republic of China and then returned to refugee camps where they organized attacks on Rwanda. They brought with them new political ideas and new insights into military strategy and tactics. In addition, the mwami and the armies, for the first time, were all outside Rwanda. If nothing else, this was a definite break with the past. Guerrilla tactics were not new to Rwanda's military traditions. They had been used against the earliest Europeans who penetrated Rwanda, during succession struggles, and were the earliest military tradition of Rwanda's Tutsi.

Mwami Kigeri V toured Rwanda and eastern Zaïre from December 2, 1959 until February 25, 1960. His purpose was to contact UNAR leaders who had fled Rwanda to escape Belgian military and judicial action against the royal *ingabo*. At Goma and Bukavu, in Zaïre, Kigeri met UNAR leaders who had begun to form exile armies. He met with two important former Tutsi chiefs who had led attacks during 1959, Michel Kayihura and Pierre Munga-lurire. In May, 1960, Kigeri had left Rwanda to take up residence at Bujum-bura. On July 25, he left Belgian Rwanda and Burundi definitely to go to Zaïre. His exile later took him to Uganda, Kenya, Europe, and China. In August 1960 Kigeri visited Bukavu where he announced that he and his parti-sans were prepared to attack Rwanda. On August 21, he met with two exile leaders of the refugees in Uganda and those in Tanzania.

During 1960, François Rukeba, a close advisor to the king, launched a guerrilla movement dubbed the Inyenzi or cockroaches. This name was chosen because, as the cockroaches, the Inyenzi attacked at night eating away at the vitals of the Hutu state. Most Inyenzi attacks were limited in scope to cattle raiding and killing Hutu officials. In September 1960 a Twa commando of four attacked Joseph Gitera who fought them off. Numerous attacks were mounted from Uganda aimed at destablizing the fledgling Hutu administra-tion. The Belgian Sûreté warned, in March 1961, "It is possible that these extremist . . . Tutsi [may] attack Rwanda. If . . . so, we can anticipate a general panic and full disarray in Hutu zones of Ndorwa and Mutara [in the northeast]."[7] The Belgians dispatched reinforcements and, in April, 1960, the Sûreté reported that the morale of Hutu in Ndorwa and Mutara was very much imporved.[8] In late April, a Tutsi wrote the Prefect and Assistant Prefect (local officials) of Byumba District, both Hutu, to threaten them:

> The Mungalurire [Tutsi guerrillas] have rifles, they will use them to kill educated Hutu, because they are destroying Rwanda with these Belgian dogs. The Belgians will soon leave.[9]

This letter alluded to upcoming decisions at the United Nations favorable to the UNAR position. Rwanda was part of a UN trusteeship territory and UNAR hoped to influence the UN to adopt resolutions to relestablish Tutsi hegemony.

Tutsi exiles in Rwanda were able to convert a Uganda-based cultural as-sociation of resident Rwandans to their cause. (Their support diminished considerably after Rwanda achieved independence in July, 1962.) This association, the *abadahemuka*, was organized by Mwami Mutara when he visited Uganda in 1956. The name is that of a traditional royal army created in the 1850s by a former mwami(Lemarchand, 1970: 207). In late March, 1961, the *abadahemuka* were staunch supporters of UNAR and distributed a tract urging

---

7   Rwanda. Service de Sûreté. *Journée du 15–20.3.61*, p. 4.
8   *Op. cit., Journée du 1–6.4.61*, p. 1.
9   *Op. cit., Journée du 20–21.4.61*, p. 1.

Rwandan refugees to arms. The tract, 'Unity and Valor,' was subtitled, "Live three days of valor rather than thirty of cowardice". The tract was in the style of precolonial epic martial poetry:

Dear valiant brothers who know Rwanda,
All of us love Rwanda,
Armed with spears and bow,
Let us go to the aid of Kigeri and of his land.
Let us surround him on all sides.
We are destined to die for Rwanda.
Kigeri, have confidence in me,
You are worthy of the troops given to you.
You are the honor of the nobility,
Upholder of that Rwanda to which all UNARists pay hommage.
Guide the Abadahemuka who have formed an army to allow
Rwanda to guard its monarchy.[10]

In spring 1961, the United Nations passed a resolution calling upon Belgium to hold new elections under international supervision, including a referendum on the monarchy and the person of Mwami Kigeri. The Tutsi guerrillas considered this a significant victory. They celebrated and guerrilla raids subsided. A select commando was instructed to murder specific Hutu and European personalities. This assassination squad was placed under the command of a university educated Tutsi refugee.[11] An attempt was made to smuggle Mwami Kigeri into Rwanda prior to the elections, but the Belgian administration intercepted the mwami and foiled UNAR's plans. Belgian troops and the Rwandan (Hutu) *Garde Territoriale* made a number of sweeps among suspected UNAR/Inyenzi sympathizers in early June, 1961, arresting hundreds.

The elections held under United Nations sponsorship in 1961 confirmed the Tutsi political and military defeat. A militant Hutu political party, PARMEHUTU, swept the elections for a national assembly. The monarchy was voted down as was Kigeri V. The Tutsi responded with an upsurge in guerrilla attacks. According to Belgian Sûreté reports, Tutsi guerrillas were sent to spy on the Belgian troops and the *Garde Territoriale* to prepare for major attacks. In early December, 1961, following the election defeat, François Rukeba allegedly visited about 12,000 Tutsi refugees to form a central guerrilla committee of two former subchiefs and two other Tutsi. A Youth Council was organized to plan attacks on Rwanda and it grouped about 100 Tutsi youths.[12]

The scale of Tutsi military operations against the new Hutu political leadership in Rwanda increased as the number of refugees swelled with increasing numbers of Tutsi prepared to fight. During the spring of 1962, prior to independence, Inyenzi carried out numerous raids in northern Rwanda. On April 3, 1962, a twelveman commando unit, armed with rifles, attacked

---

10 *Op. cit., Journée du 20.3.61,* p. 5.
11 *Op. cit., Journée du 26.4–4.5.61,* p. 2.
12 Rwanda. 0571/1337/B.I. 795, December 4, 1961.

Byumba District. They rustled twenty-five cows, killed one person and wounded another. On April 4, 1961, two armed Tutsi killed a Hutu official in Kibungu District. Another band of armed Tutsi, intercepted by Hutu, attacked and killed several of the Hutu. On April 8/9, 1961, Tutsi made another cattle raid into Byumba District. On the night of April 13/14, twenty guerrillas attacked at two places in Kigali District. They murdered a European, his wife, and two Hutu officials. The following evening, a former Tutsi subchief led a guerrilla attack into Byumba District. They killed three Hutu, wounded another, and fired three homes. Similar attacks continued through May, 1962. On June 20, 1962, the guerrilla leadership in Uganda wired the United Nations to warn of war if independence were granted to Rwanda. It was on July 1, 1962.

By July, 1962, thousands of additional Tutsi refugees swelled the guerrillas ranks, allowing the leaders to mount more impressive military campaigns. In early July, 1962, a large guerrilla band led by Jovite Nzamwita invaded Rwanda with plans to assassinate Rwanda's Hutu leaders, including President Grégoire Kayibanda. The marauders were intercepted, and six were killed. Twenty-two Inyenzi were taken prisoner and another sixty-two escaped. This was the first large group attack following Rwanda's independence.

The Inyenzi were not the only guerrilla group. There were three armies formed to group Tutsi refugees: the Inyenzi, the Intare and the Ingangurarugo (variant, Ingaguraruge). The Intare participated with Inyenzi in raiding Rwanda. The Intare were formed as a result of divisions among the Tutsi exiles over finances, personalities, and accusations that Inyenzi guerrillas failed to complete attacks launched into Rwanda. The Inyenzi were paid 100–1,000 Rwandan francs per raid. Most had to surrender their modern arms after a raid. They were recruited among the younger and jobless Tutsi refugees. The older and wealthier Tutsi led the guerrilla attacks and were permitted to keep their modern arms. They were often Intare.[13]

The Ingangurarugo were named after the warriors of Kigeri's grandfather, Mwami Rwabuligi. The name was selected as part of the guerrillas' effort to keep alive the mystique of the Rwandan kingship (Lemarchand, 1970: 200).

In late November 1963, the guerrillas made an aborted attempt to invade Rwanda: "about 1,500 refugees from various parts of Burundi, most of them armed with spears, bows and arrows, began a three-day trek towards the Rwandese border" (Lemarchand, 1970: 220). The most serious guerrilla attack was launched in December 1963, when a column of more than 1,000 Tutsi invaded Rwanda from the south. They were armed with modern and traditional weapons. Other guerrilla forces attacked from Uganda and Zaïre but were repulsed by the Rwandan army. These attacks, a threepronged invasion, were a coordinated full-scale military campaign. The Rwandan army at this time was not that much larger than the invading forces. The column of 1,000 Tutsi who entered through southern Rwanda marched to within about

---

13   Rwanda. Ministry of the Interior. Sûreté Rwandais. *Note sur les 'Invenzi'*, Nov. 21, 1961.

twelve miles of the capital city, Kigali, where they were defeated and routed by Rwanda's army.

The response of the Hutu civil authorities was patterned after Rwanda's Tutsi military tradition. The presidency, as the *ibwami* before it, sent its representatives, the ministers, to each prefecture (these had replaced the districts) to head up local militia to guard against Tutsi attack. In some areas, local Hutu authorities organized their administrees into armies who attacked Tutsi homesteads, burning and looting as they went.

Tutsi raids continued after the December 1963 defeat, but there was never any new major military operation against the Hutu regime. The exiles quarrelled increasingly over finances, personalities and tactics. Tutsi refugees were increasingly unwilling to participate in guerrilla attacks. The Belgian officered Hutu army had proved itself superior to the guerrillas, and each attack caused new reprisals against those Tutsi who remained in Rwanda. Nevertheless, the *intore* tradition lingered on among refugees and infrequent attacks into Rwanda continued until 1968/69.

Conclusion

Within Rwanda itself a modern styled army had been created with Belgian assistance, and it was building traditions of its own which blended the new with the old. The army functioned as traditional armies in that it defended the nation, but it was a standing army and not an hereditary one. Its officers were selected on the basis of merit rather than lineage, although the Belgians did practice a bias in favor of northern Hutu whom they considered the staunchest anti-Tutsi Rwandans. By 1969 Tutsi guerrilla attacks had ended with the exception of occasional cattle raids and these were not necessarily guerilla actions. In 1972 Rwanda normalized its relations with all neighboring states and obtained their agreement to prevent refugee activities aimed against the security of Rwanda. Some Tutsi military traditions have continued probably in the Tutsi refugee settlements and camps, but within Rwanda the Tutsi warrior tradition had been largely displaced.

The political situation within Rwanda deteriorated after 1965, as Hutu politicians disputed power. In 1968/69 there were serious tensions and an attempted coup d'état. President Kayibanda attempted to manipulate the army and prevent it from becoming a significant political force to avoid a coup d'état. However, in 1973 the country verged on civil war between Hutu of different regions. On July 5, the army seized power. General Habyarimana, to justify his decision, announced that the army intervened to save the nation. The army's act was in keeping with the "defender warrior" tradition, although Habyarimana's troops did not sacrifice themselves. Political power is fused in Rwanda, now that General Habyarimana has become the President of the Republic. This pattern is not new to Rwanda. However, it is not yet clear if we can identify this too strongly with the traditions of the previous mwamiship, where the mwami was the chief general as well as a political leader.

REFERENCES

ATTERBURY, Catherine
1968   *Revolution in Rwanda* (University of Wisconsin, Wisc).
BOURGEOIS, R.
1954   *Banvarwanda et Barundi: La Coutume* (Institut Royal Colonial Belge, Brussels).
Chronologie du Ruanda (Historique et Chronologie du Ruanda).
CODERE, Helen
1962   "Power in Ruanda," *Anthropologica*, vol. 4, 1, 45–85.
DES FORGES, Alison
1972   *Defeat is the only Bad News: Rwanda under Musiinga: 1896–1931* (University Microfilms, Ann Arbor).
HARROY, Jean Paul
1959   "Mutara III-Kigeri V," August 3.
HERTEFELT, Marcel d', TROUWBORST, A. A., SCHERER, J. H.
1962   *Les Anciens royaumes de la zone interlacustre méridionale: Rwanda, Burundi, Buha* (Musée Royal de l'Afrique Centrale, Tervuren).
HEUSCH, Luc de
1966   *Le Rwanda et la civilisation interlacustre* (Université Libre de Bruxelles, Brussels).
HUBERT, Jean, R.
1965   *La Toussaint Rwandaise et sa répression* (Académie Royale des Sciences d'Outre-Mer, Brussels).
LEMARCHAND, René
1970   *Rwanda and Burundi* (Praeger Publishers Inc., New York).
LOUIS, W. M. Roger
1963   *Ruanda-Urundi: 1884–1919* (Clarendon Press, Oxford).
MAQUET, J. J.
1961   *The Premise of Inequality in Ruanda* (Oxford University Press, New York and London).
NKUNDABAGENZI, F.
1962   *Rwanda Politique* (Les Dossiers du CRISP, CRISP, Brussels).
"Quelle politique la Belgique doit-elle adopter au Ruanda?" Nov. 27.
1959
VANSINA, Jan
1962   *L'Evolution du royaume Rwanda des origines à 1900* (Académie Royale des Sciences d'Outre-Mer, Brussels).
VAN HOECK, Albert
1966   *De Kraanvogel op de Vulkaan* (D. A. P. Reinaert Uitgaven, Brussels).

SECTION II:
THE WARRIOR AND VIOLENCE

The Warrior Tradition and the Masculinity of War

ALI A. MAZRUI

The University of Michigan, Ann Arbor, U.S.A.

AT THE ANNUAL meeting of the Organization of African Unity held in Kampala in July 1975, Field Marshal Idi Amin drew attention to the presence of women in a special "suicide squad of the Ugandan Armed Forces." The question arose whether African women were about to play a bigger role in African military establishments. If this were to happen, how would it affect the status of women in African societies? And how does modern military technology relate to that process?

In cultures which are otherwise vastly different, the role of the warrior has been reserved for men. "Our sons are our warriors." This is virtually universal. (Israel is no exception, in spite of contrary appearances.)

Again, in cultures which are otherwise vastly different, crimes of violence have been disproportionately committed by men. The jails of the world bear solemn testimony to the basic masculinity of violent crime.

Is there a connection between this masculinity of violent crime and the preponderant masculinity of the military profession? The barracks and the prisons have a majority of men. Is this link between *warriorhood* and *Mafiahood* accidental? Or are there organic interconnections between the two?

On Violence and Masculinity

Images of valour, courage, endurance, and maturity have, in different societies, been intimately related to the role of the male in social and military affairs. Sexual division of labour has been both a cause and an effect of a range of social symbols defining boundaries of propriety and congruence. We have discussed this in a related context of the warrior tradition in relation to the origins of the State.

Especially pertinent for politics and war is a historic link between manliness and capacity for violence. Nothing illustrates this more poignantly than the sexual ambivalence of at least one major prophet of non-violence in modern history. In this ambivalence we see that link between masculinity and martial prowess.

In his psychological study of Mahatma Gandhi, Erik H. Erikson refers to

Gandhi's tendency to see himself as half man and half woman, and his aspiration to acquire motherly qualities. Factors identified with Gandhi's bisexual state of mind range from his love for homespinning, traditionally women's work, to his self-description as a widow when a man dear to him died. We shall return to Gandhi's case later in this paper. We know that his renunciation of sexual activity, combined with a motherly interest in a young girl's physical development, added to the widespread speculation about Gandhi's psychological orientation with regard to sex.

> "He undoubtedly saw a kind of sublimated maternalism as part of the positive identity of a whole man, and certainly of a *homo religiosus*. But by then all overt phallicism had become an expendable, if not a detestable matter to him. Most men, of course, consider it not only unnecessary, but in a way indignant, and even irreverent, to disavow a small god-given organ of such singular potentials; and they remain deeply suspicious of a sick element in such sexual self-disarmament. And needless to say, the suspicion of psychological self-castration becomes easily linked with the age-old propensity for considering the renunciation of armament and abandonment of malehood."[1]

Erikson goes on to suggest in passing that increasing the mechanization of warfare would continue to decrease the equation of manliness with martial qualities. The move from the spear to the intercontinental ballistic missile amounts to some extent to the demasculation of warfare. Face to face warfare makes greater demands on individual courage than does destruction by remote control. Gandhi's nonviolence, linked to Gandhi's sexual renunciation, was a simultaneous renunciation of both the spear and the penis. In Erikson's words:

> "Here, too, Gandhi may have been prophetic; for in a mechanized future the relative devaluation of the martial model of masculinity may well lead to a freer mutual identification of the two sexes."[2]

Africa still has many societies that are within a combat culture of the spear. In such societies killing is a confrontation between individuals, and a man tests his manliness within a spear-throw of another. In such cultures martial and sexual qualities become virtually indistinguishable for the male of the species. Eligibility for marriage is sometimes tied to experience in killing – just as the war hero in developed technological societies continues to enhance his sexual appeal. There are of course differences of scale in the killing between a culture of the spear and a culture of bombs falling from B-52s. And the purposes of the violence may be intelligible to one culture and bizarre to another. What we do know is that within the culture of the spear, the effort is more deeply personal. The bridegroom revels in having known moments of violence and danger.

Colin M. Turnbull was once looking at a Dodo tribesman called Lemu, and reflected on issues of this kind in a comparative perspective.

---

1   Erikson, *Gandhi's Truth: On the Origins of Militant Violence* (New York: W. W. Norton, 1969) pp. 402–403.
2   *Ibid.* p. 403.

"Lemu's shoulders were covered with rows of weals left by cicatrization. These are cut to show the number of people you have killed, and are an indispensable prerequisite to marriage. Lemu could look pretty fierce, if all you looked at was the rows of scars, his powerful body proudly bare except for the cloak flying in the breeze, and a string of ivory beads. His ears were pierced and lined with colored seeds, though, and he often wore a tuft of antelope hair on top of his head, and his smile and his eyes were warm and gentle like those of the rest of his people. His spear was for the protection of his cattle and his family, and it was difficult to think of Lemu wishing harm to anyone."

And then, bringing home this mysterious relationship between violence and sociability, Turnbull goes on to say the following of Lemu:

"He probably wished no harm at all even to those he killed, but faced with the choice of the life of a Turkana or that of himself and perhaps those of his wife and children, he made the same choice that most of us would make, without trying to justify it in the noble terms with which we justify our essays at mass murder."[3]

Lemu belonged to a combat culture still distant from mass destruction. He was also an African untouched either by Gandhism or by Euro-Christian inhibitions and tendencies. We shall return later to the softening and demasculating consequences of Christianity in Africa. What we should note from the outset is the interplay between martial and sexual prowess in man's ancestral heritage.

The interrelationship between sexual maturity and military manhood has had wider political consequences within Kikuyu political culture. Circumcision ceremonies involving the "shaping" of the penis were also ceremonies of initiation into the virtues of endurance and valour. The spear also featured more explicitly in initiation ceremonies of a traditional kind. Kenyatta tells us about the paramount resolution of young Kikuyu boys on being initiated by ancient custom. They used to say in courageous affirmation:

"We brandish our spear, which is the symbol of our courageous and fighting spirit, never to retreat or abandon our hope, or run away from our comrades."[4]

In the Mau Mau insurrection, the Kikuyu tendency to link sexual symbolism with martial symbolism continued in an even more elaborate fashion. Josiah Kariuki, who was later to be a Minister in the Kenya government took the Mau Mau Batuni oath in the 1950s to fight on the side of the rebels. He stood naked, his penis pushed through a hole in the thorax of a goat, while he solemnly swore not to hesitate in the obligation to kill should it be necessary.

Some of the mixed symbolism of sexual and martial elements which were characteristic of Mau Mau became subjects of wide controversy. The mixture of sexual and martial ceremonies revolted some sections of international opinion, and convinced them that the movement was not nationalistic but atavistic and primitive. Pre-eminent among the controversial Mau Mau symbolism was the

---

3 Colin M. Turnbull, *The Mountain People* (New York: Simon and Schuster, 1972) pp. 104–105.
4 Jomo Kenyatta gives a version of this story in his anthropological book about the Kikuyu, *Facing Mount Kenya* (first published in 1938) (London: Secker & Warburg, 1959), p. 199.

use of female menstrual blood, sometimes swallowed by the men in the oathing ceremonies.[5]

Some of the details of these ceremonies have in fact been disputed by those who took part in them. For our purposes in this paper it suffices that an elaborate intermixture between sexual and martial symbolism formed part of the foundation of the Mau Mau movement.[6]

Political Masculinity in an African Empire

The Kikuyu – as well as the Dodo, the Turkana, the Ik, etc. – are all among the less centralized of the societies of Eastern Africa. The Amhara, who ruled Ethiopia, are among the most centralized and elaborately institutionalized of the peoples of that part of the continent. The theme of masculinity as capacity to kill continues in the culture of the Amhara and the Empire they ruled. The society is on the one hand deeply Christianized, and on the other continues to have a premium placed on martial virtues. Donald N. Levine tells about the place of the purposeful cultivation of ferocity in the process of socializing and educating young people. The Amhara youth develops skills in versification, especially of the kind which is declaimed in order to inflame the blood of the warrior. Young people memorize lines of aggressive assertion, many of which glorify the warrior and the act of killing.

> "Kill a man! Kill a man! It is good to kill a man!
> One who has not killed a man moves around sleepily."

Levine cites an anecdote. A provincial school teacher, a boy of about twenty, was walking with Levine and another Ethiopian teacher in the countryside in Ethiopia one afternoon. Levine suggests that the mountain breeze and the rugged landscape might have gone to the head of the young teacher, for he suddenly exclaimed to his fellow:

> "We are Ethiopians. Let us kill something. Let us kill a man or a wild beast."[7]

Levine sometimes sees too much in rhetorical bravado. But although hyperbolic in some of his interpretations, Levine is persuasive in the central thesis that "For the Amhara the virtues of the male are the virtues of the soldier."[8]

---

5   J. M. Kariuki, *Mau Mau Detainee* (London: Oxford University Press, 1963). Consult also my review of his book entitled, "On Heroes and Uhuru-Worship," *Transition* (Kampala), 1963.

6   Idi Amin, who later became President of Uganda, fought the Mau Mau insurrectionists as a member of the King's African Rifles. For the masculine image of Amin himself consult Mazrui, "The Militarization of Charisma: An African Perspective," paper presented at 9th World Congress of the International Political Science Association, Montreal, August 19 to 26, 1973.

7   Donald N. Levine, "The Concept of Masculinity in Ethiopian Culture," *The International Journal of Social Psychiatry*, Vol. XII, No. 1, 1966, pp. 18–20.

8   *Ibid.*, p. 18. Philip Attlee gives us a light-hearted fictional dramatization of one's first encounter with the stone phalli of Michichi in Ethiopia. "The length of the grassy glade was broken by what seemed jutting, slanting, fallen, and erect stone cylinders. We paused

In some African societies the expansion of economic and political opportunities for young people has resulted in the decline of the prestige of the profession of combat as such. But in Ethiopia the prestige of the military hero continues to exercise considerable influence on the imagination of young people. A study some years ago on Ethiopian student conceptions of culture heroes discovered that about ninety percent of the students tested "showed a preference for the 'military man' as their 'culture hero'."[9]

Levine himself also conducted research among Ethiopian students and discovered that military virtues were the qualities most appreciated in Ethiopian historical figures of the past. But in spite of the persistence of martial sentiments in a large part of the student population, Levine discovered that those who reached the upper grades of the educational system "no longer look upon military activity as sanguinely as do their traditional counterparts." The following two tables provide useful comparative perspectives in this connection.[10]

Across the border is Somalia. The Somali are radically different in political organization and social orientation from the Amhara. Politically and diplomatically there is also considerable tension between the Somali and the Amhara. But one cultural factor that they do have in common is the mystique of purposeful ruthlessness as a manly virtue where the occasion arises. This is the central element within what I. M. Lewis calls "the martial character of the traditional Somali society where the display of force, however brutal and merciless, is

Table 1

Attitudes of Ethiopian Students to War

		War is		
	N	*Needless and Preventable* %	*Necessary Evil* %	*Sometimes a good thing* %
Secondary School Males	392	46	11	43
Secondary School Females	39	46	18	36
College Males	199	45	20	35

to consider them in the bright moonlight. ...All of the tapering cylinders were over five feet long, and the largest of them towered over twenty feet. ...A tremendous gallery of erect male members, every-one loaded and ready to fire. All circumcized. For uncounted decades and centuries, they had been aimed at heaven, enduring seasonal rains and storms. ...Men had long sought the Elephant's Graveyard and King Solomon's Mines, the Golden Fleece of Jason, and the fabled delights of the Old Man's Garden, where Assassins were trained. But this was the ultimate secret, the fierce and fecund heart of Africa, where all the unspent orgasms of the world were honoured." See Attlee, *The Judah Lion Contract* (Greenwich, Conn.: Fawcett Publications, 1972) pp. 81–82.

9 This work was conducted by Dr. William Shack, an American anthropologist who worked in Ethiopia for a while, and is now at Berkeley. The study is cited by Levine.

10 See Donald N. Levine, *op. cit.*, p. 22, and Levine, *Wax and Gold: Tradition and Innovation in Ethiopian Culture* (Chicago: University of Chicago Press, 1965), p. 143.

Table 2
Attitudes of International Sample of College Students toward War

	N	War is		
		Needless and Preventable %	Necessary Evil %	Sometimes a good thing %
France	105	65	26	9
Israel	28	68	18	14
Japan	95	72	16	8
Mexico	106	51	23	26

associated with manly virility and contrasted with weakness, a quality which though despised is held to possess a certain, compensating mystical virtue."[11]

When the link between masculinity and aggressiveness is so close, almost any weapon of war becomes by definition a phallic symbol as well. The associations between combat and sexual conquest are so intimate that an easy psychological transition takes place between martial and sexual symbolism.

The war dances in many African societies become also phallic dances. Many African dances fuse the aesthetic and the athletic. The grand leap, the stamping of the feet, the vigorous movements of the warrior's body, all acquire both sexual and martial suggestiveness.

Sometimes fertility dances share movements with war dances. The orientation towards reproduction becomes interlinked with the mystique of brave destruction. Again the range of elements which feature in such dances are from chest thumping to thunderous imitations of the copulation of beasts.

In many a context, the African dancer becomes himself a phallic symbol. In the words of Lawino,

> "It is danced in broad daylight
> In the open
> You cannot hide anything...
> All parts of the body
> Are shown in the arena!
> Health and liveliness
> Are shown in the arena!"[12]

The dancer, the warrior, the lover, become indistinguishable where the heritage of imagery draws no sharp distinction between valor and virility.

The Warrior and Society

African societies differed in their modes of self-defence and security arrangements, and are certainly different in their conceptions of the rights and

---

11   I. M. Lewis, "The Politics of the 1969 Somali Coup", *The Journal of Modern African Studies*, Vol. 10, No. 3, October 1972, pp. 389–390.
12   Okot p'Bitek, *Song of Lawino*, (Nairobi: East African Publishing House, 1966) p. 34.

duties of the warrior. But certain themes have persisted in cultures within the African continent which are otherwise very different from each other. This is partly because the concept of the warrior captures some quite fundamental aspects of human organization and human symbolism. Pre-eminent among the more obvious shared aspects is, firstly, the link between the warrior and idea of *adulthood*; and secondly, the link between the warrior and the concept of *manhood*. These are quite fundamental linkages and carry a variety of implications.[13]

Adulthood is related to notions of self-reliance. The adult is he who has a capacity to earn his own living and maintain his own homestead. But adults are sometimes to be differentiated from elders. In this sense, while children are pre-adults elders are post-adults, no longer at the peak of their physical powers, though hopefully much enhanced in their mental powers. African languages differ in the way they handle the distinction between relatively young adults, with warrior duties, on the one hand, and elders, on the other.

But even if we use the term adult in its usual sense in the English language, to indicate those who are no longer children, the basic point remains that it is from the ranks of adults that full warriors are recruited. One became a warrior when one was presumed to be capable of protecting cattle, or defending land, or collectively fighting to protect the clan. A heavy element of self-reliance was thus built into the concept of warrior because of its link with the concept of adulthood.

In many African societies the process of initiation carried implications of this presumed stage of self-reliance. The generations are separated for a while. The young adults are separated from their elders. In this respect there is sometimes a closer bond between the third generation and the first, between the elders and the children, than there is between the elders and the young adults. Many African societies encourage newly grown boys to live separately in a lodge after puberty.

"The removal of the boy from parental care is a matter of separation of the generations. The boy is developing into a man, a new generation has come into being within the family. This is on an individual level. Seclusion of the whole group of initiands in their own lodge, and their reluctance to give the fathers, i.e. the parental generation, access to the lodge, also points to the separation of adjacent generations, but on a *group* level. The

---

13 For the latest debate concerning the warrior tradition and resistance to colonial rule consult T. O. Ranger, "African Reactions to the Imposition of Colonial Rule in East and Central Africa," in L. H. Cann and Peter Duignan, *The History and Politics of Colonialism, 1870–1914*, Vol. I (Cambridge, 1969) pp. 293–324; John Iliffe, *Tanganyika under German Rule, 1905–1912* (Nairobi and Cambridge, 1969); Terence Ranger, "Connexions between 'Primary Resistance' Movements and Modern Mass Nationalism in East and Central Africa," Parts I and II, *Journal of African History*, Vol. IX, Nos. 3 and 4, 1968, pp. 437–453 and 631–641. Consult also Michael Crowder, *West African Resistance* (Ibadan, 1970); and Robert I. Rotberg and Ali A. Mazrui (editors) *Protest and Power in Black Africa* (New York, 1970); Terence Ranger, "The 'New Historiography' in Dar es Salaam: An Answer," *African Affairs*, Vol. 70, No. 278, January 1971, pp. 50–61.

'oneness' of the circumcised in the lodge would seem to express the solidarity of a new adult generation...."[14]

The gulf between the parental generation and the generation of the new adult has its own tensions. Alnaes tells us about Konzo fathers who are reluctant to have their sons circumcised "too soon". This is because the circumcision ceremony converts a son in some sense into a rival in adulthood. Among the Konzo a boy eager to cross the line into adulthood might in desperation go to a Muslim to be circumcised without going through the traditional Konzo ritual. But this is a last resort. A better strategy in the face of a reluctant father is to run away and be circumcised in the traditional manner before the father manages to intervene.

"...a fair number of boys run away to be circumcised in the traditional manner and they usually manage to have the operation before the father arrives on the scene... The traditional circumcision is a symbolic transition from childhood to manhood."[15]

African societies with age-grade systems have more complex stages of social progression. The Nandi of Kenya have seven age-grades, each with a name of its own, and all operating on the basis of a recurring cycle. Every fifteen years the fighting age hands over to the age next below it. And members of that succeeding age would have been preparing themselves for the previous fifteen years to qualify for warriorhood after circumcision. The retiring age moves up to become elders.[16]

The theme of mature independence again links adulthood with warriorhood. The initiation ceremonies, both those involving circumcision and those which do not, share certain important characteristics. S. N. Eisenstadt has summarized the descriptions of these ceremonies as they abound in the literature. We might use here Eisenstadt's summary, but relate it more explicitly to the theme of self-reliance and mature independence which initiation implies:

(a) In these ceremonies the pre-adult adolescents are transformed into full adult members of the tribe, the transformation being effected through

(b) a series of rites in which the adolescents are symbolically divested of the characteristics of youth and invested with those of adulthood from a sexual and social point of view. This symbolic investment, which has deep emotional significance, may have various concrete manifestations, bodily mutilation, circumcision, taking on of a new name, symbolic rebirth, etc.;

14   Although this description refers specifically to the Konzo it also applies to a large number of similar cultures in Africa. For this particular quotation consult Kirsten Alnaes, "Nyamayingi's Song: An Analysis of a Circumcision Song," *Africa*, Vol. XXXVII, No. 4, October 1967, p. 460.
15   *Ibid.* pp. 458–459.
16   G. W. Huntingford, *The Nandi of Kenya* (London, 1953); A. C. Hollis, *The Nandi, Their Language and Folklore* (London, 1909) and E. E. Evans-Pritchard, "The Political Structure of the Nandi-Speaking People of Kenya," *Africa*, Vol. XIII, 1940, pp. 250–268.

(c) the complete symbolic separation of the adolescents from the world of their youth, and especially from their close status attachments to their mothers; i.e. their complete "male" independence and autonomous male image are articulated (the opposite usually holds true of girls' initiations);

(d) dramatization of the encounter between the different generations, a dramatization which may take the form of a fight, competition, etc., and which the basic complementariness – whether of a continuous or discontinuous type – is stressed; thus, in all initiation rites the members of different generations must act together, the ones as teachers, the others as "students". The elders sometimes assume frightening forms and stress that without them the adolescents cannot become adults. Quite often the discontinuity between adolescence and adulthood is symbolically expressed in the "rebirth" of the adolescent – in their symbolic death as children and rebirth as adults.[17]

Those communities in Africa which have had age-set systems have usually done so in relation to the military organization of the tribe. But even among the Nuer, where the age-set system is less directly militaristic, the link between adulthood, manhood, and warrior remains explicit. In Eisenstadt's words:

"When a boy passes into the grade of manhood his domestic duties and privileges are radically altered. From being everybody's servant and an inferior, he becomes an independent adult. This change of status is epitomized in the taboo on milking through which he becomes separated from women, with whom he was identified as a boy—a taboo which begins at his initiation and remains in effect throughout his life. ...At initiation the youth receives a spear from his father or uncle and becomes a warrior. ...He becomes a true 'man' when he has fought in war (battle) and has not run away, has duelled with his age mate, has cultivated his garden and has married."[18]

We hope to demonstrate later that the theme of self-reliance involved in this warrior tradition is antithetical to the dependency complex which many Africans later acquired under the impact of colonial rule. We hope also to illustrate that the struggle against dependency as exemplified by Field Marshal Amin at his best is, in an important sense, a reactivation of the ancestral assertiveness of warrior culture.

What should not be overlooked is again the sexual dimension of the warrior culture. As we indicated, an initiation ceremony was simultaneously a moment of confirmation as an adult and graduation as a man. Adulthood and manhood were sometimes indistinguishable for the male line of the tribe.

Military Technology and the Persistence of Masculinity

In the history of military technology, there was no doubt a time when muscle was directly relevant for combat effectiveness. How effectively a fighter

---

17 S. N. Eisenstadt, *From Generation to Generation: Age Groups and Social Structure* (New York: The Free Press, 1971 edition) pp. 31–32.

18 *Ibid.* p. 60.

wielded his *rungu* or his axe, how far he threw his boomerang or spear, how totally he dislocated the jaw of his opponent, were all partly determined by the physical strength and physiological prowess of the fighter. But as military technology advanced, pure muscle became less relevant. The preponderance of men in the fighting profession became less justifiable in terms of the muscular technology of combat. To press the button of a B-52 on a bombing mission over North Vietnam was an assignment which did not need a man's finger. Yet the great majority of those who fought in the Vietnam war were men.

Technology may change many aspects of culture, but so far it has not yet fundamentally changed that part of culture which assigns the warrior-role disproportionately to men.

Is the explanation biological or cultural? Are men more violent because of upbringing and socialization or because of higher biological aggressivity in their nature?

Experiments have indicated a definite difference in levels of aggressivity between male and female in other creatures.

The political power of men can perhaps be traced to their preponderance in the military profession from very early times.

In a few countries recently, women have attained high office. But here one must distinguish between:

(a) political power by delegation
(b) political power by derivation
(c) direct political power

When Elizabeth Bagaya was Foreign Minister of Uganda, that was clearly uneven delegated power. The real authority resided in President Amin.

What about Indira Gandhi? Was her original ascent to high office partly based on the credentials that she was Nehru's daughter? Was Mrs. Bandaranaike's original ascent to power partly derived from her status as the widow of an assassinated male Prime Minister? Did Señora Peron's position emanate from her late legendary husband? If so, each of these three impressive female heads of government *derived* her power partly from the stature of a man she was related to.

In the recent history of women in power, perhaps only Mrs. Golda Meir attained supreme authority without the prestige of a towering male relative. Her authority while it lasted was neither *delegated* (like Bagaya's) nor *derivative* (like Mrs. Gandhi's, Mrs. Bandaranaike's or Isabella Peron's) but *direct*.

A major reason behind the relative powerlessness of women in politics may lie in their military impotence. Sexual division of labour had reserved the role of the warrior disproportionately for the male of the species. In so doing it also helped to reserve the role of the ruler for the male also.

In the African colonies a great experimental opportunity was missed this century. Why did not the British and the French imperial governments create colonial armies made up of African women? The experiment could have been of immense value for the human race as a whole. Since the imperial powers were disrupting local cultures in other ways in any case, it might have made sense also to attempt a disruption in one of the most perennial and obstinate aspects of human culture – the masculinity of warriorhood.

Indeed, as indicated in another chapter in this collection, the French even helped to destroy in the nineteenth century that rare female class of warriors, the Amazons of Dahomey. In the process of colonizing Dahomey (now the Republic of Benin), the French shattered Dahomey's most distinctive institution.

Elsewhere in their colonies the French were no different from the other European colonial powers – they all missed an opportunity for the kind of social engineering which would have effectively enlisted African women to the profession of arms.

Such an imperial experiment might not have worked in every African country. But if it worked in any of them at all, the consequences for African politics after independence could have been epoch-making. The soldiers who took over power after independence would in some cases have been women. And some of the presidents in uniform at meetings of the Organization of African Unity would therefore have come from the female half of Africa's humanity. African women in control of armies could have started a unique experiment in the sharing of power.

This brings us to the connection between democracy and military technology. There are African societies to the present day where military skills are still assessed in terms of prowess of handling spears and in the use of the bow and arrow. The simplicity of this technology made it accessible to almost every one. In the words of the British anthropologist, Jack Goody:

> "The bow and arrow is essentially a democratic weapon; every man knows how to construct one; the materials are readily available, the techniques uncomplicated, the missiles easy to replace (though more difficult with the introduction of iron that affected even hunting people like the Hadza of Tanzania and the Bushmen of the Kalahari). With the technologies of the bow and stone-tipped arrow any kind of centralization is almost impossible. But with the introduction of metals, kingdoms are on the cards."[19]

In the case of the original West African kingdoms it was, according to Goody, the uneven distribution of raw materials which involved systems of exchange and brought about often long distance trade. This in turn necessitated systems of control and security.

With the coming of the rifle in colonial Africa, and the tank in independent Africa, military elitism became more conspicuous. The old days of military democracy, when everyone passed through the warrior stage, and when the weapons were the simple ones capable of being manufactured by the warrior himself, were now replaced by the era of military professional specialists, with weapons requiring high technological skill to manufacture and specialized training to use.

---

19 Jack Goody, *Technology, Tradition and the State in Africa*, (London, 1971): pp. 43–46.

But even in the days of the more democratic bow and arrow, women in almost all African societies were left out of combat. Only an imperial power with a higher military technology could have started quickly enough the process of militarizing womanhood. African women in charge of tanks and artillery under the colonial regimes would have been potential wielders of political power after independence.

It so happens that colonial armies were often recruited from some of the least privileged ethnic communities in Africa and from some of the most peripheral regions. There was a belief among most colonial administrators that illiterate or semi-literate Africans made better soldiers than the better educated. The better educated was sometimes distrusted as "cheeky" and not adequately obedient.

In any case, the better educated young men had other ambitions. A job as a soldier even in modern uniform – with guns rather than spears and bows and arrows – was seldom the most attractive option for an ambitious African youth. White collar work often ranked much higher.

The British and the French therefore bequeathed to their former colonies military establishments manned primarily by people recruited from some of the poorest and least influential sections of the population. When these finally took over power after independence, some balance was partially restored in their societies. The intelligentsia and the former bourgeoisie still remained influential, but no longer paramount. The *lumpen-militariat* had successfully (and sometimes brutally) claimed a share of the power.

Unfortunately, this lumpen-militariat was almost exclusively made up of men. On the basis of ethnic balance in the sharing of power, their triumph in places like Nigeria and Uganda had some democratic consequences. Previously deprived communities entered the main stream of national life. But from the point of view of restoring balance between men and women, the lumpen-militariat which colonialism created contributed nothing to the resolution of sexual injustice. The very fact that the colonial recruiting officers often insisted on physical height of five feet eight inches (5' 8") as a qualification for joining the army aggravated the discrimination against female recruits.

But given that a great experimental opportunity was lost in Africa, are there signs of a change in the future? Field Marshal Idi Amin's female "suicide squad" is at least symbolic of some basic rethinking about the role of women in war. This rethinking may have started among otherwise relatively traditionalist groups in Africa.

Less traditionalist circles include the new rulers of independent Mozambique and the experimentation in female recruitment which FRELIMO inaugurated while it was still fighting Portuguese colonial rule, and has maintained since.

It is unlikely that male political dominance in the world as a whole will end this century. But a step in that direction has to include *the increasing militarization of womanhood*. This may be a sad reflection on the human race. It is certainly a reflection of the historical linkage between statehood and the control of physical force, between politics and the instruments of coercion, between power and warriorhood. Military technology is now too sophisticated to be as democratic as the bow and arrow. But it is at least sophisticated enough to make physical height and muscle power no longer relevant in recruiting for the armed forces. While military technology is now elitist in terms of the skills needed, it is at the same time more sexually neutral than ever before. The primeval war of the sexes is about to enter its most fundamental stage ever.

Some steps have already been taken in a number of countries to deal with this potential social crisis. Promotion of women in the American armed forces has been accelerated. The Soviet Union and Israel have attempted to consolidate their relative "equal opportunity" policies. The Egyptian army is using more women than ever before.

But there is no room for complacency. On the contrary, some of the current shifts of power in the world may be aggravating the problem. The energy crisis from 1973 onwards aroused the hopes of the people of the Third World. The Organization of Petroleum-Exporting Countries had demonstrated how "primary producers", technologically underdeveloped, could put pressure on the industrial giants. Since then the movement for the creation of a new international economic order has gathered momentum, led partly by members of OPEC.

But if the politics of oil show a shift of power in favour of at least some Third World countries, that same shift is in favour of countries which are still more "male-dominated" than average. Saudi Arabia, the most influential of the OPEC countries, also has a social system in which women are not only demilitarized but also depoliticized. Most of the Gulf states have basically similar social systems. So does Iran by and large.

The Third World has good reason to celebrate the emergence of OPEC and oil power. But do the women of the world have similar reasons for rejoicing? Is not the balance of influence shifting in favour of greater masculinity as illustrated in the social structures of OPEC countries?

It is too early to be sure. The new prosperity of the oil-exporting states may gradually lead not only to the politicization of their women, but also to their militarization.

What is clear is that momentous changes are about to occur. How those changes will affect the interaction between sex and war, between technology and stratification, are questions whose answers still lie in the womb of future history.

Warrior, Rebel, Guerrilla, and Putschist

Four Aspects of Political Violence

CLAUDE E. WELCH, Jr.

State University of New York at Buffalo, Buffalo, U.S.A.

Histroy is replete with instances of violence. Yet political scientists using historical material have often minimized the role and significance of coercion. In large measure, this oversight is inherent in political science as a discipline. Its practitioners tend to view politics as conflict contained within accepted boundaries, as a form of war by other means; they equate these "other means" with articulation of concerns by interest groups, with competitive elections, with aggregation of demands by or within political parties. Political scientists thus take as a given the existence of a framework within which "legitimate" coercive powers rest with the government. Following the tradition of Max Weber, political scientists regard the state as a "compulsory association with a territorial basis", in which "the use of force is regarded as legitimate only so far as it is either permitted by the state or prescribed by it."[1] Acts of violence directed against the incumbent regime, from this perspective, are both inherently illegitimate, and of less interest to political scientists than "normal" institutions.

That Weber's formulation is an ideal type needs no elaboration. Its biases have been challenged, and partially revised, in recent years. Scholars now give far greater attention to violent political change – a heritage of the coups d'etat, rebellions, civil wars, and international embroilments that have punctuated the post-World-War II period. Eckstein, for example, counted more than 1,200 "unequivocal examples" of internal war in 1946–59 period,[2] and the ensuing 18 years have been equally fertile of political violence.

In dealing with Africa, political scientists (notably in the early and mid-1960s) tended to overlook political violence. Their neglect stemmed in part from the ease with which independence was achieved, through relatively peaceful transfers of power from European to African hands south of the

---

1 Max Weber, *The Theory of Social and Economic Organization*, edited by Talcott Parsons (New York: Free Press of Glencoe, 1964), p. 156.
2 Harry Eckstein, *Internal War: Problems and Approaches* (New York: Free Press of Glencoe, 1964), p. 3.

Sahara. Quiet self-government appeared to succeed an equally quiet colonial interlude. The purported calm of both was soon assailed. Combat in Algeria, Kenya and the Portuguese colonies made clear that external rule would not fade quietly away. Repression of opposition by newly independent African governments marked several states, and was often succeeded by military intervention or civil war – and sometimes by both. By 1968, a well-informed critic could point to "conflict and disorder" as the "most prominent features" of politics in Africa.[3]

Academic fashions thus eventually caught up with the facts of political life. Revived interest in pre-colonial combat and organized resistance to colonial rule led to the publication of several outstanding books.[4] Studies of African armed forces created a minor publishing boom. Thus intellectually resurrected, political violence became by the 1970s the dominant concern of social scientists writing on Africa.

In this article, I shall not examine at length the *status quo* bias of the Weber formulation. Much political violence is in fact initiated by political incumbents, prescribing coercive acts against their opponents. Rather than delve into government-ordained repression, I shall be concerned with the use of violence to depose incumbents or significantly alter polities they are implementing.

Successful political violence obviously brings changes in personnel and policies. How can its success be gauged, or possibly predicted? Attention must be given four factors:

1) popular disenchantment with existing government personnel and policies (delegitimization);
2) social values condoning and channeling the use of violence;
3) ability to organize and coordinate resistance to the incumbent government; and
4) access to means of training, equipping and directing combatants.

These four factors will be analyzed and applied to another quartet: the warrior, the rebel, the guerrilla, and the putschist of tropical Africa.

Warrior

The image conjured up by the word warrior is one of the valiant, intrepid individual, courageous and bold in his actions. He is, in the descriptive word

---

3 Aristide R. Zolberg, "The Structure of Political Conflict in the New States of Tropical Africa," *American Political Science Review*, LXII (1968), p. 70.
4 Major examples include Michael Crowder, ed., *West African Resistance: The Military Response to Colonial Occupation* (New York: Africana, 1971); Bethwell A. Ogot, ed., *War and Society in Africa: Ten Studies* (London: Cass, 1972): Robert I. Rotberg and Ali A. Mazrui, eds., *Protest and Power in Black Africa* (London: Oxford University Press, 1970); T. O. Ranger, *Revolt in Southern Rhodesia 1896–97: A Study in African Resistance* (Evanston: Northwestern University Press, 1967).

applied to North American Indians, a "brave". His stamina is great, his ability to withstand deprivation unquestioned, his effectiveness as a combatant enhanced by specialised training. He has gained self-reliance through his passage from youth to adult status, a transition marked by martial training.

The warrior tradition tends to be culturally specific. Each social group has its *rites de passage*, symbolizing the change of status. To be certain, culturally discrete groups may carry out similar practices, such as age-set initiations, which can (as the actions of Shaka illustrated) become the foundation for wider political and social bonds. Further, such *rites de passage* may enhance the effective coordination of fighters in battle. But this may be problematic: the "braves" of North America were among the most valorous and the least effective of soldiers. As individual, expert horsemen, they often charged when the spirit moved them, not in an effective, coordinated fashion. Military effectiveness, as Turney-High and others have stressed, rests on extensive coordination among individuals.[5] A single warrior can accomplish little; his courage must be buttressed by the joint action of his comrades in arms.

The warrior tradition usually left the tasks of protection to a restricted, totally male segment of society. Although all able-bodied men might be pressed into service during emergencies, the warrior tradition did not (with the exception of the Zulu) result in the idea of a full-fledged "nation in arms". Responsibility for defense, and the attendant social and political awareness, were vested in a small, though respected, sector of society.

The warrior tradition flowered prior to the imposition of colonial rule, and in the initial phase of resistence to it. Central to the warrior tradition accordingly was the continued legitimacy of the existing political and social order. On occasion political incumbents were ousted from power, but the system of values as a whole remained unchallenged. The warrior sought to protect what was accepted; he fought within a context of shared presumptions about the worthiness of existing institutions. Disenchantment with existing government personnel and policities existed – but delegitimization was not so widespread as to lead to extensive social upheaval. In fact, it was the protection of their societies and values that, in the early years of colonial expansion, brought warriors to contend against the invading armies.

As noted above, the acceptability of violence within an individual society rests on social values condoning and channeling violence. An expectation that violence would occur leads to its normative justification – while the existence of collective violence breeds further collective violence.[6] The question remains as to the effective boundaries of individual or collective violence. How adequately, in other words, could various groups collaborate in the face of external challenge? If small groups cling to their own patterns of opposition, and cannot

---

5   Harry Holbert Turney-High, *Primitive War: Its Practice and Concepts* (Columbia: University of South Carolina Press, 1971, second edition), p. 23.
6   Ted Robert Gurr, *Why Men Rebel* (Princeton: Princeton University Press, 1970), pp. 170, 177.

effectively coordinate their resistance, defeat is probable. Colonial history furnishes many examples of a divide and rule strategy, by means of which Europeans subdued individual ethnic groups and used tribal animosities to extend their control.

How well were African armies organized during the initial colonial penetration? The following remarks seem apposite:

> Armed forces were segmentary, pluralistic, relatively egalitarian, and usually based on recruitment at the village level. No sharp lines of cleavage or delineation separated a society from its military arm... military discipline and stratification within the armed forces were not strong... most pre-colonial African societies lacked standing armies, clearly differentiated from other social institutions. Low levels of military sophistication and weaponry coincided with low levels of political centralization.[7]

Finally, in terms of access to equipment and training, the warrior of tropical Africa decidedly came off second-best. Innovations *within* the existing technological limitations could be rapidly diffused among African societies (for example, the spread of some of Shaka's and Dingiswayo's innovations to other Nguni peoples), but the external invention of new technologies heightened disparities between Europeans and Africans. As Crowder observed, "The chief advantage of the European forces was that they had access to the most recent advances in military technology"[8] – a point more wittily put by Hilaire Belloc, "Whatever happens we have got The Maxim gun, and they have not." These disparities were further enhanced by contrasting patterns of training fighters. Again to cite Crowder, "Herein lay the second major key to the success of the European armies: using African soldiers, they were much better drilled and disciplined than most of their opponents."[9]

The warrior tradition was temporarily laid to rest with the full imposition of colonial rule. Other forms of resistance – marked by the appearance successively of the rebel and the guerrilla – came to the fore. Undergirding both these, however, was the heritage of political violence created in the warrior tradition.

Rebel

A rebel, by definition, engages in the act of rebellion – "to refuse allegiance to and forcefully oppose an established government or any ruling authority."[10]

Looking at political violence in historical perspective, one can link the warrior tradition to pre-colonial African societies and to primary resistance to European rule. This primary resistance, as noted above, was fought on a society-by-society basis, spread out in time and space, in which relatively few

7   Claude E. Welch, Jr., "Continuity and Discontinuity in African Military Organization", *Journal of Modern African Studies*, XIII, 2 (July 1975), p. 238.
8   Crowder, *Western African Resistance*, p. 8.
9   Ibid., p. 9.
10 Robert I. Rotberg, ed., *Rebellion in Black Africa* (London: Oxford University Press, 1971), p. xiii.

leaders (e.g., Samori), were able to rally warriors from many different groups. The rebel tradition, by contrast, depended on the deepening of the European impact, particularly in economic and cultural terms, within a social context considerably larger than a single ethnic group.

European colonization constituted multiple disasters for many African societies. As Barkun has stressed, social dislocation brought by invasion and the spread of new ideas necessitated the synthesization of new explanations, often with religious or magical foundations.[11] What Coleman termed "nativistic, madhistic, or messianic mass movements" emerged, serving as "psychological or emotional outlets for tensions produced by the confusions, frustrations, or socio-economic inequalities of alien rule."[12]

It is important to note that the rebel can utilize forms of resistance other than political violence. Movements of rebellion intermix social, cultural, and economic protest with political protest. There is an obvious and important cause. Leaders of rebellion must arouse a dedicated following. They often seek to preserve or restore by-gone practices, particularly practices dealing with group solidarity. They must generalize feelings of discontent: grievances felt individually must be shown to be widespread, and must be channeled into action against the political incumbents. However, discontent can be expressed through seemingly non-political channels, such as religious enthusiasm, emigration, or heightened inter- or intra-group tensions. It is when *political* ends are paramount – that is to say, the conscious directing of violence against the incumbents in order to bring changes in personnel or policies – that rebellion is primarily a political act.

The most effective rebel leaders were those who coupled prophecy with armed resistance. African history provides numerous examples of mediums sparking resistance. Such "charismatic prophet figures", as Ranger has deemed them, both built upon and departed from customary practices. His analysis of the Shona mediums in 1896–7 merits extensive citation:

> It was in a true sense a revolutionary situation, revolutionary in the sense that what was needed was the total overthrow of existing white control, in the sense that what was needed was a revolutionary fervour and commitment on the part of the rebels, and in the sense also that something was required over and above the fragmented remnants of pre-European political systems, both in order to organize a rising and to provide a vision of society when the rising had been successful. The rising could not be organized merely by making use of surviving political institutions; nor could the aims of the rising be merely to return to a state of impotent fragmentation.
>
> What one can call "traditional" religious systems could help to provide... coordination and inspiration. But perhaps a new element was required even in the field of belief... there emerged a leadership able to transform the appeal of the religious systems into something more radical and revolutionary; a prophetic leadership operating over and above all the restrictions implied by hierarchic order and links with the past.[13]

---

11   Michael Barkun, *Disaster and the Millennium* (New Haven: Yale University Press, 1974).
12   James S. Coleman, "Nationalism in Tropical Africa," *American Political Science Review*, XLVIII (1954), p. 406.

What one glimpses among successful rebels is the evocation of norms transcending individual cultures, or of ideas touching many parts of the same society. Creative adaptation of existing avenues for voicing protest – as through spirit mediums – marks rebels. Leaders thus are drawn not necessarily from traditionally martial groups or individuals, but from the traditionally prophetic. Cultural and social institutions, not political ideologies, serve as the means for coalescing individual grievances.

Let me put the contrast in even starker terms. The warrior defends his society against external *military* pressure; the rebel seeks to reassert the values of his society against external *economic, administrative, and/or social* pressures that affect the structure of the society. When invasion threatens, all can draw together, using the strong bonds of self-defense and traditional mobilization. But when the challenge is partly internal, the martial arts will not suffice; cultural synthesis is necessary. In the case of cultural change, the external challenge is more subtle, more destructive of the social fabric. The standard responses will not work, for various pressures have eroded the foundations on which the society rested. The challenges are internal as well as external, since members of the community adopt different ways. If things have fallen apart, protest must take new forms. In adaptation of existing norms – oathing, for example – the rebel counters the challenges undermining society. He uses largely cultural mechanisms to achieve political and social objectives. Military defense has proven inefficacious or impossible; only some form of "revitalization" movement[14] can provide relief.

The rebel protests not only against the insidious alien presence, but also against his own traditional patterns of leadership. Colonial governments enjoyed little legitimacy; they were the source of detested policies (taxation, corvée labor, cultivation of certain crops), and indirectly sponsored the teachers, missionaries, and warrant chiefs who weakened the social structure. But indigenous leaders seemed unable to cope fully with the challenge. They were divided, disarmed, and discredited. Popular disenchantment thus existed with both the colonial administration and the local social structure, though in markedly different degrees. No wonder, then, that the rise of the rebel bore witness to significant internal reordering within African societies. The "young-men", those who had travelled extensively (like John Chilembwe), or on occasion the demobilized soldier or disgruntled messenger, could declaim against the oppression of external rule and the inadequacy of existing leaders.

Complicating rebel protest was the deliberate demilitarization of African societies following the establishment of alien rule. *Asafo* companies were disbanded, or turned to other tasks; age-set initiations no longer emphasized preparation for combat. Punitive expeditions brought heavy retribution on villages refusing to pay taxes. Thus lacking organized means of combat, and

---

13 Ranger, *Revolt*, pp. 123–4.
14 Anthony F. C. Wallace, "Revitalization Movements," *American Anthropologist*, LVIII (1956), pp. 626–38.

knowing the marked contrast in firepower, rebel leaders turned to sublimated forms of protest. Social values condoning and channeling violence were suppressed or diverted. Protest had to take non-military forms, thereby again emphasizing the syncretistic nature of rebel activity.

The social disorganization that made rebels possible also affected their ability to carry out joint action. Disoriented individuals seek new social roots, and thus may readily attach themselves to mass movements – certainly the speculations of Eric Hoffer lead to this conclusion.[15] On the other hand, disoriented individuals cannot readily be linked for joint action; they lack both symbols and a sense of commonality. They become "primitive rebels," in Hobsbawm's phrase, organizationally incapable under most circumstances of fully adapting to change. Rebel movements mushroom, then quickly ebb in the face of opposition; though they linger in underground forms, they do not successfully challenge the externally imposed and internally changing system. Separatist churches rise and splinter; religious enthusiasts proclaim new beliefs; economic boycotts may be implemented. Individuals may be coopted into new positions, losing their fervor. When channels exist for voicing discontent, and where alteration can come about, the rebels lose their constituency. What Hopkins noted of the Nyabingi cult could be observed elsewhere: "This new participation in the formal political network seriously undermined the vicarious displacement of political sentiment previously provided by cult participation ... The sudden dislocation of the cult from its enduring role as a vehicle for political protest marked the end of co-ordinated opposition to British rule in Kigezi. No further effort was made to challenge the presence of Europeans; rather, local political energies, confirming the premise of European occupation, were channeled into a manipulation of and movement within the system itself."[16]

Finally, rebels rarely enjoyed access to means of training and equipping forces. Arms were costly, and in the colonial period trade in them tightly regulated. Potential "base areas" (as discussed in the following section) were remote from the centers of social change – and yet it was in these centers that alterations were most profound and anomie most likely to lead to protest. Where the cash economy was implanted, land alienation advanced, or immigration of other groups encouraged, tensions rose. Rarely did these explode into overt conflict, however, the rebel able to achieve widespread support did so where the repressive strength of the police or military could not be readily exercised, and such areas were well removed from the center of power.

Consideration of the capacity of the administration to counteract political violence leads us to the third category, the guerrilla.

---

15 Eric Hoffer, *The True Believer: Thoughts on the Nature of Mass Movements* (New York: Harper & Row, 1951).

16 Elizabeth Hopkins, "The Nyabingi Cult of Southwestern Uganda," in Rotberg, *Rebellion*, pp. 131–2.

Guerrilla

In historical perspective, guerrilla struggle seems linked to a tertiary stage, to that period in which a colonial power was strongly entrenched, both willing and able to counter resistance with harsh military repression.

The two key components of guerrilla warfare are 1) the use of "irregular" (i.e. non-positional) warfare and 2) emphasis on political awareness. The guerrilla fighter recognizes his initial weakness relative to a better-armed adversary, and seeks to overcome this through building a strong political foundation. The struggle is waged (in the well-worn phrase) more for the hearts and minds of men than for the physical control of territory. Actual combat should be avoided, if possible, until the requisite support is created. Mao Tse-tung bears quoting on this point: a guerrilla army like the Red Army is "an armed body for carrying out the *political* tasks of the revolution ... besides fighting to destroy the enemy's military strength, it should shoulder such important tasks as doing propaganda among the masses, organizing the masses, arming them, helping to establish revolutionary political power and setting up Party organizations."[17]

To carry out irregular warfare, a guerrilla must enjoy a redoubt or base area, usually a densely forested or mountainous region, often on the border between two territorial jurisdictions, not readily patrolled by government troops. The Aberdare Mountains for the Mau-Mau, the forest camps of the Mulelist fighters, the savannah liberated areas of the PAIGC near the Senegal and Guinea borders, provided refuges not readily controlled by the central government. Rooting out such pockets of resistance may require such heavy investments of manpower and material as to be unfeasible – and efforts at repression may backfire. In seeking to contain a guerrilla insurrection, a government might unwittingly escalate it by regrouping the populace, alienating them by ripping them from the lands to which they have been historically and economically attached, and establishing resettlement sites (alternatively worded, concentration camps) in which messages of resistance can readily be propagated.[18] Thus the handful of initial resisters may find ready supporters among the displaced population.

Political awareness for the guerrilla requires an ideology, especially an ideology that 1) explains the perceived conditions of polarization and exploitation, 2) suggests means of change through struggle, and 3) emphasizes common bases for cooperation. In other words, the "enemy" must be clearly defined, and shown to be combattable by struggle carried out jointly by the deprived group.

Seemingly the clearest example of guerrilla conflict stemming from a political ideology is furnished by the Mulelist partisans, who (in 1964–5) con-

17 Mao Tse-tung, "On Correcting Mistaken Ideas in the Party" (December 1929), reprinted in *Selected Military Writings of Mao Tse-tung* (Peking: Foreign Languages Press, 1972), p. 54.

18 Gerald J. Bender, "The Limits of Counterinsurgency: An African Case," *Comparative Politics*, IV (1972), pp. 331–60.

trolled a part of Zaire nearly the size of Belgium, in the name of the "Second Independence". The official goals of the uprising in Kwilu were shaped by Pierre Mulele, in the name of the "popular masses" – namely, "the poor, the peasants, the workers. They are like the dogs who catch game but who eat only the bones."[19] Borrowing directly from Mao Tse-tung, Mulele pointed to polarization between the working masses and the "strangers" (both European and African), who arrogated the fruits of self-government. He sought to overcome ethnic division yet found his support ethnically circumscribed, limited to the Bapende and Bambunda. In short, what he borrowed from the Sayings of Mao Tse-tung could not be readily translated into action in Kwilu.

The Kwilu experience highlights the importance of indigenous traditions of resistance. As Fox et al. emphasized, that uprising "seems to be deeply rooted in history, social structure, cultural tradition, aspirations and frustrations profoundly Congolese in nature ...."[20] Guerrilla fighters, to be the "fish in water" of which Mao spoke, must be in harmony with the society. Hence, a guerrilla outside his own cultural milieu may lack the rapport and support necessary for melting into the populace.

The four criteria indicate the difficulties guerrilla fighters confront.

The perceived illegitimacy of the regime helps make guerrilla conflict possible. Disenchantment with government policies – land alienation, corruption, and the like – testifies not only to the existence of feelings of "relative deprivation", but also to their politicization.[21] The rebel, it was suggested earlier, may find release for pent-up emotions through surrogate activities, such as messianic sects; the guerrilla, by contrast, attacks the *political* source of discontent directly.

Indigenous social values condoning and channeling violence abet the growth of guerrilla movements. In fact, exhorting individuals to take up arms in the absence of both delegitimization of the regime and a tradition of resistance may well backfire. Those who become *maquisards* do so in large measure because of the societal support given them. Thus, historical continuities in African political violence should be expected: a warrior tradition capped by active resistance against initial colonial penetration; a rebel tradition carried out through extensive protests and occasional uprisings against external rule; a guerrilla tradition developed in the face of colonial intransigence. The role of the Makonde in the political history of Mozambique indicates such continuities, as does the involvement of the Bapende of Zaire in political violence.

Ability to organize and coordinate resistance depends on a multitude of factors, which can be briefly summarized. There must exist sufficient awareness

19 Benoit Verhaegen, *Rebellions au Congo*, Tome I (Brussels: Centre de Recherche et d'Information Socio-Politiques, 1966), p. 167.
20 Renee C. Fox, Willy de Craemer, and Jean-Marie Ribeaucourt, "'The Second Independence': A Case Study of the Kwilu Rebellion in the Congo," *Comparative Studies in Society and History*, VIII (1965), p. 78. Also see Claude E. Welch, Jr., "Ideological Foundations of Revolution in Kwilu", *African Studies Review*, XVIII, (1975), pp, 116–28.
21 Gurr, *Why Men Rebel*, esp. pp. 155–92.

of the government that individuals can blame their social ills on it. A "base area" providing sanctuary, and in which training can be imparted amidst a friendly populace, is essential. Indigenous social traditions condoning violence must be drawn upon. Shared and readily politicizable grievances should form a bond of understanding between partisans and populace.

Finally, successful guerrilla struggle requires arms as well as popular support. Paradoxically, the better equipped the armed forces of the government, the greater the chances for guerrilla success. Lacking extensive equipment, the insurgents concentrate on creating a firm popular foundation; the incumbents, on the other hand, may take false comfort in their firepower superiority, and neglect creating a basis of at least tacit acceptance. The bloody, heavy-handed repressive tactics of (for example) the Japanese in China and the Germans in the Soviet Union and France during World War II sparked even greater popular opposition, from which the nationalist guerrillas quickly profited. Further, the more extensive the equipment, the easier its capture by insurgent forces. In fact, several classic twentieth-century guerrilla leaders found captured arms their chief source.

Putschist

The most common form of violent political change in contemporary Africa is the military coup d'etat. Between late 1958 and early 1974, 33 successful coups were staged in 20 different states. The following table provides details:

Table 1
Successful Military Coups d'Etat in Africa

Country	Date	Results
Sudan	17 Nov. '58	Lt. General Ibrahim Abboud ousted Prime Minister Khalil.
Togo	13 Jan. '63	President Sylvanus Olympio was assassinated by soldiers who named Prime Minister Nicolas Grunitzky as President.
Congo (Br.)	15 Aug. '63	Military forced resignation of President Fulbert Youlou. Provisional Committee of army and gendarmerie officers named Alphonse Massamba-Debat as President.
Dahomey	28 Oct. '63	Army Chief of Staff Col. Christophe Soglo assumed power.
Zanzibar	12 Jan. '64	Sultan Jamshid was overthrown by armed opposition party. Abeid Karume named as President of newly-proclaimed Republic.
Algeria	19 Jun. '65	President Ahmed ben Bella was ousted by military coup led by Col. Houari Boumedienne.
Zaire	25 Nov. '65	President Joseph Kasavubu overthrown in army coup led by Gen. Joseph Mobutu.
Dahomey	29 Nov. '65	Prime Minister Ahomadeghe forced out by Armed Forces Chief of Staff Gen. Christophe Soglo, who named National Assembly President Tahirou Congacou to head provisional government.
Dahomey	22 Dec. '65	Soglo took complete control after ousting Congacou government in bloodless coup; on 24 Dec., Soglo named himself President.

Table 1 (Continued)

Country	Date	Results
Central African Republic	1 Jan. '65	Col. Jean Bokassa ousted President David Dacko and took over as the new President.
Upper Volta	3 Jan. '66	President Maurice Yameogo was deposed in coup headed by Armed Forces Chief of Staff Lt. Col. Sangoule Lamizana, who headed new government.
Nigeria	15 Jan. '66	Maj. Gen. J. T. U. Aguiyi-Ironsi came to power in a bloody coup in which Prime Minister Sir Abubakr Balewa and other top officials were assassinated.
Ghana	24 Feb. '66	President Kwame Nkrumah was ousted by a coup led by the National Liberation Council, headed by Lt. Gen. Joseph Ankrah.
Burundi	8 Jul. '66	Prince Charles, with support of the army, ousted his father, King Mwambutsa IV. Charles became the new ruler as King Ntare V.
Nigeria	29 Jul. '66	A mutiny by northern military elements toppled the Federal Military Government; its head, Lt. Gen. Aguiyi-Ironsi, was killed. Army Chief of Staff Lt. Col. Yakubu Gowon was persuaded by fellow officers to take over as Supreme Commander of a new regime.
Burundi	28 Nov. '66	King Ntare V was ousted by his Prime Minister, Army Captain Michel Micombero, who became President.
Togo	13 Jan. '67	Army Chief of Staff Lt. Col. Etienne Eyadema overthrew President Grunitzky in bloodless coup.
Sierra Leone	23 Mar. '67	The army on 22 Mar. had arrested new Prime Minister Siaka Stevens minutes after he was sworn in; on 23 Mar. the army took power and formed a National Reformation Council, headed by Lt. Col. Andrew Juxon-Smith.
Dahomey	17 Dec. '67	Maj. Maurice Kouandete, heading a group of officers in deposing President Soglo, took over as chief of state; four days later, ex-Army Chief of Staff Lt. Col. Alphonse Alley was named as President, with Kouandete as Prime Minister.
Congo (Br.)	3–31 Aug. '68	Army deposed President Alphonse Massamba-Debat; Capt. Raoul became nominal head of the government; Captain (later Major) Marien remained as strongman.
Mali	19 Nov. '68	Young officers ousted President Modibo Keita and set up a Military Committee of National Liberation headed by Lt. Moussa Traore.
Sudan	25 May '69	President Ismail al-Azhari was ousted by army coup headed by Col. Jafar Muhammed Nimeri, who headed new Revolutionary Command Council.
Libya	1 Sept. '69	King Idris I was ousted in coup led by army officers headed by Col. Muammar Gaddafy who became President of the ruling Revolutionary Command Council.
Somali Republic	21 Oct. '69	Prime Minister Mohamed Egal was over thrown by military/police junta led by Armed Forces Commander Gen. Mohamed Siad Barre, who headed the newly-formed Revolutionary Council.
Dahomey	10 Dec. '69	Army Chief of Staff Lt. Col. Maurice Kouandete ousted President Zinsou. Kouandete then formed a triumvirate with himself, Lt. Col. Paul-Emile De Souza, and Lt. Col. Benoit Sinzogan to rule until elections could be held.

Table 1 (Continued)

Country	Date	Results
Uganda	25 Jan. '71	President Milton Obote was overthrown by Chief of Defense Staff Maj. Gen. Idi Amin, who took over as head of state.
Sudan	19–22 Jul. '71	Maj. Hashim al-Atta led army coup against President Jafar Muhammed Nimeri, who was arrested. In a counter-coup, loyal army elements freed President Nimeri and reinstated him.
Ghana	13 Jan. '72	Lt. Col. Ignatius Acheampong, Commander of the Army's First Brigade, led a coup that toppled Prime Minister Dr. Kofi Busia. Acheampong became head of state and Chairman of the newly-formed National Redemption Council.
Rwanda	5 Jul. '73	Maj. Gen. Juvenal Habyarimana, Minister of Police and Army Commander, ousted President Gregoire Kayibanda in a bloodless coup. Habyarimana became chief of state.
Niger	15 Apr. '74	Armed Forces Chief of Staff Lt. Col. Seyni Kountche outsted President Hamani Diori and took over as head of state.
Ethiopia	12 Sept. '74	Military elements forced the resignation of Emperor Haile Selassie I, climaxing a "creeping" coup that started 27 Feb. when military unrest led to the resignation of the government, to the drafting of a new constitution, and to the resignation of civilian ministers 3 Aug. '74.
Malagasy	5 Feb. '75	General Ramanantsoa handed full powers to former Interior Minister Col. Richard Ratsimandrava, who was assassinated 11 February. The following day, a 19-member Military Directing Committee was created under Gen. Gilles Andriamahazo.

Note: This Table omits both the few instances (e.g. Sudan, November 1964; Sierra Leone, April 1968) in which military-dominated governments were forced out of power by popular demonstrations or dissension within the armed forces, and the instances in which the dominant political figure reinforced his power by using unconstitutional means (e.g., Uganda, February 1966; Lesotho, January 1970).

Military intervention fits temporally as a fourth phase in African history. The warrior flourished prior to major colonial intrusion and in the initial colonial penetration; the rebel countered the extension and intensification of alien rule, particularly its economic and social consequences; the guerrilla fought for independence against strongly entrenched minority regimes. All three were countered by fellow Africans, hired by the European invaders/rulers for the military rank-and-file. As van den Berghe observed, colonial soldiers were, in effect, "armed and somewhat privileged helots, more or less compelled by circumstances to serve their foreign masters in conquering and subjugating their fellow Africans, usually from other ethnic groups."[22] Only when control

---

22 Pierre L. van den Berghe, "The Military and Political Change in Africa," in Claude E. Welch, Jr., ed., *Soldier and State in Africa: A Comparative Analysis of Military Intervention and Political Change* (Evanston: Northwestern University Press, 1970), p. 258.

of the government had passed from European to African hands could the armed forces stage coups d'etat; independence and Africanization of the officer corps were prerequisites for successful intervention.

Compared with the warrior, rebel, or guerrilla, the putschist starts with several inherent advantages. He has control over a well-armed, obedient, trained group of soldiers, likely stationed in a politically central area, facing relatively ineffective countervailing forces. He can draw upon the armed forces' sense of exclusivity, and appeal to their claim to protect the "national" interest – frequently a guise for maintenance of institutional budgets. No need exists for a base area, nor for mass mobilization. Political awareness need not be inculcated among a large number of persons; what counts is the sense among officers that they have the power, the potential, and the opportunity to take control.

Whence stems the putschist tradition? In the medley of explanations, four basic sources recur: 1) from the warrior tradition; 2) from external manipulations and/or reference symbols; 3) from personal and corporate factors within African armies; and 4) from unsettled conditions in which recourse to force is commonplace.

Other papers in this collection deal with the historical and social context of the warrior tradition. Certain African cultures have nurtured the warrior, glorifying martial skills. Take, for example, the Nubi culture, shared by Idi Amin Dada. "If ever there was a hereditary military caste," Southall has written, "the Nubi are one."[23] Nubi were attracted to army service, in the process developing a reputation as a martial group. Colonial military recruiters were sensitive to the purported prowess of various groups; hence, the emphasis on the "martial races" who furnished large portions of the rank-and-file and the non-commissioned officers. Only when individuals with such backgrounds moved into command positions could their warrior heritage be transformed into a coup potential, however. Where commissioned officers have risen from the ranks (as with, for example, Generals Amin or Bokassa), one should expect highly personalistic policies. Where commissioned officers have joined the armed forces by lateral entry based on educational qualifications, the warrior tradition is essentially irrelevant. I am not aware, for example, of academic discussion of the Ibo warrior tradition, nor of the Fanti or Ewe tradition – yet officers from these backgrounds were among the prime movers of military intervention in Nigeria and Ghana.[24]

External influences on coups d'etat take three forms, 1) direct involvement, 2) indirect involvement through reference groups, and 3) contagion. The fine hand of the CIA is often purported to lie behind military intervention south of

---

23 Aidan Southall, "General Amin and the Coup: Great Man or Historical Inevitability," *Journal of Modern African Studies*, XIII (1975), p. 88.
24 For observations on the military practices of the Ibo, see M. M. Green, *Ibo Village Affairs* (New York: Praeger, 1964), pp. 61–7. The treatment of Okonkwo in Achebe's novel, *Things Fall Apart*, also provides sympathetic insights into the lack of Ibo military structure.

the Sahara – yet, as Ruth First has noted, this species of demonology does not square with the facts. "Obsolete theories of external intervention in the Third World" should be cast aside, she suggests. "It is not a matter of a few foreign plotters springing coups d'etat or assassinations on unsuspecting states ... To make it the whole picture, or even the main ingredient, is simplistic ... In Africa, ... the primary initiative for the coup d'etat does not seem to have come from outside, but from inside the countries themselves."[25] In fact, coups d'etat more likely result from the withdrawal of external support from a regime than from direct sponsorship of intervention. Indirect involvement, on the other hand, may be extremely significant. Officers trained abroad may absorb attitudes that, transplanted home, move them toward intervention.[26] Such "allies", in First's terminology, need no further prodding to undertake political action.[27] Finally, successful intervention by one army might spark intervention by another, as illustrated by the clustering of coups d'etat in Central and West Africa in late 1965 and early 1966. However, by the mid-1970s the coup-making capabilities of African armies had been conclusively demonstrated; there was no need to show politically aspirant majors how readily intervention could be carried out.

The immediate causes of military intervention lie within the armed forces themselves. Two contrasting causes can be noted here, respectively denoted as personal and corporate causes. Individual animosities between the head of state and his commanding officer have on occasion led to early retirement of the latter (e.g. Ankrah in Ghana in 1965, Malloum in Chad in 1974), followed a few months later by the premature retirement of the head of state as a consequence of intervention. Corporate causes of intervention are linked to institutional slights, as perceived by the armed forces. Budget reductions (real or threatened), or "political" interference in matters the military perceive as their prerogatives, have provided the spark for numerous coups d'etat. The statistical analysis of Eric Nordlinger, or the speculations of Michael Lofchie, substantiate the economic and institutional factors involved in intervention.[28]

But the long-term causes of military intervention lie within the social context of individual African states. As First commented, "The basic structures of African society in new states ... hold the seeds of a coup d'etat within them-

25   Ruth First, *The Barrel of a Gun: Political Power in Africa and the Coup d'Etat* (London: Allen Lane, 1970), pp. 417, 414.
26   Although Price attempts to illustrate the opposite—that "reference group" theory moves members of the armed forces away from extensive political involvement—his speculations in fact reinforce the point made above. Robert M. Price, "A Theoretical Approach to Military Rule in New States: Reference Group Theory and the Ghanaian Case," *World Politics*, XXIII (1971), pp. 399–430.
27   First, *The Barrel of a Gun*, p. 414.
28   Eric Nordlinger, "Soldiers in Mufti: The Impact of Military Rule Upon Economic and Social Change in the Non-Western States," *American Political Science Review*, LXIV (1970), pp. 1131–38; Michael F. Lofchie, "The Uganda Coup—Class Action by the Military," *Journal of Modern African Studies*, X (1972), pp. 19–35.

selves."[29] Numerous analysts have commented the pervasive nature of political violence south of the Sahara. Zolberg, in an assertion quoted earlier, pointed to conflict and disorder and the absence of political institutions for resolving issues.[30] Few effective constraints internal to the soeciety and the political order thus preclude members of the armed forces from asserting and assuming control. The power that grows out of the barrel of a gun has not been subordinated, in contemporary tropical Africa, to civilian political institutions.

The putschist tradition draws on a fact of human existence: the historical dominance of members of the armed forces in the political arena.[31] Civilian control of the military is the exception, not the rule. The colonial conquest illustrated the primary of force, and gave birth to armies whose members today enjoy the resources to seize control. Far more than the warrior, rebel, or guerrilla tradition, the putschist tradition is the current form of political violence in Africa.

Can one envisage a fifth phase of political violence? In the long term, revolutionary conflict could emerge, pitting a government oriented toward the use of force against partisans motivated by a high degree of class or national awareness. Let me re-emphasize *long* term, however. Numerous obstacles to revolutionary transformation in contemporary Africa exist, including the penetrated economy, latent ethnic discord within states, the absence of clear class demarcations, and generally low levels of political awareness. Pluralistic societies, with some avenues for personal and/or group mobility, enjoy safety valves that impede clear polarization. The potential for revolution requires, in Lemarchand's words, "a society riven by deep and persistent ethnic, social and economic cleavages that are cumulative rather than overlapping in their incidence, and where blockages in social mobility patterns rule out all significant prospects of transition from one socio-economic category to the other ..."[32] This potential has been translated into revolutionary restratification in Rwanda, Zanzibar, and (to a lesser extent) Algeria – all of them states in which an ethnically defined minority had exercised paramount political, economic and social control. The Republic of South Africa seems to exhibit the conditions listed by Lemarchand, leading sociologists to inventive explanations for the maintenance of white control.[33]

It is easier to speak of a revolutionary tradition outside the African continent than within it. Would-be revolutionaries south of the Sahara confront

---

29 First, *The Barrel of a Gun*, p. 414.
30 Zolberg, "The Structure of Political Conflict".
31 In Mosca's maxim, "The class that bears the lance or holds the musket regularly forces its rule upon the class that handles the spade or pushes the shuttle." Gaetano Mosca, *The Ruling Class* (New York: McGraw-Hill, 1939), p. 228.
32 Rene Lemarchand, "Revolutionary Phenomena in Stratified Societies: Rwanda and Zanzibar," in Claude E. Welch, Jr. and Mavis Bunker Taintor, eds., *Revolution and Political Change* (North Scituate: Duxbury Press, 1972), p. 284.
33 Heribert Adam, *Modernizing Racial Domination: The Dynamics of South African Politics* (Berkeley: University of California Press, 1971); Pierre L. van den Berghe, *South Africa: A Study in Conflict* (Middletown: Wesleyan University Press, 1965).

the simultaneous advantage and disadvantage of having revolutionary models and ideologies ready at hand. The advantage is one of ease: explanations for government inadequacy and conflict can be found readily; ideologies can be borrowed without fear of infringing copyrights. The disadvantage is one of inapplicability: as Mulele discovered, the maxims of Mao could not be easily transferred from one sociopolitical context to another. Further, widespread awareness of revolutionary models and ideologies means that incumbents as well as insurgents can follow the prescribed strategies. Revolutionary political violence leads inexorably to counterrevolutionary political violence.

Successful political revolutions have coupled urban with rural insurrection. Writers as far removed in their political orientations as Samuel Huntington and Leon Trotsky have recognized that only uniting protest based in both the city and the countryside can bring a transformation of the total system.[34] The revolutionary transformations of Algeria, Rwanda and Zanzibar involved both rural and urban areas. These were exceptions. African history to the mid-1970s includes some instances of urban turmoil (strikes; student protests; marches and demonstrations; economic boycotts) and many more instances of rural unrest; however, these have not occurred simultaneously, nor have they necessarily been directed to the same political objectives. For revolution to occur, the delegitimization of the government must be both perceived and acted upon concurrently by city and village dwellers. The incumbents will be aware of the potential challenges to their control, and will take steps to enhance their own positions. The question then becomes one of the balance of the facilities and resources available to both contending entities.

The revolutionary tradition in Africa will be developed by those opposing indigenous governments. The rebel and the guerrilla struggled against external impacts on their societies; the warrior and the putschist sought changes of personnel and policy largely within their societies. The revolutionary thus concentrates on sweeping internal political transformation, far more extensive in scope than the alterations of the guerrilla. A heritage of political violence naturally will abet the tasks of creating a political foundation – in fact, the revolutionist may become the capstone of a tradition (as amplified and revised) of political violence.

To come full circle to the observations posed at the start of this paper, only the revolutionary can create conditions under which the nature of political violence changes qualitatively. His success in creating new political institutions leads to new norms of legitimacy. "A full-scale political revolution," Huntington has stressed, "thus involves the rapid and violent destruction of existing political institutions, the mobilization of new groups into politics, and the creation of new political institutions."[35] These new institutions enjoy a founda-

---

34   Samuel P. Huntington, *Political Order in Changing Societies* (New Haven: Yale University Press, 1968), pp. 277–300; Leon Trotsky, *The Russian Revolution* (Garden City: Doubleday, 1959), pp. 31–48.
35   Huntington, *Political Order*, p. 266.

tion of support unknown to the former institutions of government-legitimacy. As such, these institutions can prescribe the use of violence against opponents without necessarily undercutting their own legitimacy. Paradoxically, only after successful revolution might the use of violence against the government be illegitimate. I leave to future historians and political scientists the resolution of this issue.

The Cultural Roots of Aggressive Behavior in Modern African Politics

VICTOR C. UCHENDU

University of Illinois, Urbana, U.S.A.

IN A VERY fundamental way politics is warfare. The task of the political process, particularly in the new states, is to evolve a political framework that is capable of transforming "political warfare" into a new political culture that can generate and sustain new rules of the political game that are different from the traditional rules of warfare.

Political developments in Africa during the first decade of Africa's independence shocked and disappointed both critical lovers and loving critics of African politics. Some African leaders and many African scholars have been no less disturbed in their political assumptions. We are now groping, almost in the dark, to understand African political realities. What is clear is that we can no longer confuse political institutions with the institutionalization of politics. Africa inherited a large variety of the former and is now challenged to achieve the latter.

It is the contention of this paper that *consensus*, an important ingredient of traditional African polity, has been replaced by *coercion* in modern African states. This is not to suggest that a state can operate without the use of coercion, but rather to say that in traditional African polities coercion was an instrument of the last resort; and that a reversal has occurred in the decade of independence.

The following questions may well be posed: What is the character of political arena in modern Africa and what rules of the "political game" are being evolved in it? What is the "aggressive" content of this political game and how can we explain it? I will attempt an answer to these and other allied questions, not from the vantage point of an African "expert," but from the personal perspectives of an African scholar who wants to "look into" the continent from the outside.

Review of Culture and Aggression Theory and Research

We can isolate two major streams of theoretical thought which have bearing on my subject. There are what may be classified as general theories of aggression, which focus on individual and group behavior, particularly the responses to stressful situations. A large body of the social science literature, dominated by psychology, is oriented to this problem area. The second stream of theoretical thought – and it represents the underdeveloped research area, particularly in the African field – deals with political violence.

Gurr (1970, pp. 2–3) defines political violence as "all collective attacks within a political community against the political regime, its actors – including competing political groups as well as incumbents – or its policies." The assumption that aggression by human beings – whether at the level of individuals or groups (societies) – owes more to cultural influence than to any particular factor that is biological in character is a persuasive theoretical position. This assumption leads us to examine the "cultural environment" of aggression in order to understand how aggression is brought about. The literature on the subject has called attention to both the adaptive or survival functions of human aggression in many situations as well as the conscious effort by societies to either emphasize or to de-emphasize aggression as a necessary instrument of adaptation. Within this theoretical vein runs an extreme culturogical dogma: According to White,

> "Warfare is a struggle between social organisms, not individuals. Its explanation is therefore social or cultural, not psychological" (White, 1949, p. 132).

Psychologists have rightly protested this "single factor magic" in the explanation of very complex behavior patterns in individuals and societies. They recognize, and other social scientists seem to agree, that like war, "aggression begins in the mind of men" – to borrow from the Preamble to the UNESCO Constitution.

Although it tends to be single-discipline centered, the psychological analysis of aggression (human and animal) has yielded a rich harvest of theories. Both Freud and McDougall, who are among the most influential protagonists of the instinctivist conception of human aggression, left many unresolved questions to enable the so-called "New Biologists," notably Lorenz (1966) and Ardry (1966) to embark on reconstituting what Okonji aptly described as the obsolete "parliament of instincts". As it is well known, Ardry invested this parliament with much power, with aggression in the forefront.

Unlike Ardry, Scott seems to have allayed our fears. Following an impressive review of experimental evidence concerning the biocentric view of aggression, Scott suggests that:

> "There is no physiological evidence of any spontaneous stimulation for fighting arising within the body. This means that there is no need for fighting, either aggressive or defensive, apart from what happens in the external environment which is without stimulation..." (Scott, 1958, p. 62)

What do we have in the environment of an organism that can produce aggression? One of the best known attempts to answer this question is the "frustration-aggression" hypothesis. According to this thesis, frustration arises when a goal-directed response is obstructed. In this context, primary frustrations which are the result of aroused need (i.e., hunger) is distinguished from secondary frustrations which are obstructions to goal attainment. In my view, political aggression belongs more to a *secondary* than a *primary* type of aggression.

In the political domain we can isolate three types of secondary frustrations – passive, security-threatening, and strategic.

1. Passive Frustration is the type of secondary frustration which poses an insurmountable political obstacle that is not necessarily a security threat. African irredentist movements come under this. African political thought and practical politics are both cool to irredentist political aspirations. Nyerere has asserted that the inherited African state boundaries are so *absurd* that they must be treated as sacrosanct. We do not know of any serious fundamental disagreement with this dictum.

2. Security-threatening Frustration is rather obvious and is the major concern of frustration-aggression hypothesis. The question often asked is whether every aggressive act is the result of some frustration and whether every frustration instigates an aggressive response. Available evidence suggests that certain forms of aggression are not instigated by frustrations and that whether or not frustrations lead to aggression will depend on certain learned experiences and cognitive factors which affect the individual's *definition* and/or *perception* of his environment (Okonji, 1970).

3. Strategic Aggression is one kind of secondary aggression which, according to Berkowitz (1962), is not caused in any direct way by frustration. It is rather a strategem in the competition between groups for incompatible goals. The United States involvement in Vietnam cannot be rationally explained in terms of a Super-power whose immediate interests are threatened. It can be seen as a *strategic aggression* designed to prevent the disruption of a perceived political status quo in Asia. Kwame Nkrumah's political strategy in the Congo (Zaire) in the early 1960's falls within this class of strategic aggression.

Looking beyond the boundaries of psychology, we are forced to raise a question which is at the heart of aggression – man – culture problem: Is it valid to equate or better, to relate aggressive action in individual behavior with aggression between groups or classes in one society or, for that matter, between societies? If aggression is as much a *structural* concept as it is a *functional* one, is there any continuity in the structuring of aggressive behavior between two interrelated levels of social organization – the individual and the societal levels? Is there any evidence to support the proposition that individuals reared in a "peace oriented" political culture will invariably produce political leadership and institutions which will mediate their external relations in a way consistent with their cultural orientation? What impact does the specialization of political roles, particularly the concentration of political power among a ruling elite, have on the interpretation of "national interest" and therefore on internal and external political relations of either a peace-oriented culture or a highly competitive political system? I do not promise a definitive answer. I only hope that the African data will provide some insights.

Theories of Political Violence

The central assumption in recent theorizing about political violence is rooted in the emerging psychological evidence that suggests that men have a *capacity* but not a *need* for aggression. With this assumption, the task of the political theorist interested in political violence is essentially to identify and order available data about the patterns of social circumstances in which men exercise that capacity for violence collectively. Since anthropologists, who seemed to be better informed of the traditional African institutions than any other discipline, have virtually abandoned modern African polity to economists and political scientists, we have to go to the latter for guidance. Unfortunately, serious studies of violent political behavior in tropical Africa are hard to come by, though newspaper reports and journalistic observations abound. To redeem the barrenness of the field, political sociology has paid some attention to questions of "political stability and instability". I am aware of only one major study of this problem in recent times (Uche, 1971) – and that in a continent that has continuing anti-colonial struggles and has had three or more generations of military coups and two celebrated civil wars in a decade of independence.

The most comprehensive theory of political violence known to me is that of Ted Robert Gurr (1970). In his study, *Why Men Rebel,* Gurr provides an integrated social science theory of political violence which incorporates both psychological and societal variables in his model. Gurr's theory rests on three pillars. First, he traces the primary causal sequence in political violence to the development of *discontent*. Second, he calls attention to the factors which lead to the *politicization* of that discontent. Third, he discusses the *actualization* in violent action against political objects and actors.

Central to the development of discontent, its politicization and actualization in violent action is the concept, *Relative Deprivation* (RD). Relative Deprivation is defined as a perceived discrepancy between men's value expectations and their value capabilities (Gurr, 1970, p. 13). If we regard "value expectations" as the goods and services and conditions of life to which people believe they are rightfully entitled, "value capabilities" will be likened to the goods and services and life styles they think they are capable of attaining or maintaining, given the social means available to them. In this view, societal conditions that increase the average level or intensity of expectations without increasing capabilities also increase the intensity of discontent.

The political environment in modern Africa which can and has affected *Relative Deprivation* includes the value gains of competing ethnic groups and social classes within a modern African state and the promise of new opportunities which often accompany an abrupt change in government created by military take-overs. And every military coup creates new channels of political communication.

Societal conditions which decrease a people's average value position without decreasing their value expectations similarly increase deprivation, and consequently intensify discontent.

Among the societal variables that affect the focusing of discontent on political objects are the extent of cultural and sub-cultural sanctions for overt aggression, the extent and degree of success of past political violence, the legitimacy of the political system and the kind of responses it makes and has made or is perceived to have made in balancing Relative Deprivation among competing political interests in the political system. Gurr (1970, p. 13) notes that "the belief that violence has utility in obtaining scarce values can be an independent source of political violence" – an observation which recent experiences in military take-overs in West Africa seem to document.

Politicized discontent is a necessary condition for the resort to violence in new states. Particularly in tropical Africa, where politicization of issues is an important colonial heritage, discontent is just one of the many issues that are politically articulated. The dominance of society, economy, and culture by the polity cannot be divorced from conflict generation.

Africa's Political Environment

Let us examine the structural features of modern African states and Africa's past and recent historical experiences which, in my view, lead to competitive politics, exaggerate Relative Deprivation, and create an unmanageable political dis-census in a political system that lacks an effective conflict management system.

Structural Features of the Polity and Economy

Four major features of the African polity deserve attention.

1. All but ten of the 42 independent African states have gained their independence in the last decade or so. Given the newness of independence and the legitimate interests of the leaders who achieved independence to maintain their power, there is the increasing temptation to reassert monarchical tendencies as a political style, leading to what amounts to "living ancestor" syndromes in an ethnically heterogeneous political system.

2. Recent events emphasize the obvious fact that despite the political rhetorics of continental unity and Pan-Africanism, Africa is becoming increasingly nationalistic, and may probably grow more nationalistic in the forseeable future. Finding a common cultural and institutional base for this growing nationalistic movement is not without conflict in a poly-ethnic political system.

3. The *unevenness in development* and the *varying development potential* among states are probably two of the most significant facts of African experience. In a young plural society, unevenness in development, however caused, is a major source of political conflict which cannot be ignored. Three levels of *unevenness* in development can be isolated.

a. Geographically, we can see the differences in the levels of economic achievement between the forest areas and the dry savanna areas. This is not just a geographical phenomenon; what is new is the creation of new African states that are confined entirely to poor savanna regions. The consequence for development is that the complementarity between the forest and savanna regions in trade and labor mobility is being destroyed by certain policy decisions which are motivated by short-run economic problems.

b. Territorially, unevenness in development is characteristic of each state. Since African economies tend to be export-dependent, countries that lack export capacity (in terms of agricultural and/or mineral wealth) have tended to lag behind in the current pace of development. This disparity in development potential is a major obstacle to regional cooperation and an important element in relative deprivation within a region.

c. Nationally, regional differences in the distribution of resources, especially where resource endowment has an ethnic linkage, puts strains on rational economic decision-making. This factor underscores an important observation that in the African context, development implies building the society and the economy as a simultaneous activity.

4. Probably the most dramatic characteristic of the African development environment has to do with the spatial aspect of its sovereignty. *Africa has the largest number of land-locked countries of any continent.* Of the 24 land-locked countries in the world, 14 are in Africa, all of them in Black Africa. In Africa the political economy of land-locked countries deserves special attention. Land-locked economies constitute an environment which must be understood not only in development terms, but in their potential for generating frustrations and conflict.

For instance, the five land-locked countries in Western Africa have much in common. They are French-speaking, French-dependent, and are found in the savanna ecology where export potential is limited. Except Upper Volta and Central African Republic whose land areas are comparable to other states in the West Africa region, Mali, Niger, and Chad are massive, dry, continental in location, and have small population relative to available territory.

Land-locked countries in Eastern Africa are comparatively smaller in size, have sizeable population, with Rwanda and Burundi definitely overpopulated. They are also moving towards greater market integration. The experience of Uganda indicates what a land-locked country can gain through membership of a functional organization. Malawi's foreign policy and domestic political culture indicate the dilemma and the political price which a small land-locked country must pay in exercising its limited economic options. Zambia's political styles owe much to the personality of President Kaunda, but one cannot divorce this from another economic reality: a small but mineral-rich country, that can afford high political stakes.

Four land-locked countries which are tied to the political orbit of South Africa are Zimbabwe, Botswana, Lesotho, and Swaziland. Botswana in particular poses the most immediate political problem, as it is psychologically oriented to Black Africa but geographically and economically a captive of South Africa.

The political landscape of the African continent shows that two structural features of the polity must not be ignored in any attempt to analyze present and future capacity of the political community to generate conflict. First, there is a large number of small states which cannot support a viable economy but must seek some accommodations in a regional arrangement. Second, the large number of land-locked states in the continent indicates that for many countries to develop at all, we must go beyond the national "Will to Develop" and create a "Regional Will".

The Impact on Sovereignty

Let us explore the influence of sovereignty on a society's capacity to generate conflict by citing recent experiences of the Western African region.

When African leaders charge colonialism with Balkanizing the African continent, they mean that they did not inherit geographically sizeable territories at independence. But in terms of development, colonial fragmentation meant more than this. If colonial policies fostered geographical, economic, social, and institutional fragmentation, the fact of "sovereignty" has led to more fragmentation.

Take the question of political boundaries. At independence, what were formerly unimportant administrative markers became international boundaries for nine Francophone countries. Independence has led 14 countries of West Africa to follow different policies which are dictated by "national self interests" – and, as recent events have shown, these policies have tended to deviate from the Pan-African ideal. The policies are, as predictable, often independent, separate, and often conflicting, rather than continentally focused.

West Africa has its fair share of "small" countries, both in terms of area and population. Five sovereignties with very small areas and population are The Gambia, Togo, Dahomey, Sierra Leone, and Liberia. The Gambia, Africa's river country, is smaller than Connecticut, but much of the area is water or mangrove swamp. With a population of about 400,000, The Gambia has been able to avoid military coups by opting not to have an army. Togo and Sierra Leone are both smaller than Maine.

Mauritania, Niger, and Mali have small populations but much larger areas, in desert environments. Mali, Upper Volta, and Niger are three of Africa's 14 land-locked countries. Mauritania is not land-locked, but has most of the problems of land-locked countries. In view of the limited resources for development, any development policy that does not link the nine small and land-locked West African states with their neighbors would spell perpetual "aid-dependence" – and this implies perpetual conflict.

Historical Experience

No serious discussion of African political conflicts on a continental scale can fail to pay attention to politics and politicians – two critical agents that create and manage conflict at the political level.

One appalling legacy of colonial rule in Africa, particularly in the domain of political discourse, is the extremism of political language. The nationalist struggle taught the politicians that no phrase and no trick was too mean to use against the political enemy. The argument was that the sacredness of the cause of independence justified any means. Even in those African countries which pride themselves as having won independence on a golden platter, it was considered legitimate to fight the colonial enemy with all the weapons available. As long as the "enemy" was a colonial government or institution, it did not seem to matter what language, tactics, or weapons were used. But independence has changed the definition of "political enemy". In the post-independence period the political enemy has become opposition parties. Since political parties tend to have strong ethnic attachment and linkages, it is no longer clear when a party or an ethnic group becomes an "enemy" of the ruling party, and by extension, the enemy of the state.

The most paradoxical point is not the loss of a climate in which political concensus can flourish, but the fact that many African polities are indeed ripe for political extremism. Our polities exhibit a very high level of disaffection leading to three varieties of Relative Deprivation:

1. *Decremental Deprivation* in which the *value capabilities* of a political system are decreasing while the *value expectations* are constant.

2. *Aspirational Deprivation* in which the *value expectations* are rising faster than *value capabilities* of a political system.

3. *Progressive Deprivation* in which sustained gains in *value expectations* and *value capabilities* have become suddenly disrupted because of a sharp reversal in the growth curve of *value capabilities*. This trend is sometimes referred to as the "J-curve" hypothesis which argues that revolutions are most likely to occur when a prolonged period of objective economic and social development is followed by a short period of economic reversal.

Without invoking a single factor explanation for complex phenomenon, I would suggest that part of the political frustrations manifest in our political system can be traced to the performance of our economic system and the unfulfilled promises of our politicians. Social and economic development, particularly rapid elite mobility, at both the political and bureaucratic structures of our society have combined to produce a high level of mass frustration. There are numerous frustrated segments of our society who are willing to follow a leader who promises drastic action to solve all their problems quickly. I have been amused and sometimes angered by the behavior of our masses whenever there is a violent change of government. It appears that it does not matter who comes to power. A leader's mass support literally evaporates once he is no longer in power!

Our frustrated population is drawn from many ranks: the unemployed school leavers seeking non-existent jobs in the towns; the trade unionists; the school teachers; underpaid and underutilized junior civil servants and office clerks; the farmers, exploited by the cheap foods policy that benefits the towns – all seeking a new deal. All this is fertile soil for political radiaclism.

Rewards of Politics

Politics in independent Africa is the most rewarding profession for the successful politician. Everywhere government constitutes the largest industry, and in one country or more, one can make a case that it is the only industry. Is it any wonder that politics has become a zero-sum game! Unless there are other employment opportunities that are as economically attractive as politics, competitive politics will always tend to lead to aggression.

Assuming fair elections, democratic politics will not return conservatives to office in Africa; in these circumstances we expect radicals to be returned. The question is whether there will be an opportunity for meaningful elections and whether liberal or authoritarian radicalism will dominate the political scene.

Other questions may be raised. Can Africa produce leaders who are radical enough to win mass support, but liberal enough to proceed by *compromise* rather than by *arbitrary force*? Leaders who enjoy enough ethnic support to hold their own constituencies but have broad political support to win the rest of other ethnic groups who make up the nation? If there is any validity to the hypothesis of cultural continuity, one would answer these questions in the affirmative. Centuries of political experience are not lacking among some African groups. The political culture of most traditional African polities emphasized action based on *compromise* and *conciliation* after extended "palaver". All that is needed is to return to this democratic tradition.

Conclusion

We have tried to call attention to a sample of a large body of theoretical literature which has a direct bearing on aggression, particularly political violence. It is clear that the incidents of political violence in Black Africa have grown since independence, that the pattern of violence is not haphazard but patterned.

In a study of political violence in 31 independent African countries in the first decade of independence (1957–68), Uche (1971) found the following correlations which could serve as our summary:

1. General economic development has no statistically significant correlation with any type of political violence.
2. Primary education has a statistically significant positive correlation with internal war.
3. Size of the polity is correlated with all forms of internal political violence, such as internal war, turmoil, and subversion.
4. Rapid population growth has a statistically significant correlation with war.
5. Number of chief executives since 1957 is positively and significantly correlated with turmoil.

6. Defense budget is uncorrelated with any type of political violence, internal or external.

Political violence is not new to African politics (Jones, 1951). What is new is the environment of the polity – a post-colonial setting and associated inherited institutions – and the lack of agreed rules for political competition. Given this new environment, cultural continuity is not a powerful argument to explain the roots of political aggression in modern African states. My argument is that the structure and the character of the modern African polities, the distribution of the economic rewards, and the ethnic composition and the emerging class interests in the new states are factors which are directly relevant in an explanation of violence in African politics.

REFERENCES

ARDRY, R.
  1966   *The Territorial Imperative*, New York.
GURR, A.
  1970   *Why Men Rebel*, New York.
JONES, G. I.
  1951   *Basutoland Medicine Murder (Report on the Recent Outbreak of "Dirette" Murder in Basotuland)*, London.
LORENZ, K.
  1966   *On Aggression*, New York.
NIEBURG, H. L.
  1969   *Political Violence (The Behavioral Process)*, New York.
OKONJI, M. O.
  1970   *Psychological Causes of Civil Wars: The Sudanese Case*, Mss.
UCHE, C.
  1972   *Political Violence in Black Africa 1957–1968*, Unpublished Ph. D. dissertation, Department of Sociology, University of Chicago.
WHITE, L. A.
  1949   *The Science of Culture*, New York.

SECTION III:
THE WARRIOR AND CULTURE

African Dance and the Warrior Tradition

JUDITH LYNNE HANNA

The University of Texas at Dallas, Richardson, U.S.A.

THE "warrior tradition" has been characterized as capturing such aspects of human organization and symbolism as (1) the idea of adulthood related to notions of self-reliance and (2) the concept of manhood linked to violent valor and sexual virility (Mazrui 1975). In this paper I shall explore the relationship of dance to the warrior tradition: its multifarious manifestations, the Eurocolonial impact on warrior dances, and the transformation of "traditional" warrior dance in the post-colonial independence period The discussion will be introduced by some preliminary qualifications and a summary of the mechanisms or properties of dance which help to explain why this form of human behavior is so commonly a concomitant of the warrior tradition.

Qualifications. A few preliminary remarks are called for concerning the problems involved with data and generalization about the concepts of "warrior" and "tradition". Unfortunately there is no full study of the relation of dance to the warrior tradition. Rather than a diachronic thread within a single ethnic group woven from precolonial through the European imposition to the independence era, one finds scattered and often superficial descriptions of warrior dances in the literature. By the time many scholars were on the African scene, pacification had occurred.[1] Some colorful descriptions refer to mock attacks, frenzied leaping and charging, wild plunging and thrusting of spears, savage weapon brandishing, abandoned gesticulating faces, transfixing eyes on invisible enemies, dilated nostrils, perspiring bodies, nervous trembling, unflagging vigor, blood-curdling shrieks, roars of defiance, and exhilarating

---

1 Uzoigwe (1975) reports on the dearth of pre-colonial military studies. When a tradition is stamped out, it is hard to write about it. Brelsford (1959) found that there was little descriptive material on war dances in Zambia, attributing this to inspiration lost with the cessation of warfare. Since few anthropologists could observe "illegal" warrior action, many were obliged to rely on the memories of informants, some of whom glorified their history or suppressed it in accord with the values they presumed the inquirer to hold. Furthermore, the literature on war was usually written by individuals who considered dance from the contemporary Western perspective of being a segmented, "frivolous" slice of life and not worthy of attention. "They danced" is the reference *ad nauseum.*

throbbing sonic accompaniment. These are hardly useful to the serious social scientist. Warrior dance description and discussion of purpose, function, and relationships between dance behavior and other sociocultural phenomena are also limited because of the underdeveloped status of African dance studies.[2] My discussion of African dance and the warrior tradition must therefore be incomplete.

It is important to point out that on the African continent with its 800 to 1000 ethnic groups, not all have a "warrior tradition". (Cf. Welch 1975). Sometimes entire groups migrated or parts seceded from a group in order to avoid confrontation. Others surrendered to preclude it. The Lala were not alone in their behavior in the event of a raid: they would desert their villages and seek refuge in the nearby hills until marauders had left (Long 1968: 80). Through conquest or voluntary submission to a warrior tribe or nation, some groups were forced to acquire the warrior tradition.

The concept of "tradition" in dance has been misunderstood. From the evidence we have, dance seems to be characterized by change (cf. Hanna 1965, 1974a; Ranger 1975 on contemporary history). The concept of "warrior dance" refers to dance which is performed by real or symbolic warriors. "War" will be used broadly to include national battles, group raids, dyadic affrays, and the isolated manslaying to prove manhood.

The notion of the warrior tradition encapsulating adulthood and self-reliance must be qualified. Warriors achieved physical characteristics of adulthood and usually an increased detachment from their parents' nuclear family. However, in many instances, the warrior tradition was a "liminal" (Turner 1967) transitional status toward adulthood and social power. In the Samburu gerontocracy, the warrior junior age set (*moran*) was forbidden to marry and kept in a state of delayed adolescence until it could be replaced by a new age-set, the creation of which was determined by the elders. Among the Zulu,

---

2   This field is retarded because of factors related to the study of the "arts" generally, the study of dance in particular (Hanna 1975b, 1976d), and the factors of the colonial experience and historical time in Africa (discussed in the section on the European impact upon dance and the warrior tradition). The social sciences felt a need to emphasize the "science" in their disciplines and thus neglected the "arts." Discourse—verbal speech—was the primary key to human behavior. In the arts and humanities, systematic focus on nonwestern forms is also comparatively recent. With respect to the study of dance in particular, scholars reflect the cultures of their own societies and thus have tended to have ethnocentric concepts of dance. Western researchers were most active in Africa and carried with them attitudes of Victorian and Puritanical dislike of the body or shame toward it. Perhaps a voyeuristic appreciation of African dance occurred, but objective reporting may have been psychologically and socially difficult. There was a tendency to perceive dance forms different from one's own as not dance at all. Anglo-Saxon men rarely studied dance since men's dancing came to be considered effeminate or with homosexual implications. Most students of an art form have some minimal experience in it. The study of African dance has been seriously hampered by the fact that scholars were not acquainted with dance—its elements (space-rhythm-dynamics and the instrument of dance, the human body) in motion. Consequently, if there was no dislike or shame toward the body, there was often a detachment from it and inability to "read" it.

Shaka's warriors were by no means independent; they were a symbol of his independence. He controlled nearly every aspect of their conduct and careers extending the time they remained unmarried and determining the sequence of age grades that was previously regulated by the natural progress of the life cycle (Walter 1969: 148, 190).[3]

Dance. The concept "dance" refers to human behavior composed – from the dancer's perspective – of purposeful, intentionally rhythmical, and culturally patterned sequences of nonverbal body movement and gesture which are not ordinary motor activities, the motion having inherent, aesthetic value, in terms of notions of appropriateness and competency (Hanna 1976b, 1976f). Dance can be viewed from what Hatch (1973) calls the "behavioral cybernetic approach," the use of feedback and systems concepts to account for the reciprocal interactions between dance performance and psychological and sociocultural processes. It is assumed that a principle function of dance has been to control and organize social interactions. The thought, emotion, and motor properties of dance which seem to make it work along the lines discussed in this paper relate to its instrument (the human body), motion, dance as a multisensory phenomena, and the symbolic potential of dance. (For a fuller discussion, see Hanna 1975c, 1976b, 1977a.)

The human body is the simplest and earliest human form of power. Power refers to the ability to influence predispositions, feelings, attitudes, beliefs, and actions. Ontogenetic development is characterized by increasing body awareness and mastery and body control of the environment. Rooted in sensory and internal experiences, body image comprises the memory of experiences the individual has with the body and the attitudes toward or expectations about it. Body power often becomes equated realistically or symbolically to power in other domains. For example, among the Ankole, when the physical powers of the king waned through approaching age or through sickness, the kingly powers were believed to wane with them. No king therefore was permitted to age or weaken; his magicians would prepare his poison (Oberg 1940: 137).

Dance, a special form of body motion, is actual power involving the interaction of four sources force: mental energy, muscle strength, force of gravity, and momentum developed in the moving body or any of its parts. The warrior is usually viewed as having the ability to take life and to give life (sexually and in not killing). Dance, and especially warrior dance, may be a symbol of power representing self control and dominance. One kind of power such as the physical or symbolic self may be used to secure another (over others) through the dancing self or others' dancing, a substitution of proxy for self (Hanna 1976c).

Motion is generally recognized as the strongest visual attention attraction (Arnheim 1954: 361). Implicit is a change in environmental conditions which

---

3 Of course, the warrior tradition of Shaka's rule is unique; there were more than one hundred thousand warriors, a million deaths, and domination over a half million population (Walter 1969: 111).

may require a response to danger or pleasure. The intrinsic value of motion may be found in the growth and development of the human (Gardner 1973).

Dance is a complex multimodal system with the unique potential for a greater impact than many audiovisual media. The efficacy of dance lies in its capacity to fully engage the human being with the senses of sight (performers moving in time and space), sound (of physical movement), odor (of physical exertion), kinesthetic activity or empathy, and proxemics. Thus there is a potential multisensory bombardment and saturation which can lead to altered states of consciousness for the dancer and observer (cf. Ludwig 1969).

The symbolic potential of dance becomes apparent if dance is viewed as a communication system and like speech, especially poetry. In fact, dance exhibits most of the design features of language (Hockett and Ascher 1964). Dance had directional reception, interchangeability (someone can be both a transmitter and receiver), arbitrariness (many characteristics have no predictability), discreteness, displacement (it can refer to something not immediately present), productivity (messages never seen before can be sent and understood within a set of structural principles), duality of patterning (a system of action and a system of meaning), cultural transmission, ambiguity, and affectivity (expression of an internal state with potential for changing moods and a sense of situation).

There are five distinctions between dance and verbal language. First, in dance, the vocal/auditory channel is replaced by the motor/visual-kinesthetic-auditory-olfactory-proxemic-tactile channels. Whereas language is unidimensional, dance involves three dimensions in space. Second, complete feedback of language, the speaker's ability to perceive everything relevant to his speech, is not possible in the multimedia of dance. Third, the phoneme and morpheme are generally agreed by linguists to be the minimal unit. No such agreement about minimal units exists in dance. Fourth, the detailed syntax governing sequences as exists in language is yet to be worked out in dance. Fifth, specialization in language, the fact that someone need not have total involvement in the act of communication is not generally applicable to dance.

Devices of semantic encoding may include the concrete representation (e.g., an imitative reconstruction of war with advance and retreat tactics, leadership patterns, tension levels, manner of killing) an icon (a danced war god revered as the deity), a stylization (an arbitrary gesture or movement such as the V gesture for victory), a metonym (a war dance as part of a war action), a metaphor (reference to qualities of strength characteristic of war but applicable to nonmartial domains of behavior such as economics), and actuality (a warrior dancing as a warrior and treated as one). These devices of encoding meaning are signs (indications of the existence, past, present, or future of a thing, event, or condition) which may function as signals (heralding confrontations or celebrations, e.g.) when their meanings lie in the orientation they give to interactional behavior. These context based devices may operate within one or more of seven spheres: dance as a sociocultural event; total body in action; total performance; discursive performance (segmental unfolding of images or groups of images); specific movements or gestures; intermeshed with other communication modes, and a medium for song, music, costume, accoutrements, or speech (cf. Hanna 1975d).

Symbolism in warrior dances is linked to the notion of play which borrows or adopts patterns that appear in other contexts where they achieve immediate and obvious ends. The mimetic fight is divorced from the original motivation and is qualitatively distinct. There may be exaggerated uneconomical motor patterns, the sequence may be reordered with more repetition than usual, sequences may be fragmented, or not completed. The warrior dance is a playing with the body, ideas, and emotions. Play allows for distancing, safe examination of problems and the separation or merging of serious and non-serious. Play, Schechner (1973) argues, maintains a regular, crisis-oriented expenditure of kinetic energy which can be transformed from play energy into fight energy. The boundary between play and reality may, of course, dissolve.

Dance in Pre-European Independence Era

In this period, on the basis of oral histories reported in the ethnographic literature, it appears that warrior dances were status markers for groups and individuals, vehicles for sexual display, physical preparation for war, affective readying for violent encounters (incitement, communion, we/they distancing), religious behavior, displacement, and political behavior. These categories are neither mutually exclusive nor necessarily independent.

Status markers. Dancing makes manifest many social and cultural categories and value concepts and distinguishes the ordinary from the extraordinary. It is used to mark status changes, including the passage of childhood to youth or adulthood. Dances are frequently part of rites of passage in which separation, transition, and reaggregation occur. In the transitional period, dance is usually an educational medium for adult male physical and moral behavior. Military training and discipline in dance is frequently the mode of status change. Emergence dances celebrate the new maturation level and are often an emblem of the successful status change.

Although the Shilluk had no elaborate and prolonged rites of passage for youths to acquire manhood status, participation in a *cong bul* dance for warriors and their partners was the measure of achieving adult status and a symbol of reintegration with the community after a short period of segregation (Howell 1941). In Ruanda, the Tutsi kingdom had several years training for young men, the *intore* or chosen ones, who lived at the court of the *mwami* (king) or a chief allowed to recruit an army. The *mwami* asked his clients to bring to his court their sons for training. A company was constituted of 150–200 young men chosen on a wide territorial base (the herdsmen section of the army was based on kin). The youths learned the qualities of manhood – self mastery and military courage – and received instruction in war and raiding through warlike dances. They memorized and recited the poems exalting extraordinary bravery and boldness of their warrior forbears (Maquet 1961: 109, 117–119).

Among the Ndembu there were special high status cults with specific dances for killers. Hunting men or animals epitomized masculinity in a society jurally dominated by the principle of matrilineal descent. Part of the prayer at the onset of the *wuyang's* ritual, "We want a man who can sleep with ten women in one day, a great…hunter," points to the associated qualifications of virility and disregard for usual norms for a blood shedder (Turner 1957: 202, 59, 29, 380). The *mukanda* initiation rite for boys inculcated these values. *Chikoli*, a strong hard tree signifying strength, an erect penis, and masculine virtues of courage and skill, was a dominant symbol (as in other rituals). During circumcision, dancing occurred near the tree (Turner 1967: 354). On the last day in the rites of return, the *ku-tomboka* solo war dance with an axe was performed by each boy (*ibid.*: 259–260) signifying aspiration to the high status cult for killers.

Dance is also an indicator of individual achievement and prowess during victory celebrations. At the *nwole* feast of the Nuba, only the youths who have killed an enemy may take part in a special dance in which they display symbolic trophies to proclaim their feats – a shield or spear for every man killed, a gourd for every woman (Nadel 1947: 141). For the Lele, *tamo* referred to ferocity and courage, and a youth had to prove his manhood by killing a man or man-slaying animal such as a leopard and bring back proof of the deed. This allowed him to make a triumphal dance around the village to the beat of the special *nkoko* drum played only to celebrate man-killing (Douglas 1963: 187). Sonjo warriors were given prominent roles at most major rites; they were the principal dancers at the harvest festival during which they gave exhibitions of strenuous dancing (Gray 1965: 55). The Boran display their strength and skill at dancing; a proper man does not bluster or quarrel. Dancing with trophies of raids evidenced achievement, patriotism, and prestige (Baxter 1965). Raiding was the surest way of obtaining a large herd of cattle and thereby achieving or validating social status.

The influence of an Ibo "town" was measured by the strength of its able-bodied warriors. The Edda and Abam, famed for their war-making power, had strong age-grade organizations. They required taking an enemy's head as a precondition for manly status (Uchendu 1965). When an Ibo youth took a head for the first time, he joined in a public dance performed by all head-getters, holding the head in his left hand, his machete in the right, and sporting an eagle feather on one side of his head, a parrot feather on the other (Meek 1937: 49). Man-killing warrior societies, with a distinctive drum covered with human skin, had their own special dance performed on certain occasions. They would bring out the heads of people killed and place the skulls on a tray which was balanced on the head. Holding the machete between the teeth, they danced with deliberate steps or tiny rapid ones on the ball of the foot while the shoulders quivered and vibrated (Green 1964: 67). Meek reports that in former times at Ngbwidi, a title of Ogbute was conferred on any man who had killed and decapitated an enemy in war. A dance was held to announce the feat. The head was buried for about three weeks to clean it of flesh after which it was dug up and a dance of all head-getters was held in the market place (*ibid.*: 172). About some of these warriors, Nzekwu writes, "their ruthlessness was fed fat by the realisation that at the welcome dance held in their honour on their return from each campaign, they were to display the human trophies they had won" (1963: 17). Similarly, among the Yakö, only those warriors who returned from military action with the heads of slain enemies would take leading parts in the fighters' dances. They men danced around the ward squares with the heads before throwing them in the latrine. Later the teeth were removed to decorate the dancers' special fibre caps (Forde 1964: 148, 155).

Sexual display.   Women discriminate among men in terms of dance performance vigor and endurance. In *Song of Lawino*, p'Bitek (1966: 33) writes about Acholi dance: "A man's manliness is seen in the arena,/ You cannot hide anything,/ All parts of the body/ Are clearly seen in the arena,/ Health and Liveliness/ Are shown in the arena!" (p'Bitek is a social anthropologist and a dancer.) Nadel's description of the Nuba Tira tribe characterizes much of the continent. In the *hahodha* dance, young men recited their exploits in raiding and mimed their actions of skill, pugnacity, and endurance.

> In this dance, male pride and sexual stimuli are inextricably mixed. For by means of these self-praises the young men try to attract the attention of the girls, who standing in the centre of the ring formed by young men, will pick out one or the other, and throw themselves against the partners they have chosen (1947: 248).

The *dunuba* warrior flagellation dance of the Kouroussa was designed to test strength and courage. Holding a small war ax or saber in one hand and a short whip made of the plaited membrane of a donkey's penis in the other, each man wipped the man in front until blood ran. Those who could not bear the pain left the dancing ground amidst jeers from the crowd. When about four or five of the original fifteen youths remained, they danced and were nursed by the women. After they retired to rest, women and girls danced and sang their praises (Meillassoux 1968: 93). Mazrui sums up the dynamic: "The dancer, the warrior, the lover, become indistinguishable where the heritage of imagery draws no distinction between valor and virility" (1973: 20).

Physical preparation for war.   For the Zulu, according to Mahlobo (1934: 184), the different regiments would compete with each other in their dancing which was regarded as the means by which mind and muscles were kept exercised. Shaka's success was attributed in some measure to the warrior training in physical endurance and effecting mass movements (Walter 1969: 142). The "Old Style" of fighting was highly individualistic, a campaign was an "unorganized swoop" (*ibid.*: 122–123). Shaka led his dancers in the royal kraal; the men danced in drill units with mass attack strategies at the different camps. The tactics may have been the revival of practices that had died out or were derived from indigenous hunting practices in which a cresent was formed or the "horns" of the warrior unit encircled the enemy and killed everything within the circle.

Among the Kikuyu, the *kebata* and *nguro* dances were performed by warriors to display their physical fitness and dexterity in handling spears and shields and their ability in jumping high and broad while carrying their weapons. This training was considered necessary to prepare the youths to be able to meet any danger with confidence and to help the men become good runners, an important talent in the absence of mechanical travel in pursuing an enemy or dangerous animal (Kenyatta 1962: 93, 197). War dances were often regarded as a review at the opening of the campaign season as among the Chamba of Donga (Meek 1931(I): 349).

Dancing in preparation for a physical conflict has a scientific foundation as do "warm-up" exercises for athletes prior to a game. Furthermore, physiological research at Harvard suggests that palm and sole sweating in response to stress, exercise, and heat may be part of the "flight-or-fight" reaction that prepares animals, including humans, to cope with danger by running away. Sweating increases the coefficient of friction and enables animals to run better (New York Times 1976).

Affective readying.   Warrior dances often incite men to action. They frequently signalled a forthcoming raid. Boas (1955) noted the intense emotional value of music and dance and their implied heightened effects which in turn call forth an intense emotional reaction, an exciting of the passions. When the Chaga had to prepare for war, hundreds of warriors were called upon to perform the *rosi* war dance personally supervised by the chief. The dancers advanced in semicircular formation and then closed in upon each other engaging in sham duel. The simultaneous feet stamping, surging forward of the far-flung battle-line, and thunderous roars were assumed "to arouse the spirits of all and make concerted action possible" (Raum 1940: 222). Part of the incitement to action involves the preparation for the dance as well as the dance itself. For the Turkana *akimumwar* dance, all the men elaborately mud themselves with multi-colored ochre in intricate patterns and colors, fasten bells around the knees, stick ostrich feathers in the head-dress, and carry fighting sticks (Gulliver 1953: 75).

Communion, creating and alluding to solidarity through group dancing, is generally acknowledged in the literature (it is also recognized that fights often break out at occasions for the dance and during the performance). Langer (1953: 176, 190) speaks of the individual partaking of a feeling of strength in group rally and bonding, promoting combative readiness although the actual combat may be through individual skirmishes; Wepner (1973: 82), of dispelling or forgetting anxiety with a greater energy expenditure and higher fever of involvement; Zander (1974: 2), of team spirit as a "potent and invigorating tonic." He found that group success is not a permanent trait of individuals, but a motive that develops in particular group situations. The Swazi man called Sobhuza explained:

The warriors dance and sing at the *Incwala* and so they do not fight, although they are many and from all parts of the country and are jealous and proud. When the dance they feel they are one and they can praise each other (Kuper 1969: 224).

Often the precursor of war waged against external enemies, this annual ritual promoted solidarity and fortified the warriors for attack. The Zulu danced as a communal group in the image of the king reflecting his personal disposition in the movement style. Walter argues that the Zulu felt the state should be the body of the despot in "responding to his emotions and controlled by his will" (1969: 256). Dancing the king's dance was metonymical to the king's power, expressing and revivifying sentiments which sustained the combative extraordinary behavior. The incitement and communion in dance retelling success stories of warrior encounters served as motivation for continued achievement by focussing on skills which were tested and proven. The power of dance as a stimulus and sanction (shaming) is a potent weapon in many African cultures (See Gluckman 1960).

We know that Shaka conquered a number of groups and incorporated them into his kingdom and regiments. It might have been that battle unity and group integration were promoted by incorporating movements from different groups into a full corps's performance. There are no movement analyses to support this hypothesis. There is evidence among the Anáhuac of México that the dances and deities of heterogeneous conquered groups were incorporated (Kurath and Martí 1964, Hanna 1975c).

Part of affective readiness involves setting apart the fighting from the non-fighting group and the friend from enemy, adjusting behavior from one sphere of appropriateness (e.g., thou shall not kill) to the opposite through altered states of consciousness, or distancing. Wallace (1968) calls this a shift from a relaxed to a mobilized state arguing that a releasing mechanism is necessary. For many African groups the war dance serves as this kind of mechanism through being a special language code with kinetic graphic symbols evoking a disciplined response, a motivational state. Warrior dance is similar to the use of masked or possession dance which separates and defines differences between an individual's role in ordinary life and his role in another domain which sanctions extraordinary behavior and frees him from libel and similar repercussions. Thus warrior dance may create an affective state in a nonplay context in which the individual is able to commit acts of violence which are normally taboo. Often warrior dances work up to a frenzy and an ecstatic delirious state. The unusual motor qualities of swift movement through space, and vigorous accelerating activity may distort and attenuate perceptions and imbue the individual with an alien quality and a sense of a superior source of energy. Fisher (1973: 33) speaks of boundary loss, the submergence of the self in a flow. The violent change in the state of one's body may help instigate or cushion the effect of what is considered to be a radical change in the social state of affairs.

The discussion thus far has suggested that when a group goes to war there are frequently processes of separation and distancing, transition and preparation, and reaggregation and victory celebration which are marked by warrior dance (cf. Van Gennep). An example of closure is found in the Acholi perform-ance after a battle when the warriors danced the *bwola* backwards into a hut. As they entered to return the spears, a woman repeatedly poured water onto the roof above the doorway wetting them and so terminating the mobilized state (p'Bitek 1971).

Religious behavior. Dance is often a form of prayer (Nketia 1957, Hanna 1974b): to praise, thank, and invoke the deities, and to reenact cosmological events. In southwest Nigeria's Benin kingdom, there was a war ritual to honor *Ogu*, the god of iron. The warriors proceded through Benin City and then performed an acrobatic dance suspended from the trees in which the mythical war against the sky was enacted (Bradbury 1957: 58).

Warrior dance is often performed as a form of sympathetic magic. The dance becomes a kind of transformer through which currents of bodily energy are transmitted. Dance is believed to activate a supernatural essence used for curing among the Kung Bushmen, to release *jok* among the Lango, and to transform girls among the Bemba. Thus the shaking movement of the Samburu warrior dance is believed to make a man irresistible in battle; it also reflects anger, self-assertion, and manliness (Spencer 1965: 263–264). The concern among some peoples with reincarnation and lineage continuity and reenact-ment of ancestors' celebrated maneouvers may be seen as activating their power and skill.

Dance is, of course, metonymical to life. The transmission of life forces through dance is seen in the most important of all Swazi national ceremonies, the *Incwala* ritual for the hereditary king who shares power with his mother. Annually at the time of the southern summer solstice, the symbolic meaning of kinship (fertility, authority, and order) is expressed. The king is made by the people who contributed bride payment for his mother, and they sustain the regime. Nearly every male Swazi has at one time or another participated in the *Incwala*. Through warrior dance the power of life or death was harnessed to promote the common good. The Swazi were a powerful warrior nation with regiments stretching beyond the boundaries of clan and principality. Warfare was essential to sustain the kind of society that had developed. Sometimes initiated by warriors to provide the opportunity to display their courage, loyalty, and strenth, war was the vehicle for commoners to achieve power, wealth, and fame (Kuper 1969: 123).

For the especially richly costumed warriors to abstain from dancing in the *Incwala* was to withhold the power which bestowed strength and life (Kuper 1968). Held in the royal cattle byre, the dance acquired "perfect performance" by long hours of practice. The Swazi emphasized that the dance itself strengthened the king and the earth at the *Incwala*. "The people dance with vigor; here more than at any other stage they keep their king alive and healthy by their own movements" (Kuper 1969: 218). Officials urged the people: "Dance! Dance! The *Incwala* is not a thing of play. Dance!" (*ibid.*: 290). At specific times during the drama of kingship, the king himself is expected to dance with his men (*ibid.*: 209, 218). Dancing the *Incwala* secured the monarchy.[4]

From Ghana there were a number of reports of married women, whose men had gone off to battle, pantomiming war through dance as an imitative charm. The women painted themselves white, adorned themselves with beads and charms and carrying guns, sticks, and knives, they hacked paw-paw fruits as if they were enemy heads. Carrying long brushes made of buffalo or horse tails as they danced, singers made the point verbally explicit with such phrases as "Our husbands have gone to Ashateeland, may they sweep their enemies off the fact of the earth" (Frazer 1929: 26, Field 1940: 103).

Displacement. From a psychological perspective, displacement is essentially the expression of a dangerous impulse in a comparatively harmless way. Dance may reduce anxiety, emotional tension, or surplus energy by performers acting out frustrations or expending energy. Dances have been viewed as an outlet for sexual and pugnacious feelings. Like other forms of intensive physical activity, it "often provides a healthy fatigue or distraction which may abate a temporary rage crisis and thus allow *more enduring personality patterns to regain ascendancy*" (Munroe 1955: 630). A specialist in African psychodynamics put it this way:

> The rhythm, vigorous movements, their coordination and synchronization, tend to induce some degree of catharsis... The essential psychological function of the dance, in fact, is the prevention of depression and accumulation of other psychic stresses (Lambo 1965: 41).

The Ngoni use the strenuous leaping and stamping *ingoma* dances to stress responsibility and self-restraint. Young men were continuously being told by older men "to dance strongly, *usina na-mandla.*" *Ingoma* were supposed to make a youth "obedient (*wamvera*) and self-restrained (*wadziletsa*)" (Read 1938: 10).

There seems to be evidence, however, that play war-like activities sometimes lead to aggression.[5] The competitive warrior dances of display and courtship were often the occasions of fighting. There was tension between the graded Samburu age-sets over relationships with girls, honor, and prestige. Spencer notes that the course of a dance is uncertain. It either becomes a safety-valve reducing tensions and inhibitions through a release of pent-up energies in a harmless way or it becomes a fray (1965: 125). Performance of the Ubakala Ibo *Nkwa Ese* sometimes led to violence at an elderly, esteemed man's second burial. Usually an important man was a heroic warrior, as were some of his sons and other kin who are the designated participants. The dance-play reenacted the heroic deeds of the deceased, and reminders of his heroism would invoke the wrath of individuals attending from other villages whose relatives had been his

---

4 The power of dance and the polity is further discussed in the sections on political behavior.

5 In his test of two rival theories, the driver discharge model (in which warlike sports discharged accumulated and aggressive tension), and the culture pattern model (in which aggression is learned and there is a strain toward cultural consistency), Sipes found that the latter model was confirmed. War and warlike sports tend to overlap and support each other's presence (1973).

victims (Hanna 1976b). Among the Zulu, Gluckman saw men lock in armed combat because one bumped into another or became agitated in the excitement of the dance (1959: 9). p'Bitek writes, "A man's manliness is seen in the arena/ No one touches another's testicles" (1966: 33).

There are distinctions between warrior dances which are playful and those which are instrumental in violence. Among the Ga, for example, there were two distinct patterns in which the Nungawa Asafo military body grouped itself. One formation was used for going to war, to honor a new leader, or engage in public works. The other formation was created for what is called "play – drilling, training, dancing, singing, and funerals" (Field 1940: 171). Such distinctions often become blurred. In Accra many quarrels and fights derive from ancient rivalries and battle behavior boasted about in the play dance competitions: Gbese people danced "the War of the Skewer," with a fish-hook which meant, "This is very shallow water" which in turn meant "These Jamestown people are valueless and negligible." The Jamestown people retorted with a dance involving a bell which referred to "You left your bell in the war, and your power is now our power."

Political behavior. As suggested earlier, warrior dances were believed to sustain particular leaders and the political structure within a religious perspective. Warrior dances were also politically important symbolic behavior. They were a form of praise and honor toward governmental leaders. Among competitive groups, warrior dance competition successes accrued to their chiefs. For example, the Tutsi chiefs, like the king, entrusted their pages to the care of highly paid dancing teachers who instructed these youths in new movements and rhythms in secret. The leaders derived honor from hearing their warriors were the best trained (Pages 1933: 170).

Dance was the vehicle to proclaim a new government among the Kikuyu. Calling for war dances to be held in every district was considered the effective way of promulgating a new constitution. Words of the drafted constitution were put into song phrases and embodied in sonic and danced media. On the appointed day, the constitution was announced, and the warriors danced brandishing their spears and shields to welcome the newly introduced government (Kenyatta 1962: 186, 197, 200).

Gluckman has called attention to "rituals of rebellion" in Africa, in which behavioral inversions occur. Women, usually the subordinate sex, may engage in socially approved inverted and transvestite behavior which is believed to be for the common good. Girls dress as men, assume their dominant authority roles, and dance warrior dances. When the Gogo men who hold ritual responsibility for controlling human and livestock fertility fail, disorder reigns, and the women assume the men's ritual roles and become the only active agents permitted to redress the wrong. They dress as men and dance violently with spears (Rigby 1966). Warriors may mock and attack their leader in dance. At an Anuak headman's installation, the village men arrive at his homestead carrying spears and rifles and stage a mock attack. Sometimes they shout words of rebellion. They mime an attack on the dance drums which the headman controls and which when seized, mark a successful rebellion. The headman's permission is necessary for the drums to be brought out for a dance which possesses principles of communal order (Lienhardt 1957).

In these instances, I do not think it is catharsis, the controlled release of tension in which the powerful allow a contest or reversal against themselves in order to consolidate more effectively and have an orderly state of affairs, that is at issue. It may be that the temporary public sharing in high status behavior and then its loss served to emphasize the holder's superiority, reinforce the maintenance of the system, and create order. Alternatively, the rituals of rebellion may be viewed as boundary maintaining mechanisms which impose restraints on the occupants of high status positions. Perhaps these representations of conflict through role reversal and behavioral inversions are posited as a latent system of potential alternatives if contingency so warrants: a role reversal in fact, revolution or anarchy. The inverse, conversion into the opposite, can be used to present a veiled threat and prophylactic by portraying what might happen if normative bounds were violated and power abused. Thus individuals and groups are put on their mettle to serve their positions well and receive support.

European Impact

The penetration of Europeans caused an increase in warfare due to the increase of slave trade and refugeeism. Initially, dances were part of war behavior among African groups and then between African groups and Europeans. European contact set in motion a series of social, economic, and political changes.

Religion, morality, and the "white man's burden." The introduction of Christianity in Africa has had emasculating consequences on many forms of dance. Europeans recognized that dance was intertwined with indigenous religion and morality. Even though African dances often had universal themes and origins comparable to those of European folk dances, their performance was seen as the manifestation of savage heathenism and antagonistic to the "true faith."

African dance was found too licentious for the "civilized" Victorian Europeans. Gorer, who observed many dances in West Africa in the 1920s, suggested that the European perception of African dances as orgies could be traced to the perfervid daydreams of sex-obsessed missionaries "who cannot see anything in negro manifestations except illicit copulation (1962: 175–176). Malinowski thought that the early missionary was frightened of dance without ever coming near it (1936: 500). Furthermore, some Christians came to Africa as missionaries in order to escape what they considered decadence – often including dance – in their own societies.

Europeans had often perceived Africa as a "dark continent" immersed in barbaric gloom and the African mentality child-like at best. To some, the people of Africa resembled the simian genus more than European humanity, and therefore had no culture. Indeed, the "white man's burden" was to spread western civilization to "primitive" peoples.

Political behavior: order and defiance. Order was a primary concern of the European administrations. With pacification, warfare was virtually eliminated and thus the need for war dances as physical and affective preparation for violent encounters was terminated. Consequently, members of the Sonjo group changed their patterns: they would leave the home area to work in the urban area or mines where they performed their warrior dances (Gray 1965).

The colonial situation stripped to its essentials is characterized by a state of dependency imposed on a subject majority by an imported European oligarchy. Thus warrior dances could be viewed as a symbol of independence, self assertion and pride reflected as a kind of potential disorder antithetical to the dependency complex. It was a metaphor of revolution from the European perspective. At the minimum, it was a metaphor of rebellion, ousting European occupants from office and installing Africans. The Bemba believed in their rulers' omnipotence and arbitrary action (Richards 1940: 111). Shaka maintained complete dominance over his nation (Walter 1969). In this light, dances which praised African leaders were unacceptable. Throughout Africa, warrior dances usually were sequelched. So were other dances as expressions of communal life that might loosen the colonial grip.

Containment or proscription of dance is widely documented (cf. Hanna 1975e). As early as 1901 in eastern Nigeria there were proclamations about regulating "native plays" defined as "a gathering of natives in any public street or market, or in any house, building, or in any compound adjoining a public street or market for the purpose of dancing or playing native music" (Nwabara 1965: 188–189). Licenses and permission from the District Commissioner were often necessary. Northern Rhodesia Township Regulations proscribed the organization or participation in any dance "calculated to hold up to ridicule or bring into contempt any person, religion or duly constituted authority" (cited in Mitchell 1956: 12). As pointed out earlier, dances were often the occasion of fights; there was fear that these might have broader repercussions. The 1929 "Women's War," in which 32 women were killed, 31 wounded, and the British government altered its colonial policy, is the most notorious case evolving from a dance-play performance (Gailey 1970).

The *Beni* dance performed by a number of ethnic groups in East Africa is an interesting example of dance perceived as defying the European presence. In 1919 an administrator commented, "The obtrusive simulation of a superior race by the specious elegants of the youth was not an effect that was lacking" (Ranger 1975: 37). The term *Beni* refers to a popular, versatile team dance (*ngoma*) with urban origins which had recognizable features of modernity (a brass band and European dress), organization (military drill and a hierarchy or officers with European titles) and competitiveness; it also had a continuing tradition of communal dance competitions, elaborate ranks, and displays of military skills. *Beni* was so disliked and feared by the missionaries that some turned to supporting traditional dances which they had earlier tried to abolish. Europeans were dismayed at the widely dispersed Tanganyika dance society network which was centrally controlled during its early development. Communication between groups occurred through the flow of migrant labor. The potential of the degree of coordination threatening European domination was not overlooked (*ibid.*: 44, 123). The sense of oneness developed among the members of the dancing associations and the European perception of a mockery directed against themselves, dance as breeding impatience with all authority, its concealing a revolutionary conspiracy and being a spearhead of Islam and coastal Arab culture led to the disconcerted Europeans prohibiting government clerks from joining dance groups and imposing high fees to obtain licenses for publicly held dances (*ibid.*: 88, 92, 124, 130).

The warrior tradition persisted in *Beni*. It provided physical and affective military training for the African *askaris* who fought in World War I. European participants in the East African campaign admiringly described an *askari's* dancing in the battle-line to rally his men. Reporters sometimes displayed "uneasy astonishment that the suffering and death in East Africa would be responded to by a dance" (*ibid.*: 55). African support personnel were able to identify with military power and prestige by performing *Beni*. In both war and peace times, it was a status marker displaying characteristics of the elite class and modernity. Although *Beni* was a mode of identifying with European military prowess, Ranger emphasizes that it was not a submission to European power but an accommodation to power in a traditional vein. *Beni* is explained as an indigenous dance form to display self-respect and self-confidence in communal values and express the pride of a group based on locality, ethnicity, moiety, and/or class against others in a tradition of dance competitions. These dance groups traditionally had elaborated ranks, displays of military skills, opportunities for innovations, achievement of high rank, and the exercise of patronage to achieve high status. This form, historically sensitive to changing power relations, selectively borrowed from the European military and settlers in a combination of mimicry and mockery.

Not all administrators agreed to the policy of wiping out traditional culture. Destruction of traditional institutions countered the romantic conservatism of those colonial service members who believed Europeans and Africans were destined to be culturally separate and that most worthwhile resources of the Africans inhered in traditional institutions (Heisler 1974: 7). In the 1920s local traditions in Tanganyika seen as consistent with morality were encouraged by the missionaries, although earlier they wanted to save Africans from their traditional culture (Ranger 1975: 126–127).

Secular factors. Europeans also had a convenience or "efficiency" reason for banning African dances. The "noise" of these often disturbed the sleep or work of Europeans or distracted the attention of Africans who might be enticed away from their jobs to join the dances. Furthermore, the Africans might spend their resources on the related feasts and clothes and consequently be unable to pay their taxes (*ibid.*: 88, 110).

The new technology of education and mechanization tended to somewhat diminish the importance of actual physical power. Gunfire, hell fire, and book power were destructive or suppressive of the warrior tradition of pre-European intervention. For example, Christian supernatural power meshed with other western resources was seen to surpass the indigenous supernatural power of Bemba leaders (Richards 1940: 114) and the complex in which it was meshed.

Nationalism. In the nationalist period, educated Africans sponsored the growth of "traditional" consciousness in Africa. They formed ethnic groups and unions as a mechanism for mobilizing support in competition for scarce resources which became the goals of modernization – land, jobs, trade, education. Warrior dances were resurrected in nostalgia for the lost grandeur of kingdoms or a pre-European dominated way of life. They symbolically represented aspirations rather than hard and fast rules of conduct or direction of aim. In South Africa, Tracy claimed the performance of war dances was merely for the love of movement (1952: 2). It seems difficult to overlook the prideful recapitulation of history as a source of reference and set of models for current aspiration, however much stifled. The formerly dominant Tutsi of Ruanda continue to perform their *intore* nobles' dance in exile. Some groups espouse the warrior tradition in order to identify with contemporary prestigious groups which pride themselves in it. Paul Makgoba, for example, a Sotho professional dancer, singer, and actor from Johannesburg, grew up with Zulu children and observed their tribal dancing in the black townships on Sundays. He, as many others, was most impressed with Zulu dance – its "virile, manly grace" and developed Zulu warrior dance teams (personal communication). The Ndau of Rhodesia have adopted the war dance of the Nguni who dominated them from 1830 to 1900 (Moyana 1976).

Traore (1968) points out that theater arts simultaneously permit recreation and transcendence – incarnation of and escape from reality. Some dances, however, such as the *Beni*, competitive in terms of locality, moiety, or class, were viewed as divisive in the 1930s among the proto-nationalists in Tanganyika. They felt this kind of dance behavior made Africans easy prey to colonialism and tried to discourage it (Ranger 1975: 96).

Post-Colonial Independence Era

Reemergence of the warrior dance. With political independence, African leaders seek sociocultural independence and integrity by mediating modern and traditional influences, choosing selectively from an ancestral heritage, often regenerating ennobled patterns. The revival or invention, as may be the case in some instances, of warrior dances is an aspect of negritude or authenticity. Both concepts lead toward an increased consciousness of indigenous cultural values as a counter to the colonial imposition of its own values and the denigration of indigenous ones (Adelman 1975). Negritude and authenticity are most valuable to those who had experience of some type with cultural disruption and separation, not just the political, economic, and religious leaders in the urban areas, but individuals in the rural areas as well. These may be a reaction, vengeance, or more likely, a positive affirmation of self instilling pride, obtaining inspiration from the past rather than returning blindly to it (e.g., in Zaïre there is an official rejection of fetishism and tribalism). Leaders and parties may romanticize the past as a strategy of coping with change (cf. Toffler).

Political behavior. Warrior dance continues as an aspect of political behavior as it was in the pre-European contact era. While traditional offices tend to be eclipsed, the traditional symbols of power are often used by new political leaders (Lloyd 1966: 35). Authority is legitimated in the eyes of traditional masses by employing symbolic forms of independence and power such as the warrior dance. Adelabu's way to power was "to dance in the streets to the strains of Mabolaje songs that celebrated his name" (Sklar 1963: 299). Dances celebrate and pay homage to political leaders in Uganda (to Obote and now to Amin) on their visits around the country. Moreover, the ability of a local individual to mobilize popular energies around the dance is often viewed as evidence of the power he or she holds.

Kenyatta, Kenya's first president and a Kikuyu, perpetuated his ethnic group's tradition of calling for war dances in every district to promulgate a new constitution. He broadened the pattern by calling for warrior dances to be performed throughout the country, and ethnic groups from all parts of Kenya were brought into Nairobi to dance at the lowering of the Union Jack. Warrior dances are performed in one or another version at independence anniversaries throughout the continent.

Status markers and sexual display. Besides the warrior dance being a status marker of national independence, it continues to recognize individual and group achievement. I witnessed the traditional Ibo war dance described by Meek and Green performed celebrating a feat now considered equivalent to manslaying – obtaining a law degree. With "heads" placed on a tray and balanced on his head, machete in his teeth, shoulders quivering, a dancer celebrated the return of a kinsman who had just returned from his legal training in the United Kingdom. Virtually every dance team or national company has its warrior dances, memories of the positive aspects of historical times, deeds immortalized in repetitive performances. They continue to permit the display of self assertion and sexuality.

Dance has become a symbol of ethnic identity in a heterogeneous nation. It is a we/they boundary marker in independence celebrations, school competitions, national dance companies, the military, and urban areas (Meillasoux 1968, Mitchell 1956, Hanna 1973).

Physical preparation and affective readying.   Even with European pacification and national laws since independence, dance and war are still related in some areas which had a warrior tradition. The dance continues to provide physical and affective preparation for violence for a number of pastoralist groups. Samburu raids are still expected; girls bait the youths at the dance and egg them to lawlessness as a counter to the social order. They too feel suppressed and controlled by the elders in the gerontocratic system and partake in vicarious rebellion (Spencer 1965: 122, 125).

Conclusion

In order to understand the relation of dance to the warrior tradition in modern Africa, we have taken a diachronic perspective. The significance of dance appears more fully through an examination of some of its various manifestations interlaced with other sociocultural phenomena in different historical eras. (These are not fixed categories, for behavior often extends beyond the boundaries of historical events.) During the pre-European independence era there was a pervasive but not universal dovetailing of valor and virility with prestige in African societies. These qualities permeated the warrior dances which were status markers for groups and individuals, vehicles for sexual display, physical preparation for war, affective readying for violent encounters (incitement, communion, we/they distancing), religious practice, displacement, and political behavior.

Some of the contingencies which contributed to the transformation of traditional patterns and the creation of new ones in the European colonial era and independence period were explored. The European impact upon warrior dances was constraining. Christians found it antagonistic to the "true faith" and immoral. Missionaries and administrators found these dances a challenge to their dominance and also an inconvenience. Supportive of dance they were not. Africans themselves, saw the alternative to the physicality of the warrior tradition, and its dance, in Western education and technology, and they defected. Warrior dances rise phoenix-like with nationalism and independence when their symbolic value becomes apparent. There are transformations in style and structure or continuities in different contexts such as the battle of the barrister training and its celebration or illegal raids for female approbation. Warrior dance as a vehicle of display of strength and self affirmation, as a status marker, and as political and symbolic behavior are pervasive structures.

I tried to suggest the properties of dance underlying the product and process of the dance-warrior tradition interaction. In brief, my argument is that the power of dance lies in its multimedia thought, emotion, motor, and aesthetic capability to create moods and a sense of situation for performer and spectator alike. The manipulation of the body through movement and gesture in purposeful, intentionally rhythmical, attention riveting discrete cultural patterns presents a dramatic, powerful statement which can influence predispositions, attitudes, beliefs, and actions.

Acknowledgements

Thanks are due Alexander Alland, Jr. and William John Hanna for their helpful comments on an earlier draft of this paper. I appreciate the comparative source material suggested by Jane Bennett Ross, Anthony Shay, David Lindner, and Margaret Drewal.

REFERENCES

ADELMAN, Kenneth Lee
    1975   "The recourse to authenticity and Négritude in Zaïre." *Journal of Modern African Studies* 13 (1): 134–139.
ARNHEIM, Rudolf
    1954   *Art and visual perception: a psychology of the creative eye.* Berkeley: University of California.
BAXTER, P. T. W.
    1965   "Repetition in certain Boran ceremonies." *In* M. Fortes and G. Dieterlen, eds., *African Systems of Thought.* London: Oxford University, pp. 64–78.
P'BITEK, Okot
    1966   *Song of Lawino.* Nairobi: East African Publishing House.
    1971   *Religion of the Central Luo.* Kampala: East African Literature Bureau.
BOAS, Franz
    1955   *Primitive art.* New York: Dover (1927).
BRADBURY, R. E.
    1957   "The Benin Kingdom and the Edo-speaking peoples of south-western Nigeria." *In* Daryll Forde, ed., *Ethnographic Survey of Africa, Western Africa,* Part 13. London: International African Institute, pp. 18–171.
BRELSFORD, W. V.
    1959   *African dances of Northern Rhodesia* (The Occasional Papers, No. 2). Lusaka: Government Printer for the Rhodes-Livingstone Museum.
DOUGLAS, Mary
    1963   *The Lele of the Kasai.* London: International African Institute.
FIELD, M. J.
    1940   *Social organization of the Ga people.* Accra: Government Printing Dept.
FISHER, Seymour
    1973   *Body consciousness: you are what you feel.* Prentice-Hall: Englewood-Cliffs.
FORDE, Daryll
    1964   *Yakö studies.* London: Oxford University.
FRAZER, Sir James George
    1929   *The golden bough: a study in magic and religion,* I. New York: The Book League of America.
GAILEY, Harry A.
    1970   *The road to Aba: A study of British administrative policy in Eastern Nigeria.* New York: New York University Press.
GARDNER, Howard
    1973   *The arts and human development: a psychological study of the artistic process.* New York: John Wiley.
GLUCKMAN, Max
    1959   *Custom and conflict in Africa.* Glencoe: Free Press.
    1960   "The rise of a Zulu empire." *Scientific American* 20 (4): 157–168.
GORER, Geoffrey
    1962   *Africa dances.* New York: W. W. Norton (1935).

GRAY, Robert F.
1965   "Some parallels in Sonjo and Christian mythology." *In* M. Fortes and G. Dieterlen. eds., *African Systems of Thought*. London: Oxford University Press, pp. 49–63.
GREEN, M. M.
1964   *Igbo village affairs* (2nd ed.). London: Cass.
GULLIVER, Pamela and P. H, Gulliver
1953   *The central Nilo-Hamites*. London: International African Institute.
HANNA, Judith Lynne
1965   *Africa's new traditional dance*. Ethnomusicology 9: 13–21.
1973   "The highlife: a West African urban dance." *In* Patricia A. Rowe and Ernestine Stodelle, eds., *Dance Research Monograph One*. New York: Committee on Research in Dance, pp. 138–152.
1974a   "African dance: the continuity of change." *Yearbook of the International Folk Music Council*. Vol. 5: 164–174.
1974b   *Kinetic symbolism and the supernatural in Africa*. Unpublished paper.
1975a   "The anthropology of the body (Association of Social Anthropologists' Conference)." *Dance Research Journal* 7 (2): 39–43.
1975b   "The anthropology of dance: reflections on the CORD Conference." *Current Anthropology* 16 (3): 445–446.
1975c   "Dances of Anáhuac—for god or man? An alternate way of thinking about prehistory." *Dance Research Journal* 7 (1): 13–27.
1975d   *Toward symbolic analysis in dance: Searching for meaning with a semantic grid*. Paper presented at York University Dance Department Seminar in Research and Writing.
1975e   *The urban ecosystem of dance*. Paper presented at the Conference of the Committee on Research in Dance and Society for Ethnomusicology, 1974. Summary of revision in Comparative Urban Studies 3 (2): 40.
1976a   *The anthropology of dance: a selected bibliography*. School of Arts and Humanities, The University of Texas at Dallas, Richardson, Texas.
1976b   *The anthropology of dance ritual: Nigeria's Ubakala nkwa di iche iche*. Unpublished Ph. D. dissertation, Columbia University. Ann ARBOR, University Microfilms.
1976c   *Danced rites as political conceptualization and behavior*. Paper presented at the Third Annual Conference on Social Theory and the Arts, SUNY Albany.
1976d   *Movements toward a dance anthropology*. Unpublished paper.
1977a   "To dance is human: some psychobiological bases of an 'expressive' form." *In* John Blacking. ed., *The Anthropology of the Body*. New York: Academic Press (forthcoming).
1977b   "Toward a cross-cultural conceptualization of dance and some correlate considerations." *In* John Blacking, ed., *The Performing Arts: Music Dance Theater (World Anthropology)*. The Hague: Mouton (forthcoming).
HATCH, Frank White
1973   *A behavioral cybernetic interpretation of dance and dance culture*. Ph. D. dissertation. Ann Arbor: University Microfilms.
HEISSLER, Helmuth
1974   *Urbanisation and the government of migration: the interrelation of urban and rural life in Zambia*. New York: St. Martin's.
HOCKETT, Charles F. and Robert ASCHER
1964   "The human revolution." *Current Anthropology* 5: 135–168.
HOWELL, P. P.
1941   "The Shilluk settlement." *Sudan Notes and Records* 24: 47–66.
KENYATTA, Jomo
1962   *Facing Mt. Kenya*. New York: Vintage.
KUPER, Hilda
1968   "Celebration of growth and kingship: *Incwala* in Swaziland." *African Arts* 1 (3): 57–59, 90.
1969   *An African aristocracy*. London: Oxford University Press (1947).

KURATH, Gertrude and Sameul MARTÍ
    1964   *Dances of Anáhuac: the choreography and music of precortesian dances.* Chicago: Aldine.
LAMBO, T. Adeoye
    1965   "The place of the arts in the emotional life of the Africa." *AMSAC Newsletter* 7 (4): 1–6.
LANGER, Suzanne
    1953   *Feeling and form: a theory of art developed from philosophy in a new key.* New York: Charles Schribner's.
LIENHARDT, Godfrey
    1957   "Anuak village headmen." *Africa* 27 (4): 341–355.
LLOYD, P. C.
    1966   "Introduction." *In* P. C. Lloyd, ed., *The New Elites of Tropical Africa.* London: Oxford University, pp. 1–64.
LONG, Norman
    1968   *Social change and the individual: a study of the social and religious response to innovation in a Zambian rural community.* Manchester: University Press.
LUDWIG, Arnold M.
    1969   "Altered states of consciousness." *In* Charles T. Tart, ed., *Altered states of consciousness.* New York: John Wiley, pp. 9–22.
MAHLOBO, G. W. K. and E. J. KRIGE
    1934   "Transition from childhood to adulthood amongst the Zulus." *Bantu Studies* 8: 156–191.
MALINOWSKI, B.
    1936   "Native education and culture contact." *International Review of Missions* 25: 480–515.
MAQUET, Jacques
    1961   *The premise of inequality in Ruanda.* London: International African Institute.
MAZRUI, Ali A.
    1973   *Phallic symbols in politics and war: an African perspective.* Paper read at an Interdisciplinary Colloquin on "African Systems of Form," African Studies Center, University of California at Los Angeles.
    1975   "The resurrection of the warrior tradition in African political culture." *Journal of Modern African Studies* 13 (1): 67–84.
MEEK, C. K.
    1931   *Tribal studies in Northern Nigeria.* London: Kegan Paul, Trench, Trubner.
    1937   *Law and authority in a Nigerian tribe.* London: Oxford University.
MEILLASSOUX, Claude
    1968   *Urbanization of an African community: voluntary associations in Bamako.* Seattle: University of Washington.
MITCHELL, J. Clyde
    1956   *The Kalela dance* (Paper No. 27). Manchester: University Press for the Rhodes-Livingston Institute.
MOYANA, Tafirenyika
    1976   "Muchongoyo: a Shangani dance." *African Arts* 9 (2): 40–42.
MUNROE, Ruth L.
    1955   *Schools of psychoanalytic thought: an exposition, critique, and attempt at integration.* New York: Holt, Rinehart and Winston.
NADEL, S. F.
    1947   *The Nuba: an anthropological study of the hill tribes in Kordofan.* London: Oxford University.
New York Times
    1976   *Sweating on palms and soles.* March 7, p. 7.
NKETIA, J. H. Kwabena
    1957   "Possession dances in African societies." *Journal of the International Folk Music Council* 9: 4–9.
NZEKWU, Onuora
    1963   "The Edda." *Nigeria Magazine* No. 76: 16–28.

NWABARA, Samuel Nwanko
    1965   *Ibo land: a study in British penetration and the problem of administration, 1860–1930.*
            Ph. D. dissertation, Northwestern University. Ann Arbor, University Microfilm
OBERG, K.
    1940   "The Kingdom of Ankole in Uganda." *In* M. Fortes and E. E. Evans-Pritchard,
            eds., *African Political Systems.* London: Oxford University Press, pp. 121–164.
PAGÈS, G.
    1933   *Un royaume Hamite au centre de l'Afrique: au Ruanda sur les bords du lac Kivu.* Bruxelles:
            Librairie Folk Lils (HRAF trans., Bernard Scholl).
RANGER, T. O.
    1975   *Dance and society in Eastern Africa 1890–1970.* Berkeley: University of California.
RAUM, Otto
    1940   *Chaga childhood.* London: Oxford University.
READ, Margaret
    1938   "The moral code of the Ngoni and their former military state." *Africa* 11: 1–24.
RICHARDS, Audrey I.
    1940   "The political system of the Bemba tribe—Northeastern Rhodesia." *In* M. Fortes
            and E. E. Evans-Pritchard, eds., *African Political Systems.* London: International
            African Institute, pp. 83–120.
RIGBY, Peter
    1966   "Dual symbolic classification among the Gogo of central Tanzania." *Africa* 36 (1):
            1–17.
SCHECHNER, Richard
    1973   "Drama, script, theatre, and performance." *The Drama Review* 17: 5–36.
SIPES, Richard G.
    1973   "War, sports and aggression: an empirical test of two rival theories." *American
            Anthropologist* 75 (1): 64–86.
SKLAR, Richard L.
    1963   *Nigerian political parties.* New Jersey: Princeton University.
SPENCER, Paul
    1965   *The Samburu: a study of gerontocracy in a nomadic tribe.* Berkeley: University of California.
TOFFLER, Alvin
    1970   *Future shock.* New York: Bantam.
TRACY, Hugh T.
    1952   *African dances of the Witwatersrand gold mines.* Johannesburg: African Music Society.
TRAORE, Bakary
    1968   "Meaning and function of the traditional Negro-African theatre." *In Colloquium:
            Function and Significance of African Negro Art in the Life of the People and for the People*
            (March 30–April 8, 1966), 1st World Festival of Negro Arts, Dakar. Paris: Présence
            Africaine, pp. 481–493.
TURNER, Victor W.
    1957   *Schism and continuity in an African society: a study of Ndembu village life.* Manchester:
            University Press.
    1967   *The forest of symbols: aspects of Ndembu ritual.* Ithaca: Cornell University Press.
UCHENDU, Victor D.
    1965   *The Igbo of southeast Nigeria.* New York: Holt, Rinehart and Winston.
UZOIGWE, G. N.
    1975   "Pre-colonial military studies in Africa." *Journal of Modern African Studies* 13 (3):
            469–481.
VAN GENNEP, Arnold
    1960   *Rites of passage.* Chicago: University Press.
WALLACE, Anthony F. C.
    1968   "Psychological preparations for war." *In* Morton Fried, Marvin Harris, and
            Robert Murphy, eds., *War: the anthropology of armed conflict and aggression.* New York:
            Natural History Press, pp. 173–182.

WALTER, Eugene Victor
    1969   *Terror and resistance: a study of political violence*. New York: Oxford University Press.
WELCH, Claude, Jr.
    1975   "Continuity and discontinuity in African military organization." *Journal of Modern African Studies* 13 (2): 229–248.
WEPNER, Franklyn
    1973   "The theory and practice of orientation therapy." *The Drama Review* 17: 81–101.
ZANDER, Alvin
    1974   "People often work harder for group than for selves." *Institute for Social Research Newsletter* 2 (3), 7.

Manhood, Warriorhood and Sex in Eastern Africa

Perspectives from the 19th and 20th Centuries

DENT OCAYA-LAKIDI

Makerere University, Kampala, Uganda

THE TERM "tradition" as used here has two related meanings. In its narrower sense it refers to warrior *practices* and *values* handed down from generation to generation in any particular society. In this sense it is descriptive and, to a large extent, realistic. It concerns itself with how a particular society can be expected to recruit and train its warriors, how the warriors can be expected to behave, especially in wars; and how they might be organised and armed. In other words we are here concerned mainly with *military* tradition.

More broadly, however, the term refers to the consequences and significance of military values and practices for society as a whole. The main concern here is with relationships and meanings. For example, how does war and warriorhood relate to and affect the economic, political, social, aesthetic, and psychological life of a society? What is the significance of the war dance or a war song? What is the link between manliness or masculinity and warrior values? Do these values have any implication for the status of women in the societies concerned? The problem becomes even more challenging when we try to explain contemporary African behaviour by reference to indigenous norms. For example, how much of the behaviour of modern soldiers and liberation fighters in Africa to-day is affected by traditional concepts of the warrior? Were the "Mau Mau" revolt in Kenya in the 1950's, *the Maji Maji War* in Tanzania at the turn of the century, or the Pare protest against colonial authority in the 1940's in the same country a resurgence of the warrior tradition? How has modernisation in the technology of war affected indigenous warrior values?

It is quite clear that such questions do not lead themselves to easy matter-of-fact answers. We have to probe, analyse, and often guess at answers. The task is a challenging one given the state of historical studies of war, warriorhood and the warrior especially in tradition Africa, to date. Only recently, the historian Bathwell Ogot (1972: 1) called this a "little-studied aspect of African history." More recently still, an eminent scholar with a particular interest in the military in Africa has complained that "Comparative study of military organisation in Africa remains surprisingly limited in scope. With the exception of the Yoruba and the Zulu, and of the societies set forth in books edited by Crowder and Ogot, the impact and modalities of conflict have rarely been subjected to systematic, comparative analysis cutting across several groups" (Welch, 1973: 3). These difficulties should be born in mind by the reader of this paper.

But whether we are dealing with tradition in the first or the second sense, a decidedly sociological approach and interdisplinary method of analysis is suggested, particularly for Africa. By a sociological approach we mean studying the warrior and war in terms of the dynamics of society as a whole paying particular attention to the social, political and economic processes and institutions vital for the particular society concerned. This is in contrast to an approach which would concentrate on the warriors as constituting an army, a distinct institution within society, to be studied in terms of military technology organization, strategy and logistics.

A few societies in pre-colonial and colonial Africa did evolve interesting military organisation, strategy and tactics. G. C. K. Gwassa (1972) has suggested that during the Maji Maji war, for example, three-pronged attacks were prevalent among the indigenous warriors and that these could be explained in "traditional" terms. "It may well be that among these people," he writes, "three is a ritual number: that is, in order for payer of ritual to be effective, the doer must repeat each act three times. Thus the number three, or anything representing it, becomes a symbol of success for the doer and for others of his faith..." (p. 141).

Though explainable, at least partially, in religious terms, the strategy made a great deal of military sense, as the Germans found out to their cost. Gwassa gives us this interesting illustrative example:

> One morning at Samanga Ndumbo, Maji Maji fighters came in and uprooted cotton. Of hearing of this action, *Kinoo* or Steinhagen, together with the *akida* and some askaris, marched to and attacked the Africans. After a short fight the Africans retreated into the interior. Later in the afternoon they came back and took up three positions—the Kinjumbi road, Kilwa road and Mohoro road *lita pos*. As the Germans were expecting an attack from Kinjumbi, this *litapo* charged first and Steinhagen hit back very ruthlessly. But that *litapo* retreated, pursued by most of the Germans; simultaneously the Mohoro road *litapo* moved into the attack. A remnant of askaris and supporters had to fight the Mohoro *litapo* which in turn retreated and was hotly persued by the Germans. This left Samanga Ndumbo undefended, so the Kilwa *litapo* moved in and burnt the settlement down... (Ibid.: 141).

The same interesting pattern is seen in the guerilla methods of warfare used in areas where they were suitable during the same war. With the highly sophisticated *kalinguli* method, after the enemy had been located, an ambush was laid, arranged in a 'V' formation with the apex away from the enemy: "The *Kalinguli* or spy then went out, and when he was a reasonable distance from the enemy, he fired at them and ran back as quickly as possible towards the apex of the 'V'. On seeing the *Kalinguli* the Germans nearly always pursued him mistaking him for a lone attacker. In this way the askaris gradually became engulfed in the 'V' formation, and as they reached the apex they were attacked by fighters at that end along the sides of the 'V'. As fighting developed, those along the 'V' closed in behind the askaris... and attacked from behind. It was in this manner that Sergeant Josef Schober was killed at Mbombwe on 2 October 1905 by one Abdallah Tosa..." (Ibid.: 143).

Shaka Zulu's famous military formation in terms of a central, compact, large group or "head" and "chest, with two smaller flanks, or "horns", deployed into encircling arms (Ritter, 1969: 42), is too well-known to need a fuller description here, as also his anticipation of the commando technique. The same methods were later to be copied and used by the Swazi. Further north the Masai are known to have evolved a similar kind of strategy, though less sophisticated.

Military technology remained everywhere, till the coming of the gun, simple and unsophisticated. Emen Shaka's deadly invention, the stabbing *assegai*, relied more on the strategy and toughness of the Zulu warrior than on any sophisticated feature for its success. In fact it was one of the simplest of weapons. In the rest of Eastern Africa the spear was the traditional weapon. As for military organisation, some societies such as the Zulu under Shaka and the Nyoro under Kabalega did have standing armies. Others like the Ganda had a more feudal military arrangement; the Kikuyu and the like tribes organised militarily through the age-set organisations. Finally in the non-centralised societies in which age-set organisations were not very highly developed, there were no military organisation to speak of. There was instead something akin to a peoples' militia.

These matters, though interesting and worthy of study, however, do not take us to the heart of things as far as the warrior tradition in the broadest sense of the term, goes. For this we must examine the warrior within the context of society as a whole; except/for the brief colonial interlude. African warriors have always been and continue to be inseparable members of their societies. With very few exceptions, Shaka's Zulu being the most outstanding, the warrior in pre-colonial Eastern African was not a *specialist* apart from the society in which he lived (not counting the very young, the very old and the women) either in the weapon he used, the way he lived, or the training he received as a warrior. He was not, in the words of that eminent nineteenth century Prussian military philosopher Karl von Clausewitz, "levied, clothed, armed, trained, he did not sleep, eat, drink, and march merely to fight at the right place and the right time." As we shall see later, in most of these societies warriorhood was in *addition* to being a full man, in every aspect of the term, in society.

In the post-colonial era the warrior or soldier has indeed become part of a specialised institution apart from society. He is now indeed "levied, clothed, armed, trained, he sleeps, eats, drinks, and marches..." At the same time his mission and functions are now almost wholly internal to his own society. The mere opportunity to fight a war is often lacking and, in any case, in the underdeveloped world where political instability is a constant reality, the military more often has to be assigned the task of maintaining internal order than the task of repelling or deterring foreign invaders (Grundy, 1968: 5). This means that the soldiers are always physically present within society instead of being away at the remote borders of the country. But even more important, the question of inter-ethnic cleavages and inter-ethnic violence becomes significant, given that the armies of independent African countries are both multi-ethnic and not very well integrated internally. It thus becomes imperative to ask how warrior and military values relate to ethnicity and sub-national identities. In other words we are brought back to consider the military in the context of society as a whole. Grundy is thus quite right when he argues that:

> It would be fallacious to view the military and politics separately. Particularly in the developing countries the militaries are part and parcel of contemporary politics and cannot be divorced from it in theory, reality, or analysis.... (Ibid.: 1.)

Warrior Integration Into Society and Warrior Tradition in Pre-Colonial Days

The most important single determinant of the warrior activities and behaviour and, therefore, of their collective image, and also the factor that is most likely to explain these, is the extent to which the warriors are integrated into society. On the whole, the more integrated the warriors or soldiers are into society, the more positive their collective activities and image – by any reckoning.

Political Integration

In looking at the warrior or the soldier within his own society, the concept of integration has, first of all, a political implication. John D. Chick and Ali A. Mazrui have identified the two aspects of integration in this regard as relating to *national integration* on the one hand, and to the *consolidation of political authority* on the other:

> Soldiers become nationally integrated when they became capable of recognising bonds of shared nationality and respect the rights of fellow citizens. Soldiers become absorbed into the system of authority when they learn to measure physical force according to legitimate need, when they recognise their place in the pattern of roles and functions within the social system, and learn to respect socially sanctioned frontiers of authority (1970: 12).

The warriors of pre-colonial Eastern Africa were highly integrated into their societies on both counts. This achievement was made possible by three related factors. First of all by a mode of socialisation which successfully combined instruction in skills, including military skills, with inculcation in fundamental social values (Ocaya-Lakidi, 1974; Ocaya-Lakidi and Mazrui, 1973). Among the category of values given prominence in socialisation were those relating to how people ought to live together in society (political values). Secondly, the philosophy and structure of political power synchronised well with these values and skills so that the one strengthened the other. Finally, there was a super-natural basis to society and, therefore, to the values so inculcated. Without this neither social values nor the structure and philosophy of power would have proved adequate in maintaining an integrated society, even when operating together under the best of conditions. We shall presently return to a consideration of training in military skill and the place of the super-natural in socialisation generally. For the moment let us take a brief look at the manner in which socialisation in political values synchronised with the structure of power.

Among what are commonly called the Plains and Highland Nilotes, for example, the Teso, Jie, Karamojong, Turkana, Masai, Sebei and Pokot of eastern Uganda and western Kenya, inculcation in political values synchronised with a political structure based on the age principle institutionalised into age-set organisations. Here we discuss the system as it operated among the Bantu-speaking Kikuyu of Kenya.

The whole Kikuyu society, Jomo Kenyatta (1938: 106) has written,

> is graded by age and the prestige which accompanies a status in age grouping and this is done in such a way that even small children know it... It determines the different salutations used, the manners people may adopt in homestead or garden, it rules habits of dress or demeanour in the community and it explains the rights of different people in judging cases, in exercising authority in the clan or family, in ceremonial or religious pre-ceedings. *It is in relation to this social ladder that the child's education must be studied if it is to be understood...*"
> (Emphasis added)

From the political power-structure perspective the gist of the matter is that any Kikuyu, including the warrior, was indeed totally absorbed into a highly structured system of authority which his socialisation made sure he recognised and abided by. His ascendency to political power was inseparably tied up with those of his generation set and a generation set had to wait its turn to govern, for "At any one time, political authority was regarded as being vested in the elders of one generation, and a generation of elders handed over to its successor in intervals of somewhere about thirty years" (Goldthorpe, 1958: 62). The young Kikuyu went through many stages in his upward mobility till *ituika*, the handing over ceremony, "one of the highlights of the traditional system ("Goldthorpe, Ibid.: 62) at which time, power changed hands between generations.

The point of entry at the bottom of the social ladder was marked by initiation into manhood. This conferred upon the young man full rights of citizenship, including the right to be a warrior. But as a warrior his freedom to participate in politics, or more precisely to exercise political power, was circumscribed by two institutions: the one, social and all embracing, his age-set, and the other, political, the warrior council. Kenyatta has described the set, up as follows:

> From the governmental point of view the whole of the warrior class, composed of several age-groups, was divided into two sections, from which the two councils of senior and junior warrior were formed. Each group had its village, district and national leaders... who acted as spokesmen in all matters concerning the welfare of the group and the tribe.

These leaders were chosen by their particular groups at the general assembly. They were men who had proved by their own actions, their capability of leadership; they had shown bravery in wars, impartiality in justice, self-sacrifice, and above all, discipline in the group. A man with these qualities was able to attain a high position and esteem in the community, especially when he had retired from the activities of the warriors. Judges and responsible elders... were chosen from such men... (Ibid.: 200).

It is significant to note here that successful warriorhood was a credential for political leadership; but the exercise of political power itself often came after warriorhood. The point in time at which one finally left warrior activities was determined by age, or more precisely, by the "Cage" of one's age-set. The path passed through various stages of elderhood, beginning with the first stage. This could be combined with warriorhood. Such men, however, were not yet elders or rulers in any sense. They were learners of the elder's procedures and were debarred from the privileges of the elders such as the eating of kidneys, spleen, or loin of animals.

Entry into the proper elders grade, constituting the Council of Peace and therefore the governing council, was a great achievement after so much waiting and preparation. At long last the individual had achieved the pinnacle of power. But, once again, such power was not individually enjoyed, but was collectively exercised; the initiation ceremony for entry into the *Kiama* (elders' Council) itself made this clear by insisting on a pledge by the initiate "to keep the secret of the kiama, and never to reveal it to anyone who is not ritually initiated into the age-grade... It is only when they have taken this solemn oath that the secret matters and procedures, including the etiquette of the Peace Council, are revealed to them..." (Kenyatta, *Ibid.:* 202). Very few ever became members of the highest council concerned with religious ceremonies.

It is clear from the account that Kikuyu traditional society achieved a high level of political integration. With respect to the consolidation of political authority, Goldthorpe has summarised the position very well as follows:

The system was in one sense thoroughly democratic; to be more precise, it was strongly egalitarian, for everyone enjoyed an equal opportunity to rise to positions of social standing and political power. It was also extremely conservative; it ensured that only old men ruled, and, since an individual was judged on a whole life's history of conformity to custom, everyone had a vested interest in the system and stood to lose by any changes. For example, when a man's application was being considered for admission to a senior grade of elders, his whole life and career would be reviewed. Did he shrink from the circumcision knife? As a warrior did he fight bravely? Has he learned the customary law, and are his judgements sound? It is obvious that in such a society a man had every incentive to conform to what was expected of him according to traditional ideas (Ibid: 63–64).

From the point of view of national integration, socialisation emphasised the collective, even as it recognised individual ability. Leaders, we have already seen, were chosen from men of proven leadership ability, men who had shown bravery in wars, impartiality in justice, and self-sacrifice, but above all those *disciplined in the group*. The council system also worked towards this end. In a large measure, therefore, Kikuyus in precolonial time could not help but recognise the bonds amongst themselves of shared nationality and respect for the rights of fellow citizens.

In pre-colonial Buganda and in Zululand under Shaka the political integration of the warrior into society was achieved in a way much different from that of traditional Kikuyu. In Buganda three mutually supportive principles formed the basis of this integration. They were: despotic kingship, equality of opportunity for upward mobility, and Ganda sense of nationalism.

The significance of kingship for integration is clearly shown in the fact that Buganda itself became a single powerful country with the increase in royal power under Katerega, Mutebi and Mawanda (who died about 1734). Under these three Kings Buganda was increasingly ruled directly by the king through personally appointed chiefs; the powers of the hereditary chieftains (i.e. clan heads) were reduced, and the clan heads themselves were increasingly replaced; the clans were weakened; so was the religious class. By the nineteenth century despotic kingship had been firmly established in Buganda (Kiwanuka 1971 (a): Chapter 5, 1971 (b)).

The successful establishment of despotism had two direct consequences for national integration and these, in turn, had consequences for the growth of Kiganda national consciousness. *Horizontally* it encouraged the free settlement and the free mixing of the population regardless of clan identity. Being the king's subject, sure of protection by the strong king anywhere in the kingdom, no one need longer confine himself to a clan area among Clansmen. *Vertically* despotic kingship generated and maintained equal opportunity for upward (as well as for downward) mobility. The royal family alone was regarded as superior to and separate from other classes by virtue of their birth. With this single exception, any member of a clan could rise to the highest position in the land, if he succeeded in making himself conversant with state affairs, was brave in warfare and shrewd in council (Roscue, 1911: 246). It was the despot who made this possible and so prevented class formation. (Fallers, 1959) has postulated the phenomenon as follows:

> The relationship which... obtains among these elements (i.e. despotism, status culture, and social mobility) is as follows: despotism is related to social mobility in that one of the aspects of the despots arbitrary authority is his ability to grant and withdraw favoured positions without regard to the person's status at the time. Furthermore, the more the despot exercises his authority in this way, the less likely it is that marked status cultures will persist.

And because the system did not develop rigid social class, the individual felt he had a fair chance to rise to an important position. This is why Buganda developed into a society, in the words of C. C. Wrigley (1964).

> in which there was strongly marked differentiation of wealth and status but at the same time something like equality of opportunity. Ambition was general and unlimited, for no position in the state, except the supreme power was in principle out of reach of the humblest youth. Inequality seemed natural to the Baganda; it aroused envy but not resentment; and this attitude reflected not (as in most neighbouring Kingdoms) passive

acceptance of immutable inferior status, but the knowledge that advancement was open to any clever and energetic man.

The individual did use all means at his disposal to gain his ends, including intrigue, alliancies, and *kuloopa* (malicious tale bearing). But far from these things leading to the disintegration of society, they actually worked to strengthen solidarity and national integration. As Apter (1967: 17) has pointed out:

> Precisely because these factions are relatively fleeting and do not congeal into major power blocks for very long, the presence of faction and competition among faction leaders prevents widespread raptures in the social body. Few people dare stand against the system. There are no rebels in that sense. Quite the contrary, each person sees accomplishment in participating in the system, and except for problems raised by elections in the Lukûko (Parliament), personalised factionalism has led to basic unity in Buganda...

The whole thing hinged, as we have already said, on autocratic monarchy. A monarchy which could be tyrannical and brutal, but which actually catered for Baganda's deepest sentiments, strengthened their sense of nationhood. Fallars (Ibid.) has described the whole mechanism as follows:

> A faithful chief... would be rewarded by being given *Carte blanche* to plunder the estates... of one who had fallen into disfavour. This "pay off" to the King's loyal Servants goes far in explaining the King's legitimacy which the Kabaka enjoyed, despite his arbitrariness and cruelty. In fact there was a definite "pay off" for the nation as a whole: the ever more frequent wars against neighbouring peoples, in which more than one hundred thousand men might take part, were essentially raids for plunder, in which everyone who took part received a share. In addition, the nation as a whole received the psychic satisfaction which came from national aggrandizement at the expense of their neighbours. In the context of this ideological and economic commitment to aggressive expansion, the despotic behaviour of the Kabaka added to his legitimacy rather the reverse.

As among the Kikuyu, success in military activities was one way to political power. It was King Katerega who first broke with tradition in replacing indigenous chiefs by his successful war generals (Kiwanuka, *Ibid.*: 99 100). Thereafter successful warriorhood, especially when combined with shrewdness in Council and conversance with state affairs, became a sure path to great chieftainship. But as with the Kikuyu, the former-warrior-now-chief could not attain the highest or absolute political power. This was reserved for only a limited class of people: the so-called princes of the drum; i.e. the immediate male offsprings, brothers and sons of brothers of the King (Southwold, 1966). This principle was so entrenched in Kiganda tradition that a general rebellion or revolution by the populace at large against the King was out of the question. The Baganda did of course, overthrow their Kings often in a violent exercise. But they did so under the banner of an aspiring prince. Since such a prince was always one of the few people in Buganda who was traditionally allowed access to supreme political power by becoming the King, it is clear the entrenched principle debarring the majority (including almost all the warriors) from supreme power, was always adhered to. And in traditional Nkore, Karugire has found that "there were no 'pretenders' in the history of the dynasty of Nkore..." (1972: 16), a statement which is most likely true for most traditional interlacustrine Bantu societies.

Among the small-scaled, less centralised societies, successful warriorhood was rewarded by social, rather than by political benefits. This was so, firstly, because the specifically *political* aspects of society were hardly pronounced in social values and organisation so that society was governed by social rather than by political factors. Secondly, social leadership was, in most of these societies, naturally determined by traditional mores within the lineage. But even such leadership, because of the size of Society never concentrated in itself sufficient 'power' or even status to make it the envy of the male members of the community generally.

The Lwo speaking Nilotes of Eastern Africa illustrate this set-up well. Among the Acoli of Northern Uganda, chiefdom warriors were often led by "Twon Mony", War Bull or War Leader. Chiefs rarely led their warriors. But more significantly successful warriorhood did not lead to social leadership. Chiefs "grew", as it were, naturally from among their lineages, while successful warriors were esteemed for their deeds, but had no prospect, because of this, to become chiefs, except where they would have become chiefs anyway. In many of these societies it was not uncommon for a man to decline the honour of becoming a chief or for a regent to hold the position (for a young successor not yet of age) without any challenges from usurpers. All these are indicative of the extent to which leadership of society as a whole was not an intensely sought-after position. There were, of course, exceptions to this.

On the whole, therefore, Eastern African societies were not *politically* threatened by their warries qua warries. The combination of effective socialisation in political values and appropriate power structures made this possible. Among the Acoli and related people, political power itself was only rudimentarily developed. Prize to be competed for Access to what little power there was depended on tradition within the lineage *rather* than merely on personal (of military) ability.

Where power was centralised, and, therefore, prized, as among the Baganda and the Zulu under Shaka, the very force or agent responsible for the centralisation always had sufficient power (or was well-enough protected by tradition) not to fear the armed population. Again, the combination of successful value inculcation coupled with an appropriate power structure did the trick.

Finally the Kikuyu and other similar societies coupled socialisation with a power structure based on the age principle and collective action. The system not only ensured equal opportunity to all to rise to the most honoured position in society, it also descentralised power itself so that there was never any mature age-group lacking political power. Consequently the warrior class never exercised violence for political reasons within their own society. In contrast, the Dinka warrior, whose society was similar to the Kikuyu at least in outward form, did use a great deal of violence for political purposes within his own society. Deng (1971) has pointed out that

> Usually... the warrior age sets provoke and fight wars even in opposition to the chiefs and elders. Where, for instance, members of an age set compose songs defamatory of other subtribes, or where they violate territorial boundaries in grazing, there are civil

means of remedying the wrong. However, the age sets would consider it unmanly to wait for any peaceful settlement. The wars they provoked are not fought by them alone. All, young or old, must then join... (p. 55).

The reason for this, he argues, is to be found in the warriors' relative deprivity in the exercise of political power.

All these manifestations of excessive violence could be constructed as compensation for being deprived by the established persuasive strategies. It is the age set's only form of participation in power. We noted that if a young warrior happens to participate in the decision process as a chief or any such authority, he suddenly becomes opposed to violence (Ibid.: 56).[1]

It is significant to note that even here there was a limit beyond which the warriors would not step. As Deng points out, "It would... be a mistake to overemphasize the competitiveness of the younger generations, as individual warriors or as groups. Essentially, even their opposition does not amount to questioning the basic structure of power... (Ibid.).

Why was this so? And why was it that the Kikuyu warrior elder obediently stayed clear of the juicy morsals of kidney or spleen? And why did not the Ganda warrior rally an army to declare himself King?

The answer is to be found in the place of the supernatural in the maintenance of traditional African societies and Busia (1967: 1) is right when he wrote: "The contemporary problems of Africa must be seen in the context of Africa's own cultural heritage. That heritage is intensely and pervasively religious". In the context of our discussion, religion was the ultimate internal control in the behaviour of the warrior, quite apart from the fact that it also sanctioned both traditional values and traditional distribution of power.[2] Turnbull (1966: 212) has argued the point most forcefully as follows:

The greatest force towards law and order comes from inside each individual. The strength of this force is such that when even a minor disaster strikes an individual or his family he will go at once to the doctor, or diviner, and confess all the things he has done that might possibly have brought disaster to him as a punishment...

He did this in the belief that:

the ancestors will punish any transgression directly without any trial or chance to plead excuses. The punishment may not come at once. It may come years later. One can never be sure...

---

1   The aggressive group of Masai warriors, the "Empikas", operated somewhat differently. According to Sankan (n.d.: 41) the "Empikas" was "an aggressive delegation whose members use force to obtain whatever they want. They neither request nor beg—they merely take away whatever they came to look for. They go round fully armed as though for war." He points out that the purpose of the aggressive delegation was "usually to... repatriate any unwanted elements in the society. They also act(ed) as a press-gang for recruiting warriors into the manyatta".

2   It is significant that both Shaka Zulu and Mutesa I of Buganda sought to bring the priestly class under their political control. See Ritter, *op. cit.* and Kiwanuka (n.d., *op. cit.*)

This, he argues, was the real controlling force in traditional Africa. It ensured that even without courts, and without "law" as we think of it, there is a powerful force compelling people to lead their lives properly. The real driving force comes from within, from the knowledge that every wrong act, however slight, will bring its punishment. The real force then is religious belief.[3] The Kikuyu elders and the Kings of Buganda and the Zulu, as intermediaries between the ancestors and the people, were thus quite secure from the ambitions of the power-hungry in their societies.

What happened to Kabaka Mwanga in 1888 becomes clear. C. C. Wriggley's account (1964) of the overthrow of Mwanga in terms merely of the power of the gun misses the point, in the opinion of this writer. He writes:

> In Buganda those who managed to acquire a firearm during the 'seventies' and 'eighties' of the nineteenth century were at once set apart from the mass of the population—not merely from the rank and file but also from the territorial chief, the leaders of the now almost obsolete militia. Instead of being diffused through a hierarchy, power was now concentrated in the hands of a small organized group consisting of the new praetorian cohorts which came into being at the capital. The personnel of these cohorts was drawn in the main from among the palace pages, the youths who were being trained at the capital for the service of the state. It thus consisted of those who would in any case have formed the next generation of the governing class. But the new military system opened up new and swifter avenues to power...

This is the context in which, he argues, in September 1888 "the guardsmen used their weapons to carry out a coup d'etat, expelled the Kabaka, and made themselves masters of the state."

The impression is given by Wriggley that the coup can be accounted for, in large measure, by the so-called cohorts' perception of the superiority of their power. But vis-a-vis whom? In relation to the Kabaka a group of pages armed or not were always stronger than the king alone. This stands to reason. In relation to society at large Kiwanuka (N.d: 23) is closer to the truth when he writes that: "There was no standing army in Buganda. Even after the introduction of firearms, the Baganda did not organise a standing army similar to that of Kabarega in Bunyoro. What was developing just before the British intervened was that chiefs were in the process of becoming war lords. They had begun to organise their followers and to arm them."[4]

If relative military superiority is not the answer, what is? A clue to the answer is supplied by the "religious composition" of those who carried out the coup. They were young Moslems and young Christians! In other words the coup was carried out by those who no longer had any faith in traditional Kiganda religion.[5] Before the coup they had already established a tradition of

---

3   Alan Wells (1970: 251) has put the matter more generally as follows: "...We may regard religion as being, like other social institutions, a means of orienting a person in society..."

4   See also Southwold's private communication to Wriggley cited in Wriggley (Ibid.) which is in agreement with the views expressed by Kiwanuka.

5   A. B. K. Kasozi (1976) has argued that foreign religions had gained the ascendency in Buganda precisely because traditional belief forms had already been undermined by internal factors by the late 19th century.

disobeying the wishes of the Kabaka when these were, in their views, unchristian or irreligious (Faupel, 1969). It is more than likely these pages would have overthrown Mwanga anyway, guns or no guns. Mere spears would not have been adequate.

This point is worth bearing in mind in considering the political roles of modern armies in Africa.

Finally, on the question of socialisation, particularly socialisation in Sacred Values, the factor of *time* needs to be taken into account. Socialisation, if it is to lead to successful institutionalisation, takes a long time. This point, too, is worth bearing in mind in thinking about modern African politics.

Military Integration

Jack Goody (1971: 42) has argued, drawing on West African experiences, that military technology can somehow be correlated with distinctive political organisations.

> These various political systems are correlated not so much with differences in ownership of the means of production (nor yet in the objects of production themselves) but rather in the ownership of the means of destruction and in those means.

After identifying the basic West African military technologies as: (i) bow and arrow; (ii) spear and sword, (iii) horse, and (iv) gun; he continues:

> The bow and arrow, the characteristic weapon of the aschapalous peoples of the area, was used not only in warfare but also in hunting... The bow and arrow is essentially a democratic weapon; every man knows how to construct one; the material are readily available; the techniques uncomplicated; the missiles easy to replace (though more difficult with the introduction of iron)... With technologies of the bow and stone-tipped arrow, any kind of centralisation is almost impossible. But with the introduction of metals, Kingdoms are on the cards... (Ibid.: 45–46).

The most important point from the quotation above, for our purpose, is that relating simplicity of weaponry to democracy. We are interested in this point mainly from the perspective of the more embracing concept of military integration, the meaning of which will become clear presently. *But before we discuss the subject of military integration as it relates to traditional Eastern Africa, it is necessary to streamline some of Goody's statement in the light of Eastern African experiences.*

First of all, the bow has generally been little-used in this area and then mostly as a hunting weapon rather than for warfare. The most widespread weaponry both for war and for hunting has been the spear, often with an accompanying shield, so much so that an eminent student of African culture has categorised most of the societies in this area under the title of "the civilization of the spear" (Jaques Maquet, 1972). Generally speaking, therefore, these societies in their military technology were mainly metal-using societies.

Secondly, political centralisation has hardly correlated with weaponry using iron or metal parts. In northern Uganda, for example, many Acoli societies were using iron-tipped spears perhaps by the 17th century, (Webster, et al: 1970). Yet by the close of the 19th century centralised political communities had not emerged. Goody's essential argument is that the use of metal: especially iron, leads to centralisation:

> First, because the distribution of raw materials is uneven and involves systems of exchange (often long distance trade) which can be brought under control... Secondly, because the process of manufacture are relatively complicated... But quite apart from the increase in productivity which the use of metal offers (and hence the possibility of maintaining a more complex administrative system), it is possible to supervise the technology itself... (*op. cit.*: 46).

In Eastern Africa the raw material (i.e. iron ore) was always found locally and the blacksmiths were local specialists or else accessible to local people. This is certainly true of most of Uganda (Haden: 1970, White: 1969, Wilson, 1970, Webster, et al: 1970). But even where the king did have a group of state "blacksmiths", as it were, the implication, clearly, is that the king was able to do this *because* of the concentration of political power in his own hands. In other words centralisation of power in the state preceeded rather than came after the control of the technology for warfare by the state or king.

Nevertheless the main thrust of Goody's argument remains valid, especially when placed and looked at within the concept of military integration. The concept of military integration has at least three important aspects: weaponry, organisation and training. It demands the examination of such questions as: did the warriors constitute an institution apart from society, a standing army? did they monopolise weaponery superior to that held by the rest of society at large; and did they undergo special military training not available to the rest of society?

Generally speaking East African societies organised more in terms of militias than in terms of standing or professional armies, the age-set societies not withstanding. This means that training in military skill was a general social process rather than a professional affair.[6] This in turn affected (and may in turn have been affected by) the level of available military technology in society.

Written sources are very scanty on military training in traditional Africa; in general, training dealt with military skills on the one hand, and with military ethnics, on the other. Where military training in the modern sense of the word was absent, which was the case in most of Africa, military skills tended to be acquired in three phases: during youth by play, during adolescence by apprenticeship, and during adult life by experience.

Among the Acoli, for example, a game such as "lawala" (lit = circle) taught boys hunting techniques. A twig was fashioned into a wheel and the wheel was then, with a great deal of force, sent spinning among a line of boys with long sticks (for spears) at hand. The challenge was to place the stick inside the surging wheel, which would then stop dead. A "kill" had been registered.

Later the boy was trained on the spear, usually by accompanying his father about.

---

6   In Zululand under Shaka there was formal military training, as is very well known.

When a boy is about eight years old he can accompany his father to the garden to dig, although very often he is excused to come home earlier than his father... In the early evenings he may go with his father for a walk round the fields or in the jungle to collect some logs. During their walks in the evening, father and son carry spears. A father will tell his son to carry a spear, or two, whenever he goes to the jungle, in case an animal or an enemy appears. He tells the young boy all he knows about the behaviour of certain dangerous animals, and what to do when they appear... (Anna Apoko) 1967: 63–4).

As he becomes sure of himself the young man may accompany those older than himself on communal hunts. This kind of hunting was a good training and also an introduction to warfare, since fighting often errupted among the various clans or sub-tribes during such hunts. The young man is thus gradually made a warrior.

Finally, he accumulates experiences depending on how active he is in wars and how frequently he as joined in them.

This sequence of development was generally followed, with minor local variations,[7] even in societies in which entry to warriorhood was via a formal initiation rite. The most significant point, as far as we are concerned, is that military training was part of the general socialisation available to all.

Military ethics, on the other hand, were taught more indirectly through songs and orally narrated stories, as we shall see when we consider the more social aspects of the warrior tradition in pre-colonial Eastern Africa.

As for military organisation, most of the Eastern African societies operated in terms of the militia rather than the standing army, though significant exceptions such as the Zulu under Shaka and the Nyoro under Kabalega should be noted.

In Buganda "military organisation was based on the concept that every able-bodied male was a potential soldier" (Kiwanuka, n.d.: 22). Among the Nandi all the males of fighting age were warriors (Mair, 1962: 84); and in Ethiopia:

"The farming population's sense of participation in and continuity with Ahmara polity was also strengthened by the diffusion of military ideals and values throughout the land-holding peasantry, for military ethos set before lay farmers image of opportunity for all through military service. It was characterised by its pervasiveness and its essentially unspecialised nature. It entailed a way of life, a mode of achievement and a state of soul which was held appropriate not to some of the people (the elite) all the time, but to all of the people (except the clergy) some of the time" (Hoben, 1970: 212).

And among the Kikuyu, as we have seen, to become a man was automatically to become a warrior. Examples could be multiplied endlessly.

Even where warriorhood seemed restricted to only a relatively few in society, a closer examination soon reveals that this is not necessarily so. In traditional Rwanda, for example, warriorhood was restricted to the aristocra-

---

7 In Ankole, for example, a great deal of emphasis was placed on dexterity in the use of the stick for self-defence, while among the Karamojong trekking techniques were developed into a superb art.

cy.[8] Only the cattle-owning Tutsi were warriors; "their young men received a specialised training and only Tutsi were allowed to enter military organisation" (Maquet, 1970: 95). A closer look, however, reveals that here, as elsewhere, all *citizens* were warriors. It is simply that the agricultural Hutu and the marginal Twa traditional hunters, constituting some 80 per cent of the population of traditional Rwanda, had been defined non-citizens in Rwanda, as much as the Greeks in classical times defined as non-citizens a large portion of their population. In Rwanda this is clearly illustrated by the fact that "Government, at almost all levels except the lowest ones, was for the Tutsi exclusively" (Maquet, *op. cit.*).

Furthermore, even where there was a standing army, as in Zululand under Shaka, we are not justified in thinking that the warriors constituted an elite group superior in training and weaponry when compared to the rest of society, for here too the warriors were society, in the sense that recruitment into warriorhood was almost universal. Shaka's standing army, for example, embraced virtually the whole of Zululand's males of fighting age.

Militarily, therefore, the warriors were well integrated into society. Since, as we have seen, they were also politically fully integrated into society, the way was firmly closed to the use of the warriors as the mere instrument of statecraft, except for the Zulu experience. Acting as the military instrument of the state or a monarch constituted the least important of the functions of the warrior. Since the warriors and society were almost inseparable, the warriors actually functioned according to the dynamics of society and Society's interest – which were also their interests. Among these was the need to defend the family, relatives and society at large. Other interests and needs were economical, social and psychological.

Harry L. Shapiro (2956: 35) has described intertribal warfare among what he calls "primitive" peoples as imbued with a lot of sporting spirit. "Such organised conflict," he argues "is a dangerous game in which glory may be won and lives lost...", but "In none of these cases is warfare an instrument of tribal or national policy."

The only quarrel with this statement is that it does not give economic motives due weight as the reason for wars in such societies. In Eastern Africa (succession wars apart), war was generally waged and the warriors willingly participated for no other reason than to acquire booty: slaves, women and especially cattle. The partly agricultural and partly cattlekeeping Lluhya, for example, saw war in decidedly economic terms. According to Mair, "Their warfare had two objects, to increase their hards and to extend the area a vailable to them for cultivation." This was never achieved by formal conquest but rather "by intimidating their neighbours so that they would think it safe to keep their homes and fields at a distance" (Mair, *op. cit.*: 54). Hilda Kuper (1947) records a similar experience among the Swazi;

---

8 For a discussion on the relationship between "Warrior Societies" and aristocratic values consult Maquet (1972: 116–118).

even in Buganda in the nineteenth century where warfare did lead to the extension of territory it is clear that the impulse for such wars was often primarily economic (Kiwanuka, n.d.: 22).

Generally, therefore, the warriors were, in their military attributes and activities, part and parcel of society.

Socio-economic Integration

The concept of socio-economic integration might perhaps be looked at from three related perspectives.

The most significant of these, the economic, concerned production, consumption and the relative levels of wealth. On the whole, the warrior in traditional Eastern Africa produced what he consumed – as did anyone else. War could, of course, increase a warrior's wealth directly through the acquisition of booty or indirectly by increasing his capacity to produce, through additional war slaves, wives and children. But this did not necessarily lead to a class structure based on different levels of wealth between the warriors and the others. Traditional redistribution mechanism saw to that. In any case, the opportunity was open to most able-bodied adults in society.

The fact that warriors were basically ordinary productive members of their societies in turn had an impact on the very nature of war itself. It had to be brief and, as far as possible, not interfere with the major economic activities. In Buganda "Men went to war whenever there was a war and once it was over, they demobilized and returned to their villages" (Kiwanuka, n.d.: 22). If on demobilization the warrior did not appear to engage in the routine process of producing food, it was not because he was a warrior. The explanation is that such work was left to the women soon after the first breaking of ground and planting by the men (Wriggley op. cit.: 23). Even the chiefs did not function solely as professional war leaders. "Every chief besides being an administrator as well as a magistrate... was a war captain in times of war. He would lead his regiment or division into battle..." (Kiwanuka, n.d: 22).

In traditional Ethiopia the Ahmara armies "came quickly into being, performed erratically and dissolved in a moment. Their potency was due, not to the perfection of a specialised institution devoted to the art of warfare, but rather to the extent to which Ethiopian society as a whole was pervaded by military skills, virtues and ambition" (Levine, n.d.: 6).

Even where the warriors were quartered in barracks such as with Shaka's standing army or the Masai *manyattas*, they were not parasites feeding on the labour of their own people. Among the Zulu a great deal of the cattle and grain on which the army fed came from "foreign" wars or from the produce of the female wing of the army. Similarly the Masai warriors acquired their needs through cattle raids. Without strict central discipline, however, the distribution between "foreign" and "home" sources of livelihood was liable to be ignored. Ganda warriors, Melvin L. Perlman (1970: 139) has noted, "helped themselves to anything they found on route, even in their own country". And Kiwanuka (n.d.: 22) has written of the same people: "War was a man's job and soldiers lived on the land, which made them unpopular, even in their own areas".

The only way in which the warriors were beneficiaries of the sweat of others occurred in the context of royal despotism, as we have already seen with respect to Buganda. In Zululand, too, the king often took from those who had fallen out of grace to give to the people and the army. The parallel with the economic war in Uganda in 1972 under a warrior-president is unmistakeably clear.

The second area of socio-economic integration relates to the issue of functional occupation, but has an especially psychological implication. Because warriors were full productive members of society, they did not feel a sense of being functionally redundant; of looking on while other people carried out the really important functions in society. The warriors felt completely part of society and were not alienated from it. The consequences of such alienation can easily be imagined by drawing on the example of the consequences of political alienation among the Dinka young warriors.

Finally, we might think of social integration as relating to the style of life. Traditional Eastern African warriors shared a life-style in common with others, differencies in the level of wealth acquired as a result of war notwithstanding. There were, of course, exceptions, especially where standing armies existed or where warriors were quartered in barracks or special warrior kraals during at last part of their career as warriors.

To summarise this section, we have argued that the extent of warrior integration into society is a good indication of how positively or negatively they are likely to function in society. The standard we have used to assess the warrior-society relationship has been functional, political, economic, social, military and psychological harmony. We have noted that effective socialisation coupled with an appropriate structure of political power has meant that warriors have not been a threat to the political stability of their societies. Indeed they acted positively to maintain stability. We have also argued that traditional Eastern African warriors were militarily and socio-economically fully integrated into their societies, with some few exceptions.

Manhood, Warriorhood and Sex in Pre-colonial Eastern Africa

Strictly, the relationships which obtained among manhood, warriorhood and sex in traditional African societies are too complex to be fully captured in a written analysis. It is something better experienced to be appreciated. If such experiences must be communicated, this is better done by poets than by political analysts. What follows is thus a very sketchy description of what might have been.

Men, Women and Wars

There can be no wars without warriors and warriors, before they are, trained and armed, must be born. This is a most fundamental, if indirect, relationship between sex and war, and was instinctively, as well as, consciously recognised by the traditional Eastern societies. Kenyatta (Ibid.: 1974–5) has put the matter well as follows:

> For economic and political reasons every family was expected to be able to protect its own interests and at the same time help to protect the common interest of the tribe from outside attack. To do this effectively and to command the respect of the tribe it was necessary for every family to have a number of male children who could be called up for military service in time of crisis and alien aggression...

Both in agricultural societies, where the routine production of foods tended to be the responsibility of the women folks, as well as in the pastural societies where herding though a man's job was akin to war, the emphasis was placed on sons above daughters.

The high incidence of patrilineality and patrilocality in these societies are also related to this emphasis, and, to a large extent, to warfare.[9] But patrilineality and patrilocality themselves posed problems for the woman's sense of belonging in society. Her position became at best ambiguous. At her parents' home she was not valued much compared to her brothers. The latter were expected to stay-put and be available for warfare while she would soon be on her way to the homes of strangers. At her husband's home, she was, indeed, an alien who had to accommodate to the ways of her new environment. In this patrilineality worked to make her almost marginal to society.

It becomes tempting to see women in these societies as the property of men and men's beast of burden: to produce sons and food. This is to a certain extent true. In Zululand under Shaka where women formed part of the army their activities were economic and, at certain times, sexual.[10] In Acoli a war alliance was struck only after the chief, being asked for military assistance, had accepted the *lapii* of the requesting chief. The "lapii" was a young but mature girl who became the wife of the receiving chief.

But these practices did not necessarily mean that women were second-class citizens or unesteemed in society. In Acoli in 1859 the Palaro chiefdom, having found the Atyak chiefdom militarily too tough for them, turned to the centrally placed and more powerful chiefdom of Payira for help. The *Lapii* who was accepted by Rwotcamo of Payira became the mother of Awic, perhaps the most famous of all the Acoli Chiefs (1954: 32). In many of these societies women were central figures in war ceremonies both before and after wars. More indirectly patrilocality was ultimately the basis of military alliances. By being married away from home women widened the social ties of their original communities and made new friendships and alliances. The real argument against regarding women as unfavoured citizens, however, rests on the fact that women had their own arena of importance directly related to warfare if not in physical combat – as we shall shortly see.

---

9   For an interesting treatment of this theme see: Peter Farb (1971).
10 Having killed in battle it was traditional for Zulu warriors to "sula izembe", to "wipe the axe", that is, to have sexual intercourse with a woman as an act of purification.

Masculinity, Warriorhood and Sex

The fact that warfare demanded the production of sons and that war itself was a manly activity, led the Eastern African societies to place undue emphasis on masculinity and manliness, the one to be tested sexually and the other in hot combat. Ultimately, however, the two kinds of tests were one.

Sex was the test of masculinity in at least three ways. Physically the real man was ideally expected to be tall, well-built and, if possible, magnificent in appearance. In any case he should not look effeminate. In addition he had to be physically strong. And, finally, a great deal of emphasis was placed on virility, perhaps as an indirect way of determining fertility. These attributes markedly determined a woman's choice of a male partner in many Eastern African societies. And some of them even the Acoli, for example, only the "man in deed" could have proper, physical, sexual access to his girlfriend. The girl did secretly visited the boy-friend in his hut in a secret rendezvous at night. Once inside the hut she sat at the edge of the bed, a locally constructed contraption. Thereafter it took a strong man to get her to lie on the bed and yield. A weak man had to "keng ki ngwece", as the Acoli said, "be content with the smell". The principle behind such visits and pre-marital sex was to test the man's fertility indirectly by gauging his virility and potency. Failure to perform adequately meant the break-up of the friendship, since the girl was unlikely to marry a man who might not be sexually strong enough to make children, especially sons.

War, too, put manliness to test by questioning the individual's physique, courage and the ability to secure victory from the enemy. The more manly, the more warriorlike. The Kikuyu, for example, instead of testing masculinity separately and privately in a darkened bachelor hut, and manliness on the battlefield, combined the two tests – at least formally. The lengthy initiation rite gave ample opportunity for gauging a man's masculinity, while the supreme pain of circumcision tested his manliness and suitability for warriorhood. This is why becoming a man meant access to physical sex and to warriorhood at the same time. The uninitiated youth were not allowed to be warriors and in matters of sex could legitimately go only as far as "Ombani na ngwe-ko" (platonic love and fondling). This was thought necessary in order not to suppress entirely the normal sex instincts of the boys and girls. Given the slippery nature of the boundary between Platonic and physical love, however, Kikuyu society sought to protect the prerogatives of the initiated diligently. Kenyatta tells us that:

> If a man is detected by a girl trying to loosen her garments during the night of *ngweko* she generally reports the matter to all her friends in the district. The matter is taken to the age-group meeting... such a man would be ostracised by his friends and would be debarred from having *ngweko* with other girls... (*op. cit.*: 160).

Graduation into manhood did indeed satisfy society's curiosity about masculinity; but did sex and warriorhood necessarily go together? Shaka Zulu, at least, did not think so. His army was deliberately denied sex, except by permission of Shaka himself usually for the purpose of "wiping the axe"; and when this permission was granted, the king himself provided for the warriors from the parallel female regiments. He preferred warriors to marry only at retirement from warriorhood though he did have married regiments in the army.

What was left to an individual king to decide in Zululand, the Masai institutionalised into a normal routine. For warriors who had served their term to graduate into elderhood, a special initiation rite, *Eunoto*, was performed. At this ceremony one of the leaders of the initiates, the *Olutuno* "is asked to choose any of the girls he might prefer for a wife... He chooses whichever girl he wants and she is obliged to marry him. This symbolizes a new phase for he now graduated young elders, for they are thenceforth permitted to marry" (Sankan, *op. cit.:* 30).

Warriorhood, Sex and Literacy

In an atmosphere in which the ideal tribal virtue consisted of manly excellence enduring courage and bravery at war, and masculinity at home a question mark hangs over the position of three categories of people.

They are: (a) those who for biological and physical reasons could not possess these values or, if they had them, might not be allowed to demonstrate them – the women; (b) the males who had these values in excess, and (c) the males who lacked them.

The position of women was, on the whole, clear cut. They were not expected to have these values. Most of these societies shared an attitude to women very close to what Kuper (Op. Cit.: 139) has attributed to the Swazi:

> As in other primitive societies, the major division of labour is based on sex. Different psychological and physiological qualities are attributed to men and women as *intalo yabo* (their nature) to explain the allocation of particular occupations. Instilled in Swazi from childhood is the theory that "the strength of woman does not equal that of man". The male is considered to be born "hard" and "firm", a leader in the fight and council, while the "nature" of women is "weak" and "soft"...

But this does not mean that women did not relate to the ideal male values in some significant manner. As far as manliness and warfare is concerned, women related in at least two significant manners. First of all, by not being expected to have these values and to have the opposite values instead, women, or rather their characteristic qualities, constituted a set of standard against which manliness could be measured in absolute terms. To be accused of being "like a woman" was to be denied manliness, even manhood. But more significantly, for our purpose, women were often the most effective amplifiers, and therefore popularisers, of these values in a verbal and literary sense. It is in this context that warfare and sex have consequences for literacy in society. Professor Mazrui (1974) has ably argued that militarized language can have inspirational and organisation functions in military affairs. The otole dance and songs had just such functions among the Acoli. The war dance and war songs could not help but stir men to aggressive spirits. As Okot (*op. cit.:* 15) has pointed out:

"Even to-day these stirring poems still arouse feeling among former enemies". For example, "the football match between the Acoli and Lango has always been very fiercely fought." Part of the Acoli war song arising out of a 19th century war in which the Acoli were victorious over the Langi always brought to the football field (instead of the battlefield), to the stir the Acoli to aggressive spirits, went something like thi:s

Tong romo ki wedi ye,	Spear met spear, oh;
Ilamo lapii kwe,	In vain you invoke your luck;
Oboke Olwedo,	The leave of the olwedo tree;
Oboke olwedo mukonyi;	It was the leaves of the olwedo tree that saved you;
Lweny ma Ogwal lameny ywa, ye,	The battle that was led by Ogwal Lameny
Oweko Omiro owanyi mac Ame pura...	The Omiro[11] were in the fire like Kongonis...

It is no less true, however, that warfare can have very inspirational effects on oral literature in society. In the breasts of emotional young women, the exploits of war were intertwined with the qualities of the warrior and the man into stirring love songs. The songs were sung in the fields, on the way to the water springs or as accompanying music for grinding millet. They became part of society.[12]

As for the males of society who did not quite make the mark, it is interesting to note that the Cheyenne of North America solved this problem in a remarkable way. According to Selby (1969: 19–20):

These persons donned women's clothes and took up women's labours... They were called *berdaches* and held an important place in society. Sometimes they were credited with greater spirit-vision or they were acknowledged masters (or mistresses) of women's skills... Theirs was an honoured place, and women would send their girls to them to learn the trades from those who know best. They were, of course, liberated from the dangers of the battlefield, but war parties liked to have their company, not only for their medical skill, but also because they were socially graceful and entertaining... In short, though deviant in the sense that they were incapable of carrying out the role of the judicious warrior, they were not relegated to a place of dishonour among their fellows, on the contrary, they were given a place of esteem and tasks of difficulty...

Eastern African societies do not appear to have been very accommodating on this issue. The Kikuyu uncircumcised man, *kehee*, could not go to the battlefield, but had to stay at home and defend the homestead with women. His position was not a very honourable one. Among the Dinka "to fear to fight in... a war is one of the most shameful things a Dinka can do, and such a person may never enjoy the company of his fellowmen" (Deng, *op. cit.:* 55). And in Acoli to show cowardice in war was to invite the label of "woman". Among the Masai if an army was defeated, the warriors removed their sandals before they got to their homes. All the sandals were collected and put in one

---

11   The Langi.
12   For the literary contribution of Zulu women to their nation's cultural life see Ritter (*op. cit.*)

heap. As soon as the warriors returned home they had to shave off all their hair – the hair of defeat (Sankan, *op. cit.*: 23–24).

The only category of "deviant" males accommodated appear to have been the disabled. It is interesting to note that such men often enough, like women, contributed to the war efforts literally and poetically. In 1947 Wright, then District Commissioner of Acoli, ordered Eliya Aliker, chief of Payira, to construct a new road.[13] Aliker, in turn, passed the order to the people of Labongo chiefdom, who had earlier been placed under the Payira chief by the British. The people of Labongo refused, saying, "what white ant ever eats across a stream" – by which they meant that there was a sovereign territorial boundary between the chief of Payira and that of Labongo and that Aliker should confine his activities in Payira. Aliker went in person to enforce the order, thereby challenging, according to the Labongo men, their manliness. The Labongo warriors rose in anger to meet Aliker and instantly killed his bodyguards. The chief shot one man and fled for his life. In retaliation Wagstaff, a British officer, led colonial mercenaries and the warriors of Payira against Labongo. They killed many people and captured many cattle. But the Labongo warriors counter-attacked, killed many Payira warriors, and recaptured their cattle. In a song composed by a Labongo poet, the Payira warriors were compared to women. In contrast the Labongo warrios were men indeed:

Aliker, kel dyanga	Aliker, return my cattle
Ka ilwor	You coward,
Mony Gala	Tell the army of the white man,
Cung Ikura	To stop and wait for me
Waci waromo Lamola	We shall meet at Lamola;
Iyoo, iyoo	O yes. O yes,
Muloji lwor	Muloji is a coward
Dako loyo	Even a woman defeats him
Muloji lwor	Muloji is a coward
Muloji lwor	Muloji is a coward
Dako loyo...	Even a woman defeats him...

But in 1938, when a blind man from Lamogi chiefdom had to react to a colonial order to have all able-bodied males from the area go to Gulu on forced-labour, he could not defend his and their insulted manhood by fighting. He hit back with a "nanga" song in which he made himself triumph over the colonial hierarchical system of authority in the most absolute manner imaginable:[14]

Cuna mito telo	My penis wants to get erect
An anongo min jago	When I find the sub-chief's mother,
Agero benebene;	I will fuck her all night long;
Ee, cuna mito telo,	Ee, my penis wants to get erect,
An ayenyo min rwot,	When I find the chief's mother
Agero i dye yo;	I will fuck her in the middle of the road.

---

13 This story is narrated in Okot p'Bitek, *Horn of My Love* (1974: 14).
14 From Okot p'Bitek (*op. cit.*: 12).

Ee, gira mito telo,	Ee, my penis wants to get erect,
An aito wi lela	I am mounting the bicycle,
Alaro Gulu;	I am hurrying to Gulu;
Ee, cuna mito telo,	Ee, my penis wants to get erect,
An Anongo min Dici	When I find the District Commissioner's mother.
Agero i bar Pece;	I will fuck her in the football arena at Pece
Ee, cuna mito telo,	Ee, my penis wants to get erect,
An abedo ing kwateng	I will sit on the back of a kite,
Watuk benebene;	We shall fly all night;
Ee, cuna mito telo,	Ee, my penis wants to get erect,
An anongo min king,	When I find the king's mother,
Jal, agero wi got.	Man, I will fuck her on top of a hill.

With regard to "deviants" at the other end of the scale, i.e., those who sought to overdramatise the warrior values, these societies do not appear to have been duly threatened by their existence. Either they perished in war in attempting to overexcel or, if they were always successful, rose to position of eminence in the context of the socio-political set-up, as we have already seen.

Colonialism and the Soldier in the Contemporary Eastern Africa of Warriors, Soldiers and Freedom Fighters

> Students of African history distinguish among types of military combattants. Soldiers of pre-colonial forces are usually denoted warriors—a proud title suggesting independence in combat, personal prowess, and a high degree of individual initiative. Soldiers of colonial armies are branded with titles like "black mercenaries" or "armed and somewhat privileged helots". Finally, those who fight for national liberation are termed "freedom fighters", with connotations of political commitment and foresightedness. These contrasts in nomenclature thus clearly differentiate those who defended or continue to defend their societies against external attack, and those who upheld an alien, colonial form of government... (Welch, *op. cit.*: 1)

In fact this is far too simplified a classification, at least as far as Eastern Africa is concerned. Nineteenth century Langi combatants were clearly warriors in the traditional sense; yet some of them served as mercenaries under Kabalega of Bunyoro in his liberation war against the British and their collaborators. Similarly the Mau Mau war was a one of freedom. But it drew a great of its inspirational and organisational techniques from traditional sources, often the very same ones employed by pre-colonial Kikuyu warriors (Rosberg and Nottingham 1970: 211). On the other hand it is only from a strictly "objective" point of view that it can be said that black colonial soldiers were instruments of alien rule (Welch, *op. cit.*; Welch: 1970). Some of these soldiers, at least, were proud to be engaged in combat against, for example, the alien Germans, in the name of "our freedom", under the great King George. For how else have these armies, for the most part, remained "colonial" in mentality? And yet, again, there is John Okello, an "alien" in Zanzibar who led African Zanzibaris against Arab Zanzibaris.

The most that can be said with certainty is that colonialism has been a great but ambiguous force in the history of combat and combattants in Eastern Africa. But two broad categories of reaction to it and its accompanying forces are discernable: the one embodying a great deal of the traditional with 'some elements of modernity, the other reversing this emphasis. The embodiment of the first is the warrior and freedom-fighter, and of the second the modern soldier.

The Warrior, Freedom-fighter

The warrior, freedom fighter displays three significant characteristics. Firstly, he is part of a general military mobilization of his society. Secondly, he operates in a situation in which mobilization itself, as well as military organisation, depend on some form of ritualistic affirmation of commitment and of belonging by each and every combatant. Finally, the weaponry involved is often not systematically organised but depends on availability. There is a general state of armament, but the arms are assorted, not centrally issued or controlled, and are often inferior to those of the enemy. There are, of course, exceptions to this rule.

The best Eastern African examples are the Mau Mau, Maji Maji, Okello's revolution in Zanzibar, and the guerilla freedom fighters of South-eastern Africa. In all these cases the ideal has been to involve all able-bodied persons, sometimes including women, in the war. In many of them the use of some form of ritual for mobilization and organisation has been central. The best example of this is, of course, the phenomenon of oathing among the Kikuyu during the Mau Mau uprising. In the Maji Maji rebellion it was Kinjikitile and his *maji* (special water) who provided the unifying ideology:

> His *maji* was not to be a war medicine of or for a single group of clan, but of and for all people; his was a universal war medicine having a universal appeal. Thus his message through the *maji* became the basis of a revolutionary commitment to mass action against the Germans (Grassa, *op. cit.*: 131).

A little later on (Ibid.: 137) Gwassa writes: "It will be seen that *Maji* movement as ideology, provided for and made possible, mass involvement in Maji Maji, and that without it, it is unlikely that the war as a mass movement would have taken place".

During the Zanzibar revolution, "the nearest thing to a people's revolution" was in East Africa (Mazrui, 1972: 273), Okello who led the revolution was like "an Old Testament character". Okello's "Ten Commandments" which he gave to his followers in mid-1964, as well the many dreams that he claims inspired him (Okello, 1967), certainly bear this out.

The Okello revolution also illustrates well what has been said about the weaponry of the warrior, freedom-fighter, at least in the Eastern African context. Until they took over the important armoury at Ziwani in Zanzibar, the revolutionaries, according to Okello's account of events, were armed only with the traditional bows, arrows, spears and *pangas*! The taking over of the armoury decisively tilted the military balance in their favour and also illustrates how easily the modern can be pressed into the service of the basically traditional. The introduction of firearms in Acoliland in the 19th century, for example, did not bring about revolutionary changes in pattern of warfare. In similar manner in the same area, the gun as a weapon for hunting has continued to be used side by side with the spear, even in the same communal hunt!

In all these cases revolutionary warfare drew its inspiration ultimately from deep seated values values which could be activated by oathing, ritualistic drinking of Maji, or Okello's "Ten Commandments".

Colonialism and the Modern Soldier

Three sets of factors explain fairly adequately the behaviour and nature of the modern soldier in Africa. They are: (a) those relating to technology and the organisational forms that necessarily accompany it, (b) those relating to basic values and primordial sentiments, and (c) those having to do with professionalism. Each of these sets of factors have had varying degrees of impact on the politics and socio-economic life style of Eastern African countries.

To take politics first, it has been suggested that advanced military technology, introduced into Africa during the period of colonisation, has had the effect of tilting the balance of power in favour of organised armed men, especially in favour of the armies maintained by the state. Professor Ali A. Mazrui has argued persuasively that:

> With the coming of the rifle in colonial Africa and the tank in independent Africa, military elitism became even more pronounced. The old days of military democracy, when everyone passed through the warriors stage and weapons were simple ones capable of being manufactured by the warrior himself, were replaced by the era of professional military specialists, with weapons requiring a high level of technological skill to manufacture and some specialised training to use. The Uganda Army might not have a monopoly of certain types of firearms... But in the totality of concentrated technological power of destruction, the army in an African country like Uganda is in a position to assert special rights of primacy (Mazrui, 1972: 266–267).

Though persuasive, this argument cannot by itself explain the tendency of African soldiers to *actually* intervene in politics and often to assume the rein of government themselves. If it did, we would be at a loss to explain why in pre-colonial period, the Kikuyu warriors, for example, did not take over from the Council of Elders and rule Kikuyuland. The argument hinges squarely on the point that it is preponderance in, rather mere possession of, military technology that is critical. All mature male Kikuyus had each their own disspears. But might not a group of warriors using no more than ordinary spears arm them?

The military overthrow of Kabaka Mwanga of Buganda is even more illustrative. There existed in Buganda at this time something like "military democracy", not in context of ruler-ruled relationship, but rather with regard to relationship between the supreme and the peripheral powers: the Kabaka vis a vis his great chiefs. According to Southwold (1964):

> When he began to receive guns in significant quantities, Mutesa created a special department (Kitongole), the *Kijasi*, to have charge of them. Its head, the *Mujasi*, had charge

of the Kabaka's armoury, and commanded the men of the department who formed a special body of musketeers (baserikale)...

Kabaka Mwanga who followed Mutesa established three more *bitongole* and these later deposed him.

The significant thing, however, is that, "... the chiefs, or at any rate the more senior of them, also appointed similar offices: each chief had his own *mujasi*, in charge of the chief's own guns and musketeers" (Southwold: *Ibid.*). The youth who acted and overthrew Mwanga did so in a situation of relative "military democracy", since they did not possess superiority in weaponry.

It would appear that two additional factors are necessary to explain *certain* and *successful* intervention in politics by the soldiers. In Eastern Africa both have owed their genesis to colonial rule. One of these was so very dramatically illustrated by the voice of the soldier who announced the coup in Uganda on January 25, 1971. He ended his announcement with the words "Power is now handed over..." Power must be in a certain *form* to be taken over. The political and administrative structures created and evolved by colonial rule and continued by independent African countries make it possible for power to be "handed over". "It has proved infectious, this seizure of government by armed men, and so effortless;" Ruth B. First (1972: 4) has written. "Get the keys of the armoury; turn out the barracks; take the radio station, the post office and the airport; arrest the person of the president, and you arrest the state."

Many writers have attempted to relate successful coups to the supposed fragility of African socio-political institutions (Greene, 1970). Even President Nyerere of Tanzania could say in 1960: "These things cannot happen here," giving as his reason the fact that "we have a very strong organisation, TANU" (Mazrui, 1968: 1). Both implicitly and explicitly, it is argued that the reason the military have not taken over in the so-called developed countries is because they have strong developed institutions. The question: what could these institutions possibly *do* if the soldiers did turn their guns on society? is never asked.

In fact, in the final analysis, what secures these countries from take-overs is not the strength in their socio-political institutions but, rather, the strength of the tradition of non-intervention in their armies. This is the third dimension our analysis should take into account. Guns by themselves are useless until and unless fired (or threatened to be fired). The fundamental question then is: what holds back the soldiers of the developed nations from doing so; and do African soldiers not have these restraints? The question cannot be answered contextually, as Welch (1970: 164) and Ruth First (*op. cit.*) have done, i.e. in terms of the failure of politics, declining economy, etc., in the African countries concerned. We have to look, instead, at the concept of socialisation and integration proposed by Chick and Mazrui already referred to earlier. The low level of integration pointed out by these two writers, we wish to suggest, is itself a consequence of three things, two of them by-products of colonialism.

First, colonialism destroyed the political *context* of the old loyalties, but without destroying the loyalties themselves. Secondly, it built up an unfamiliar political structure to which these old, often ethnic loyalties, have not been able to adapt successfully. Finally, the successors to the colonial state have not had the necessary time to re-orient either the colonially-created structures or the now-inappropriate loyalties to the needs of to-day. The results have been all too clear.

But a qualifier is in order here. Professor Mazrui has written regarding African national armies' sense of national commitment that at least, "There is a built-in inclination on the part of a national army to engage in active prevention of separatism." (1972: 267). This might suggest that these armies have at least a certain sense of national loyalty and that the foregoing analysis needs to be qualified. This is true. It often happens that, though the army as a whole is conservative and traditionalist in outlook, its leaders can be forward-looking and nationalistic. But the phenomenon can also be explained away in strictly professional terms as Professor Mazrui himself does when he continues, "...In the absence of external warfare and preparation for distant military adventures, national armed forces in Africa very often find a special sense of mission in seeking to keep the inherited territory intact" (Ibid.). In other words the phenomenon, and possibly many like it, is really a soldier's reaction to what he sees as a military problem.

But what happens to soldiers when they do not have the primary responsibility to govern and are not engaged in putting down secessionist movements? How do they, in other words, relate to the socio-economic life of society?

Military Professionalism, Manhood, and Sex

The fact that the soldier is now a military professional has had consequences which may be viewed from two broad perspectives. From the functional perspective there is the problem of boredom arising out of a sense of functional redundancy. Professor Mazrui (1971) has suggested that this might be one of the causes of coups in Africa. But might it not lead, also, to exaggerated activities along the line suggested by Clausewitz for a standing army: clothing, armament, training, sleeping, drinking, marching, and – in the African context – sex, but without war? The consequences of some of these things for society can be left to the reader to imagine. But political commentators and African governments themselves have often been worried about them. There have been suggestions that African armies should be made more directly economically productive. Writing as early as 1962, Lucian Pye thought that there were good reasons why this might be possible:

> In all societies it is recognised that the armies must make those who enter them into the image of a good soldier. The underdeveloped society adds a new dimension: the good soldier is also to some degree a modernized man. Thus it is that the armies in the newly emergent countries come to play key roles in the process by which traditional ways give way to more Westernised ideas and practices (p. 299).

In West Africa the colossal size of the Nigerian army, which has grown from 8,000 in 1966 to 250,000 today, for example, is already beginning to generate thinking in that country along these lines. As Peter Enahoro (1975) has reported, "... there have been suggestions already that 100,000 soldiers should be demobilised and put to other use. Another suggestion was that the army should take over construction jobs like road building..." In Uganda soldiers are being encouraged to participate in the economic life of the country in a double sense. Recently President Amin (1975) revealed at the end of the Budget speech: "If you see a slight increase in the defence budget it is because we are training soldiers to become farmers. Every battalion will have its own farm to feed itself and the country. The army may even export its agricultural produces outside Uganda."

But the Ugandan soldiers have also been involved in the economy as some of the beneficiaries of the Economic War, the expulsion of the Asians and the distribution of their businesses to indigenous Ugandans. Because of this both political power and economic power can be said to have become held by the same class. Professor Ali Mazrui (1972 (a)) has argued that the embourgeoisement of the military has positive consequences for the stability of the state in Africa. This remains to be seen.

But the fact that military training per se as well as the gun as a weapon of destruction are somewhat irrelevant in the great tasks that face most African countries does not mean that these things have ceased to be used. They are. And in a situation in which foreign wars are a scarcity, they are increasingly used internally against the citizenry. Two possible reasons for the manner in which military techniques and technology are used in this context have been given. The one hinges on the fact that soldiers are not appropriately trained for what really ought to be police work. In this connection Professor Mazrui has argued:

> We prepare our soldiers to fight wars and deal with enemies when in fact their usual duties have nothing to do with foreign wars in distant lands but are concerned with fellow citizens in the same country. There is a danger that the skills of fighting enemies are not suitable for dealing with civilians who are fellow citizens. The roughness of combat training could be misplaced when handling your neighbours (1971).

The second reason is an extension of the first. Because African armies are nationally poorly integrated, ethnic groups within them tend to relate one another as indeed "foreigners" to be treated according to the rules of combat applied in foreign wars (Chick and Mazrui, *op. cit.*).

But might there not be a third reason, connected this time with the very nature of modern military technology itself? In the Marxist world view of history advanced technology of production has an ambiguous role to play, depending on the socio-political context in which it is employed. Where it is used as a profit-maximising technique under capitalism it leads to human degradation. But under communism it is the very instrument which, by taking care of basic needs with the minimum of human labour, leads to man's realisation of his manhood, in the sense that he is left free to engage in the kind of creativity that leads to self realisation. What of advanced technology of destruction?

Advanced technology of destruction has had (given Africa's traditional warrior values) the disastrous effect of making sex and therefore manhood as irrelevant in combat as women are as men.[15] Consequently men have felt themselves womanised, as women have become men. Human nature being what is, the men have fought back to regain manhood. Unnecessarily brutal use of the gun on fellow countrymen may be a way of compensating for lost manhood. The other strategy has been the arbitrary exclusion of women from the army.[16]

Ethnic politics, too, has been decisively affected by the introduction of advanced military technology into Africa. The stage for this was prepared by the colonial military recruiting pattern. The British, for example, tended to recruit from what they had believed to be either warlike, courageous tribes or tribes more easily amenable to discipline. The outward signs of these qualities, they erroneously believed, were tallness and a good build. Thus in India they recruited mainly from the remote Sikhs, in Pakistan, from the rural Punjab and Pathans, in the Sudan from the northern Arabs, in Nigeria from the Moslem north, and in Uganda from the Acoli of the north (Zanowtiz, 1964).

The predominance and entrenchment of certain ethnic groups in the colonial armed forces was to have a decisive effect on politics during the post-colonial era. In Uganda, for example, the southern Bantu-speaking tribes ultimately lost political power to the northern Nilotics, and one of the criteria used to recruit even more northerners into the armed forces and to exclude almost all but a few southern Bantus was physical height and general physique. Few Southerners measured the 5 feet 7 inches required of a recruit into the armed forces.

Yet military technology made it easier than in the pre-colonial days of spears, shields and courage, for a 5 foot man to make as good a soldier as a taller man. The insistence on irrelevant recruitment standards must therefore be put down to a technique to monopolise military power as an avenue to political power.

Conclusions

This paper has attempted a bird's eye view exploration of the warrior tradition in Eastern Africa from just before colonisation to the present. It has been argued that socialisation and the structure of political power are critical factors in these traditions. What these suggest is that contemporary African societies must look again critically at the whole question of integration as it relates to the military in society. Ideally, the soldier, like the traditional warrior, should be an integral part of his society economically, politically and socially instead of standing apart and above society.

---

15   Recently in Kampala, Uganda, a combined male representatives from the Ghana and Uganda armed forces had the humiliation to be beaten by female representatives drawn from the Uganda Police and Prisons' Services.

16   In Uganda President Amin has thrown the door open for women to join the Uganda army. In Tanzania women have been receiving military training as part of the militia for years. President Nyerere's wife herself has undergone this exercise.

REFERENCES

AMIN, President, Idi
1975   Uganda T.V. Address, June, 12.
APOKO, Anna
1967   "At Home in the Village: Growing Up in Acholi," in Lorene K. Fox, ed., *East African Childhood* (Oxford University Press).
APTER, David E.
1967   *The Political Kingdom in Uganda* (Princeton, Princeton University Press).
BUSIA, K. A.
1967   *Africa in Search of Democracy* (Routledge and Kegan Paul, London).
CHICK, John D., and Ali A. Mazrui
1970   "The Nigerian Army and African Images of the Military." A Paper prepared for delivery at the VIIth World Congress of Sociology at Varna, Bulgaria, 14–29 September.
DENG, Francis Mading
1971   *Tradition and Modernisation: A Challenge For Law Among the Dinka of the Sudan* (Yale University Press, New Haven and London).
ENAHORO, Peter
1975   "Nigeria: Gowon's Quiet Coup", *Africa* (London) January.
FALLERS, L. A.
1956   "Despotism, Status Culture and Social Mobility in an African Kingdom", *Comparative Studies in Society and History* 2: 11–32.
FARB, Peter
1971   *Man's Rise to Civilization* (Paladin).
FAUPEL, J. F.
1969   *African Holocaust:* The Story of the Uganda Martyrs (Geoffrey Chapman, London).
GOLDTHORPE, J. E.
1958   *Outlines of East African Society* (Department of Sociology, Makerere University, Kampala).
GOODY, Jack
1971   *Technology, Tradition and the State in Africa* (Oxford University Press).
GREEN, Fred
1970   "Toward Understanding Military Coup." In living Leonard Markovitz, ed., *African Politics and Society* (The Free Press, New York: Collier-Macmillan Ltd., London).
GRUNDY, Kenneth W.
1968   *Conflicting Images of the Military in Africa* (East African Publishing House).
GWASSA, G. C. K.
1972   "African Methods of Warfare During the Maji Maji". In Bathwell A. Ogot, ed., *War and Society in Africa* (Frank Cass, London).
HOBEN, Allen
1972   "Social Stratification in Traditional Ahmara Society." In Arthur Tuden and Leonard Plotnicov, eds., *Social Stratification in Africa* (The Free Press, New York; Collier Macmillan Ltd., London).
KASOZI, A. B. K.
       "Why Did the Baganda Adopt Foreign Religions in the 19th C?", *Mawazo*, Vol. 4, No. 3. (Forthcoming).
KENYATTA, Jomo
1938   *Facing Mount Kenya*, (Secker and Warburg, London).
KIWANUKA, S. M. S.
1971a *A History of Buganda From the Foundation of the Kingdom to 1900*, (Longman).
1971b *The Kings of Buganda* (East African Publishing House).
n.d.   "The Kingdom of Buganda" (Mimeo Department of History, Makerere University, Kampala).

KUPER, Hild
    1947   *An African Aristocracy: Rank Among the Swazi* (Oxford University Press).
LEVINE, Donald, N.
    n.d.   "The Military in Ethiopian Politics" (Unpublished Manuscript). In: Allan Hoben, *op. cit.*
MAIR, Lucy,
    1962   Primitive Government (Penguin).
MAQUET, Jacques
    1972   *Civilizations of Black Africa* (Tr. Joan Rayfield, Oxford University Press).
MAZRUI, Ali, A.
    1971   Interview with *Sunday Nation*, (Nairobi), July 11.
    1972   *Cultural Engineering and Nation-Building in East Africa* (Northwestern University Press, Evanston, Illionois).
    1974   "Language in Military History: Command and Communication in East Africa", *Mawazo*, Vol. 4, No. 2: 1935.
OCAYA-LAKIDI, Dent, and Ali A. MAZRUI
    1973   "Secular Skills and Sacred Values in Uganda Schools: Problems of Technical and Moral Acculturation." A Paper presented at the Conference on Conflict and Harmony Between Traditional and Western Education in Africa. School of Oriental and African Studies, University of London, March.
OCAYA-LAKIDI, Dent
    1974   "The Modernisation of Education in Uganda: From Initiation Rites to Graduation Ceremonies", *Mawazo*, Vol. 4, No. 2: 87–110.
OGOT, Bathwell, A. ed.
    1972   *War and Society in Africa* (Frank Cass, London).
OKELLO, John
    1967   *Revolution in Zanzibar* (East African Publishing House).
OKOT, p'Bitek
    1974   *Horn of My Love* (London, Heinemann).
PYE, Lucian, W.
    "Armies in the Process of Political Modernisation", in: Claude E. Welch, ed., *Political Modernisation* (Wadsworth Publishing Company, Inc. Belmont, California).
RANOWITZ, Morris
    1964   *The Military in the Political Development of New Nations.*
ROSCOE, John
    1911   *The Baganda* (London, 1911).
SELBY, Henry
    "Elite Selection and Social Integration: An Anthropologist's View", in: Rupert Wilkinson, ed., *Governing Elites: Studies in Training and Selection* (New York, Oxford University Press).
SHAPIRO, Harry L.
    1956   *Man, Culture and Society* (Oxford University Press).
SOUTHWOLD, Martin
    1966   "Succession to the Throne in Buganda", in: Jack Goody, ed., *Succession to High Office* (Cambridge University Press).
WEBSTER, J. B., et al.
    1970   *Acholi Historical Texts* (Mimeo. Department of History, Makerere University, Kampala).
WELCH, Jr., Claude E.
    1973   "Continuity and Discontinuity in African Military Organisations." A Paper submitted to the International Congress of Africanists, 3rd Session, December 9–19, Addis Ababa, Ethiopia.
    1970   "Soldiers and State in Africa", in: Marion E. Doro and Newell M. Stultz, *Governing in Black Africa: Perspectives On New States* (Prentice-Hall).

WELLS, Alan
    1970   *Social Institutions* (Heinemann, London).
WHITE, R. G.
    1969   "Blacksmiths of Kigezi", *Uganda Journal*, 33, 1, 65–73.
WILSON, J. G.
    1970   "Notes on the Use of Naturally Occurring Minerals in Karamoja", *Uganda Journal*,
           34, 1, 81–82.
WRIGLEY, C. C.
    1964   "The Changing Economic Structure of Buganda", in: L. A. Fallers, ed., *The
           King's Men* (New York, Oxford University Press), pp. 16–63.

The Bankruptcy of the Warrior Tradition

AIDAN SOUTHALL

University of Wisconsin, Madison, U.S.A.

CULTURAL RELATIVITY is one of the chief cards played by anthropologists against the besetting sin of ethnocentrism, but the moral relativity entailed is one of the dilemmas with which thoughtful anthropologists perennially wrestle. So for once I will be bold and state my conviction that the warrior tradition is neither relevant nor useful for contemporary Africa. It inevitably summons up the colonial image of the noble savage, poised on one leg in *nilotische stellung*, fierce, courageous, independent, every inch a man and visibly male, honest and clean, lion-spearing, the virtuous though primitive contrast to the lying, thieving, spoilt "mission boy". On the one hand it is a beguiling fantasy, – *alter ego* to discontented, disillusioned, frustrated, civilized, urban man; on the other hand a compensatory antidote to the troublesome real life native for the harassed imperial administrator.

The adulation of the warrior image never hampered the efficient suppression of resistance to the spread of imperial rule by local patriots fighting to preserve their freedom. Such local valor was soon quashed, and quite forgotten by later foreigners who came and found the Pax Colonia remarkably stable, and on the surface peaceful, so that its more violent and stern beginnings lay conveniently buried until recent Africanists dug them up again out of the archives and popularized them as "primary resistance movements," (Ranger, 1968).

In so far as the warrior tradition continues to find expression in the verbal bellicosity and excessive military spending of some African leaders, it is a suicidal mockery, effectively destroying any hope of sound economic development and threatening nobody except fellow Africans, whether inside or outside the states which perpetrate it. Now that effective warriorhood depends directly on economic strength, which is Africa's greatest weakness, martial posturing becomes a transparent exercise in vain machismo.

Furthermore, the African peoples whose poverty and economic backwardness are exploited to perpetuate the sentimental warrior image, on cinema and television screens, in game parks and tourist shows, or white men's entertainments in South African mine and factory compounds, are not for the most part even those who posed the greatest military threat to the establishment of the Pax Colonia, nor yet those who in the previous era had been themselves the most successful warriors in military expansion. They are, rather, those who have been left high and dry in inaccessible and inhospitable areas, far from the sources of new wealth, power and change, so that *faute de mieux*, their primal existence has continued colorful and unchanged.

There are deep and insidious dangers, as well as intellectual fallacies, in fostering the warrior image as a positive symbol in contemporary Africa and, as an example of it, flattering Field Marshal Hajji Idi Amin Dada as a mystical heir of Shaka the Zulu. Prancing about with tanks and guns may be a suitable posture for a charismatic army commander inspiring his soldiers in combat situations, – a General Patton seriously playing a boyish game as a grown man at the right moment, – but it is totally inappropriate for the head of a poor nation, as even Amin has increasingly had to discover, and as Nasser, Nimeiry, Boumedienne, Mobutu, Gowon and other African Soldier leaders had done before him, not to speak of Castro in Cuba or Suharto in Indonesia.

It is too early to tell clearly whether, or in what respects, Amin will destroy Uganda, (as the Economic War appears to be doing so far), but to justify Amin by certain positive and mostly unintended results of his rule would be like the German people justifying Hitler and eulogizing their own defeat on the grounds that Hitler restored their ethnic and racial pride, wounded in World War I, and that their destruction in World War II enabled them to rebuild their economy as the most powerful productive machine in Europe. The ultimate threat to Amin must come from within the warrior tradition which he has tried to revive. As highly educated and technically expert young officers come back from training in Russia or Libya they are bound in the end to insist on taking over the régime and introducing a more genuine modernization and efficiency, provided they are not all systematically eliminated on their return for this very reason, as has already been rumoured.

The Amin-Shaka identification commits the error of confusing the three domains which Social Scientists have always had to keep clearly distinct for analytic purposes: the personality system, the cultural system and the Social System.

There is also the empirical error that the Warrior Image does not, in fact, appear to be important in African states today. Soldier statesmen have not used it, as already pointed out. A Zairois scholar has characterized the successful image construction of General Mobutu Sese Seko Waza Banga (to give him his full, though fabricated name, as it must be used in Zaire, though rarely elsewhere) as *la deification d'un chef*. Even more recently, Mobutu has made it quite plain that his Party has, indeed, taken the place of the church. The images of chief, of divine King, of mystical supernatural power, are those which seem to be more often used. The naked power is palpable enough in many African states today. What it needs, even from the cold perspective of power maintenance, is not further emphasis by Warrior imagery, but sanctification. Of course, the images which are projected internally and externally need to be carefully distinguished and separately manipulated.

President Jomo Kenyatta, despite his radical and revolutionary past, dress-

es up in leopard skin robes which obviously hint at the results of coronation.[1]
Perhaps to suggest that he is the mystical heir of the Nuer leopard skin chief
would be less far fetched than the Amin-Shaka analogy. President Kamuzu
Banda of Malawi is said to open his allocutions with the utterance "I am not
only Banda" – followed by a pause generating excited expectancy, – "I am
Kamuzu." Kamuzu in the Cewa language is said to suggest "doctor", with that
powerful ambiguity which covers not only Banda's medical career in Scotland,
which is no longer highly relevant to his present role, but the much more
telling African image of the personage with mystical and supernatural as well
as curative powers.[2] Examples could be multiplied. Heads of state who survive,
which implies successful elimination of competitors, wish to develop a father
image which, I would argue, is radically different from the warrior image, and
is calculated rather to dress the wolf in sheep's clothing than to reveal his teeth
and claws. Thus we have the erudite scholar-poet father in Léopold Sédar
Senghor and the benignly providing capitalist father in Félix Houphouet-
Boigny. Needless to say, the warrior image is totally inappropriate to states with
serious socialist goals, such as Tanzania or Guinea. One need hardly recall
that neither Russia nor China ever place warrior symbols or personages at the
pinnacle of power, and that Marshal Tito never stressed his warrior qualities.

I believe there is a deep and general significance to this. There is not space
to develop the argument fully here, and it is done elsewhere, but it can be
shown with very far flung evidence that in the long evolution of political
society there is a general change in the quality of emphasis on ritual and political
factors. In societies where the relationship between technology and natural
resources is such that very little surplus can be mobilized as a basis for centralized power, ritual beliefs, practices and institutions provide the widest scale
basis of order and solidarity and the major sanctions which support them.
Where richer resources and more efficient technology makes possible the
mobilization of a firm material base for centralized power, that power obviously
becomes more purely political and less ritual in its mechanisms and its sanctions,
so that ritual concepts and practices are employed more to sanitize and sanctify
the already firmly established power system than to provide its main support. It
naturally follows from this that in many political systems ambivalent expression
is given symbolically to these two variously balanced aspects.

Thus the Alur chief, whose power and resources were severely limited, but
who certainly laid claim to all the political authority he could, was ambivalently
regarded: on the one hand as ng'u (lion or leopard), a ferocious, carnivorous
beast capable of tearing people to pieces and destroying them if angered or
slighted. In real life he acted in this capacity, either when besought by petitioners whose claims he wished to support and enforce, or when he felt his own
authority and honor grossly flouted. In either case he would mobilize persons

---

1   At the time of writing, the Sunday Times of London reports that Kenyans now popularly
    and habitually refer to Kenyatta and his close kin and affines as "The Royal Family".
2   See Philip Short (1974) Banda, pp. 87, 89, 316.

and groups most loyal to himself and attracted by the prospect of plunder, as well as factions and groups supporting the petitioners and naturally disposed to act against their enemies. With such a composite force he would go to the scene of dispute and settle it by adjudication or by coercion as required, living off the country meanwhile. The point was that the chief's judgment and power to enforce it were felt by his people to be sometimes indispensable, but both plaintiff and defendant, together with all their local groups, suffered gravely from invoking it. They would have much of their stock of food and livestock consumed, quite apart from the fine which a guilty party and his kin would have to pay, usually in cattle and women. So the chief's authority was regarded as necessary, but feared, and never lightly invoked. But on the other hand, the chief was equally essentially regarded in quite a different light, as the sacredly ritualized embodiment and guarantor of the harmonious balance of man and nature, of the benign climatic balance of rain and sun, making the earth fruitful and bringing sustenance and fertility to animals and man.

Fanon has emphasized the sanctifying and ritualizing of contemporary African leadership by invoking and trying to re-enact the hallowed unity of the struggle for independence, but with no suggestion of recapturing a precolonial warrior tradition. He insists that leaders invoke the glories of the past, not as a stimulant to restore manhood to action, but rather as a diversionary soporific to evade the present. "The leader pacifies the people......we see him reassessing the history of independence and recalling the sacred unity of the struggle for liberation. The leader......asks the people to fall back into the past and to become drunk on the remembrance of the epoch which led up to independence During the struggle for liberation the leader awakened the people and promised them a forward march, heroic and unmitigated. To-day, he uses every means to put them to sleep, and three or four times a year asks them to remember the colonial period and to look back on the long way they have come since then. Now it must be said that the masses show themselves totally incapable of appreciating the long way they have come. The peasant who goes on scratching out a living from the soil, and the unemployed man who never finds employment do not manage, in spite of public holidays and flags, new and brightly colored though they may be, to convince themselves that anything has really changed in their lives" (1967, 135–6).

The irrelevance of the warrior tradition in contemporary Africa is clearly shown by a glance at the fortunes of reputed warrior peoples during the last century or so. In Uganda there is no doubt about the unanimous opinion of early European travellers that the Baganda and the Banyoro were essentially fighting peoples, nations of warriors, as Ashe (1889, 1970, 295) said of the former. Yet, in opposite ways the warrior tradition proved useless, or disastrous, in both cases. The Banyoro under their warrior King Kabarega in fact put up the only significantly strong resistance to British conquest and occupation of any Ugandan people. The result was a long guerilla war (Thomas & Scott, 1935, 34–38) with the eventual defeat and exile of the King and the ruin of Bunyoro society from which it has not recovered to this day. It lost the greater part of its territory, it was for thirty years denied the honors and privileges granted to other kingdoms in Uganda and it went into an economic, cultural and demographic decline as though its people had simply lost heart. They gained a moral and political victory with the return of part of its lost territory from Buganda in 1964, (Southall, 1975, 93–6) thereby precipitating the crisis which led directly to the dismantling of the Buganda Kingdom. The Banyoro are no worse off than any other ethnic group in Uganda today, but there is absolutely no sign of their old warrior tradition and no hint that it could be of any value to them if there were.

The warrior tradition of the Baganda stood them in very good stead at first, as their generals and armies were used by the British to subdue the rest of Uganda. But, throughout Africa, the states which made the best deals with the colonial powers at the establishment of colonial rule provided the greatest obstruction to the attainment of political independence in the 1950s and 1960s. Buganda, Ashanti, Sokoto and Barotse are all good examples. After 1900 the Baganda soon lost their warrior reputation completely in exchange for that of education, professional advancement and large scale farming. The attempt of the Kabaka to use ex-servicemen in 1963 and his courageous but hopeless resistance in the second Battle of Mengo on 24th May, 1966, were both disastrous failures in the end ('King Freddie', 1967, 168–9). Not only has no one regarded the Baganda as warriors, or fighters, for many decades, – quite the contrary, – but both their material advancement and any possible psychological rehabilitation and regaining of confidence which may be desirable for them, lie in quite different directions.

No other Ugandan peoples put up concerted or effective resistance to British penetration, although there were many local and sporadic outbreaks like the so-called Lamogi Rebellion in Acholi in 1911 (Adimola, 1954) or the Nyabingi Movement in Kigezi during the first quarter of this century, (Hopkins 1971), all requiring punitive expeditions to be mounted against them but all suppressed without serious difficulty.

In the First World War, as is well known, East Africans were used, and lost their lives, in large numbers, but as porters rather than as warriors. By the Second World War the colonial stereotypes of the divergent propensities of the various Ugandan peoples had crystallized and some of the northern peoples, expecially the Acholi, were sentimentally regarded as warriors by Europeans because of their good record of service in the King's African Rifles. By the post-war period the peoples of Karamoja began to show up prominently as by-passed by the economic development and social change occurring in the rest of Uganda. They still had nothing but their cattle, which they had to defend, naked, with their spears against raids from the Suk and Turkana in Kenya. Unbeknown to them, they began to provide the prototypical image of the noble savage in the latter day colonial system, an image appropriately confused with those of the exhilarating wide open spaces, big game hunting, the development of game parks and the tourist's Africa.

This type of warrior image has to be considered as part of the genre although there is something pathetic and false about it. It is clearly incompatible with economic development. Only those who had no cash crops and no other attractive avenues to wealth were willing to go into the army or to stand on one leg leaning on their spears by the roads leading to the game parks to collect tips from passing tourists.

The point at which most African peoples began to regain their confidence in themselves and their future, not of course on the basis of their old ethnic groupings but on the larger scale of the new nation, was when the post war politicians began to organize effectively to "fight" for self government and independence. But they neither fought as warriors nor in the image of warriors. They suffered harassment and imprisonment but they never attempted to fight as warriors, either in image or reality. As everyone knows, the struggle for *uhuru* in most of Africa during the 1950s and 1960s was remarkably peaceful, though not without suffering or heroism. This was because the colonial authorities were by this time prepared to opt, if pressed, for a new type of less direct control. Of course, all political movements, all election candidates, use some of the metaphors of fighting and struggle, but this has nothing to do with the warrior tradition. The more violent examples, Mau Mau in Kenya, the Simba in Zaire, the Zanzibar revolution, the rebellion in Madagascar and the guerilla movements in Algeria, Guinea-Bissau and Southern Africa, will be considered later.

The exception which proves the rule in the Uganda case is that of the one ethnic group without a territorial base in the country: the Nubi. I have told the story of the Nubi in some detail (1975) and only wish to point out that they are the only group in Uganda who can be said to have maintained a continuous warrior tradition since the nineteenth century, because they were forced into it by a strange concatenation of events and kept in it by British policy which tended to keep them isolated from other advantageous outlets. So the oppression of Uganda by the army with its strong Nubi core is the strongest case for the relevance of the warrior tradition in Africa today, but not one which will commend itself greatly to most scholars, inside or outside Africa. Even here, although the bitter joke has worn thin, let us not forget Amin's frequently reiterated and never retracted assertions that his régime is a temporary caretaker government cleaning up the country in preparation for a return to civilian rule. Thus, even where the warrior tradition reigns supreme, it lacks the self-confidence to declare itself as such. Indeed, the image of the simple soldier which Amin suffers from the world press is hardly the one of his own free choice. On the other hand, it is hardly convincing to suggest that Amin's posturing has restored the damaged ego and wounded masculinity of Ugandan men, for he has emasculated more than he has rendered potent.

It may thus be said that in Uganda none of the warrior traditions of the peoples of the country survived, or proved of any practical use or psychological value. The only warrior tradition which did have continuity during the colonial period was one essentially foreign to the country, which, on achieving supremacy in the coup of 1971, has steadily led the country to new depths of degradation and underdevelopment. Of course, this is a delicate issue. The understandable desire to keep the ranks closed has prevented most African leaders or scholars, with a few prominent exceptions such as Nyerere and Kaunda, from openly criticizing Amin until recently. There is no reportage of actual events inside Uganda any more except by the process of rumor mongering, which is itself a capital offence. The only possible criticism by Ugandans is by refugees, since they could not critize inside and remain alive. As long ago as May 1973 Joseph Kityo wrote in Africa Magazine (p. 7) that while to Africans outside Uganda Idi Amin is great, a true revolutionary, to be supported by all black people throughout the world, to Ugandans he has devalued the African Revolution, quarrelled with all his five African neighbors and kept in power by intimidation and systematic elimination of educated Ugandans.

Kenya had no traditional states or centralized societies of any significant power and therefore no warrior traditions of any significance in opposing European penetration. But the foreigner's romantic image of the noble savage warrior has nowhere been more powerful than in Kenya, sustained by the outsider's perception of its warlike cattle nomads, symbolized most strikingly in the always photogenic Masai, but also fed by the other Nilotic and Cushitic pastoralists: the Galla, Rendille and Somali; the Turkana; the Kipsigis, Nandi, Suk (Pokot), Tugen (Kamasia), Elgeyo and Marakwet, – all peoples of the newly emerged colonial tribe of Kalenjin (Southall, 1970).

Undoubtedly these peoples would have chosen to continue their traditional way of life largely as it was, had they been offered a genuine choice in the matter in the 1890's, but their interests were in conflict with those of the new masters. The Masai, who ranged over vast areas of good pasture and some good arable, including fine forests also, were swindled of over half their territory and cut into three parts, divided from their Samburu brothers in the north by the White Highlands and from the Tanganyika Masai by the colonial boundary. Apart from the Kipsigis, who were assisted in transforming themselves into highly productive mixed farmers by the 1950's, most of the other pastoralists were disarmed as much as possible, forcefully deprived of their surplus cattle from time to time in the name of anti-erosion measures, and otherwise permitted to continue with little change. The attempt to force them into wage labor on European farms was largely a failure, except for small numbers of cattle herds and grooms. The fact was that the European warrior image of the Kenya pastoralist served many useful purposes. It convinced the rulers that they were justified in putting their lands to more commercial use as European farms, since the noble warriors were too conservative to change or progress. The romantic idealization of the Masai as beautiful but impossible people fitted the policy of isolating them and leaving them relatively free of interference within the limits of their reduced territory, the prohibition of warfare and the payment of tax. This hands off policy reflected and to some extent salved the guilt feelings of an administration which knew that it had broken its word (Leys, 1924, cap. IV).

It is significant that the Kikuyu did not share in this expatriate warrior tradition, and were never looked upon as noble warriors by the colonial administration, but rather as crafty thieves. They did, of course, share a form of generation cycling and age-grading system with the pastoralists, which did inculcate the values of courage and fortitude and was a mechanism of mobilization for defense against the Masai. But it is important to note that the conventional translation of the young men's grades as junior and senior warriors is a mistranslation which is useful for the European warrior myth. The vernacular term *moran* used for these grades by the Masai, Samburu and Kalenjin peoples does not mean warrior.

The Kikuyu reaction to European control was quite different from the start. It owed nothing to the indigenous warrior tradition, which was neither appealed to by them as a focus of solidarity nor attributed to them by Europeans. The precise links between the new secular resisters like Harry Thuku and the more traditionalist defense of clitoridectomy, is a matter of debate, but the two were clearly fused together to some extent in the organization of independent churches, schools and resistence movements which later blossomed into Mau Mau.

Obviously there was an important warrior imagery in Mau Mau, but it was the modern imagery of General China with its oriental leftist echo, rather than any direct appeal to a warrior tradition in the age organization, although the culture of oathing and the mechanism of mobilization and organization certainly had some kind of continuity with the former age organization which was otherwise generally defunct by then.

The Mau Mau movement, despite its broad potentialities, was successfully contained by the colonial security forces, so that, however nationalist its aims may have been and however much sympathy other ethnic groups in Kenya may have had with them, Mau Mau never in fact succeeded in becoming a movement of national resistance in Kenya. It remained an essentially Kikuyu movement at its core, as was finally proved in the awful moment of truth when Kenyatta himself, as nationalist leader, had to disown it again and again, like St. Peter, and suppress the forest freedom fighters.

In Kenya, therefore, there was a kind of warrior tradition and there was a powerful European warrior myth, but it was not only irrelevant to the nationalist movement, playing no part in the effective rehabilitation of the African ego, it was actually one of the psychological props perpetuating the colonial system. Kenyatta's choice of his picture as a Kikuyu "warrior" dressed in a monkey skin and fingering his spear, when he published Facing Mount Kenya in 1938 only heightens the contrast with the image which he sedulously fostered thirty years later as Head of State, when he became a Kikuyu *elder, not warrior*, on informal occasions and on formal ones quite obviously a monarch in his leopard skin head-dress and regal robes.

The Europeans accorded something of a warrior image to the Kamba also, not simply from their prominence in the King's African Rifles, but also because of their reputation for manual dexterity and mechanical skill, which also stood them in good stead as soldiers, as well as in the great railway workshops of

Nairobi and in their pioneering of the East African trade in wood carvings. (Elkan 1958). The strong association of the Kamba with the army has been maintained to this day, with conspicuous representation in the higher ranks of the Officer Corps, but far from being the basis of a warrior tradition to be fostered and encouraged, it has been one of those delicate problems of potential alternative centers of power which President Kenyatta has had to use all his manoeuvering skill to contain and defuse.

In Tanzania also it is equally plain that there was no continuity in the warrior tradition through the colonial to the *uhuru* period, nor was there any attempt to resucitate it. On the contrary, it was precisely those peoples who had some claim to a genuine warrior tradition, like the Hehe, who under their ruler Mkwawa had led the fiercest resistance to the German conquest, who presented Julius Nyerere with the most delicate problem of incorporation. Mkwawa's skull was brought back home with honor from a German museum and his descendant was given high office, but it was very clear that the Hehe warrior tradition was only a threat, not a strength, to modern Tanzania. In the Zanzibar revolution self-styled Field Marshal John Okello's soldier image was fleeting, sadly almost comical, soon superseded by the quite different militant image of the proletarian left.

We do not find the warrior image invoked or effective anywhere in Africa today. It is only in the most oppressive, isolated, non-ideological and economically retrograde states, such as Amin's Uganda or Bokassa's Central African Republic that a blood thirsty warrior image, *faute de mieux*, comes closest to relevance. But its more bizarre expressions have been satyrically pilloried by a Kenyan humorist: "But Joe", I said, "this business of cutting off ears – I thought that was done and gone hundreds of years ago." "That's why it has to be resurrected," Joe said. "You forget that President Bokassa is an African socialist whose pride is in African traditions... Modern African socialists must copy African traditions because that is the only way they can fulfil their Africanness. They must cut off a thief's something. Being socialists, they cannot cut off a person's hands, for that would interfere with his productivity. So they cut off his ears, since these in a socialist society are purely of ornamental value" (Hilary Ng'weno, 1972).

The military right stresses the divine king image or the Sandhurst gentleman. The civilian right stresses an almost imperial dignity with the underlying suggestion of supernatural powers. Both military and civilian left are committed, – as long as they remain true, – to essentially secular, non-traditional images.

But it may well be thought that in the African guerilla movements we have the real thread of continuity in the warrior tradition. This would be a misinterpretation. Ben Bella and Boumedienne in Algeria, Cabral in Guinea Bissau, Mondlane and Samora Machel in Mozambique, Sithole in Zimbabwe, do not invoke warrior traditions. Not only would warrior traditions have been divisive, because they refer to specific ethnic groups which guerilla leaders are trying to weld together into larger nationalist entities, but they have all been looking forward rather than backward and, even when they did not begin that way, have been forced by the geo-political logic of their situation to look left for help and inspiration, so that their models have had to be Castro and Che Guevara and Mao-tse-tung, or even the Palestine Liberation Movements and the Irish Republican Army, but not Shaka the Zulu. Equally obviously Shaka has not provided inspiration, example, or moral strength to Nelson Mandela and the underground resistance in the Republic of South Africa. It is rather in the mines and big factories and the tourist parks that White South Africa keeps alive, in travesty, the image of the Zulu Warrior. In these contexts, where the Black South African *industrial worker* is induced to perform as a colorful dancing warrior, he serves to emphasize how harmless and irrelevant the warrior tradition of the old Africa is, while at the same time deluding the White visitor that he is happy in his degradation.

Analogies between the personal destinies or weaknesses of Shaka and Amin are fascinating and worthwhile as a literary, symbolic exercise, but they have no empirical, historical, psychological or political link with one another or with contemporary Africa. Outside the literary field, the warrior tradition is a dangerous toy to play with. Lacking any ideological anchor it degenerates easily into fascism, but worst of all is its technological atavism and anachronism. The effective warrior of today, in nuclear submarine, supersonic fighter plane or heavy bomber is not a terribly moral or desirable image to foster in any case, but certainly in Africa its fruits are poverty, dependency and bloodshed.

For the visible future, despite the shift in the geo-political balance of the world wrought by the oil crisis, Black Africa will remain relatively weak in sophisticated military force. For the moment Black Africa has a phony, somewhat illusory yet highly significant influence through her still increasing bloc of votes at the United Nations. However, this phony strength is a product of the fundamental weakness of Africa's disunity. To blame this on the imperial powers may be psychologically comforting but will in no way increase Africa's strength. In historical reality, the imperial powers left Africa composed of larger political units than they found, although they destroyed most of the largest states of the old Africa and in some cases finally sabotaged larger political entities such as the federations of French West and French Equatorial Africa. The inescapable point is that the indigenous peoples of Africa are quite numerous enough and their territory and resources quite large and varied enough to provide ample markets for every kind of large scale manufacturing in both light and heavy industry. If Africa were united she could be quite as self sufficient as China. Blaming neocolonialism for disunity is unhelpful, however true, for without the collusion of African leaders neocolonialism would be relatively impotent. The potency of African men and African peoples will be restored when Africa unites and stands on its own feet despite all external opposition and internal sabotage. Resuscitating warrior traditions will delay not hasten this victory.

POSTSCRIPT

The recent self-elevation of Jean Bedel, later Salah Eddine Bou-kassa, into the Emperor Bokassa I, further strengtkens my argument (Jeune Afrique, 832, 17 December 1976, 19),

REFERENCES

ADIMOLA, A. B.
    1954   "The Lamogi Rebellion of 1911–12", *Uganda Journal*, 18, 2, 166–177.
Africa Magazine, 28, Great Queen Street, London, W.C.2.
ASHE, R. P.
    1970   *Two Kings of Uganda, or, Life by the Shores of Victoria Nyanza, being an account of a residence of six years in Eastern Equatorial Africa*, Cass. (1st publ. 1889).
Banda, Hastings Kamuzu, biography by Philip Short, q.v.
ELKAN, Walter
    1958   "The East African Trade in Woodcarvings", *Africa*, 28, 4, 314–24.
FANON, Frantz
    1967   *The Wretched of the Earth* (1st publ. 1961), Penguin Books.
HOPKINS, E.
    1970   *The Nyabingi Movement of Southwestern Uganda*. Robert J. Rotberg and Ali A. Mazrui (eds.) Protest and Power in Black Africa, 258–357, Oxford University Press.
KENYATTA, Jomo
    1938, 1961   *Facing Mount Kenya, the tribal life of the Gikuyu*, with an introduction by B. Malinowski.
"King Freddie"
    1967   Desecration of My Kingdom, Constable.
LEYS, Norman
    1924   *Kenya*, Hogarth.
NG'WENO, Hilary
    1972   In: *The Daily Nation*, August 7. Nairobi.
RANGER, T. O.
    1968   "Connexions between "Primary Resistance" Movements and Modern Mass Nationalism in East and Central Africa." *Journal of African History*, 3, 437–453; 4, 631–41.
SHORT, Philip
    1974   *Banda*, Routledge and Kegan Paul.
SOUTHALL, A. W.
    1970   The Illusion of Tribe", *Journ. Asian and African Studies*, 5, 1–2, 28–50.
    1975   General Amin and the Coup: Great Man or Historica l Inevitability?" *Journ. Mod. African Studies*, 13, 1, 85–105.
THOMAS, H. B. and R. SCOTT
    1935   *Uganda*, Oxford University Press.

SECTION IV:
THE WARRIOR AND LIBERATION

Gandhi, Marx and the Warrior Tradition

Towards Androgynous Liberation

ALI A. MAZRUI

The University of Michigan, Ann Arbor, U.S.A.

IN THE STRUGGLE for equality and liberation in this century three forms of resistance have been particularly important in Eastern and Southern Africa. One form is rooted in indigenous culture and has sought comfort in African symbols and drawn inspiration from African heroes. This is the form of resistance associated with the warrior tradition.

The second form of struggle has been partly inspired by the whole tradition of passive resistance as dramatized by the techniques used by Mohandas Gandhi against white racism in South Africa and British imperialism in India.

The third form of struggle has been inspired by the Marxist revolutionary tradition and has so far found its most successful fulfilment in the former Portuguese colonies of Mozambique, Guinea-Bissau and Angola.

The warrior tradition was at play in some of the very earliest instances of resistance against the penetration of the white man in Southern Africa. These early struggles are now sometimes referred to in the literature as cases of "Primary resistance".

Partly as a result of stimulation provided by the Dar es Salaam School of African History, increased attention has recently been paid to this phase of "primary resistance" when Africa first had to confront western intrusion. The argument of scholars like Terrence Ranger for Eastern Africa and Michael Crowder for Western Africa identifies those early armed challenges by Africans against colonial rule as the very origins of modern nationalism in the continent.[1] By this argument Tanzania's ruling party and its function as a liberating force has for its ancestry both the Maji Maji and the pre-Maji rebellions against German rule from the 1880's onwards. African struggles against colonial rule did not begin with modern political parties and western trained intellectuals, but originated in those early "primary resisters" with their spears poised against western military technology.

---

1 Consult especially T. O. Ranger, "Connexions between 'Primary Resistance' Movements and Modern Mass Nationalism in East and Central Africa," Parts I and II, *Journal of African History*, Vol. IX, Nos. 3 & 4, 1968, pp. 437–453; and pp. 631–641.

This author is basically in sympathy with the Dar es Salaam School of African historiography, but with one important difference. While the Dar es Salaam historiography regards the Nkrumahs and Nyereres of modern Africa as the true heirs of those primary resisters, we believe that it is much more the liberation fighters in southern Africa that have really carried the mantle of the original primary resisters.

But it is more the fighters in the field rather than the westernised leaders who have shown affinity with Africa's ancestral combat culture. The rural recruits into liberation movements have often been steeped in traditional norms and perspectives. Their concepts of valour and honour, their conceptions of solidarity and loyality, have all been partly conditioned by important aspects of African culture. That is one major reason why "tribalism" or ethnicity has been so resistent among liberation fighters in Southern Africa, especially in Angola and Zimbabwe (Rhodesia).

Historians have used the term "primary resistance" chronologically, applying it to the earliest times of confrontation between the indigenous fighter and the foreign intruder.

But it is at least as defensible to use the term "primary resistance" in a *cultural* rather than a chronological sense. In this cultural meaning primary resistance could be taking place today – provided it is a form of resistance which draws its "primary inspiration" from indigenous symbols and values. The Mau Mau insurrection was therefore in part a case of primary resistance in this cultural sense although chronologically it took place almost on the eve of Kenya's independence. Similarly UNITA (The National Union for the Total Independence of Angola) was nearer to being an instance of primary resistance in its use of indigenous values and symbols than was MPLA (the Popular Movement for the Liberation of Angola). This was partly because UNITA was much more of a rural movement than MPLA.

If we accept this cultural sense of "primary" we may then relate the warrior tradition to *primary resistance*, the Gandhian tradition to *passive resistance* and the Marxist tradition to *revolutionary resistance*.

In earlier chapters we examined linkages between military and sexual symbols. Virility and valour were often intertwined in cultural terms.

In this chapter we have to note that primary resistance is connected with masculinity, passive resistance with feminine techniques and revolutionary resistance with *both*. The warrior tradition once again asserts its manliness, Mahatma Gandhi displays feminine virtues and Karl Marx becomes a prophet of androgyny or sexual parity.

Let us examine these three dimensions as we relate them to the African struggle for social justice in its wider implications.

Masculine Warriorhood and Primary Resistance

The Mau Mau movement, in rebellion against British rule and white settler occupation of African land in Kenya, constituted the first major resurrection of the warrior tradition in recent East African history. The Kikuyu mobilized themselves into armed rebellion against European settlerdom. The Kikuyu fighters in the forests and the hills of the Aberdares became for a while true heirs of that heritage of primary resistance. The Kikuyu went back to reactivate primeval symbolism, and resurrect important elements of traditional Kikuyu virtues as a basis for establishing a military solidarity against the colonial presence in Kenya.

The connection between martial symbolism and sexual symbolism remains a major aspect of the oath of allegiance demanded from the Mau Mau warriors. We have details of the Batuni oath. The new warrior initiate was first stripped naked, and seated facing the oath administrator. Then a long strip of goat's meat was placed around the neck of the new initiate. One end lay across the chest of the naked man and the other dropped down his back around his waist several times, and then between his legs. The new initiate was ordered to hold this end of the goat's meat up against his penis. On the floor were the two eyes of an uncastrated he-goat, called a "Kihei". The word itself meant "uncircumcised youth", but paradoxically it was used during the Mau Mau insurrection to refer to a man who had taken the Batuni oath.

The oath itself did not demand total sexual abstinence, but forbade the use of prostitutes and the seduction of "other men's women". These particular prohibitions were to discourage the danger of betrayal by temporary sexual companions, such as prostitutes. They were also designed to discourage the warriors from fighting with each other over women. But once the Mau Mau fighters were in the forests, total sexual abstinence was demanded among some groups. And in some of the detention camps, where the possibility of having intercourse with women detainees was possible, special codes were self-imposed by the detainees against sexual relations while they were all behind bars.[2]

The Mau Mau did use aspects of that old discipline which Shaka had demanded of his own warriors but the movement did not push the particular discipline to total extremes.

There were other instances in the Mau Mau movement linking sexual with martial symbolism including the use of menstrual blood for certain oath-taking ceremonies in at least some sections of the movement. What was happening was an attempt to provide a sense of sacred awe to counterbalance belief in the invincibility of the white man which the colonial experience had so far consolidated. Let us remind ourselves that the warrior tradition earlier in the century had been badly damaged by two terrors which had come with the white man – the terror of gunfire and the terror of hellfire. The terror of gunfire was what the new military technology of the white man was all about. Those early primary resisters against the European intrusion discovered before long

---

2 Consult Karigo Munch, *The Hard Core* (Richmond, B.C., Canada: LSM Information Center, 1973), pp. 19, 22, 43; Don Barnett and Karari Njama, *Mau Mau from Within* (New York and London: Monthly Review Press, 1966), and J. M. Kariuki, '*Mau Mau*' *Detainee* (London: Oxford University Press, 1963).

the overwhelming superiority of the cannon as against the spear, the gun as against the bow and arrow. In the words of the English writer, Hillaire Belloc:

> "Whatever happens we have got
> The Maxim gun, and they have not."[3]

European technology soon overrode and demoralized the resisters. The new terror of gunfire initiated the decline in the warrior tradition.

The decline was reinforced by the terror of hellfire which came with Christianity. Death for millions of Africans was now given a new meaning. African ancestors were cut down to size, denounced as insignificant by the missionaries of the new religious order. A new god was proclaimed, and a new fear of damnation was propounded. Some African Christians, like many other Christians before them, accepted the concept of hellfire at its face value; others equated it simply with the threat of damnation after death. Whatever interpretation, literal or symbolic, the new religion had come with a new system of punishment and rewards. The power of all indigenous beliefs began to decline; the authority of the village medicine man was struggling against the challenges of local missionary schools. The old order was partially disintegrating – and with it, the warrior tradition.

Movements like that of Mau Mau had to invent new forms of ritualized damnation in order to outweigh the combined demasculating effect of the fear of the white man's gunfire and the Christian priest's hellfire.

Christianity had in addition damaged the warrior tradition in Africa by proclaiming the ethic of "turning the other cheek". Meekness was regarded as a virtue even for otherwise virile and valiant men. A version of Christianity which had hardly even been truly implemented in Europe, and which had in part become anachronistic on its home ground, was now bequeathed to African school-children and peasants. The god of love was mobilized behind the task of "imperial pacification." The message of Christianity discouraged Africans not only from fighting each other but also from resisting the colonial presence.

Again, a movement like Mau Mau had to help Kikuyu Christians transcend the conditioning of "turning the other cheek," as well as overcome the terror of external Christian damnation. Those oaths of Mau Mau combining sexual symbolism with militant commitment were part of the process of countering the demasculating consequences of the colonial experience.

The Mau Mau movement was militarily defeated by the British. But it was clearly a victory of the vanquished. The political triumph went to the African people, even if the military successes were retained by the colonial people. The stranglehold of the white settlers on Kenya was at last broken and before long Kenya was preparing for independence.

The Mau Mau movement was also the first great African liberation move-

---

3   Stavrianos links Belloc's cynical observation and the literature of self-righteous power to Social Darwinism as an ideological movement. See L. S. Stavrianos, *Man's Past and Present: A Global History* (Englewood Cliffs, N.J.: Prentice Hall, 1971), pp. 270–273.

ment of the modern period. All the efforts which are now being made in Southern Africa to consolidate resistance, organize sabotage, and seek to dispel white power and privilege, have for their heroic ancestry that band of fighters in the Aberdare forest of Kenya. The warrior tradition was at least temporarily revived at a critical moment in Kenya's history.

The revival of primordial symbolism – which was so striking in the history of Mau Mau – has also been discerned in more subtle forms in the struggle for the liberation of Rhodesia since Ian Smith unilaterally declared its "independence" in 1965. As in the case of Mau Mau, a return to cultural ancestry has included in Zimbabwe a return to aspects of indigenous religion as well. Hostility to Christianity has also reared its head among the liberation fighters. In the rural areas the internecine fighting among the rival nationalist parties has included the burning of churches. And many a young man has re-established contact with the experience of spirit possession.[4]

Basil Davidson has also drawn our attention to the fact that an oath taken by guerrillas in the names of the great spirits of Chaminuka and Nehanda forms part of a "truly impressive" continuity.[5]

The Zimbabwe nationalist, Nathan Shamuyarira, has also observed the effort often made to give meaning to the Zimbabwe struggle through the utilization of the African heritage itself.

> "In rural areas meetings become political gatherings and more..., the past heritage was revived through prayers and traditional singing, ancestral spirits were evoked to guide and lead the new nation. Christianity and civilization took a back seat and new forms of worship and new attitudes were thrust forward dramatically..., the spirit pervading the meetings was African and the desire was to put the twentieth century in the African context."[6]

A grandson of a rebel leader killed in 1897 invoked the memory of Chaminuka, the great prophet who provided the focus of Shona solidarity in the nineteenth century.

Joshua Nkomo, the Zimbabwe leader, on arrival back home from abroad in 1962, was met at the airport by a survivor of the 1896–9 rebellion. He presented a spirit axe to symbolize the martial succession and the transmission of the warrior torch.[7]

In their campaign in northern parts of Rhodesia more recently the liberation fighters have reportedly shown respect for traditional beliefs and customs, and this has helped the movement to build a more effective infrastructure of

---

4   Reverend S. Madziyere "Heathen Practices in the Urban and Rural Parts of Marandellaz Area," *Themes in the Christian History of Central Africa*, eds. T. O. Ranger and John Weller (London, 1975), pp. 76–82. I am greatly indebted to Professor Ranger for stimulation and for bibliographical guidance.

5   Basil Davidson, *The Africans: An Entry to Cultural History* (London, 1969), p. 255.

6   N. S. Shamuyarira, *Crisis in Rhodesia* (London, 1965) pp. 68–9.

7   Shamuyarira, *ibid*. See also Ranger, Connections between 'Primary Resistance Movements and Modern Mass Nationalism in East and Central Africa," Part II, *op. cit.* pp. 635–6.

popular support. Some of the campaign zones have at times been named after senior spirit mediums. Indeed, some of those mediums have been known to operate from guerilla camps. The link between the warrior and the prophet has often been permitted to persist in these movements. Manliness, valour and some degree of ancestral devoutness have gone alongside the spirit of modern liberation.

Feminized Warriorhood and Passive Resistance

Almost inevitably the strong connection between masculinity and warfare has resulted in a similar connection between kindliness and femininity. The example of Gandhi we mentioned earlier is certainly a case in point. The great prophet of nonviolence found himself torn between serving as a father figure and acting as a mother symbol. At a more personal level Gandhi had played this second role for a young orphan girl named Manu. The girl had previously been adopted by Gandhi's wife Kasturba. Kasturba on her death bed had asked her husband to take her place as a mother to Manu. Gandhi took this role so seriously that he assumed the task of teaching the girl about womanhood, and watching her physical development, and later actually sharing a bed with her as if Gandhi was another woman. The young woman's memoirs captured this strong maternalism in Gandhi's relationship with her when she entitled her book, *Bapu, My Mother*.[8]

Erikson points to a "persistent importance in Gandhi's life of the theme of motherhood, both in the sense of a need to be a perfect and pure mother, and in the sense of a much less acknowledged need to be held and reassured, especially at the time of his infinite loneliness." But to the extent that the loneliness might have been aggravated by a long period of sexual renunciation, we have in the story of Gandhi an illustration of the tense relationship between celibacy and masculinity, nonviolence and manliness.

The same problem arises with regard to Christianity. Is Christianity, in the ultimate analysis, a feminine religion? Does the centrality of forgiveness make the Christian God less manly than the Jewish Jehovah? Is the transition from the Old Testament to the New Testament a process of the demasculation of God? Does the centrality of love as a divine attribute make the Christian God less manly than Islam's Allah? Before he was assassinated and became a black martyr, Martin Luther King was sometimes denounced by some of his more militant black critics as "Martin Luther Queen."[9]

What we have in these questions is the prior question of whether certain symbols are counter-phallic. Are there aspects of Christian imagery which go almost purposefully against phallic symbols without being sexually neutral?

---

8 Manubehn Gandhi, *Bapu, My Mother* (Ahmedabad: Navajivan, 1949). Erikson, *Gandhi's Truth, op. cit.*, pp. 403–4.
9 For Gandhi's influence on King consult for example, Martin Luther King, *Stride Toward Freedom* (New York: Ballantine Books, 1958). pp. 76–77.

It may have started with the whole concept of a virgin birth. Intercourse was not necessary to produce Mary's baby boy. And yet the very insistence that the conception of the baby was "immaculate," the very consciousness of virginity as the basis of this supreme miracle, is indeed counter-phallic. God did not really have to send His son as His own price for forgiving the human race. And even if He did send His son, the son did not have to be born at all. And if He had to be born and have a human mother, why not also a human father? The two natures of Jesus Christ on earth could still have been maintained without the notion of a virgin birth. But the basic counter-phallicism of Christian mythology starts precisely with the virgin birth.

Later on the emphasis on celibacy for the priests of the church prior to the reformation was a continuation of the counter-phallic tradition.

The coming of the Christian religion in Africa has included these counter-phallic themes. To a certain extent Christianity has softened African masculinity. Some might even argue that it initiated a process of demasculation. The movement of "pacification" which imperialist powers helped to initiate reduced tribal confrontations. The idea of "loving thy neighbour", though still painfully unfulfilled in Africa, denuded warfare of some of its previous mystique.

"Turn the other cheek!" – This was the most feminine imperative of them all. Only a woman turned the other cheek upon being punished by her man. And even a woman attempted at times to shield herself with her arms. But the principle of turning the other cheek was part of the feminine baggage that came with Christianity.

Then there was celibacy for those who entered holy orders, and monogamy for everybody else. Sexual richness which had been so much a part of Africa before the onslaught of neo-Victorian prudery was now to be drastically circumscribed. The missionary schools were the great champions of a new prudish civilization. Suitably "modest" uniforms were devized for girl students; suitably "smart" uniforms came into being for the boy. The boys and girls were usually in quite separate schools. Visits across the sexual divide were either strictly discouraged or rigidly controlled. Most African forms of dances were abolished altogether, for the movements were interpreted as "sinful". Phallic dances retreated before the accusing finger of the new self-righteous creed.

Behind it all was the virgin birth of the son of God, when the male was dispensable. Behind it all was also the celibate life of Jesus, when female sexual companionship was dispensable. The counter-phallic stream of Christianity had begun to erode the banks of Africa's masculinity.

And yet Gandhism was clearly not an exercise of "turning the other cheek." It was not even a case of nonviolence broadly defined. Gandhism was a philosophy of nonviolent *resistance*. The idea was not to accept injustice meekly, but to fight it nonviolently.

It was between 1906 and 1908 that a civil disobedience campaign was launched in South Africa under the leadership of Gandhi, directed against laws in the Transvaal which required Indians to carry registration certificates. The movement did have an impact on African opinion in South Africa. Leo

Kuper has reminded us of a series of Gandhian protest experiments in South Africa in those early years. African women in Bloemfontein used the technique of civil disobedience in 1913 in their protests against the extension of pass laws to them by municipalities in the Orange Free State. The women's movement spread to other towns, and continued for a few years. In 1919 the African National Congress started experimenting with these techniques in Johannesburg. The Communist Party in Durban in 1930 also went "Gandhian". The Indians in South Africa resisted in 1946 in a similar way in protest against the Asiatic Land Tenure and Indian Representative Act. Meanwhile the struggle in India itself was helping to give Gandhian tactics global visibility and capturing the imagination of politically conscious Blacks in South Africa, as well as elsewhere. Then came the South African campaign for the Defiance of Unjust Laws of 1952, again using Gandhian techniques of civil disobedience. But in the very wake of such tactics, the system in South Africa was closing up and getting more intolerant.

The Gandhian resistance in South Africa in the early 1950's was an alliance between Blacks and Indians in the Union. It was in July 1951 that the African and Indian Congresses and the Franchise Action Council of the Coloureds appointed a Joint Planning Council. The aim was to coordinate the efforts of Africans, Indians, and coloured peoples in a mass campaign for the repeal of the pass laws, the Group Areas Act on racial segregation the Separate Representation of Voters Act which was moving in the direction of further curtailment of the political rights of Coloureds, and the Bantu Authorities Act seeking to ensure a re-tribalization of Africans. The campaign was successful in terms of the degree of involvement of the three groups, but a failure in terms of its aims. The failure was even more significant as an indicator of the limits of Gandhism, and the implications of this for pacific socialization in Africa at large.

Meanwhile strategies of resistance to racial domination in South Africa were regionalist rather than purely national. In September 1958 there had come into being further north a movement called the Pan African Freedom Movement of East and Central Africa (PAFMECA). The aim of the organization was to coordinate nationalistic movements mainly in British West and Central Africa and ensure periodic consultations on strategy and methods of agitation for self-government. At that time nationalism in British Africa was still significantly under the influence of Gandhism.

Yet today, Southern Africa especially presents a mixture of domestic and international violence related to the wider international environment.

Violence in Southern Africa has been both *inter-racial* (white against black) and *intra-racial* (black against black). Angola, especially since April 1974, has been a particularly acute case of black intra-racial violence. The Angolan tragedy illustrates the fragility of any sense of nationhood in the country; indeed, it illustrates how easily violence against colonialism could then lead on to an acute primary struggle for power among black nationalists themselves.

Rhodesia (Zimbabwe) has encompassed both inter-racial violence (black against white) and periodic eruptions of internecine black violence.

The contemporary political morality in Black Africa is supportive of anti-colonial violence and, to a large extent, of violence directed against domestic white minority rule. But this supportive African attitude towards inter-racial violence in the name of national liberation is a relatively recent development. The earlier phases of African nationalism showed a strong African distrust of violence as a strategy of liberation.

In this regard the ideological history of President Kenneth Kaunda of Zambia is particularly telling. Fergus Macpherson, Kaunda's biographer, reminds us that Kaunda's early nationalistic ideas were greatly influenced by Mohandas Gandhi. Kaunda saw that violence was indeed a tempting strategy for those who were denied alternative means of correcting injustices. But Kaunda insisted on the need for *passive* resistance (Satyagraha):

> "I could not lend myself to take part in any (violent) campaigns. *I reject absolutely violence in any of its forms as a solution to our problem.*"[10]

Although Kaunda was not basically a philosopher he did place his attachment to nonviolence in the context of a broader philosophical view of the world. Curiously enough Kaunda seemed to believe that there was something unnatural in being nonviolent. He did not share the romanticism which saw man as being essentially peaceful. On the contrary, Kaunda felt that "Man, just like any other animal, is violent."[11]

Like the late Martin Luther King of the United States, Kaunda virtually saw Gandhi as playing Lenin to Jesus's Marx. Just as Lenin had operationalized the teachings of Marx in a concrete political situation, so had Gandhi operationalized the teachings of Jesus and converted them into a political strategy. The theme of Gandhism as a politicisation of the love-ethic of Jesus recurs in Kaunda's intellectual growth. This is related to the conversion of Kenneth Kaunda – "Gandhi and Jesus had a special magnetism for the twenty-four year old Kaunda. He saw them as realists with a vision and rejected the popular notion that this was contradiction in terms."[12]

Alice Lenshina's Lumpa Church posed the most serious domestic challenge to Kaunda's "nonviolence" soon after the attainment of self-government; while liberation movements in "Portuguese Africa" and the implication of Ian Smith's U.D.I. later posed external challenges to Kaunda's legacy of Gandhism. Alice was one woman who served as prophetess to new religious warriors in Zambia.[13]

Macpherson discusses the struggle against the Lumpa Church, Kaunda's

---

10 Kenneth Kaunda and Colin Morris, *Black Government* (Lusaka: United Society for Christian Literature, 1960). The emphasis is original.
11 See the journal, *New Africa*, Vol. 5, No. 1, January 1963, p. 4.
12 Fergus Macpherson, *Kenneth Kaunda of Zambia: The Times and the Man* (Lusaka and London: Oxford University Press, 1974), p. 105.
13 Consult Andrew D. Roberts, "*The Lumpa Church of Alice Lenshina*," in Robert I. Rotberg and Ali A. Mazrui (eds.), *Protest and Power in Black Africa* (New York: Oxford University Press, 1970), pp. 513–570.

initial demand for Alice Lenshina "dead or alive", and his more conciliatory attitude later on. But Kaunda's biographer does not fully understand this Lenshina shock to Kaunda's universe of values. He does not even directly relate it to Kaunda's concept of the state, which is part Weberian, part Marxist, part Christian and part Gandhian. In Kaunda's words as cited by Macpherson:

> "Gandhi tried to organise things in such a way that the state must eventually wither away—for the whole state machinery has in it the seeds of violence—when man would do to others what he would like them to do to him."[14]

In this short quotation from Kaunda we have the Marxist concept of the state as an instrument of class oppression; we have Weber's idea that the state exercises a monopoly of the legitimate use of physical force; we have Gandhi's distrust of the state in favour of village industry and general decentralization; we have the marxist idea of the withering away of the state and its replacement with a classless society; and we have Jesus's Golden Rule as something which can only be adequately realized when Marx's dream of a classless society is finally brought to fruition.

As head of state, Kaunda was inevitably in charge of something which had the seeds of violence. Alice Lenshina shocked Kaunda into experiencing what state-management was all about.

By 1975, Kenneth Kaunda seemed to be in a diplomatic alliance with Prime Minister Vorster of South Africa in pursuit of a constitutional settlement in Rhodesia. The President of Zambia was even prepared to meet and have discussions with the prime minister of the most racist regime in Africa's history. The word *détente* had entered the political vocabulary of Southern Africa, affirming the need for white and black to live together in relative peace. Prime Minister Vorster was the chief architect of the principle of détente, and Kenneth Kaunda was perhaps his most sensational convert.

Was Kaunda returning to Gandhism? Had he rediscovered *Satyagraha*, or "Soul Force", which Mohandas Gandhi had espoused as an alternative to violent resistance?

If Kaunda had rediscovered Mahatma Gandhi through John Vorster, history had once again indulged its own mischievous sense of humour. It was after all in South Africa, as we have noted, that Gandhi had first experimented with *Satvagraha* much earlier this century. We know that within South Africa the Gandian experiment failed. Kenneth Kaunda later became one of the Mahatma's most enthusiastic black converts. Kaunda retreated from *Satyagraha* partly in the face of domestic violence in Zambia after independence, and partly in response to hardening attitudes in Southern Africa as a whole. The question which has arisen in the 1970's is whether a new Gandhian mood is in the air in the region – a readiness to try alternative pressures on the remaining racist regimes in Southern Africa, and let "Soul Force" destroy *apartheid* in the fullness of time.

---

14   See Macpherson, *ibid*. pp. 105–6.

In reality, the chances of a peaceful transition to social justice in South Africa and Rhodesia without additional violence are remote. The region is likely to need *Gandhians*, *Warriors* and *Radical Guerillas* before racial equity finally prevails.

But of even longer-term consequence than inter-racial violence will be the cleavages of black against black. These are likely to be the most obstinate. They are also likely to tax the ingenuity of Africa to find both preventive and curative measures. Violence as a form of political pathology will need more than traditional witchdoctors or modern psychiatrists. It will need a long but vital process of creating self-discipline and establishing self-policing techniques to govern Africa's relations with itself.

In this quest for new approaches to problems of violence, Kenneth Kaunda's name looms large. More a strategist than a theoretician, more a statesman than a philosopher, Kenneth Kaunda gropes for answers about some of the most basic questions of man's relations with man. Kaunda is a nationalist who is ready to give the oppressor the benefit of the doubt; he is a humanist capable of supporting armed and violent insurrection; he is a world figure who is capable of being concerned about a village; he is a political warrior who is capable of bursting into tears.

Yet in those very tears we are back to feminine symbolism in culture. The convert to Gandhism has retained the supremely feminine prerogative of unabashed capitulation to tears on relatively casual emotional stimulus. The sublimated maternalism of Gandhi has found its African counterpart in Kenneth Kaunda.

Androgynous Warriorhood and Revolutionary Resistance

It is with the intrusion of modern revolutionary ideas in Southern Africa that androgynous warriorhood became at last a serious aspiration for some of the liberation movements. We define androgynous warriorhood as a principle which seeks to end masculine monopoly of the skills of war. Historically, before total European control was established, Angola had indeed known strong women with warrior skills, from a warrior queen to peasant fighters. But on balance the principle of masculine monopoly of the war-machine was the order of the day in Angola as elsewhere.

Perhaps more fascinating was the Dahomean experience with women fighters, especially in the nineteenth century. It started earlier when the Kings of Dahomey had at times conscripted some of their wives as armed palace guards, especially in times of emergency. In the nineteenth century the practice became institutionalized. After a dynastic coup in 1818 the royal pretender, King Gezo, selected from among non-Dahomean captive girls a corps of fighters to defend him in case of further trouble. These women had certain privileges as both his soldiers and his wives, and their loyalty to the king was on the whole strengthened by their vested interest in his survival.

King Gezo died in 1858. In the years which followed recruitment into the

Amazons' Corps was no longer restricted to captive girls, but was extended to Dahomean women, some of whom came from high ranking families.

Another significant change took place. The Amazons in time became not merely the monarch's civil guard but important units in the Dahomean army. From about 1840 onwards they started getting involved in foreign wars, and soon earned a reputation as particularly ferocious and often cruel fighters.

Psychological explanations of their ferocity have included the sexual frustrations which emanated from their being all the wives of a single man – the king.

> "These female soldiers had all the privileges of important royal wives; they lived in the royal palaces, they had their food prepared for them; anyone who met them on the roads had to make way for them. They had also to obey the regulations which governed the lives of the King's wives. The most onerous of these was that, although they could only enjoy the favours of their royal spouse infrequently, they were forbidden any relations with other men. Any deviation from this rule was punishable by death. No doubt this enforced state of chastity goes a good deal towards explaining their ferocity."[15]

In the course of much of the rest of the nineteenth century the "standing army" of Dahomey had regular male and female units. At its peak the size of the army in an emergency rose up to twelve thousand warriors, nearly half of whom were women.

The Amazons of Dahomey were destroyed as a fighting force by the French colonizers in 1892. The male units of the Dahomean army were almost equally decimated. One of the most dramatic experiments in androgynous warriorhood anywhere in the world came abruptly to an end.

And yet the Dahomean experiment was not an ideal instance of androgynous warriorhood. In the first place the fighting units of men and women were kept separate. But even more fundamental was that the primacy of the male in the political system as a whole was not in question. The Amazons were after all the king's wives. And while the monarch could have more than four thousand wives at a time, a wife could enjoy the favours of another man only on pain of death.

Androgyny as a negation of sexism cannot therefore be credited to the Dahomean experiment. As an ideological ideal androgyny is a child of both western liberalism and western socialism. Afterall, both John Stuart Mill and Karl Marx championed the liberation of women in the nineteenth century.

In much of colonial Africa it was western liberalism which began to influence events in the direction of greater equality for women. Girls were encouraged to go to school, polygamy was sometimes taxed by the colonial master, and female circumcision where it was practised fell under the shadow of Christian and imperial disapproval. There is little doubt that in much of Africa important new areas of feminist freedom were opened up by the imperial order itself.

------

15 David Ross, "Dahomey" in *West African Resistance: The Military Response to Colonial Occupation*, edited by Michael Crowder (London: Hutchinson and Co., 1971), p. 149.

Yet warriorhood even under western liberalism continued to remain a preserve for the male. Could this military monopoly by men be reconciled with a genuine liberation of women?

It is among the leftist regimes of Africa – especially those in former Portuguese colonies – that the principle of androgynous warriorhood is *beginning* to be seriously entertained. FRELIMO in Mozambique had begun to use women in the struggle against the Portuguese by the late 1960's. The radical nationalist thrust in Guinea-Bissau under the Cabrals had initiated similar experimentation. MPLA in Angola as an initially urban movement began to tap sophisticated urbanized female talent in ways which were less dramatic than but still comparable to those which had once been used by the National Liberation Front (FLN) in Algeria in their war against the French. In the vivid words of Franz Fanon, who shared the experience of fighting for Algerian resistance:

> "Three metres ahead of you the police challenge a veiled woman who does not look particulary suspect. From the anguished expression of the unit leader you have guessed that she is carrying a bomb, or a sack of grenades, bound to her body by a whole system of strings and straps. For the hands must be free, exhibited bare, humbly and abjectly presented to the soldiers so that they will look no further."[16]

But with the conversion of the veil into a military camouflage the enemy gradually became extra alert.

> "In the streets one witnessed what became a commonplace spectacle of Algerian women glued to the wall, over whose bodies the famous magnetic detectors, the 'frying pans' would be passed. Every veiled woman, every Algerian woman became suspect. There was no discrimination. This was the period during which men, women, children, the whole Algerian people, experienced at one and the same time their national vocation and the recasting of the new Algerian society."[17]

Fanon may have been exaggerating, but he certainly captured the androgynizing tendency of revolutionary resistance. Women gradually become radicalized. And if the revolutionary resistance lasts long enough, the androgyny may become a conscious morality and not merely a side-effect of sustained struggle.

Yet the patron saints of modern socialist revolutions, Marx and Engels, drastically underestimated the relevance of *military* factors for the status of women in society. The two thinkers were such consistent economic determinists that they saw relations between men and women in primarily economic terms.

They argued that it was because men controlled the means of production that the women had become servants and serfs. In the words of Engels:

> "Today, in the great majority of classes, the man has to be the earner, the breadwinner of the family, at least among the propertied classes, and this gives him a dominating

---

16 Franz Fanon, *Studies in a Dying Colonialism*, translated from the French by Haakon Chevalier (New York: Monthly Review Press, 1965), pp. 61–62.
17 *Ibid.*

position which requires no special privileges. In the family, he is the bourgeois; the wife represents the proletariat."[18]

Engels assumed too readily that where women were effective economic producers, they attained high status. He thought "savages" and "barbarians" with economically active women respected their women more than western men respected western women:

"That woman was the slave of man from the commencement of society is one of the most absurd notions that have come down to us from the period of Enlightenment of the eighteenth century. Woman occupied not only a free but also a highly respected position among all savages and all barbarians of the lower and middle stages and partly even of the upper stage.... People whose women have to work much harder than we would consider proper often have far more real respect for women than our Europeans have for theirs. The social status of the lady of civilization, surrounded by sham homage and estranged from real work, is socially infinitely lower than that of the hard-working woman of barbarism...."[19]

What Engels did not seem to realise is that it is possible for women to work hard and be economically productive – and still enjoy low status in society. Kikuyu women work much harder than western women. They are economically more productive in relation to their society than western women are in relation to their own. But it is far from self-evident that Kikuyu women enjoy higher social status than do their western counterparts.

Engels did see the coming of the patriarchal family as a major disaster for women. But how did men manage to control the means of production in the first place? Did they not first have to control the means of *destruction* – the instruments of violence? Was it not masculine superiority in the skills of *physical* coercion which tilted the balance in the first place?

In the essay on "Armed Kinsmen and the Origins of the State" we have argued more fully that it was military factors rather than economic ones which initially gave men control over the political system. Primacy in the means of destruction rather than ownership of the means of production is the ultimate factor in the origins of sexism. This may not be neatly compatible with economic determinism but it explains a wider range of societies. The economic role of women varies enormously in different societies, while the military role of women is rather constant. Low status for women is almost universal; so is their limited military involvement. The subjection of women correlates much more neatly with the degree of their demilitarization than with the degree of their involvement in economic production.

Twentieth century Marxists are perhaps a little more sensitized to the importance of controlling the means of destruction than Marx and Engels seem to have been, inspite of the Paris Commune of 1871.

---

18 Frederick Engels, "The Origin of the Family, Private Property and the State," (1884), Karl Marx and Frederick Engels *Selected Works* (New York: International Publishers, 1972), p. 510.
19 *Ibid.*, pp. 489–490.

In the course of World War I Lenin hoped that if the fighting in Europe continued long enough the bourgeois regimes might start enlisting women. Such enlistment could help to bring the revolution closer.

"Today the imperialist bourgeoisie militarises not only the adults, but also the youth. Tomorrow it may proceed to militarise the women. To this we must say: All the better! Go ahead faster! The faster it goes, the nearer shall we be to the armed uprising against capitalism."[20]

Lenin then remembers a "certain bourgeois observer" of the Paris Commune who, writing to an English newspaper in May 1871, said: "If the French nation consisted entirely of women, what a terrible nation it would be." Lenin himself went on to observe:

"Women, and children of thirteen and upwards, fought in the Paris Commune side by side with the men. Nor can it be different in the forthcoming battles for the bourgeoisie. The proletarian women will not look on passively while the well-armed bourgeoisie shoot down the poorly armed or unarmed workers. They will take arms as they did in 1871..."[21]

This is the revolutionary fervour of which androgynous warriorhood is made. Leninist ideas are now slowly penetrating such countries as Mozambique, Guinea, Angola and Guinea-Bissau. A major sexual revolution in African conditions may be under way if such ideas do take root after a while.

And yet even in Lenin's own country true androgyny as a refutation of sexism is far from a reality as yet. Russia has discovered that the liberation of the proletariat is easier than the liberation of Russian women. And Mozambique and Angola may also discover that national emancipation is an easier target than equality between the sexes – least of all on the battlefield.

Conclusion

We have sought to demonstrate in this essay that three forms of resistance have been particularly important in Africa in the twentieth century. These are passive resistance, as championed by Mohandas Gandhi, primary resistance as manifested in the warrior tradition, and revolutionary resistance as embodied in the Marxist tradition.

Mahatma Gandhi's influence in Africa lasted mainly from the 1930's to the 1960's. In the 1930's the Indian nationalist movement was already being followed with close interest in other parts of the British Empire. Politically conscious young Africans – especially in West Africa – were already drawing inspiration from the struggle in the Indian sub-continent.

By the 1940's the African struggle itself was gathering momentum. Kwame Nkrumah of the Gold Coast (later Ghana) was toying with Gandhi's ideas on

---

20 V. I. Lenin, "War Programme of Proletarian Revolution" (1916) *Selected Works*, Vol. I, (Moscow: Foreign Languages Publishing House, 1960), pp. 820–821).
21 *Ibid.*

non-violent campaigns, and dreaming about translating them into what Nkrumah called "positive action" in his own fight against British rule. Nkrumah was aware that Gandhi had first used his technique in South Africa. What had not worked against white racism in South African might work against British colonialism elsewhere. Gandhian ideas thus helped to influence Nkrumah's approach to the struggle.

In 1958 – when Nkrumah hosted the all-Africa Peoples conference in the newly independent Ghana – neo-Gandhism was still relatively popular in much of Africa. The Algerian National Liberation Front – then engaged in an armed insurrection against the French – had a hard time persuading the Accra conference to give their armed struggle legitimacy and support.

In Southern Africa the most distinguished and most explicit disciple of Gandhi was Kenneth Kaunda of what was then Northern Rhodesia (now Zambia). Kaunda since then has become reconciled to violence under certain circumstances. Nevertheless, his flirtation with the idea of "détente" with white-dominated South Africa has probably been partly due to a residual neo-Gandhian faith that Kaunda has retained.

The late Albert Luthuli's belief in non-violent struggle against *apartheid* in South Africa was more a heritage of Christianity and the strategy of "turning the other cheek" than a product of conscious conversion to the ideas of Mahatma Gandhi. Yet who was to say where Christianity ended and Gandhism began in a politically conscious African in the second half of the twentieth century?

Since the 1960's Gandhism has drastically declined in prestige and importance in much of Africa. In Angola and Guinea-Bissau the anti-colonial struggle was gradually radicalised – and revolutionary resistance came into being. In Angola the triumph of MPLA (with Russian and Cuban support) also signified the victory of revolutionary forms of struggle. These radical forms of resistance have been substantially influenced by the Marxist tradition. It is true that Marx himself was more concerned with proletarian revolutions in industrialised countries. It was Lenin early in the twentieth century who came to address himself to the nature of imperialism. And it was Mao Tse-tung, Ché Guevara, Ho Chi Minh, Franz Fanon and Amilcar Cabral whl took the analysis further into the nature of struggling against imperialism.

All these philosopher-soldiers were influenced in varying degrees by Karl Marx and his ideas concerning class struggle and the necessity for revolution.

But affecting both passive and revolutionary resistance in Africa has been the resilience of primary resistance. We use the term here in the sense of struggle deeply imbued by aspects of indigenous military culture and African tradition generally. The colonial experience may have destroyed a large number of things in Africa, but many aspects of African culture have survived through it all. Colonialism was more successful in destroying organised African institutions than African values. It is true that the westernised Africans have, by definition, lost a substantial part of their culture. But these are only a small minority in their societies. Among the masses many traditional values and perspectives persist – including special definitions of such militarily relevant concepts as adulthood, fear, courage, discipline, honour, loyalty and enemy. When these norms are in a certain relationship with each other, and are sanctified by cultural ancestry and usage, they add up to at least part of the warrior tradition itself.

But combat and resistance reveal more than the attributes of the two sides in a fight. They tell us more than the nature of the fight itself. Combat and resistance reveal an additional piece of information seemingly unrelated to the fight – a piece of information which touches upon something as old as the origins of the human species. More important perhaps than the tension between the nationalist and the imperialist, between the socialist and the capitalist, is the relationship between men and women. How wars are fought is partly a lesson on how men and women relate to each other on issues of power.

It is because of that that the analysis in this essay has linked forms of resistance to forms of sexual arrangements and division of labour in society.

The warrior tradition in Africa – in spite of such exceptions as the Amazons of Dahomey – is a self-consciously masculine tradition, preserving warriorhood for relatively youthful males, and emphasising such hard virtues of manliness as valour and physical endurance. Primary resistance in this sense is therefore an undertaking overwhelmingly for men.

Passive resistance may be undertaken by either men or women but its values are culturally defined as feminine. They include the softer virtues of non-violence, love, and on accasion "turning the other cheek." Passive resistance is in part a politicisation of "sublimated maternalism."

Mohandas Gandhi had a "motherly" side to his personality, as we indicated. So perhaps does Kenneth Kaunda of Zambia.

It is with revolutionary resistance that androgyny as a refutation of sexist differentiation becomes at last a conscious aspiration. The term itself belongs more to women's liberation than to socialist thought, but the desire to liberate women was probably as strong in the philosophy of Marx and Engels as it is among radical feminists today.

> "The ideal towards which I believe we should move is best described by the term "androgyny". This ancient Greek word—from *andro* (male) and *gyn* (female)—defines a condition under which the characteristics of the sexes, and the human impulses expressed by men and women, are not rigidly assigned. Androgyny seeks to liberate the individual from the confines of the appropriate."[22]

Has female participation in the skills of violence been excessively regarded as "inappropriate"? Has the role of men in war been too "rigidly assigned"?

The militarisation of women in Southern Africa has at best only just started. The legacy of the Amazons of Dahomey will perhaps be radicalised in the southern parts in the continent in the years ahead. If the warrior tradition

---

22 Carolyn G. Heilburn, *Toward a Recognition of Androgyny* (New York: Harper and Row Publishers, 1974), p. x. Consult also Linda Jenness, (ed.), *Feminism and Socialism* (New York: Pathfinder Press, 1972) and Alfred G. Meyer, *Marxism and the Women's Movement* (Mimeo), Department of Political Science, The University of Michigan, Ann Arbor.

in Southern Africa does get androgynised, a new dimension would be added to liberation itself. As colonies have got their independence, races their dignity and classes their rights, the women have so far been *passively* awaiting their turn. But now it is time for a change. In the words of a famous American musical "Annie, Get your Gun!" – for that is where power resides.[23] Or so old Chairman Mao once told us.

---

23 In the musical *"Annie, Get Your Gun"* the woman could not be both a good shot and attractive to the man she loved. So she deliberately disguised her firing skills in order to win his love. In real life Annie should retain her fire power—if she wants liberation.

Armed Resistance and Counter-Insurgency*

Reflections on the Anya Nya and Mau Mau Experiences

LOUISE PIROUET

University of Nairobi, Nairobi, Kenya

It IS OFTEN assumed that in a conflict there are two sides in opposition to one another, and that a person who is not actively committed to one side must be supporting the other. During the course of a conflict leaders on both sides will use this argument to gain active support from the "crowd".[1] In reality conflicts involving more than two persons usually have more than two sides, and if a resistance movement is to be successful, propaganda and politicization are essential. It is the purpose of this paper to examine the "crowd" to whom propaganda needs to be directed, both during the course of the conflict and in relation to its possible outcome. Answers to the following questions will be sought:

(i) How will people be placed along the spectrum of commitment which stretches between active resistance at the one extreme, and active support of the regime at the other?

(ii) Why do people take the stand they do, and do they always remain in the same place on the spectrum of commitment?

(iii) If the conflict ends in a negotiated settlement, how shall we expect people to fare who have occupied particular positions on the spectrum mentioned above?

(iv) What are the alternatives to a negotiated settlement?

In order to find answers to these questions we shall look at three African resistance movements: Mau Mau in Kenya, the Anya Nya in Sudan, and resistance in Rhodesia/Zimbabwe. It will be maintained that these three conflicts are comparable and that they share many features in common.

In these three conflicts the issues were complex, but they can all be explained in the same basic terms. The issues were in part perceived as being *racial*. In Kenya and Rhodesia blacks suffered racial discrimination at the hands

---

* A first draft of this paper was presented to the East African Universities Social Sciences Conference, December 1975, held in Nairobi.

1 Ogot p. 135.

of whites; in Sudan black Southerners suffered racial discrimination at the hands of Arab Northerners (the racial issue in Sudan has been fiercely contended,[2] but since the conflict was perceived by many in racial terms, this will be accepted without further analysis. What was felt to be the case is at least as important as what actually was the case). The racial issue was by no means the only issue, and was not necessarily the most important. In each conflict *economic* factors were also involved, resistance occurring amongst a group which was being economically exploited. On another level of interpretation these conflicts can be explained partly in terms of the *class* conflict. There were as well *religious* overtones in each. In Sudan Southern resisters were sometimes spoken of as Christians defending themselves against Muslim Northerners.[3] The white minority regimes in Kenya and Rhodesia claimed to be upholding the values of Christian civilization and the resisters were labelled atavistic.[4] But whereas the categories of race, economic well-being and class all bear some relation to the facts, the religious labels distort the facts, and appear to do so deliberately for propaganda reasons. In Sudan the South was 90% pagan at the beginning of the conflict, and from the beginning some resistance leaders were Muslim, though the majority were Christian because mission schools offered almost the only opportunity for education in the South. The Northern Sudan, against which resistance arose, is not uniformly Muslim in belief or culture. Neither in Kenya or Rhodesia did the white regimes have a monopoly of Christian belief or practice.

Possibly the most important single factor in all three conflicts was the *political*. Seen in political terms, the conflicts appeared somewhat less insoluble than when seen in terms of race, economics or religion. Certain *spiritual values* – human dignity, freedom, equality – were displaced from the religious into the political sphere, perhaps because of the misuse of religion as a propaganda weapon. All three conflicts had their roots in the *colonial situation*. In Sudan there was a kind of double colonialism: British colonialism prior to 1956 gave way to the domination of the South by the North after independence. The achievement of formal independence from the colonial power does not necessarily end the subservience of one section of society to another.

The situation, conduct, and perhaps also the sequel of these conflicts have much in common. In each case resistance arose among people living at or near to subsistence level. In each case the resisters used the tactics of guerrilla warfare.

---

2   cf. Verona Fathers, Albino and Scherf.
3   An attempt was made after independence to unify Sudan on the basis of Arab-Islamic culture. References to Sudan as an Islamic state were being made as late as 1971, although Sunday had been restored as the official day of rest in the South some years earlier. One such reference appeared in the preamble to a submission to a UN agency for aid in that year. Moderate Northerners recognized that this policy was ill-advised, and it has been withdrawn, and freedom of religion guaranteed by the basic law granting regional autonomy to the South in March 1972.
4   A Fr. Lewis who is a USPG missionary is one of Smith's most ardent supporters and is often quoted on Rhodesian radio. BBC *Summary of World Broadcasts*, passim.

In each case the regime was able to recruit into its counter-insurgency forces large numbers of people from the same population group among which resistance arose, and it made constant use of this in its propaganda.[5] In all these cases the resisters had difficulty in "nationalizing" resistance. In Sudan and Rhodesia there has been chronic factionalism among the resisters; in Kenya the Kikuyu failed in the main to get other Africans to join the resistance.

The major differences between the conflicts lie in *when* they took place rather than in *why* they occurred or *how* they were conducted. The Kenyan conflict was the earliest. In the post World War II era it was among the first major conflicts involving the use of guerrilla warfare and counter-insurgency measures. The only major conflict of this type to precede it was that in Malaya. Kenyans had gained experience of this type of warfare during World War II in the Far East. At the time of Mau Mau few countries had achieved independence from colonial rule. India had done so, and Gandhi's non-violent tactics had won wide acclaim. Kenyans were acutely aware of India's achievement because immigrants from the Indian sub-continent formed a significant minority in the Kenyan population. Most of Africa was still under colonial domination and there was no way in which most Africans could give formal support or recognition to the Kenyan cause such as is given today to Rhodesian nationalist aspirations. An exception to this was Egypt whose radio gave vociferous encouragement to Mau Mau. If the Kenyan conflict was too early to receive such support, the Sudan conflict was too late. After the failure of the Round Table Conference in 1965 a number of Southern leaders took the pessimistic view that only secession could guarantee Southern rights and freedoms[6] (the Round Table Conference had discussed federation). But Sudan was an independent state, and a member-state of the OAU which was pledged to non-interference in the internal affairs of other member-states, and to upholding existing territorial boundaries. This meant that no other African state could formally view the resistance movement in the Southern Sudan other than as a rebellion (though the question whether a conflict of such dimensions can be considered an internal affair can legitimately be raised). Some African countries gave the Anya Nya the same kind of unofficial support which the Sudan government was, in its turn, giving to comparable movements in Chad and Ethiopia. The Rhodesian conflict occurred at what may, perhaps, be described as the "right" moment in time: resistance movements there are recognized formally by other African states and by the OAU as legitimate nationalistic movements. It is arguable, therefore, that the main difference between the three conflicts lay, not in their aims, nor in the manner of their conduct (nor even, perhaps, in the manner of their resolution) so much as in the moment in history at which they occurred.

We will now attempt a characterisation of resistance movements based on

---

5 Maxey pp. 33–5; Kamunchuluh pp. 203–4.
6 However, the door was never officially closed on the possibility of negotiation. See for instance Albino p. 132.

the cases of Kenya, Sudan and Rhodesia/Zimbabwe. It will be shown that when a resistance movement arises among people living at or near to subsistence level the resistance movement will find difficulty in gaining a wide measure of active support, and may be an "unpopular grass-roots movement".[7] It will be suggested that the distribution of the "crowd" along the spectrum of commitment to resistance is likely to form a curve of natural distribution, with relatively small numbers at each end actively committed to resistance or to its suppression, and the bulk of the "crowd" somewhere in between, until politicization and counter-insurgency measures alter this distribution. The reasons for the original pattern of distribution and the types of change that are likely to take place need to be examined carefully.

Firstly we have to recognize that the average subsistence-level agriculturalist or pastoralist will want to remain uninvolved so that he can get on with the business of living.[8] When a state of war disrupts his way of life and makes his livelihood more precarious, he will at first be more, not less, desirous of being left in peace. He may find it difficult at the best of times to produce a sufficient surplus to cover the expenses over and above subsistence which make life worthwhile. A little extra clothing, a more permanent house, a measure of education for his children are the sorts of things he will want to spend his surplus on. Both the resistance movement and the counter-insurgency forces will require him to pay for their services, either in cash or in kind, and this will tend to dissipate his surplus and eat into his subsistence. In the three conflicts discussed here, that in Sudan probably generated most hardship. By 1971 insecurity and military activity had been joined by drought, famine and epidemic disease, and Southerners living in Anya Nya territory suffered a severe lack of medical, educational and agricultural facilities, in spite of efforts by the Anya Nya to maintain these services.[9] Those Southern Sudanese living in areas of the South controlled by the Sudan government were not much better off. Yet a good many people had to pay taxes of some sort both to the Anya Nya and to the Sudan government, and these sometimes took the form of food levies extorted from an unwilling population. Programmes of politicization aimed at improving this situation.[10]

Counter-insurgency measures usually follow a now familiar pattern, and make the peasant's life more difficult still. "Villageization" is one of the first measures to be carried out. These villages have been variously called "peace-villages" (Sudan), "protected villages" (Rhodesia), "aldeamentos" (Mozambique), "Bantustans" (Republic of South Africa). The name itself is in part

---

7   This is Dr. Nelson Kasfir's phrase. For what follows, however, he must not be blamed.
8   A. H. M. Jones: *The Decline of the Ancient World* London 1966 pp. 367–8 describes the reluctance of ordinary folk to put up much in the way of resistance to the barbarian invasions.
9   Personal communications from Southern Sudanese. Reports from the UNHCR and aid agencies on conditions obtaining in Sudan immediately after the establishment of peace.
10 See, for example, the pamphlet *Anya Nya: What we Fight For*, n.d. intended for distribution to the Anya Nya.

propaganda since the aims of these villages are to prevent the population from supplying the insurgents with food, arms and recruits, and to protect those willing to support the regime from reprisals. If the regime is able to do so, it may provide the villages with amenities to make them more tolerable, since carrots as well as sticks will be needed in what is often described as a "hearts and minds" campaign. But initially there is invariably a measure of resistance to villageization, not only because people want to be free to support resistance, but also because villageization disrupts normal patterns of living, separates people from their ancestral lands and burial places, and is naturally repugnant. Counter-insurgency meets its first obstacle here. Its chosen tactic will drive some hitherto uncommitted people into commitment to resistance rather than submission to villageization.[11] The success of the regime will depend to some extent on the nature of the terrain and its size. Villageization met with little success in Sudan because people were able to flee into a huge, unmapped countryside, where communications were exceptionally poor, and much of which was virtually inaccessible during the eight rainy months of the year. A population of about four million was scattered over a territory of some 480,000 square kilometers. The Sudan government could not provide adequate food for the peace-villages, let alone other amenities. It was estimated that in 1970 some 75% of the Southern population had "voted with their feet" by successfully eluding villageization.[12] In Kenya under the Mau Mau emergency the regime was able to carry out its programme more successfully. A large number of people was closely packed into a relatively small area. One of the first things the regime did was to open up more roads. The alternative to accepting villageization was to flee into the forests. Moreover, although at first the villages were starkly dreadful, this situation improved, and amenities made life more bearable.

Secondly we must consider those who will be found at either end of the spectrum of commitment, and firstly those who will be the initiators and active supporters of resistance. The leaders are likely to be those with more than average political ambition and awareness who have been frustrated and who turn to violence in desperation. Then there will be those who have been deprived in other ways by oppressive rule, and who can find no alternative satisfaction. The landless, the unemployed in the towns, and those who have failed to get the educational opportunities they felt were their due will all be willing to follow the first group without much persuasion.[13] The resisters will also be joined by those forced into outright opposition to the regime by "successful" counter-insurgency operations. Villageization will be likely to have this effect, as we have seen. So will the inevitable declaration of a state of emergency (or

---

11 Kamunchuluh p. 201; Maxey pp. 44–5, 153.
12 Russell and McCall in Wai, pp. 102–3.
13 A large number of Southern Sudanese refugees were schoolboys who fled either at the time of the schools strike or when the schools were closed down.
    Kariuki p. 21; Kamunchuluh pp. 201–2.

its equivalent), detention without trial, and the imposition of a curfew. Counter-insurgency often includes punishing the non-combatants for the successes of
the resisters, and this is as likely to force people into opposition as it is to deter
them.[14] Relatives and friends of activists who are killed or detained are as
likely to be incited to active resistance as to be restrained from it. Then there
will be those who can be persuaded by the resistance leaders to join them. The
success of politicization programmes will depend in part on the degree of education and the sophistication of the leadership, and partly on the sparseness or
density of the population. It is normal practice today for resistance movements
to operate from bases outside their own country, and this may mean they can
use radio transmissions.[15]

It is common to find that a resistance movement resorts to coercion as well
as persuasion. It is usually accepted that in Kenya oathing was sometimes
coercive.[16] Attacks carried out on "protected villages" in Rhodesia can best
be explained as attempts to coerce villagers into non-cooperation with the
security forces, or as punishments for previous cooperation.[17] In Sudan food
was at times obtained by coercion.[18] This use of coercion often shocks observers,
and this is made use of by the regime in propaganda. Coercion is also, of
course, used in traditional warfare, though it can then be legalized, and
cooperation is more easily enforced.

Those involved in resistance will also include a "thug" element whose
behaviour may embarrass the responsible leadership of the movement,[19] but
sometimes remains unrecognized by outsiders because of the high idealism
which may be professed by the movement as a whole. All societies are faced
with the problem of channelling the activities of the more energetic and
adventurous of their members, and of dealing with the thugs. In the Middle
Ages in Europe they were sent crusading; in more modern times they have
sometimes joined the French Foreign Legion. They become an embarrassment
to a resistance movement when that movement wishes to turn from "terrorism"
to "respectability". An obvious recent example is the Palestine Liberation
Organization which has had great difficulty in dealing with its more extreme
and uncontrollable elements. When the term "highly-disciplined" is used to
describe a resistance movement, it is both a tribute to the effectiveness of the
leadership, and also an admission of the difficulty. The membership of Mau
Mau, and separate incidents during the emergency, need to be examined with

---

14 Maxey pp. 79, 105, 127–8, 138–140. It was commonly reported from Sudan that the
    inhabitants of "peace-villages" suffered reprisals for successful Anya Nya actions.
15 Kaggia p. 111; Maxey p. 116 et seq.
16 Kariuki p. 32: "There is no question that at times the oath was forced upon people who
    did not want to take it, though these were nothing like so many as the government
    spokesmen would have had us believe". Wanyoike p. 191 describes people caught
    between two fires.
17 Maxey pp. 134–7.
18 Sudan documentation.
19 Kamunchuluh p. 208; Maxey pp. 137–8.

this in mind. Among the active supporters, and closely allied to the thugs, will be those who want to pay off old scores and settle old grievances. A state of guerrilla war will offer plenty of opportunity for doing this. Work on Mau Mau has shown that certain incidents fall into this category, notably the Lari massacre.[20]

A person may actively support resistance for one or more of these reasons, and the flux of events may make him shift his position along the spectrum of commitment from time to time. A number of those described above may have had a low level of commitment, at least to begin with. Much will depend on efficient discipline within the movement, and on successful politicization.

At the other end of the spectrum are found those who actively assist the regime to suppress resistance. These cannot all be lumped together as stooges; the reasons for their "loyalism" must be examined seriously. They will, of course, include opportunists who are only interested in saving their own skins, and who would support whoever was the highest bidder, and there will also be a thug element here.[21] There will be some who may be genuinely persuaded that the regime is not as bad as it is made out to be, or that no government is ideal and that it is better to try and modify what exists than to risk violence and the possibility that what follows will be no better.[22] Those who are better off or hold positions of influence will be more easily persuaded to these points of view than others. Some who work with the regime may desire to bring about radical change from within, and still others may use their positions to subvert or undermine the regime. Whoever the persons were who leaked Sudan government documents to the Anya Nya during 1971/2 perhaps fall into this category. An oppressive regime can never be quite sure about its collaborators.[23]

The motives of those who actually join the counter-insurgency forces are

---

20 Sorrenson 1967, pp. 100–101.
21 Kariuki p. 38; Sudan documentation.
22 In April 1971 Alier began to supersede Joseph Garang in matters concerning the South although the latter was still Minister for Southern Affairs. In May Alier, not Garang, met the All Africa Conference of Churches and the World Council of Churches delegates to Sudan who discussed, among other things, reconciliation (AACC/WCC typewritten summary of this meeting). After the coup/counter-coup of July 1971 Alier replaced Garang as Minister for Southern Affairs, and immediately set up committees to work on draft documents relating to autonomy for the South. These committees began work as early as 6 August. Their final draft proposals seem to be those dated 1.10.1971.
23 Kariuki p. 38: "...we learnt of one way in which the Home Guard had done well. The British soldiers, naturally, found it impossible to tell the difference between a 'Mau Mau' Kikuyu and any other... Fortunately the Home Guards... tried to prevent them killing ordinary citizens... we decided, when the Emergency was over, that the detainees would not allow any revenge on these Home Guards because they had at least tried to save many people. Most Home Guards had, anyway, taken the oath and several used secretly to help as much as they could."
cf. Maxey p. 34.
Daily Nation 13 September 1975: "Secret Weapon led to Victory..." "Only now can it be seen in South Vietnam just how riddled with Vietcong were the ranks in the pro-American administrations in that country..."

also likely to be very varied. In the round-about-subsistence-level conditions envisaged here, they may simply join for the sake of the pay and the rations.[24] Some may be more or less forcibly recruited from areas easily dominated by the regime.[25] None of these categories is likely to provide very reliable "loyalists". It is normal practice in counter-insurgency operations to allow troops such as these to do as much of the "dirty-work" as possible. Once men have been employed thus, they will not easily be forgiven by the resistance leaders, and so will become increasingly committed to the regime in order to save their skins. The fact that they are actively involved against the resistance movement makes excellent propaganda.[26]

Among the collaborators there may be found people who object on ethical or religious grounds to the use of violence. They may sympathise with the aims of the movement, but not with its methods. They will not be found in the main counter-insurgency forces any more than in the ranks of the resistance fighters. But there are ways in which they can be used (by either side). It is well-known that during Mau Mau, Christians who objected to the use of violence, and elders who found the methods of the movement contrary to tradition, played a large part in the Kikuyu Home Guard. This was formed to protect people against coercion and attack by Mau Mau, and it was intended to act defensively. As Oginga Odinga says: "The Home Guard Movement was begun to *turn men into* collaborators" (emphasis added).[27] People usually find it easier to square defensive violence with their consciences than offensive violence. The energies of conscientious objectors could, in theory, be harnessed to the resistance movement as well as to the forces of the regime. Cases are known to the writer from Sudan of men who objected to using violence and who acted as medical workers, teachers, and in other civilian capacities under the overall direction of the Anya Nya. It seems rather uncommon for resistance movements to accommodate conscientious objectors in this way, and the more idealogically oriented the less accommodating it is likely to be. The alternative to accommodating such men may, however, be a head-on collison with a very stubborn and not easily cowed group, and a collision which will not enhance the reputation of the resistance movement.[28]

---

24 Maxey p. 34; Leakey p. 115.
25 Kariuki p. 36 describes those who obeyed government orders reluctantly. Note the suggestion in Leakey pp. 115–6 that if you were not actively against Mau Mau you must be for it.
26 A. Hastings: *Massacre in Mozambique—Wiriyamu* London and Nairobi 1974. The DGS agent's name is given as Chico Kachavi and the command to kill is transcribed as "Phani wense". This indicates African as well as Portuguese involvement, though this is not brought out in the book. Could this be a reason why Frelimo never commented on this episode?
27 Ogot p. 136–7.
28 Kariuki pp. 37–9 shows the gradual transformation of the Home Guard from a poorly-armed, defensive group to a more professionally trained part of the counter-insurgency forces. Rosberg and Nottingham (p. 294–5) comment that "those whom the European missionaries viewed as *Kikuyu* martyrs were *Christian* martyrs to the Kikuyu". Kamun-

A dilemma of conscience will also be found among those who might be expected to support the regime in power. There will be some who object on principle both to the oppression being practised and to the tactics of the counter-insurgency forces. Others will find the continuation of oppression foolish for pragmatic and economic reasons. Resistance leaders are usually only too happy to exploit this division in the ranks of their enemies. Some may even decide that they have friends on the other side. The extent of draft evasion in the Vietnam war became an important factor in ending it. Draft evasion in Rhodesia has been a constant problem of the Smith regime.[29] Among the main critics of the Smith regime have been the Todds (under house arrest for long periods) and the Roman Catholic Justice and Peace Commission,[30] though the majority of white Catholics have been no different in outlook from most other whites. In the Sudan war there were prominent Northerners who quickly seized on the chance to make peace rather than pursue the conflict, and who, in 1971, went ahead to draft proposals which most Northerners at first thought of as a sell-out.[31] The Corfield Report on Mau Mau speaks in horror-struck tones of misguided leftists who sympathised with Kikuyu grievances and said so openly.[32] In every conflict of this kind there comes a time when the cost of counter-insurgency begins to seem too high.

We must now look at the process of reaching a settlement, and at the alternatives to this. If a negotiated settlement, or an informal bargain, is reached, it seems clear that those who find themselves placed towards the middle of the spectrum of commitment will be the ones best placed to make contact with the opposite side. It is usual for the regime to try and do its bargaining with the moderates only, and to hope to win sufficient support for this for the remaining radicals to be "isolated and more easily crushed".[33] An attempt to do this was made in Sudan in 1970. And there seem to have been last minute attempts in 1971/2 to by-pass the negotiating process or to modify it.[34] After an attempt

chuluh uses the expression "conscientious objectors" of some "loyalists". This writer has heard Sudanese and Rhodesian Africans speak with deep regret that they have been forced into the use of violence. For the Balokole in Sudan, v. Albino p. 73.

29   Maxey pp. 32, 36, 159–162. The writer has met white Rhodesian draft evaders in the UK.

30   *Daily Nation* 24 October 1975 p. 10. An article here reports comments made by the Secretary-General of the International Commission of Jurists whom it describes as being invited to Rhodesia by the Roman Catholic Justice and Peace Commission of Rhodesia. v. also Maxey pp. 138–140.

31   eg Dr Ali Bakheit whose proposals for regional autonomy were published on 9 September 1971, and M. O. Beshir, known for his conciliatory stance and writings.

32   Chapter X, pp. 221–4. Something of the same admission is found in Leigh pp. 216–7 (this is an exceptionally bigotted settler account).

33   Quoted from a letter from Barbara Haq, then secretary of the Movement for Colonial Freedom which was at that time (1970) engaged in an attempt at mediation. The letter is also quoted by M. O. Beshir 1975 p. 102–3, but the words "and more easily crushed" are there omitted. The copy of the letter in the writer's possession was given to her by B. Haq with permission to publish.

34   The reference is to attempts made in late 1971/early 1972 to persuade refugees (including students at Makerere University) to return to Sudan, and to attempts by the Sudan

by Smith to do just this in August 1975, when he made the fundamental mistake of announcing publicly his intentions and the intended result, the moderates and radicals promptly closed ranks against him for the time being. The moderates are always a useful barometer of public opinion: what they will not accept at any price no one will, hence there are usually attempts to test their reactions. In August to October 1971 there occurred in Sudan what appears to have been a particularly elaborate attempt to do this, and it is widely reported that by the time the two sides in this conflict met together for the final stage of negotiation, each knew what the other would and would not accept.[35]

In the event of a settlement, formal or informal, the moderates are likely to be in the majority in the group that comes to power. A settlement will involve a measure of compromise, power-sharing and gradualness, and its successful implementation will thus be in the main the work of the moderates. The moderates of both sides will probably have had contacts with each other already. Because they are essential to the early stages of implementing a settlement, they will have access to power. Those who achieve positions of power seldom relinquish them willingly. In this connexion a clear distinction must be made between the *conflict situation* (when the regime is fighting for the maintenance of the status quo, and the resistance is committed to a return to the status quo ante before oppression began, or to a new state of affairs whose details will have to be worked out in the future, or to a mixture of these two), and the *post-settlement stage*, when the first objective of whatever government comes to power will be that it should remain in power, and so be able to govern.[36] During the first stage when the conflict is still in progress, radicals will provide the driving force of the resistance movement, and hard-liners the energy behind the counter-insurgency operations. During the second stage, stability, not momentum, will be required, and both radicals and hard-liners will be distrusted unless they modify their attitudes.

But there are alternatives to reaching a settlement. If, instead of coming to an agreement, the resistance movement fights through to an outright military victory, then the radicals rather than the moderates will be likely to come to

---

government to obtain promises of aid to returnees before a peace agreement was reached. At the time when these attempts were being made, new refugees were still arriving in Uganda, fleeing from the usual dry-season attacks on Anya Nya bases which occurred about a month earlier than usual. This sort of activity usually precedes serious peace negotiations as each side jockeys for position.

35   v. note 22 above. Alier's committees worked over Bakheit's proposals as soon as they became available, modifying them considerably. Much of what they deleted was reinserted into the document used in negotiation in Addis Ababa the following February. It was then negotiated out again in the peace talks. It looks as if the Sudan government may have prepared a safe line of retreat by this method. The Southern Sudanese used almost exactly the same tactics at preliminary talks in London in December/January 1971/2.

36   For a more elaborate analysis of protest movements v. Mazrui, pp. 1185–1196 in Rotberg and Mazrui: *Protest and Power in Black Africa*, N.Y. 1970.

power.[37] If this happens, the basis of power may be narrower than if a settlement is reached, as the radicals may have unity forced on them by one very strong leader (the reasons for this will be adduced below). An awareness of this possibility may be a decisive factor in determining whether the resistance movement opts for a settlement or for an attempt to win an outright victory. Before the MPLA victory in Angola it was stated by one observer that "not a single African liberation organisation has taken over a country militarily" and that "this kind of placid attitude contrasts strongly with the aggressiveness of other liberation fighters as are to be found in south-east Asia".[38] The commentator from whom these remarks are quoted apparently regretted the lack of aggressiveness. Leaders of African resistance movements may be more hesitant to try for an outright victory because it would involve the violent suppression of collaborators, with whom strong ethnic ties are felt to exist, and most African liberation struggles have been directed primarily against racial oppression, ideology usually playing a subsidiary role.

Whilst it is very difficult to lose a guerrilla war, it is also very difficult to achieve an outright victory, and to decide to try and do so involves taking certain risks. The first of these is that war-weariness may set in and the regime be successful in striking a bargain with the moderates which wins sufficient support to isolate the radicals, as happened in Sarawak in 1974. Secondly victory may turn out to be overcostly, its price being destitution. Thirdly there is the danger of an increasing reliance being placed on outside aid, and this proving detrimental. The victory may then turn into a new defeat by reducing the victors to a new dependence which is little better than the old subservience. If rival movements accept aid from rival sources, they run the risk of fighting a civil war which suits outside interests better than their own.

It is always difficult for resistance movements to remain united and to operate on a national scale. The ultimate aim of a resistance movement and the exact shape of the state it hopes to inaugurate are likely to be imprecise. It is easy to unite people in opposition to oppression; much less easy to achieve agreement on the details of the polity which is envisaged instead. The greatest divergences are likely to appear when the end is in sight. It is then that quarrels over positions of power are most likely to occur. A further impediment to unity may be the difficulty of communication over wide areas of country in a war of the kind we are considering. Enormous distances may be involved, and the resistance movement may not have control over the lines of communication. This was very marked in Sudan.[39] Guerrilla warfare invariably involves informers on both sides and an extremely high level of suspicion and distrust. The greatest unity will be achieved among people who know each other fairly well, and therefore among people who live in the same locality and speak the

---

37 They may not remain in power. cf. Algeria and Ethiopia.
38 Chege Mbitiru in the *Sunday Nation*, editorial entitled "Last Train from Zimbabwe..." 31 August 1975.
39 For an account of factionalism in Sudan v. McCall 1969, Oliver Albino 1970.

same language. Charges of tribalism made against resistance movements or segments of them sometimes amount to no more than this. Integration is easiest at the local and regional level. If some areas of the country suffer more acutely from the oppression than others, it may be difficult to persuade the less oppressed groups to commit themselves fully to the conflict. This was a major reason for the failure of Mau Mau to spread among peoples other than the Kikuyu. Resistance movements sometimes, and increasingly often (but not always) seek outside military aid in the shape of weapons, training opportunities and advisors. Aid is most easily obtained from the enemy of one's enemy.[40] But the enemy of one's enemy may have entirely different reasons from one's own for experiencing that enmity. For the Sudan government, Egypt was a natural ally, and the USSR became involved through Egypt. The Southerners naturally turned to the enemy of Egypt and the USSR – Israel. Israel's main concern was not justice for the Southern Sudanese but the wasting of Egyptian, Soviet and Sudanese arms, men and money, and for a small outlay she could get large results. By 1971 there was a real danger of the Middle East conflict spreading into Eastern Africa. Mau Mau received no such support, and no legitimation from outside Kenya. If this meant that it was less efficient in one respect, it also meant that Mau Mau did not take on other people's quarrels or adopt their stances, which may have made it more efficient in another respect.

One way in which a resistance movement can find unity is for it to receive outside aid from only one source, and for all of this to be channelled through one leader, who is thus enabled to control factionalism. In the case of Sudan, Israel, the only supplier of arms, decided to channel all aid through Colonel (now General) Joseph Lagu, who then quashed dissident elements. Had the Anya Nya fought through to a military victory, his position might have been that of a virtual dictator.

There are then four possible outcomes to a conflict of the nature we have been considering: a negotiated settlement made with the resistance leaders, such as ended the war in Sudan, and three alternatives. One of the alternatives is a military victory by the resistance movement, but, as we have already seen, this involves the risk of a settlement being reached with the moderates only which then wins general acceptance for negative reasons (war-weariness), or positive reasons (the settlement turns out to be sufficiently attractive), or a mixture of the two. The second alternative is an unofficial or informal settlement, and it will be suggested that such a settlement was reached in the case of Mau Mau. The third alternative is the settlement made with the moderates only which has been mentioned. Theoretically there ought to be yet another possibility, namely the outright victory of the regime. But Malaya seems to offer the only example of this, and there the circumstances were exceptional, and proved the rule. The insurgents were Chinese and failed to win popular support from the Malay inhabitants. It was therefore possible to isolate them by villageization without antagonizing the indigenous Malay population.

---

40   Russell and McCall in Wai 1973 p. 116.

Tactics evolved in Malaya have become the pattern for other situations where the same conditions do not exist.

A settlement negotiated between the leaders of the resistance movement and the regime is likely to see moderates occupying many, but not all, positions of power because of the need for power-sharing, moderation and gradualness. But this will include power-sharing with the radicals. An outright victory will see the radicals in power, perhaps under a dictator, and with the moderates ineffective. It has been suggested that rather a lot of people will tend to be only moderately committed, so this may involve rendering ineffective a large proportion of the population. Dissident radicals may also find themselves without a say. A settlement made with the moderates only is likely to result in the radicals being left out in the cold (but there may be rather fewer of them).

This needs some substantiation. In Sudan a settlement was negotiated with the leaders of the resistance movement. Whilst the moderates now hold a good many positions of power, with Abel Alier (a "Unionist") as second Vice-President and President of the Regional High Executive Council in the South, they do not hold all of the power. More of the radicals could have shared power than actually do so: one was offered a place on the negotiating team which went to Addis Ababa, but boycotted it;[41] another is aware that he holds a less important position than he might have done if he had not been so hesitant in accepting the Agreement. It is difficult to know whether to classify some leaders as radicals or moderates: Mading de Garang and Lawrence Wol Wol both spent much time during the war years winning support for and representing the South Sudan Liberation Movement overseas, but it was also through them that the first approaches to peace were made. Both hold considerable positions. It seems to be by his own choice that General Joseph Lagu holds a military rather than a political position. Angelo Voga, his official representative in Kampala during the war, was a member of the negotiating team in Addis Ababa, and was appointed a First Secretary in the Sudanese Embassy in Kampala immediately after the war. There is, therefore, a fair measure of power-sharing, which includes people who occupied very varied positions on the spectrum of commitment. Two Southern politicians in exile refused to consider autonomy as an alternative to secession or federation even when it became clear that the Addis Ababa Agreement granted what amounts to quasi-federal status to the South, and voiced their opinions in public. They were immediately threatened with deportation by the government of Zaire, and are still in exile.[42] It is, of course, rumoured that personal ambition and a promise of continued military aid lay behind their refusal to accept the Agreement.

In Kenya the radicals appear to have virtually no place in the current establishment. Would it be correct to deduce that a settlement, albeit an informal one, was made with the moderates only, and that this then won a

---

41 Sudan documentation.
42 These were Gordon Muortat Mayen and Francis Mayar Akon. *East African Standard*, Nairobi, 29 February 1972.

sufficient degree of general acceptance to hold, at least for the time being? The radicals remained in the forest, but because this informal settlement won fairly general acceptance, they were cut off from supplies of food, arms and recruits which continued counter-insurgency measures directed against the population in general might have been expected to push their way? If so, the work of Professor Sorrenson, which deals with the land grievances of the Kikuyu, may point to the core of the political issue. In spite of its shortcomings, and these may have been more serious than Sorrenson allows, the attempt to reallocate and develop Kikuyu land was a major factor in making the informal settlement with the moderates acceptable. The work of Guy Wassermann points strongly in the same direction.[43]

Currently[44] in Rhodesia we have a situation which echoes in a measure the situation in Sudan after the failure of the Round Table Conference in 1965. The failure of negotiations with moderates led to a resumption of violence and the rise of a spirit of despair among some Southerners which only made the conflict more difficult to end. The likelihood of a Sudan-type settlement ever being reached in Rhodesia seems remote indeed.

Conclusions

In situations such as we have been describing, the methods usually employed to counter insurgency are largely self-defeating. This is true both of the propaganda and the military tactics employed. The propaganda used obscures the real nature of the conflict, and hence renders more unlikely the possibility of a solution being arrived at. Because of the variation in commitment to resistance which has been noted, the regime will be able to claim correctly that only a minority is willingly committed to violent action, and is likely to underestimate the extent of passive support. In a situation characterized by racial oppression, the regime cannot count on "loyalty" and seems bound to lose what is often described as its "hearts and minds" policy. Nevertheless, the regime is usually able to persuade itself without much difficulty that its counter-insurgency measures are primarily aimed at protecting "loyalists", and it will state correctly that resources being spent on counter-insurgency could be redirected to development if only the violence were to cease. But in the conflicts we are here concerned with, economic deprivation is one element only in the situation. Disenfranchisement rather than economic development is the root cause of the conflict, and it is argued that if enfranchisement were achieved, changed economic policies would be bound to follow. Military victories by the regime are as likely to drive people into overt opposition as to deter them from it. Particularly useless is the villageisation policy, unless accompanied by redress of grievances. In the case of Kenya, land was so close to the root of the political problem that redress of grievances was a possibility in this important sphere.

43   Wassermann p. 148.
44   April 1976.

Communal punishments, the imposition of a curfew, and detention without trial are all commonly resorted to, and again are as likely to aggravate the situation as they are to help contain it.

The propaganda war is not likely to be confined to the country in which the conflict occurs. Although the regime will claim that the conflict is a purely internal matter, it is most unlikely that it will be allowed to get away with this. The misuse of religion stems in large part from a desire to achieve international respectability.

It seems correct to conclude that the greatest danger to those committed to resistance comes, not from the regime, but from the tendency to disunity among themselves. It is sometimes argued that for this reason those involved in resistance need to be united by an ideology. On the evidence so far available from Africa, the adoption of an ideology is as likely to intensify conflicts among the resisters as it is to overcome them. People struggling to win freedom from oppression are not likely to appreciate having an ideology forced upon them. The fallacy that people can be united through having a religion or ideology forced upon them is one with a long history from which nothing seems to have been learnt.[45] When a conflict is internationalized, further possibilities of disunity are opened up. Whatever its shortcomings, Mau Mau had the merit of receiving no material aid from outside, and this source of disunity was therefore eliminated.[46] The Southern Sudanese received limited military aid from one source only, and it was all channelled through one person, General Lagu. The Rhodesian conflict has been more seriously beset by divisions and by disagreements over tactics. It remains to be seen whether divisions in Rhodesia will become as serious as those in Angola.

The regime will, of course, be able to exacerbate these divisions. It is not likely to find this task too difficult, and the more outside attention is directed towards the conflict, the greater the tendency for divisions to be perpetuated. It was stated earlier that the Rhodesian conflict occurred at the "right" time; at a time when the nationalist movements there could receive publicity and support from elsewhere. It is certain that no nation ought to be allowed to treat a civil war as a purely internal matter. Yet attention from outside is a two-edged weapon, and may not help towards a solution. Here a distinction

---

45   The best-known failure in history is perhaps that of the Emperor Constantine in the 4th century AD. Sudan's policy of Islamization seems to have had the effect of stiffening resistance; Mau Mau's use of some of the techniques of traditional religion, especially oathing, was no more successful. The resulting division is well described by Wanyoike:
...many of these loyalists were just simple but honest men and women who, after weighing the whole situation, decided to tolerate the colonial set-up until peaceful negotiations could bring the desired political changes.
If this view had been pursued, *Uhuru* might have taken longer to come; on the other hand, there would not have been so much bloodshed in the country.
Chapter 7 entitled "Conflict of Loyalties", pp. 193–4. The adoption of socialism by MPLA in Angola has not brought unity either as yet.

46   The same point was made by Professor Ali Mazrui in a public lecture at the University of Nairobi in March 1976.

must be drawn between the kind of attention paid by international groups such as Amnesty International, the International Commission of Jurists, the United Nations High Commission for Refugees, or truly international religious bodies, and the kind of outside attention paid by nation-states who undertake to supply arms and who will certainly be largely self-seeking in their intervention.

Finally it would seem possible to draw certain conclusions about the bargaining process. When a bargain is being struck, whether formally through a negotiated settlement, or informally, it is extremely unwise for any parties to the conflict to allow themselves to be excluded from the bargaining process, by their own intransigence or otherwise. It is equally unwise, of course, for the bargainers to enter into bargaining without making every effort to see that no significant element is excluded, and so has no stake in helping to keep the peace. It is worth backing down from strongly held positions if it means that those who would otherwise be excluded, can be brought in. The regime will always try to make a bargain with the moderates only, but if it succeeds, it may only be storing up trouble for a later date. All this demands a high degree of rationality, and an astute sense of timing.

REFERENCES

Information on *Rhodesia/Zimbabwe* is drawn mainly from:

BBC Monitoring Service: *Summary of World Broadcasts* Part IV, Africa, March 1974–July 1975.
GOOD, K.
    1974   "Settler Colonialism in Rhodesia", *African Affairs* 73, No. 290, January, pp. 10–36.
GRANT, G. C.
    1972/3   *The Africans' Predicament in Rhodesia*, Minority Rights Group, London.
KIRK, T.
    1975   "Politics and Violence in Rhodesia" *African Affairs* 74, No. 294 January, pp. 3–38.
MAXEY, Kees
    1975   *The Fight for Zimbabwe*, London.
SLATER, H.
    1975   "The Politics of Frustration: The ZAPU/ZANU Split in Historical Perspective"
        Kenya Historical Review, 3, 2, pp. 261–286.
WILKINSON, A. R.
    1973   *Insurgency in Rhodesia 1957–1973 An Account and Assessment*, International Institute
        for Strategic Studies, Adelphi Papers No. 20 London.

Information on *Kenya*:
CAROTHERS, J. C.
    1954   J. C. Carothers: *The Psychology of Mau Mau*, Nairobi.
CORFIELD, F. D.
    1960   *Historical Survey of the Origins and Growth of Mau Mau*, London and Nairobi.
LEAKEY, L. S. D.
    1954   *Defeating Mau Mau*, London.
LEIGH, Ione
    1954   *In the Shadow of Mau Mau*, London.

(These four have been used mainly for the evidence they give—reluctantly—on external
    sympathy for Gikuyu grievances and the Home Guard).

FURLEY, O. W.
    1971   "The Historiography of Mau Mau" *Hadith* 4, Nairobi, pp. 105–133.
KAGGIA, Bildad
    1975   *Roots of Freedom, 1921–1963*, Nairobi.
KAMUNCHULUH, J. T. S.
    1975   "The Meru Participation in Mau Mau" *Kenya Historical Review* 3, 2, pp. 193–216.
KARIUKI, J. M.
    1963   '*Mau Mau*' *Detainee*, London and Nairobi.
OGOT, B. A.
    "The Revolt of the Elders" *Hadith* 4, pp. 134–149.
ROSBERG, C. and J. NOTTINGHAM
    1966   *The Myth of Mau Mau*, London and Nairobi.
SORRENSON, M. P. K.
    1967   *Land Reform in Kikuyu Country*, Nairobi.
    1968   *Origins of European Settlement in Kenya*, Nairobi.
WANYOIKE, E. N.
    1974   *An African Pastor*, Nairobi.
WASSERMAN, G.
    1973   "Continuity and Counter-Insurgency—the Role of Land Reform in Decolonising
           Kenya 1962–70". *Canadian Journal of African Studies*, VIII, 1, pp. 133–148.
WELBOURN, F. B. and K. E. M. Students
    1961   *Comment on Corfield*, Makerere University College 1961 cyclostyled. A shortened
           version was published in *Pace*, London, May.
WISEMAN, E. M.
    1958   *Kikuyu Martyrs*, London.

Information on *Sudan*:

ALBINO, Oliver
    1971   *The Sudan: A Southern Viewpoint*, London.
           Anya Nya, periodical publication, London 1971–1972.
BESHIR, N. O.
    1968   *The Southern Sudan: Background to Conflict*, London.
    1975   *The Southern Sudan: From Conflict to Peace*, London.
EPRILE, C. B.
    1972   *Sudan: The Long War*, Institute of Conflict Studies, London.
    1974   *War and Peace in the Sudan*, London.
GINGYERA-PINYCWA, A. C. G.
    n.d.   "The Border Implications of the Sudan Civil War" in Wai, *op. cit.* pp. 123–136.
KAMANU, O. S.
    1974   "Secession and the Right of Self-Determination—An OAU Dilemma" *Journal of
           Modern African Studies*, 12, 3, pp. 355–376.
McCALL, R. S.
    1969   "The Rise of a Provisional Government in Southern Sudan," USSC Paper,
           Nairobi.
MORRISON, G.
    1971   *Sudan and Eritrea*, Minority Rights Group, London.
ODUHO, J. and W. DONG
    1963   *The Problem of the Southern Sudan*, London
RUSSELL, P. and R. S. McCALL
    1973   "Can Secession be Justified? The Case of the Southern Sudan" Seminar paper,
           Makerere University Kampala 1970. A revised version appeared in D. M. Wai
           (ed): *The Southern Sudan and the Problem of National Integration*, London, pp. 93–122.
SCHERF, Theresa
    1971   "The Sudan Conflict and its History and Development" World Council of Chur-
           ches, Geneva, cyclostyled.

The Grass Curtain, periodical publication, Southern Sudan Association, London 1970–1972. Verona Fathers

1964   *The Black Book of the Sudan—An Answer*, Verona.

Personal communications from Sudanese informants, correspondence and documents. These were given under a guarantee of confidentiality for the most part.

The Nigerian Civil War and the Angolan Civil War

Linkages between Domestic Tensions and International Alignments

J. ISAWA ELAIGWU

Ahmadu Bello University, Zaria, Nigeria

Introduction

THE TWENTIETH CENTURY has witnessed many changes – changes which have also affected the structure of the International System. There has been a "communications revolution" which has not only made the world a smaller place, but which has also relatively diluted the rigidity of the boundaries of the modern "nation-state" or "state-nation".[1] The effect of such a communications revolution on the sovereignty of the territorial "nation-state" has been extensively discussed by John Herz.[2]

Similarly, there has been a great population explosion which has caused much concern to some people. In fact, the question of family planning has become increasingly a crucial moot-point in international conferences. From the "balance of power" concept of the international system, there has been a move to a "bipolar" structure and then a "multipolar" structure. Also, the world has witnessed a new phenomenon. If the post-1945 global system witnessed alignments in the international system based on military capability, there has emerged a very important element – economic capability of new states. The effect of the recent Arab oil embargo on the West demonstrates the importance of economic capability as an instrument of international politics. Thus, it can be seen that military might alone is not enough of a criterion for international alignments. The new states which have oil have demonstrated

---

1 Sheldon Gellar makes a strong case about the development of Nation-States and State-Nations. In rejecting the tribe-tonation approach, Gellar shows that where a "Nation" precedes the "State", we have a "Nation-State". On the other hand, when a "State" precedes the development of a "Nation", it could be called a "State-Nation". Thus Nigeria may be regarded as a "State-Nation" while Guinea (Bissau) may be regarded as a "Nation-State". Refer to Sheldon Gellar, *State-Building and Nation-Building in West Africa* (Bloomington, Indiana: International Center, Indiana University, 1972) Occasional Paper, pp. 40–41. Also, Mostafa Rejai and Cynthia Enloe "Nation-States and State-Nations," *International Studies*, 13, No. 2, (June, 1969), p. 143.

2 John Herz, "Rise and Demise of the Territorial State," *World Politics*, (July, 1957), p. 473.

their "might" in the international system. At least, Arab oil was able to dilute the strength of support of the United States for Israel.

For new states, however, there are many problems of political development within the new international context. The relative isolation in which Britain, the United States and France, were able to resolve their problems of political development with little or no external interference is gone. The Congo (Zairean), Nigerian and Angolan experiences illustrate this point – not to mention experiences in Indo-China.

Furthermore, there has been a struggle among the major world powers over spheres of influence. Such desires for spheres of influence take into consideration the political and economic capability of the new states. In a world in which the 1973 energy crisis affected the industries of some major powers and imposed on them the necessity to conserve energy, the presence of oil in a new State excites interests external to its borders. Often such interests form strong undercurrents of ostensible ideological conflict among major powers.

Another important point, is that new states or developing nations face certain challenges of political development – state-building, nation-building, participation and distribution.[3] Whereas older countries, such as Britain, had the chance of coping with these problems sequentially, new states have to deal with them simultaneously. Very often, as in the former Congo (Leopoldville) and Angola, these states hardly had the opportunity to establish themselves before becoming arenas of international conflicts. The Vietnamese experience shows that such conflicts punctuate, if not halt, the process of development within the state.

In many cases, such international conflicts in new states have their domestic linkages. Domestic tensions get aggravated because of subtle or overt external intervention. In this paper, we shall be dealing with the linkages between domestic tensions (i.e. tensions among groups within a state) and international alignments among states. The Nigerian and Angolan Civil wars provide interesting case-studies.

This paper attempts a discussion of these linkages in the Nigerian and Angolan cases, the similarities and differences between the two cases, and the role of post-civil war Nigeria in the Angolan crisis.

---

3   *State-building* refers to the ability of the central government of a State to penetrate and control subnational groups. By *Nation-building*, we refer to the issue of creating unity among the various groups in a state. The challenge of *Distribution* deals with how to distribute allocatable resources relatively equitably among subnational groups. And the challenge of *participation* deals with the extent to which the citizens of a state are allowed to feed an input into the policy and decision-making institutions of a state. Refer to— Gabriel Almond and B. Powell, *Comparative Politics: A Developmental Approach* (Boston: Little, Brown, 1966); L. Binder, L. Pye, J. Coleman, P. Verba, J. La Palombara and M. Weiner, *Crises and Sequences in Political Development* (New Haven: Princeton University Press, 1971).

The Nigerian Civil War and International Alignments

On 1 October, 1960, Nigeria attained her independence from the British. The first five years after Nigeria's independence witnessed a number of political conflicts among various groups. The disputes over census exercises of 1962 and 1963, the crisis in the Western Region of 1962, the 1964 Federal Elections, and the 1965 Western Region Elections – are examples of issues of conflict which posed challenges to Nigeria's conflict resolution mechanism.

In response to the political tensions in Nigeria, the military intervened in the country's politics in January 1966. The nature of the January 1966 coup and subsequent events led to the massacre of people from the former Eastern Region (particularly the Ibos) in May 1966. Intramilitary suspicions and conflicts led to another coup in July 1966. The July coup is important because it failed to establish the authority of the Federal Government over the Eastern Region. The Eastern Region became quite autonomous in its relations with the Federal Government. Attempts to bring about a peaceful settlement of disputes between the Federal Government and the Government of the Eastern Region failed. The Aburi peace talks in Ghana (January 4–5, 1967) did not resolve the conflict.

Given the rising political temperature in the country and anxiety among the populace, many Nigerians felt the country was drifting into a greater crisis. Thus, when the Eastern Region declared its secession from the rest of Nigeria – as the Republic of "Biafra" – it was an anti-climax. Most people had expected that secession was only a few poles off. But the secession itself was symptomatic of the failure of Nigeria's conflict resolution mechanism to cope with, or resolve, the conflicts which pestered the life of the state. The secession itself was a challenge to Nigeria's statehood; it questioned the legitimacy of the central government to represent the geographical territory known as Nigeria.

In response to the declaration of secession, the Federal Government pledged to "crush the rebellion". The result was the civil war which lasted 30 months (July 1967–Janaury 1970). Given the domestic tensions which had climaxed in a civil war, what were the international ramifications of Nigeria's position?

What linkages may be identified between the belligerents in the Nigerian Crisis and other states within the international system? What was the nature of alignments in the international system in relation to the Federal Government and the secessionist "Biafran" Government?

In discussing the linkages between Nigeria's domestic tension and the external environment, two distinctions may be made. We shall discuss those linkages which are external to Africa (extra-continental), and those within the African continent (intra-continental).

Extra-continental linkages in the Nigerian Civil War

As mentioned earlier, the present nature of the international system and the communication revolution of the second half of the twentieth century, make it difficult to isolate local conflicts. Conflict situations which may be regarded as local, soon take on international dimensions.

The position of the major world powers on the Nigerian Crisis, varied from one power to the other. The *United States* made its policy clear at the beginning of the conflict. The U.S. Government would recognize only the Federal Government of Nigeria.[4] However, it declared that it would not sell any arms to any of the belligerents in the Nigerian Civil War. In fact, the United States refused to give Nigeria export permits allowing the purchase of arms on a commercial basis from U.S. manufacturers ostensibly because "the United States was basically opposed to interference in the internal affairs of another state."[5] Furthermore, the U.S. Secretary of State, Mr. Dean Rusk made it clear that "Nigeria was a British responsibility."

These statements drew angry responses from the Federal Military Government of Nigeria. The Federal Government pointed out that Nigeria never applied for military aid, as had been publicized in the United States. The government expressed its scepticism with regard to the reasons which the State Department gave for denying Nigeria export permits. In fact, a few days after the U.S. Government denied the Federal Government export permits, there were reports of three C130 Hercules transport planes with 150 personnel and 45 paratroopers sent to Zaire (Congo) to help Mobutu fight against rebels, by the United States.[6] Given the U.S. stand on Nigeria, this could be regarded as an "interference in the internal affairs of another state".

The Federal Government of Nigeria reacted quite angrily to Dean Rusk's statement. It reminded the United States that Nigeria had become an independent and sovereign State. It was no longer a British colony.[7]

To the Federal Government, the U.S.'s refusal to allow Nigeria to buy arms from manufacturers was an indirect way of supporting the secessionists, who would (in any case) buy arms from the "black-market". As far as the U.S. was concerned, it would supply relief to both sides engaged in the civil war. But as Cervenka aptly pointed out, the U.S. policy of "carrying out our moral obligations to respond effectively to humanitarian needs and not involving ourselves in the political affairs of others" did not work out that way.

> The U.S. humanitarian intervention in the conflict had distinctly political implications. First of all, it involved direct dealings with the Biafran authorities, which considerably strengthened the status of Biafra in striving for recognition. Secondly, the establishment of contact with Ojukwu's regime led to an increase of the pressure by the Biafran lobby in the U.S. for some kind of diplomatic relationship.[8]

4   This U.S. position seems to have been heavily influenced by its Ambassador, Elbert Mathews, who was known to have been very pro "One Nigeria".
5   *Christian Science Monitor*, Boston, 7 July, 1967; Zdeneck Cervenka, *A History of the Nigerian War: 1967–1970* (Ibadan: Onibonoje Press, 1971), p. 108.
6   Cervenka, *op. cit.*, p. 109.
7   It is understood that Dean Rusk apologized for this statement when he welcomed Dr. Okoi Arikpo, Nigeria's External Affairs Commissioner, to his office in Washington, in 1967.
8   Cervenka, *op. cit.*, p. 112.

Of course, it is important to note that there were pressures from within the Congress and among the American populace that the U.S. Government should change its policy. That the U.S. refused Nigeria permits to buy arms from its "traditional" source in time of trouble, signalled to Nigerian decision-makers that the U.S. did not wish their country well. The relationship between Nigeria and the U.S. reached a near-freezing point. That the U.S. gave no open recognition to the secessionists consoled the Federal Government. It would seem, however, that the U.S. really regarded Nigeria as being in the British political sphere. Its policy may be summed up as "trailing the British policy in Nigeria" while sitting on the fence. Moreover, Nigeria was not of "vital interest" to the U.S., as some State Department officials saw it.

The *British* were even more indecisive about their position at the initial stages of the conflict. The British adopted a "wait and see attitude". As the Minister of State in the Commonwealth Office told the Parliament on 25 Janauary, 1968 – "we are neutral to both sides.... We certainly are not helping one side or the other."[9]

The British Government was not going to stop the "traditional" supply of arms to Nigeria, even though it was not going to sell combat planes to Nigeria. After the invasion of the Midwestern State of Nigeria, the British policy of sitting on the fence faced a new challenge. As the British Foreign Secretary put it to the House of Commons on 12 June, 1968, to cut off aid to Nigeria would be a way of telling the Federal Government:

> We have put you in a position where you are heavily dependent on us for the instruments of power. Now when you are faced by a challenge to your authority, we will put you at a very serious disadvantage.

Such a policy would hurt British interests in Nigeria which had been estimated at 568 million dollars – about 53% of all foreign investments in Nigeria.

There was no doubt that British Government officials were quite aware of the delicate position of Britain in the Nigerian Civil War. This was evident in Mr. Maurice Foley's[10] address to the Parliament on 13 March, 1969.

> We have links extending over 100 years, we have 16,000 people in Nigeria, great invest-ments and much trade of enormous mutual benefit to Nigerians and ourselves. We have no other honorable option.

True, Britain's options were few. It had become clear that the Organiza-tion of African States stood for maintaining the territorial integrity of Nigeria. Only a few African States had recognized Biafra by the end of 1969.[11] The British Foreign Secretary could not have been more correct when he told the House of Commons on 13 July, 1969, that to cut off arms sales to Nigeria

---

9 Lord Shepherd in the Parliament, *The Times*, London, 26 January, 1968.
10 Maurice Foley was the Parliamentary Under-Secretary to the Foreign Office. Quotation is taken from Cervenka, *op. cit.*, p. 94.
11 These were Tanzania, Zambia, Ivory Coast and Gabon.

"would certainly have been a profound estrangement of ourselves from Nigeria and from Africa as a whole. It would have involved a great risk to the British people and to British interests in Nigeria."

Moreover, it had become clear that Nigeria was going to buy arms from the Soviet Union. Britain was afraid of being displaced as the main source of arms supply to Nigeria. In fact Nigerian Government officials made it clear that British interests would suffer if she cut off arms supplies to Nigeria. Chief Anthony Enahoro, Nigeria's Information Commissioner, made this clear in his letter to the Parliament.

> The first (effect of the stoppage) as I have indicated, would be to compel the Federal Government to turn to other sources of supply. The second is that the stoppage would confirm in the Nigerian mind allegations that the British Parliament and people do not really care whether or not Nigeria remains a United Country.[12]

The British Government's initial policy of vacillation changed to one of support for the Federal Government. There was no doubt that British arms contributed to the Federal Government's military performances in the Civil War. The British case illustrates the relationship between national self-interest and foreign policy. In a sense, it may be suggested that Britain's non-recognition of secession in Nigeria, might have kept the U.S. from recognizing "Biafra".

Another major support for the Federal Government came from the *Soviet Union*. Nigeria had been cold to the Soviet Union, and in fact the Federal Government had banned the distribution of Soviet literature in the country. During the Civil War, Nigeria turned to the Soviet Union for the purchase of arms, having been denied export permits to buy arms in the U.S. and the right to buy jets from Britain – her two main sources of arms supply.

The Soviet Union was anxious to maintain a "One Nigeria" against what it regarded as the attempts by imperialists to balkanize Africa for greater exploitation.[13] Its calculation of support for Nigeria might have been based on the assumption that African States would not take kindly to foreign interference. Moreover, Nigeria offered a new foothold for Soviet influence in Africa – a chance to effectively oppose "Western imperialists".

Nigeria sent a delegation to Moscow in June, 1967, and on 2 August, 1967, Nigeria and the Soviet Union signed a "cultural" pact – for exchanges in education, arts, sports etc. between the two countries. This was a prelude to the supply of the famous Russian Mig fighters to the Federal Government. Nigeria's

---

12   *The New York Times*, New York, 8 July, 1968, p. 34.
13   The *Izvestia*, 11 October, 1968, carried an outline of Soviet Policy—"If one approaches the present situation from the only correct standpoint, then one must say in all certainty that Biafra's secession is advantageous only to the imperialists... The interest of consolidating Nigeria's independence... and this can be achieved only by taking an anti-imperialist position... demands the preservation of the country's unity... a United Nigeria, within the principles of equality would be strictly observed for all nationalities... will more successfully resist the imperialists' pressure than a Nigeria fragmented and rent by tribalism..." (Quoted in Cervenka, *op. cit.*, pp. 106–107).

new Russian connection made many Western nations "schizoid". Rumors of Soviet adventure in Nigeria filled the pages of the Western press. Of course, Britain and the United States did not hide their anxiety. Western anxiety extracted a historical allusion from General Gowon (then Nigeria's Head of State). "Going to the Soviet Union, I assure you," General Gowon said, "was just a way of dealing with Ojukwu's threat. After all, Ojukwu started the air war. Even Abraham Lincoln went to Russia for help to win his own Civil War."[14]

On the other hand, *France* did not hide its support for the secessionists, even though it stopped short of recognizing "Biafra". France gave the impression, initially, that it was concerned with the humanitarian aspect of the war, yet it emphasized the right of peoples to self-determination.

France's position could not have been put more succinctly than by President De Gaulle. On 9 September, 1968, General De Gaulle remarked:

> It is not certain that the concept of a federation, which replaces in certain areas to a certain extent the concept of colonization, is always very good and very practical, and particularly in Africa—but not only in Africa, for in fact, that consists in automatically putting together very different peoples, sometimes very different indeed, and who, in consequence do not like it at all. One sees this in Canada, one sees this in Rhodesia, in Malaysia, in Cyprus, and one sees it in Nigeria.... In this affair, France has aided, is aiding Biafra as far as possible. She has not carried out the act which would be decisive, the action of recognizing the Republic of Biafra, because she considers that the management of Africa is above all an affair for the Africans.... This means that as far as France is concerned, the decision which has not been taken cannot be excluded in the future.[15]

It is not exactly clear why France aided the secessionists. It could be De Gaulle's fear of Nigeria in Africa – expecially in relation to Francophone African Countries. A huge and economically buoyant Nigeria may challenge the position of France in West Africa. That France vigorously opposed any equal treatment of Nigeria with Francophone Countries associated with the E.E.C. seems to indicate this fear. There also have been talks of the secessionists entering agreements with French *Safrap* Oil Company for monopoly over "Biafran" oil. In fact, one could also hypothesize that the balkanization of existing sovereign states had great appeal to De Gaulle – as illustrated by his parochial exhortation to French Canadians – "Long Live Quebec".

There was no doubt that French collaboration with the secessionists encouraged them in their fight. But it also led to strained relations between France and Nigeria – a relationship which took time to heal after the war.

Other actors on the secessionists' side come to mind. These include *Portugal, Israel, South Africa* and *China*. Portugal provided a European base for the secessionists; many of them flocked to Portugal after the Civil War.[16] The Federal Government claimed that a number of South African and Chinese

---

14 *Time*, New York, 4 July, 1969.
15 *Africa Research Bulletin*, London, Vol. 9, No. 5, October, 1968, p. 1186.
16 See N. U. Akpan, *The Struggle for Secession in Nigeria, 1966–1970: A Personal Account of the Nigerian Civil War* (London: Frank Cass, 1971).

mercenaries fighting for the secessionists had been killed during the Civil War. Israelis were said to have trained "Biafran" soldiers for the "Biafran" army. Portugal might have supported the secessionists because a fragmented Nigeria provided a more favorable climate for their colonies in Africa. Nigeria's support for the U.N. resolution asking Israel to leave all Arab-occupied land, may have turned Israel against the Federal Government. The Chinese position is still fairly unclear – especially since mercenaries do not necessarily represent their home governments.

What was the international line-up in Africa?

Intra-continental Linkages in the Nigerian Civil War

After the declaration of secession, the Federal Military Government took pains to point out its implications for other African States. It pointed out that if secession succeeded in Nigeria, other African States could also face the threat of disintegration. The Sudanese conflict, the Eritrean secessionist bids in Ethiopia, the Ewe irredentism in Ghana, and the Somalis in Kenya and Ethiopia – illustrated Nigeria's case.

Nigerian Government officials tried to convince other African States that balkanization of existing States in Africa would make them more amenable to exploitation by forces external to Africa. Moreover, the Federal Government emphasized Nigeria's success over secession would prove to the world that black men could rule themselves.

On the *bilateral level* of inter-state relations, only four African States recognized the secessionist "Biafran" Government. These were – Tanzania, Zambia, Ivory Coast and Gabon. It is not clear why Tanzania which had enlisted Nigeria's help in 1964 should be the first African country to recognize the "Biafran" Government. It would seem, however, that Nyerere did not see the use of force as the best way to solve Nigeria's crisis. He regretted the fact that Nigerian sovereignty was at stake. "The break-up of Nigeria is a terrible thing," he said, but "it is less terrible than that cruel war."[17] Both Tanzania and Zambia claimed to have recognized the secessionist government for humanitarian reasons.

On the other hand, *Ivory Coast* and *Gabon* might have succumbed to pressures from the French Government. The writer has no direct evidence to support this view. However, in De Gaulle's statement of 9 September, 1968, he made capital out of the fact that "there are States of East and West Africa which have recognized Biafra. Others will, perhaps, recognize it."[18] One wonders if De Gaulle could not have purposely encouraged Ivory Coast and Gabon to give recognition to the secessionists – thereby setting the platform for formal French recognition of Biafra. Of course, De Gaulle was quick to

---

17 N. M. A. Kirke-Greene, *Crisis and Conflict in Nigeria* (Ibadan: Oxford University Press), Vol. II, Document 218, p. 429. Also see, Julius Nyerere, "Why We Recognized Biafra" in *The Observer*, London, 28 April, 1968.
18 *Africa Research Bulletin*, London, Vol. 5, No. 9, October, 1968, p. 1187.

point out that "the decision which has not been taken cannot be excluded in the future."

It is not clear how far Presidents Houghouet-Boigny of Ivory Coast and Bongo of Gabon view Nigeria as a threat to them. A large Nigeria may threaten their positions in Western Africa. But there is no concrete evidence regarding such feelings of insecurity in these two countries.

At various points, some other African countries tried to table the Nigerian crisis at international conferences. Such suggestions by Gambia and Ghana received great disapproval from the Nigerian press. Generally, even those African countries which were against the Civil War did not come out to give recognition to Biafra. This brings us to the role of the Organization of African Unity.

The *Organization of African Unity* played an important part in the Nigerian crisis. At the Kinshasa summit in September 1967, the O.A.U. recognized the situation as "an internal affair, the solution of which is primarily the responsibility of Nigerians themselves." It expressed confidence in the Federal Military Government, and set up a Consultative Committee[19] to see the Head of the Federal Military Government. This Committee pointed out that any solution to Nigeria's problem must be in the context of a United Federation and that secessionists should accept the twelve-state structure of the country.

This was virtually an adoption of Nigeria's conditions for peace. The O.A.U. summit meeting at Algiers called on "all member states of the United Nations and the O.A.U. to refrain from any action detrimental to the peace, unity and territorial integrity of Nigeria."[20] The O.A.U. stand, it may be suggested, acted as a curb on the actions of many countries outside Africa which would have liked to recognize "Biafra". It is interesting that Britain, the United States, the Soviet Union and France – all recognized the importance of an African solution to the crisis. It seemed as if none of the major powers wanted to alienate African States. In fact, the O.A.U. appealed "to all governments, international organizations, humanitarian institutions as well as to all political, moral and religious bodies in the world to facilitate the implementation of the present resolution and to desist from any action, gesture and attitude likely to jeopardize the efforts of the O.A.U. in finding a solution to the Nigerian crisis."[21]

If the O.A.U. was unable to stop the four African countries from recognizing Biafra, if it was unable to effect any settlement of the Nigerian crisis at the Kampala, Niamey and Addis Ababa Peace Talks, it was at least able to restrain extra-continental forces from interfering blatantly in the Nigerian crisis. The concept of "Pax Africana" might not have been very successful when applied, in practice, to Nigeria, but it did dissuade non-African forces from imposing a solution on Nigerians.

---

19 This Committee of six Heads of State—Cameroon, Zaire, Ethiopia, Ghana, Liberia and Niger—visited Lagos on 22 and 23 November, 1967. Presidents' Mobutu of Zaire and Tubman of Liberia could not make it to Lagos.
20 Cervenka, *op. cit.*, p. 147.
21 *Ibid.*, p. 148.

Thus, given the stand of the majority of African States on the Nigerian crisis, extra-continental powers waited for Africans to provide a solution. Was the O.A.U. able to use its moral force to prevent such extra-continental intervention in Angola?

The Angolan Civil War and International Alignments

Foreign intervention in African conflicts is not new, especially when the country concerned has vast economic and strategic value, like Nigeria, the Congo and now Angola.[22]

On 11 November, 1975 Angola attained her independence after centuries of Portuguese colonial rule. It was unique because "for the first time in Africa, the metropolitan power abandoned a former colony to its own devices, without even the indulgence of its blessing on a new authority..." In his farewell speech, Admiral Cardoso, the Deputy High Commissioner, told the press that he had "ardently desired to leave sovereignty in the hands of a government of national unity, but it was not to be."[23]

Of course, after years of fighting the colonial power, Angolan nationalists had also started to fight one another. Intra-nationalist rifts deepened with the prospects of independence (precipitated as it was) and greater intervention by extra-continental forces, in what became known as the Angolan Civil War, after independence.[24]

At independence, three political movements became dominant in the Angolan political system. The Popular Movement for the Liberation of Angola (MPLA) established its headquarters in Luanda. Its leader Agostinho Neto had been sworn in as President by his Deputy on the central committee of the MPLA; Neto declared "The Peoples Republic of Angola" shortly afterwards.

The other political movement, the Front for the Liberation of Angola (FNLA) under the leadership of Holden Roberto, had its headquarters at Carmona. It drew its following largely from among the Bakongo tribe, in the North.

The third party, the National Union for the Total Independence of Angola (UNITA) drew its support from among the Ovimbundu. Under its leader, Jonas Savimbi, the movement had entrenched itself in the Southern part of the country, with its headquarters at Huambo.

On 11 November, 1975, FNLA and UNITA formed an uneasy alliance.[25]

---

22 *The Sunday Telegraph*, London, 21 December, 1975, p. 13.
23 *West Africa*, 17 November, 1975, p. 1362.
24 It was generally regarded as a war of liberation before independence.
25 We have not gone into details on the historical development of those movements. However, it may be noted that Jonas Savimbi and Holden Roberto were members of the same movement until their rift in the early 1960s. In this alliance, FNLA was to provide the President and the Military Commander, while UNITA was to provide the Prime Minister. The "Council of Revolution"—the political expression of this uneasy alliance was to have its temporary seat at Nova Lisboa (Huambo). *West Africa*, 17 November, 1975, p. 1362. A very interesting account of the Angolan situation is contained in *Afriscope*, Vol. 6, No. 7, February, 1976, pp. 43–48.

They declared the "Popular and Democratic Republic of Angola", with its capital at Carmona.

Unlike Nigeria (which had had six years of post-independence experience before a civil war), Angola had no single central government. It hardly became independent before being transformed into an arena for international conflict. What were the external linkages of these nationalist movements which laid claim to political power in Angola? We may start our discussion again from the extra-continental (i.e. extra-African) pattern of alignments.

Extra-continental Linkages in the Angolan Civil War

In discussing the Angolan Civil War, the *Soviet Union* comes into limelight – far more than in the Nigerian Civil War. It seems as if the Soviet Union had learnt lessons from its half-hearted involvement in Congo (Kinshasa) in the 1960s. Soviet support for the MPLA pre-dated independence. As pointed out by *West Africa* of 11 December, 1975, "Soviet aid to the MPLA dates back to well before independence and, while deplored by some, can be excused to some extent by the responsibility to continue to support her friends....."

The Soviet Union had consistently supported MPLA. It had provided arms and ammunition to MPLA, although its exact quantity is not available to the writer. In fact, the *Sunday Telegraph,* of 21 December, 1975, reported that Russian warships and 20 Mig fighters were being held in readiness to intervene in Angola, if the South African squadron of mirage fighters was used to support UNITA and FNLA forces.[26]

The Soviet Union did not deny its support for the MPLA. In an obvious response to U.S. criticism of the Soviet Union's role in Angola, Brezhnev declared:

> Some bourgeois leaders raise a howl over the solidarity of Soviet Communists with the struggle of other peoples... détente does not in the slightest abolish or alter the laws of the class struggle [and] no one should expect that because of détente Communists will reconcile themselves with capitalist exploitation.[27]

He went further to say – "We make no secret of the fact that we see détente as the way to create more favorable conditions for...communist construction."[27] The Soviet official newspaper pointed out that "as an important principle of Soviet foreign policy, Soviet aid to Angola will continue."[28]

Soviet support for the MPLA generated shivers in the State Department of the *United States* Government. The United States had complained about a Soviet guided missile carrier and tank loading-ship heading for Angola. On the other hand, a report by a "reputable international organization", (published by *The Observer*, London, 11 Janaury, 1976, pp. 1 and 2) claimed that the United States involvement in the Angolan conflict was greater than realized. It claimed that an American "task force", led by aircraft carrier "Independ-

---

26   *The Sunday Telegraph,* 21 December, 1975, p. 6.
27   *Newsweek,* 8 March, 1976, p. 10.
28   Quoted in *The Sunday Times,* London, 28 December, 1975, p. 6.

ence", supported by a missile cruiser and 3 destroyer exorts – had been placed on contingency orders between 15–23 November, 1975.[29]

Despite denials by the Pentagon, the report claimed that the "'Independence' sailed out on 27–28 November, 1975, for a mission in the Angolan conflict." The report went further to show that the U.S. played a direct role in operations in the central front of the Angolan War, parachuting supplies to the South African columns. This report, if true, shows how deeply involved the U.S. was in the Angolan War.

There was evidence to show that the United States had covertly (through the C.I.A.) supplied the FNLA with money and arms.[30] In fact, Henry Kissinger told the Senate that one-third of the emergency aid recently provided for Zaire was meant for "the non-Communist factions in Angola."[31] This sort of aid was classified as "a legitimate covert operation" to help pro-Western elements in Angola.

As far as the United States was concerned, Angola was not just going through a period of "Cubanization", but a period of witnessing the Communist spread of influence in Africa. It had to be stopped. The United States carried out a diplomatic offensive in Africa, through its Assistant Secretary of State for African Affairs, William Schaufele. William Schaufele had visited some African countries to convince them of the necessity to withdraw all foreign troops from Angola and for the formation of a "government of National Unity".

While the United States Government was pro-FNLA/UNITA, and wanted a more active role in the Angolan crisis, the Vietnam experience (based on a similar "domino" theory) dissuaded the American Congress from approving another possibly catastrophic international adventure.

On the other hand, *Britain's* role was not very clear. It had been rumored that Britain was pro-UNITA, but the British Government had taken care to prevent giving such an impression openly. As the *Sunday Telegraph* pointed out, "Officials in Washington believe that differences over Angolan policy have caused the first rift in the strong friendship between Mr. Callaghan, Foreign Secretary and Dr. Kissinger, American Secretary of State."

Dr. Kissinger had hoped that "Britain would bring influence to bear on Black African Governments" to turn away from their support for the MPLA. But instead, "Mr. Callaghan had taken the line that Britain could not afford to be linked with Rightist elements in Angola, partly because this would mean siding with South Africa."[32] Mr. Callaghan had told NATO Ministers in

---

29 The "Independence" carries 90 F-4 phantom jets and after 15 November, was reported to have been armed with "several tons of napalm sidewinder missiles and anti-personal fragmentation bombs in pods." *The Observer*, London, 11 January, 1976, p. 1.

30 *The Sunday Telegraph*, 21 December, 1975, p. 13.

31 *West Africa*, 13 November, 1975, p. 1368. *Newsweek*, 19 January, 1976, p. 8, claims that Washington had spent $25 million on FNLA/UNITA. *The Sunday Telegraph*, 21 December, 1975, p. 6, reported that Kissinger was asking Congress for $35 million for Angolan operations. The Senate turned down the request.

32 *The Sunday Telegraph*, 21 December, 1975, p. 24.

December 1975, that all foreign forces should withdraw from Angola and that the West should support OAU peace moves.

Unlike Britain's unclear "sit-on-the-fence" policy over Angola, Cuba came out strongly for the MPLA. Cuban forces in Angola had risen from an estimated 5,500 in mid-December, 1975 to about 11,000 in early February 1976. Prime Minister Castro told a news conference on 15 January, 1976, with regard to Cuban forces in Angola:

> The United States was fighting in Vietnam against the revolutionaries (who were) against imperialism and foreign aggressors. Our presence there [Angola] is a source of satisfaction and pride for us.[33]

As far as Cuba was concerned, she was merely helping fellow revolutionaries to gain control over their land.

On the other hand, *France* supported the FNLA. Not only had mercenaries been recruited from France, she was said to have given FNLA 1 million (pounds sterling) interest free loan. France is also reported to have backed the Front for the Liberation of Cabinda Enclave (FLEC) to detach Cabinda from Angola.[34] Incidentally, Zaire, where French ties are reportedly very good, is a strong supporter of the FNLA.

An interesting case, is that of *China* (Peking). From 1964, China had started to support FNLA.[35] Peking seemed to have reacted to the Soviet Union's support for the MPLA. Although China cautiously withdrew "its instructors from anti-MPLA camps", it is reported to have continued to supply arms and was strident in its denunciation of the Russian presence."

As the *Sunday Telegraph* commented:

> Pretoria and Peking make strange bedfellows, but the Angolan situation has thrown into turmoil alliances, allegiances and sympathies, not only throughout Africa but across the globe.[36]

What was the nature of alignments among African States on the Angolan issue?

Intra-continental Linkages in the Angolan Civil War

The alignments of States on the Angolan issue were interesting. In the first place, *South Africa's* role was most important to some African States. Unlike in the Nigerian case, South Africa invaded parts of Angola in alliance with UNITA/FNLA forces.

South Africa was reported to have sent 1,000–1,500 men, through Namibia, into Angola, on 23 October, 1975. The second regular unit (between 1,000 to

---

33 *International Herald Tribune* (Paris), 6 February, 1976, p. 2.
34 Patrick Wilmot, "Angola: Denouncement of a Tragedy," (Mimeograph, p. 6), Department of Sociology, Ahmadu Bello University, Zaria, Nigeria.
35 S. G. Ikoku, "Angola: A Case Study in Neo-Colonialism," in *Afriscope*, Vol. 6, No. 2, 2 February, 1976, p. 45.
36 *The Sunday Telegraph*, 21 December, 1975, p. 13.

1,500) was committed to action on 15 November, 1975. This was equipped with 100 French AMX-13 and US M-41 Walker Bulldog tanks. Its mission was to give support to mercenary columns in combat. South African troops, operating from Namibia, used C-130 planes to drop supplies to columns and later used airports at Sa da Bandeira and Silva Porto (UNITA and FNLA headquarters) in its fight with the MPLA.

The South African Prime Minister expressed his country's concerns thus:

> It is obvious that South Africa is concerned over blatant Russian and Cuban intervention in Angola. We are concerned because we know that the aim is... to endeavor to create a whole row of Marxist States from Angola to Dar es Salaam, and if it is at all possible, to divide Africa into two in that way. A Marxist Angola... undoubtedly enables the communists to stand astride the Cape Sea route and to act at will as they find it necessary to the detriment of the free world and the West. South Africa is concerned about these dangers and problems.[37]

It would seem that South Africa feels insecure now that the two former Portuguese colonies (which had acted as its buffer against independent African countries) have attained independence. While South Africa had been schizo-phrenic about communism, its present fear seems to lie in the potentiality of traumatic changes within the Apartheid Republic.

The involvement of South Africa in the War changed the stance of many African countries. *Nigeria* which had openly supported a "government of National Unity", turned round to support the MPLA. *Tanzania* also attacked South Africa's attempt to create a "client State in Angola now that it has no Portuguese ally in the country."[38] Even anti-communist Sudan backed MPLA. *West Africa* could not have been more correct when it described South Africa as "still the bogey-man of Africa."[39]

On the other hand, there were other African countries which supported the establishment of a "government of National Unity" in Angola. Notable among these were *Zaire* and *Zambia*. Zaire had been in favor of FNLA – for a long time.[40] Zambia, like Zaire, is worried about who controls the Benguela railway, and the port of Lobito. Zambia's support for UNITA may be regarded as an attempt to safeguard its national interest since it is a landlocked country.

Senegal's stand is hard to explain. It may have been influenced by the United States. Or in fact, Senegal might have differed with Nigeria on principles. For the first time, the OAU abandoned its traditional compromise solutions to issues. Consensus among African States in the OAU was abandoned as MPLA supporters and supporters of a "government of National Unity" had equal votes – with Uganda and Ethiopia remaining neutral.[41] Both countries recognized MPLA after the OAU meeting. In fact, following the meeting between Zaire's President Mobutu and MPLA's Neto, (under the auspices of

---

37　*The Guardian*, London, 18 January, 1976, p. 6.
38　*Ibid*.
39　*West Africa*, 15 December, 1975, p. 1516.
40　Holden Roberto is the brother-in-law of Mobutu of Zaire.
41　Line up at the OAU Meeting on Angola.

Marien Ngouabi), Zaire recognized the MPLA Government of Angola. Zaire was to expel UNITA and FNLA movements and to prevent FLEC from operating against Cabinda. In exchange, 6,000 former Katangan policemen in exile in Angola were to be repatriated at Mobutu's request.[42]

At the time of writing, over two-thirds of the African States have recognized the MPLA Government in Angola. Recognition of the MPLA Government from outside Africa has also been on the increase. The association of FNLA/UNITA with South Africa had stigmatized them in the eyes of many Africans – as "sell-outs" and "imperialist agents". As the Reuters News Agency reported on 25 February, 1976, "MPLA and the new People's Republic have won the day and Africa and the rest of the world are hastening to back the winner."[43]

Nigerian and Angolan Experiences in Comparative Perspective

Nigeria, like Angola, is a large country in terms of its area. Nigeria has an area of 356.7 square miles as compared to Angola's 481.4 square miles. While Angola occupies a larger area than Nigeria, it has less population (about 6 million by the 1976 estimate, compared to Nigeria's 63.87 million[44] by the 1969 estimate).

For MPLA	Neutral	Government of National Unity
Algeria	Ethiopia	Botswana
Benin	Uganda	Central African Republic
Burundi		Egypt
Cape Verde		Gabon
Chad		Gambia
Comoros		Ivory Coast
Congo Republic		Kenya
Equitorial Guinea		Lesotho
Ghana		Liberia
Guinea		Malawi
Guinea (Bissau)		Mauritania
Libya		Morocco
Madagascar		Rwanda
Mali		Senegal
Mauritius		Sierra Leone
Mozambique		Swaziland
Niger		Togo
Nigeria		Tunisia
Sao Tome		Upper Volta
Somalia		Zaire
Sudan		Zambia
Tanzania		

42 *The Times*, London, 1 March, 1976, p. 4; also *West Africa*, 8 March, 1976, p. 324.
43 *Reuters*, 25 February, 1976, 0804, (WAF 522 EPB992).
44 Keesing's Research Report, 6, *Africa Independent* (New York: Scribner and Sons, 1972), p. 104.

Both countries are economically wealthy. Nigeria's chief products include petroleum, groundnuts and groundnut oil, palm produce (oil and kernels), cocoa, tin and columbite, and timber. Angola has diamonds, petroleum, iron ore, coffee, sugar, wheat, sisal and tobacco. But even more important is Angola's strategic position. The *Sunday Telegraph* described Angola's position quite succinctly:

> Angola is a rich prize, probably the first prize in Africa. Its natural resources, including oil and other minerals, its abundance of water and timber and its port commanding the approaches to the South Atlantic give it an economic and strategic potential greater than that of South Africa.[45]

The political background of the two countries is also different. While Nigeria attained independence from the British without any physical fight for it, Angolans fought for over ten years to attain their independence from the Portuguese. If Nigeria had the luxury of six years of indigenous rule before her Civil War, Angola hardly had that luxury. In fact, the Angolan Civil War posed two problems. After independence, there was not only the problem of giving recognition to the Angolan State in international bodies like the United Nations, there was also the problem of agreement on which political movement should form the central Angolan Government.

In a way, the Angolan crisis was similar to Nigeria's. Both emanate from the inability of the government at the center to control all parts of the country – a challenge to the state-building process. Just as Gowon's Lagos-based Government lacked any effective authority over the former Eastern Region, so was the MPLA Government ineffective in exercizing control over FNLA and UNITA controlled areas of the north and the south. In Nigeria, it took a Civil War to re-establish this control. In Angola, it is taking a Civil War to establish MPLA control over the whole country, for the first time.

On the other hand, the issue in the Nigerian Civil War was secession. In Angola, it is an attempt by each of the rival movements to establish its authority over the whole country, and to form a central government. So far, none of the movements has declared secession, Ojukwu or Tshombe-style. In fact, Ethiopia tried to make this distinction when it gave "full recognition to the new State

---

45 *The Sunday Telegraph*, 21 December, 1975, p. 13.
The Federal Government of Nigeria also recognizes Angola's important position. In his speech to the National Conference on "Nigeria and the World," in Lagos, on 27 January, 1976, the Federal Commissioner for Industry, Col. Wushishi said:
"Angola should not, under normal circumstances, be of strategic importance to Africa more or less than any other African country but for certain exceptional considerations.... By virtue of her navigable rivers and traditional slave trade routes, including the Benguela Railway into the hinterland, she is able to control the flow of trade from certain Central African countries such as Zaire, Zambia and Rhodesia to the sea. Furthermore, Angola occupies a very strategic position on the South Atlantic sea route to and from the Cape of Good Hope which is a vital link between the highly industrialized countries in Europe and their markets in Africa and Asia. The riches of Angola—diamonds, petroleum, copper and coffee to name a few, have been of special interest to West European countries which exploited the territory during colonial administration...".

forming an indivisible unit within its present geographical and political boundaries."[46] Ethiopia was thus avoiding (at least for a while) having to choose between the movements but setting herself against secession.

More interesting is the nature of international alignments in both cases. While the United States virtually towed British footsteps in the Nigerian Civil War, Britain refused to go along with the United States' stand on the Angolan issue. It was no wonder that Kissinger "felt let down or disappointed with British reaction to his stand over the supply of arms to Right-wing factions in Angola."[47]

The position of France seems quite consistent in both cases. Just as it supported Biafra's secession, so did it encourage the separation of Cabinda from Angola by its support for the FLEC. In both Nigeria and Angola, the Soviet Union did back the horse which was eventually to win. The most interesting case was Peking's strange bedfellow in the Angolan War – South Africa. Peking must have backed FNLA mainly because of Soviet support for the MPLA – some sort of ideological clash carried over to an African arena. Peking's quiet withdrawal must have been in response to anti-South African feelings in Africa. Tanzania's recognition of "Biafra" had led to the break in diplomatic relations with Nigeria in 1968; the Angolan situation saw both countries in one camp. Both countries vigorously opposed the South African invasion of Angola, and both recognized the MPLA Government in Angola. On the other hand, the alliance between Tanzania and Zambia in the Nigerian Civil War when both recognized Biafra, became diluted. Zambia, in its desire to protect its interests opted for a "government of National Unity".

It is not exactly true to claim that those African countries which recognized the MPLA were communist countries. Sudan is the most anti-communist in Africa, given Nimeiry's 1971 experience of a communist coup attempt. Nigeria cannot easily be called a communist country. Even countries such as Tanzania and Mozambique which have strong links with the Chinese, supported the MPLA Government.

One glaring difference between the Nigerian and Angolan Civil Wars was the mode of external involvement. Unlike the Nigerian case, Cuba actually sent troops to fight alongside MPLA forces on Angolan soil. While there had been talks of South African mercenaries on the Biafran side of the Nigerian Civil War, in Angola South African Government troops actually invaded Southern Angola. By invading Angola, South Africa turned many countries which would have otherwise supported a "government of National Unity", into pro-MPLA camps. While "Biafran" friendship with Portugal made some African countries cold to its cause, in the Angolan case, Portugal had virtually cleared its bad name among African countries.

Why did Angola excite greater direct international intervention than Nigeria? The first reason lies in Angola's strategic position. Not only is it well-

---

46 *West Africa*, 17 November, 1975, p. 1363.
47 *The Sunday Telegraph*, 21 December, 1975, p. 24.

placed on the sea route to South Africa, East Africa and Asia, it borders directly with Namibia (under South Africa's control). For the racist regimes of Rhodesia and South Africa, the former Portuguese countries provided "buffers" against liberation movements, and against insurgency activities by independent black African States.

As far as the United States is concerned, Soviet influence in Angola threatened her interests in both Angola and South Africa – and these interests are quite enormous. The anti-communist propaganda being fanned by America's "domino theory" in Indo-China may be a facade for her larger interests. It was no wonder then that the U.S. Senate refused to approve Kissinger's request for 35 million dollars to help anti-communist forces in Angola. Senator Mike Mansfield might have been speaking the mind of many Americans when he said recently – "It would be better to keep our mouth a little more tightly shut and our powder a little more dry." In response to a question about Cuba's possible invasion of Rhodesia, Senator Mike Mansfield retorted – "It is not for us to say who should or should not become involved. Certainly we shouldn't (become involved)."[48]

Another reason for the international concern over Angola is to be found in the issues at stake. In the Nigerian case, it was the issue of secession. Many African countries face similar threats. It was therefore not difficult to get OAU consensus to pass a resolution supporting the federal military government. Moreover, it was not difficult to see that it was an internal affair of Nigeria. In Angola, there was no "Angolan Government" to protect its interests.

In Angola, the issue was not just secession. It dealt with i) the sensitive issue of liberating African countries; and ii) a similarly sensitive issue of South Africa trying to establish a "client state" (as some States saw it) in Angola, to perpetuate' apartheid and racism. The South African issue made a whole lot of difference. The Organization of African States split into two – abandoning its traditional approach of relative consensus among most states. To some countries, the Congo experience of 1960 was still verdant in their memories. Africa was not to be an arena for international conflict again – a situation some African countries felt would emerge under a "government of National Unity". It is interesting that none of the countries which supported a "government of National Unity" recognized FNLA/UNITA.

If in the Nigerian Civil War, the OAU stand prevented blatant external intervention, in the Angolan case, there was hardly an accepted OAU stand – beyond withdrawal of all foreign forces in Angola. The split in the OAU does not indicate the failure of that Organization. It does indicate that African states have attained such a level of political maturity that they can now agree to disagree. The "strictly cooperative" attitude among African states on African issues indicated Africa's insecurity in relation to the outside world. The new trend, if channelled along constructive paths and limited to certain levels

---

48   *New Nigerian*, Kaduna, 30, March, 1976, p. 12.

of hostility, may augur well for the future. This brings us to Nigeria's role in the Angolan crisis.

Post-civil War Nigeria in the Angolan Civil War

From her 30-month Civil War, Nigeria emerged stronger than she had ever been. But until recently, Nigeria's foreign policy had been moderate. She has been described many times as the "sleeping giant" in Africa.

As late as 23 November, 1975, Nigeria still supported a "government of National Unity" in Angola. Joe Garba, Nigeria's Commissioner for External Affairs – pointed out that Angola had become a sovereign state and that the OAU could not make decisions without the consent of all the liberation movements in Angola.[49]

Yet two days later (25 November), Nigeria announced her recognition of the MPLA as "truly representing the interests of the people of Angola."[50] Why did Nigeria change her position on Angola so dramatically, given her criticism of the Soviet Union's premature recognition of the MPLA?

After Angola's independence, Nigeria had hoped that pressure would be brought on the rival movements to unite. As Colonel Joe Garba put it:

> Then, last week we had evidence—very, very positive evidence—of the direct involvement of South Africa on the side of FNLA and UNITA command... We were left with no option but to recognize the MPLA because... apart from being the most organized of the liberation movements they have the overwhelming support of the population. If you look at the long term objectives of Africa, to do away with apartheid in South Africa, they are the ones who actively pose a threat [to it].[51]

Thus, the main reason for Nigeria's change of her position was the invasion of Angola by South Africa. Secondly, it has been suggested that Nigeria's recognition of the MPLA could be seen as a new form of competition for leadership roles between Zaire and Nigeria in Africa. Both countries have often been referred to as the "two giants" of Africa. A Nigerian official was quoted by *Africa* to have said – "we cannot stand aside and let Zaire expand its sphere of influence into Angola."[52] Hence, Nigeria's support for MPLA could be seen as an attempt to curb Zaire's ambitions. Yet, it may be suggested, that Angola provided the Mohammed government with an opportunity to take a new approach to African affairs – a role of leadership which Nigeria had been too shy to undertake in the past.

Once the Nigerian Government had made up its mind to support MPLA, it backed its decision up with active diplomatic canvassing. The Nigerian Government sent her envoys to Ghana, Niger, Libya, Chad and other African countries to persuade them to recognize MPLA.

---

49   *Sunday Times*, Lagos, 23 November, 1975, p. 1.
50   *West Africa*, 1 December, 1975, p. 1462; *The Nigeria Standard*, Jos, November, 1975, p. 1.
51   *West Africa*, 8 December, 1975, p. 1502.
52   *Africa*, No. 54, February, 1975, p. 13.

The Nigerian Government seemed most angered by the United States' canvassing in Africa. It seemed as if the main diplomatic "battle" was between Nigeria and the United States, at a point. President Ford's letter to African Heads of State worsened the situation. Not only did Nigeria publish the contents of President Ford's letter, she sent a strongly-worded reply to the letter. Nigeria accused the United States of "arm-twisting" and of "insulting the intelligence" of African leaders. She reminded the United States that the days when Africa would bow to the "overbearing" dictates of super-powers had gone.

At the OAU summit on Angola, Nigeria led pro-MPLA forces. She pointed out the dangers of allowing the South African threat to African States to go unchecked. Nigeria even went as far as offering financial aid to the MPLA Government in Angola.[53] The recognition of the MPLA Government by the OAU and its acceptance as a member state was seen by most Nigerians as a success for the Federal Military Government in its new foreign policy. As Colonel Wushishi rationalized the Nigerian stand on Angola:

> Independent Africa is committed to work to bring all dependent territories on the continent to a stage of responsible independence. Africa cannot therefore afford to be indifferent or sit on the fence whilst the territorial integrity and sovereignty of a nation which has fought hard for its independence is being violated.[54]

There is no doubt that Nigeria, given its resources and size, has taken a new role of leadership in Africa. For a large country of its size, with its economic resources, Nigeria must tread gently along as it acts out its leadership role. Smaller African States are not likely to accept Nigerian imperialism in place of extra-continental forms of imperialism. Nigeria's capability in handling intra-African affairs, in such a way that it provides safeguards for the interests of smaller States, while standing firm on extra-continental forms of exploitation, may be the greatest test of its political maturity. The ECOWAS provides a non-crisis situation for displaying Nigeria's ability to provide leadership for African States.

Conclusion

Diplomatic recognitions and victory in the battlefields are not the only aspects to ending a Civil War. The Nigerian experience shows that the "battlefield" is only an aspect of the Civil War. The more difficult task is one of reconciliation.

The MPLA in Angola may eventually succeed in warding off South African aggression. It may have succeeded in uprooting the FNLA, and may finally bring the whole country under its authority. It does seem that the MPLA may

---

53   The actual amount of aid given to Angola is not available to the writer at the time of writing.

54   Speech by Federal Commissioner for Industries, Col. Wushishi at the opening of the National Conference on "Nigeria and the World," held at the Nigerian Institute for International Affairs, Lagos, 27 January, 1976, p. 6.

have to display a more conciliatory attitude to the other Angolan movements which have lost in the battlefields. The aim should be one of bringing all Angolans under the political umbrella of a single government for the development of the country. In this light the necessity to forgive and forget cannot be over-emphasized.

If Nigeria has emerged from her Civil War only to take an active role in another country's civil war – the end of the Angolan Civil War may be just the beginning of its role in African politics. Many African States expect that Angola, like Mozambique, would take an active part in the liberation of the rest of Africa. Angola may be expected to take a leading role in Africa's relations with the outside world in the future, given its strategic position. It is not likely to be an easy role to fill.

Our discussions in this paper show how domestic tensions take on international dimensions. The nature of international alignments among States vary, depending on the issues and the situations. It only confirms the popular adage in English diplomacy, that only the interests of nations are perpetual; the nature of alignments are subject to change.

The Angolan Civil War shows that Africans have agreed to disagree. It remains to be seen how African nations can limit the extra-continental ramifications of domestic tensions within the individual African state in the future.

Soldiers as Traditionalizers

Military Rule and the Re-Africanization of Africa*

ALI A. MAZRUI

The University of Michigan, Ann Arbor, U.S.A.

AN EARLIER generation of political scientists working on Africa tended to draw from their work in West Africa conclusions about black Africa as a whole. Much of what occurred in West Africa was regarded as evidence of likely trends elsewhere in the continent. Such predictions were sometimes vindicated. The growth of modern nationalism in West Africa from the 1930's onwards did spread to other parts of Africa. The emergence of one-party systems in West Africa found imitators within a few years in other African countries. Even the application of a particular analytical concept to a West Africa situation – like David E. Apter's analysis of Kwame Nkrumah as a "charismatic leader" – soon led to a more dubious scramble to identify other "charismatic" figures in Tanzania, Zambia, Kenya, Malawi, Uganda and elsewhere.[1]

If on at least some matters West Africa once provided evidence of likely trends elsewhere on the continent, is it possible that East Africa's experience in other domains might now be similarly assessed as a traffic indicator for the rest of the continent? Are there aspects of recent East African history which should raise questions about likely trends in other African regions?

What is at stake is partly the *methodology of hypothesizing*, perhaps as part of the methodology of research. Would it be fruitful to frame a hypothesis for testing in Gabon or Niger on the basic conclusions drawn from research in Uganda? As a *comparative Africanist* this author is of the opinion that comparative politics as a whole means nothing if it does not include readiness to use evidence from one part of Africa as potential material for formulating Africa-

---

* This paper was originally presented at the annual convention of the Canadian Association of African Studies, York University, Canada, February 1975. A version of it has since been published in *World Politics*, Vol. XXVIII, No. 2, 1976.

1 Influential works of that period include James S. Coleman, "Nationalism in Tropical Africa", *The American Political Science Review*, XLVII, No. 2, June 1954; Coleman, *Nigeria: Background to Nationalism*; David E. Apter, *The Gold Coast in Transition* (Princeton: Princeton University Press, 1955); Gabriel Almond and James S. Coleman (eds.) *The Politics of the Developing Areas* (Princeton: Princeton University Press, 1960) and Martin Kilson "Authoritarian and Single-Party Tendencies in African Politics," *World Politics* Vol. 15 No. 2 January 1963.

wide hypotheses. It would then be up to other researchers to test some of these hypotheses against empirical findings elsewhere in the continent.

The recent behaviour and policies of a number of military regimes in Africa are raising new questions about the role of the military in the dialectic between tradition and modernity. My own most concentrated research on this subject has focussed on Uganda, but the Ugandan experience raises wider questions which other researchers elsewhere may wish to pursue further. This is particularly so when we allow for the possibility that the Ugandan experience may be less unique than the personality of Idi Amin may at first give us to understand.

If General Idi Amin of Uganda is indeed as "atavistic" as he seems to be, can he also be a modernizer? Is the cultural nationalism of General Mobuto Sese Seko of Zaire developmental or retrograde? Is General Bokassa of the Central African Republic an incongruous warrior in the wrong century? Is Colonel Quaddafy of Libya anachronistic? Before we grapple with these issues, let us first return to an older generalization.

An Older Hypothesis: Soldiers as Modernizers

The 1960's witnessed among social scientists an increasing belief that the armed forces were agents of modernization. An early convert to this view was Lucian W. Pye. Pye drew a legitimate distinction between the army as a modern organization and the army as a modernizing force. He conceded that the status of the army as a modern organization was clearer than its modernizing impact on the rest of the society. He saw the military establishment as something which came "as close as any human organization can to the ideal type of an industrialized and secularized enterprise." Most of the colonial armies were based on western military technology, and had used the World War II type of army as their model. To that extent they had utilized a form of organization peculiar to a highly industrialized civilization. The need for discipline within the armed forces, the necessity for them to relate means to ends, the need for technical skills and co-ordination of effort, all converted the military establishment into a modern organization.

The question which arose was whether it was also a modernizing agency, helping to change the rest of the society away from traditionalist preconceptions and towards a pattern of behaviour more characteristic of modern societies. On balance, Pye was optimistic about the modernizing capabilities of the armed forces in developing countries.[2]

This approach to the study of the military was applied more directly to African situations by a number of scholars, and continued to influence scholarly assessments of the impact of the military in African societies right into the the 1970's. Ernest E. Lefever put the point of view at its most extravagant when he asserted:

2   Lucian W. Pye, "Armies in the Process of Political Modernization," in *The Role of the Military in Underdeveloped Countries*, edited by John J. Johnson (Princeton University Press, 1962) pp. 80–89.

"African armies tend to be the most detribalized, westernized, modernized, integrated, and cohesive institutions in their respective States. The army is usually the most disciplined agency in the State. It often enjoys a greater sense of national identity than other institutions. In technical skills, including the capacity to coerce and to communicate, the army is the most effective agency in the country... A more vivid symbol of sovereignty than the flag, the constitution, or the parliament, the army often evokes more popular sentiment than a political leader."[3]

But voices of dissent concerning the developmental capability of the armed forces have increasingly been heard. Sometimes these voices distinguish between modernization and political development. The same voices might concede that the soldiers were indeed agents for modernization without necessarily accepting that they therefore contributed towards the political development of their societies. This Huntingtonian distinction between modernization and political development has been quite influential. Modernization has been viewed as the complex process of social and economic change caused by and manifested in the growth of new towns and cities, the spread of mass education, the extension of mass communication, and the process of industrialization. Political development, on the other hand, is seen as the process by which a society acquires an institutional capability to handle the political and social pressures which are generated by the process of modernization.

It is conceivable for the military to play a critical economic role which speeds up industrialization and accelerates urbanization. There have been military regimes which, because they were less socialistically oriented than the civilian governments they overthrew, and because they were more concerned with bread-and-butter issues than with long term ideological formulations, have performed better economically than their predecessors. New links strengthened with the western world, greater encouragement of investment, greater promotion of indigenous enterprise, have in such cases helped to accelerate both urbanization and industrialization. In this special sense then, such regimes might be deemed to have contributed to the modernization process. And yet, if part of the effect of these changes is to make the construction of viable and legitimate political institutions more difficult than ever, and create the potentiality of social and economic restlessness on a wide scale, it could indeed be inferred that the modernizing impact of the military is not necessarily in the direction of consolidating political development.

But even on the modernizing front, voices have questioned whether the

---

3   Ernest W. Lefever, *Spear and Sceptre: Army, Police and Parliament in Tropical Africa* (Washington: The Brookings Institution, 1970) p. 21. For a prophetically more cautious approach see Morris Janowitz, *The Military in the Political Development of New Nations: An Essay in Comparative Analysis* (Chicago: University of Chicago Press, 1964). For further comparative purposes consult Daniel Lerner and Richard D. Robinson, "Swords and Plough-Shares: The Turkish Army as a Modernizing Force," *World Politics*, Vol. xii No. 1, October 1960, pp. 19–44, and Manfred Halpern, *The Politics of Social Change in the Middle East and North Africa* (Princeton: Princeton University Press, 1963) especially pp. 251–280.

military were indeed any more effective than their civilian counterparts in developing countries. In the words of Claude E. Welch:

"It is clear that the armed forces have not fulfilled the predictions of some social scientists, put forward during the early 1960's, that their organization, modernity and nationalism would make them the leaders of the modernization process in their countries. On the other hand, their performance as rulers in this regard has possibly not been much worse than that which might have been achieved by the available civilian alternatives."[4]

Across the Atlantic in Britain, J. M. Lee was sceptical about the modernizing effect of military rule even earlier. He did not see African armies as being necessarily motivated by a desire to provide efficient administration.

"There is little evidence to indicate that African armies make better instruments of 'modernization' than their civil servant counterparts. Indeed, all the organizations of the State appear to face a common threat of problems."[5]

Our own purpose in this paper is to take the discussion even further. We propose neither to assert the modernizing impact of the armed forces, nor to claim that the armed forces are no different from that point of view from their civilian counterparts. There is a third area of investigation which needs to be undertaken with special regard to African soldiers. This area is captured by the following questions: are African soldiers agents for retraditionalization? are they carriers of values that might contribute to a partial resurrection of indigenous political cultures? are African soldiers agents for the grand process of the re-Africanization of Africa at a new level?

As I indicated, most of my own field work has been in East Africa, sometimes as a participant observer in national politics, especially in Uganda. My findings indicate that there may indeed be a traditionalizing role for military rulers in Africa. This proposition is not inconsistent with the assertion that there might also be a concurrent and paradoxical modernizing role. In situations of cultural and institutional fluidity, the impact of the soldiers could be multi-variant, and might carry significant sociological contradictions. My own position in this research note is that we do not know as yet whether or not African soldiers are better modernizers than African politicians, but there is increasing evidence to suggest that they may be greater traditionalizers than their old civilian counterparts. It is conceivable for the modernizing competitive records of politicians and soldiers to be evenly balanced, while the contradictory but concurrent record of renewing faith in certain aspects of traditional culture

---

4 See Claude E. Welch, Jr. and Arthur K. Smith, *Military Role and Rule: Perspectives on Civil-Military Relations* (North Scituate, Massachusetts: Duxbury Press, 1974) p. 256. Welch has pointed out elsewhere that the "modern" organizational characteristics of the armed forces could readily break down after the army has captured power. "In short, coup leaders face the same difficulties over which their civilian predecessors stumbled— without necessarily benefitting from greater advantages." Claude E. Welch, Jr., (editor) *Soldier and State in Africa: A Comparative Analysis of Military Intervention and Political Change* (Evanston, Northwestern University Press, 1970) p. 59.
5 J. M. Lee, *African Armies and Civil Order* (London: Chatto and Windus for the Institute for Strategic Studies, 1969) p. 184.

remains one which gives greater weight to the performance of the men in uniform.

Western commentators who have often discerned a conservative streak in "the military mind" in their own societies have at times chosen to ignore this when analyzing the role of the armed forces in developing countries.

We shall first address ourselves to this theme of conservatism as it relates to the behaviour of African soldiers in situations of culture conflicts and normative fluidity. We shall then examine the degree to which "retribalization" under military rule in African countries is an aspect of retraditionalization. We shall then relate this to the rural origins of African soldiers and the relevance of these origins for the resurrection of certain aspects of indigenous political cultures. Finally, we propose to relate this whole discussion to the distinction between political development and political decolonization and the manner in which they are affected by the dialectic between westernization and African cultural nationalism.

Political Conservatism and Social Tradition

What happens when a military establishment based on western organizational concepts, and conditioned by a western approach to military professionalism, seeks to operate in the culturally different conditions of African societies? Certainly the military profession in its modern forms in African countries has overwhelmingly borne the stamp of the metropolitan power. In Uganda the organization of the armed forces was solidly patterned upon the British model. The whole military ritual, including the pattern of drill, the categories and terminology of ranks, and the very music of the armed forces, all remained defiantly British in tone and style. Occasions of military ceremony, ranging from the funeral of a former President to the celebration of independence, from the commemoration of a military event to a preparation for combat, have still retained their ancestral connection with the metropolitan power.

To the extent to which these rituals and British traditions are upheld, this could be seen as a form of conservatism. But clearly in relation to the values of African societies, such exercises in Anglocentric militarism are by definition a departure from the indigenous normative order, rather than an exercise in its conservation.

It was Edward Shils who captured in an early essay an important distinction with regard to the new military establishment in the developing countries. The military establishment, to the extent to which it was derived from western models, was by definition non-traditional. But this did not prevent the sympathies of soldiers from being in favour of local traditions. The military establishment might indeed be a modern organization, but the attitude of the soldiers to the wider society might be more deeply conditioned by traditionalist sympathies than by the modern characteristics of their particular profession. As Shils put it:

"Military organization has little to do with the structure of traditional society, from which it is set off by its technology, most of its ethos, its organization, and its training—all of which are either imported or follow foreign models.... Yet it probably remains a fact that the military have a feeling of sympathy for tradition, not only for their own military tradition but for the traditional style of society as well. Hierarchic dignity, respect for superiors, solicitude for subordinates, solidarity, and conventionality produce in professional soldiers an attachment to the same phenomena in civilian society. Their humble origins and their separation from urbane pleasures and indulgences sustain this sympathy."[6]

In a situation where the soldiers are recruited from among the least westernized of former colonial subjects, at times directly from the narrow world of villagers and their simple beliefs, this distinction between the military establishment as a modern organization and the individual soldier as a traditionalist could be of considerable dialectical implication.

Western analysts who have been concerned with "the military mind" have at times transferred the scientificity of the military organization and attributed it to the mind of the military man. In the formulation of Samuel Huntington:

"Military and civilian writers generally seem to agree that the military mind is disciplined, rigid, logical, scientific..."[7]

Even if it were true that the military mind in the West was "logical and scientific" – Huntington himself is not absolutely sure – the field is still open for a Field Marshal Idi Amin in Uganda or a General Mobutu Sese Seko in Zaire to be "intuitive and even superstitious".

What is more likely is that the military establishments that these leaders have inherited from the colonial experience might indeed remain scientific at least with regard to technology, and logical with regard to systems of co-ordination, while the individual men in uniform remain relatively steeped in primordial beliefs and traditionalist tendencies. The military as an organization might in part be a carrier of scientificity, while the soldiers remain carriers of more primordial habits.

For as long as an African army is subordinate to civilian authority, and is consulted mainly on issues concerning security and the interests of the military organization, the impact of the traditionalism of individual soldiers on policy-making might be negligible. On the contrary, it might conceivably be the scientificity of the military organization that remains of most direct relevance to the society in a situation of civilian supremacy. The soldiers might be ordered to participate in nation-building and civic activities, and they may thus possibly have a demonstration effect in terms of co-ordination and discipline on at least sections of the wider society. What this means is that, in a situation where

---

6 Edward Shils, "The Military in the Political Development of New States," John J. Johnson (editor), *The Role of the Military in Underdeveloped Countries, op. cit.*, p. 31. Consult also Henry Bienen, (ed.), *The Military and Modernization* (Chicago and New York: Aldine Atherton, 1971).

7 Huntington, *The Soldier and the State* (Cambridge, Massachusetts: The Belknap Press of Harvard University Press, 1967), p. 60.

the soldiers have not as yet intervened and captured power, it is at most their "scientific and logical" ethos which reveals itself to the wider public.

But upon assumption of ultimate power, and the initiation of policy-making on a wide range of issues, do the more primordial aspects of their normative orientation acquire both greater feasibility and a greater impact on policy? The record in Africa so far is mixed but experience in Eastern Africa suggests a trend towards selective re-traditionalization.

Clearly this has connections with the rural origins of most African soldiers, and it is to this aspect that we must now turn.

Turning Ploughshares into Swords

This writer and others have drawn attention to the tendency for armies in developing countries to recruit from some of the least privileged sectors of the population. As the colonial presence consolidated itself, and new classes and social ranks began to emerge, there was a decline in the prestige of martial qualities.

The old days when warriorhood was, in many East African societies, a high status occupation were now receding into history. In some indigenous political systems the warrior stage was inseparable from the status of adulthood. Some societies linked the status to circumcision ceremonies, other societies invoked alternative methods of initiation. The moment of initiation marked a boy's transition, "From the culturally disvalued role of a boy... to the culturally valued role of the warrior."[8]

But three processes contributed to the decline of the warrior tradition under European colonial rule. One process was precisely connected with the discouragement of that tradition by both colonial administrators and Christian missionaries in East Africa. The colonial administrators had a vested interest in discouraging warriorhood for obvious reasons connected with a desire to monopolize the legitimate use of physical force in their colonies, and protect the stability of the colonial order. The Christian missionaries discouraged warriorhood partly because of a presumed inconsistency with Christian love, and partly because it was associated with the "heathen cultures" which the Christian gospel was out to eliminate.

A second process which helped to reduce the prestige of the warrior tradition concerned the intellectualization of African political culture under the impact of a more literate civilization. The coming of the written word in many East African societies, the establishment of missionary and state schools, and the rise of a white-collar class, all these competed effectively against the old indigenous prestige of warriorhood, and pulled young men in their millions towards classrooms indoors away from war dances in village compounds.

The third, and related process, concerned the economic diversification of

8 Satish Saberwal, *The Traditional Political System of the Embu of Central Kenya* (Nairobi: East African Publishing House for Makerere Institute of Social Research, 1970), p. 17.

East African societies. Many of these societies no longer felt that the ultimate economic roles for young people lay either in settled agriculture or in herding cattle. There were now the additional opportunities of urban employment, work in the mines, jobs as domestic servants and farm assistants, and the whole range of white-collar occupations available to those who had acquired some of the literary skills of the new metropolitan culture.

Against this background of new opportunities, a job as a soldier even in a modern uniform and with guns rather than spears or bows and arrows, was now seldom at the top of the scale of preferences for ambitious young men. Those who could go to school, and move on towards white-collar jobs, normally preferred such prospects to the opportunities of being recruited into the army. The colonial armed forces therefore increasingly turned to the most disadvantaged sector of society for their soldiers.

There was a related factor which made colonial recruiting officers inclined more towards the less literate of their subjects for use in the armed forces. This was simply the conviction among many colonial administrators that illiterate or semi-literate East Africans made better soldiers than the better educated. The better educated were sometimes distrusted as "cheeky" and not adequately inclined towards the level of obedience that the armed forces required. An illiterate tribesman could, it was assumed, be trusted to be more automatically obedient than a product of a secondary school.

The less educated Africans were in their general orientation and attitude more rural than the educated. Indeed, western education in East African conditions was a process of psychological deruralization. The educated African became in a fundamental sense a rural misfit in his own village. His parents were often people who had made sacrifices to improve the career opportunities of their child. When he graduated from school, his parents did not expect him to continue living with them, tending the cattle, or cultivating the land. Many parents assumed that the whole purpose of education was occupational improvement. They were therefore inclined to regard any insistence on the part of their educated son to remain with them in their village as something approaching filial betrayal. If their son was going to remain in the rural areas, why were all those sacrifices necessary? White-collar jobs in the villages were few and far between, and precisely because of that their son would become a rural misfit.

The illiterate or semi-literate village boy, on the other hand, maintains a compatibility with his rural environment. And upon being recruited into the army, he takes into the armed forces many of the predispositions, attitudes and even superstitions that are characteristic of the rustic community from which he springs.

It is true that once the young rustic is himself in the army, he becomes subject to certain westernizing influences. After all, as we indicated, the army is still substantially organized on the basis of a western model, utilizes western military technology, and is partly influenced by western military values. Lucian Pye compares the acculturative impact of military training with the acculturative influences involved in the urbanization process. On balance, Pye regards the army as a more potent influence for culture change within individuals than living in a city.

On this issue Pye is less than persuasive. The range of influences at work in urban centres, partly because of their very diffuseness, might constitute a more potent force for psychological reorientation than military training *per se*. This is particularly so when the urbanization process is combined with formal education in a western type of school. The peasant boy who goes to the barracks and receives military training is primarily being inducted into new skills, and secondarily into new values. And even these new values are often limited to a small area of experience, the values of combat and military co-ordination, with a few derivative normative tendencies. Even after years of experience in the army, semi-literate or illiterate African soldiers are much further from a secondary school graduate living in a city in their level of westernization than Pye's assumptions might imply. The urbanized secondary school graduate is simply more comprehensively, and perhaps even more deeply, acculturated than the peasant warrior in uniform in the barracks.[9]

As for secondary school graduates who enter the armed forces, and later receive additional training, these in turn are on balance at a lower level of normative westernization than civilian university graduates in Africa.

Many of the first waves of African rulers were in some sense products of the intellectualization of political culture in the colonies. A few of those leaders, including such figures as Kwame Nkrumah and Milton Obote were basically intellectuals in their capacity to be fascinated by ideas and in their ability to handle some of those ideas effectively. Some of the soldiers who have replaced them bear a more modest impact of western intellectualization than they did.

From the point of view of the immediate risks to rational policy-making, and the utilization of careful intellectual criteria in determining policy choices, the fact that most military leaders are less intellectual than their civilian predecessors might have a political cost. On the other hand, from the point of view of the long-term reduction of intellectual dependency in Africa and the partial resurrection of indigenous cultural ways, the soldiers might prove to be greater agents for the re-Africanization of Africa than their civilian predecessors.

Scholars like Aristide R. Zolberg have therefore been mistaken in their refusal to recognize any significant differences between military and civilian rulers in African conditions.

> "Beneath their uniforms, the Gowans, Lamizanas, Bokassas, and Mobutus are men with the same range of virtues and vices, wisdom and foolishness as the Balewas, Olympios, Yameogos, and Nkrumahs they replaced.... As a category, the military governors of Africa are unlikely to rule better, or more justly, or more effectively than their civilian predecessors."[10]

---

9   Lucian W. Pye, "Armies in the Process of Political Modernization," *op. cit.*, pp. 81–83.
10 Zolberg, "The Military Decade in Africa," a review article, *World Politics*, Vol. XXV, No. 2, January 1973, p. 319.

In fact, the range of vices and virtues has not been identical. On balance, the level of political brutality and violent sanctions against offenders has been higher under military rule in countries like the Central African Republic, Uganda, and in a special sense even Nigeria. The invocation of physical force had tended to increase in such countries. It is therefore not clear why we should not regard this as a moral cost when men specialized in a profession of violence and combat assume supreme authority. On the other hand, the potential influence of the soldiers on the process of re-Africanizing African political culture might be regarded as a moral benefit. What is important is to stop the easy equation of relatively less educated soldiers with relatively westernized African intellectuals in power. Idi Amin of Uganda is simply not Milton Obote, nor is Achiempong of Ghana either Busia or Nkrumah.

In the struggle to give aspects of African culture greater respectability, young Africans themselves might have to start with the most ambitious of the tasks – the prior struggle to conquer African self-contempt. This in turn requires the growing toleration of some of the least respected, in western terms, of those aspects of indigenous culture. If an East African intellectual can begin to concede dignity to the physical nakedness of the Karamajong men, or to the use of red ochre on the skin of the Masai, or the invocation of supernatural forces to help determine an election, that African intellectual is on his way to transcending his own cultural self-contempt.

Some of the soldiers in power provide precisely that kind of challenge to the new generation of westernized and semi-westernized Africans.

Field Marshal Idi Amin has been a particularly severe test for large numbers of African intellectuals. Many seem to have been more ashamed of Amin's "superstitions" than of his political brutality, more worried by Amin's distance from normal western diplomatic style, than by how many Ugandans he had detained or eliminated, even more ashamed of Amin's "brazen polygamy" than his political arbitrariness.

David Martin, in his book, *General Amin*, has drawn attention to the prevalent nature of witchcraft and sorcery among Africans in different parts of the continent. Martin has also reminded us that it is not unusual to find "highly educated Africans visiting witch-doctors" in a bid to ensure promotion to better jobs. But, according to Martin, Amin had "taken his belief in occult powers to a ridiculous extent". He refers to a Zambian seer Dr. Ngombe Francis, who claimed to have predicted the overthrow of President Milton Obote. After the coup the Zambian prospered significantly, and became Amin's soothsayer and prophet. There was also the Ghanaian mystic who claimed power to raise people from the dead. The mystic was flown to Uganda, and Amin later asserted that he had had an opportunity to talk to a man who had so risen from the dead.

As for Amin's innumerable dreams, these have ranged from a dream about when precisely he would die, to his assertion that God had told him in a dream to expel the Asians from Uganda and launch a national economic war.

David Martin, a westerner, regards Amin's beliefs in occult powers as "ridiculous". It would be illuminating, were it possible, to find out how many of the less educated and less westernized Ugandans would share David Martin's views on the matter. It is conceivable that every time Amin has proclaimed a major dream, it has at best been Ugandan intellectuals that have laughed secretly. Some of the other Ugandans might dispute the validity or authenticity of this or that particular dream claimed by Amin, but perhaps the great majority would not dispute the proposition that some dreams are intended to be guides for action, and that supernatural forces might at times be in communion with a leader.[11]

But is it good for political culture in East Africa to have such beliefs resurrected? Would it add to the viability of East African political systems to invoke occult powers for policy-making?

This writer, as a westernized or semi-westernized African intellectual, has strong reservations about some of Idi Amin's political "superstitions". It is arguable that such beliefs from Africa's indigenous heritage deserve to die quietly, just as similar beliefs died previously in most parts of Europe. And yet, the very "ridiculous" nature of such beliefs to westernized African intellectuals provides a challenge to their own cultural self-contempt, and might at least increase their sympathy and understanding for many of their rural compatriots.

The late Oxford political philosopher, John Plamenatz, once asserted:

"The vices of the strong acquire some of the prestige of strength."[12]

As the rustic soldiers have acquired power, and demonstrated their political strength, perhaps some of the prestige of that strength might rub off on the peasant warriors' cultural "weaknesses".

The current generation of adult westernized African intellectuals might never be able to fully transcend their cultural self-contempt, but the next generation of educated Africans might have learned from their military rulers the capacity to understand and sympathize with certain aspects of the culture of the villages. Some of these beliefs in occult powers might die a natural death before long, but when African intellectuals can respect these, they will learn to respect other aspects of African culture as well.

Re-Africanization of Africa and Militarized Ethnicity

A related issue connected with the traditionalizing impact of the military on African societies concerns the whole issue of ethnic affiliation and loyalty. Does military rule aggravate or mitigate ethnic resurgence? How much "retribalization" takes place under the pressures of a politicized army? Again we must examine East Africa partly with a view to assessing likely trends elsewhere in the continent.

The colonial authorities in East Africa sometimes avoided certain com-

11   Consult David Martin, *General Amin* (London: Faber and Faber, 1974), p. 16.
12   Plamenatz, *On Alien Rule and Self-Government* (London: Longmans, 1960).

munities in recruiting for the armed forces. The exclusion of such communities might have been motivated by considerations which ranged from a presumption that certain communities did not have either the valour or the physique for soldiers, to an imperial calculation that such communities when equipped with arms might create problems for the colonial order.

Persistent in the imperial mentality was the simple assumption that martial prowess was ethnically distributed. Some tribes were simply better warriors than others, they believed.

In the course of World War II, a new attempt was made in different parts of Africa by the colonial powers to assess the martial qualities of different communities, partly with a view to determining priorities in recruitment for the imperial armies against Germany, Italy and Japan. In East Africa some kind of research was conducted in this direction. The Chief Native Commissioner of Kenya asked that a census be undertaken to determine "the soldierly qualities of the members of the various tribes composing the East African Force." The issue was referred to a conference of governors of the East African colony, and a questionnaire was worked out and sent to each commanding officer in 1941.

> "Each of the countries in East Africa was to furnish the Native Commissioner with names of tribes, giving provinces, districts A similar survey, but a hasty one, had been carried out in 1932 'in order that opinions of K.A.R. Officers might be obtained with a view to deciding which tribes were likely to make the best soldiers.'"[13]

Tarsis Kabwegyere reminds us of the questionnaire and the qualities which were looked for. These included adaptability, reaction to discipline, steadiness under bombing, stamina and staying power, powers of leadership, intelligence, esprit de corps, cleanliness and turnout, capacity for hard living, general health, ability to fraternize, and fighting qualities. There were in addition some special qualities and skills which were to be ascertained. Each ethnic group was assessed, and a system of scores for each was devised.[14]

But soldierly qualities had to be balanced against other considerations. Although in the early days of the colonial presence in Uganda the Baganda was still regarded as a martial community, there was an understandable reluctance among colonial administrators to recruit disproportionately from the Baganda into the armed forces. The Baganda were already becoming among the best organized and most politically conscious of the communities of the country. The imperial power naturally hesitated on the issue of militarizing the Baganda by giving them a disproportionate present in the imperial armed forces.

Both those who were excluded from the armies and those who provided the bulk of the army were chosen substantially in terms of ethnic categories. This basis of recruitment was to have considerable repercussions in the relations between soldiers and civilians after independence.

The different communities and tribes themselves entertained stereotypes

---

13 Cited by Tarsis B. Kabwegyere, *The Politics of State Formation: The Nature and Effects of Colonialism in Uganda* (Nairobi: East African Literature Bureau, 1974), p. 115.

14 *Ibid.*, pp. 115–117.

about each other, sometimes influenced by considerations about which community was capable of providing better soldiers. In Nigeria, the armed forces had recruited from both the north and the south, yet within the armed forces themselves mutual ethnic stereotypes conditioned interaction between different sections and ranks in the army.

> "Northern soldiers obeyed orders from Ibo officers, but there was a residual feeling in their minds that the Ibo were not really a martial race—they considered the Ibo people too articulate for warriors. 'Maif ada ba zai yi surutu ba'—'The warrior is not talkative'—is a common Northern proverb; they regarded the martial qualities of the Easterners rather as the British other ranks regarded those of the Italian, or the Punjabi regarded those of the Bengali or the man from Madras."[15]

Against this background both of an ethnic basis for the recruitment of soldiers into the armed forces and the persistence of ethnic stereotypes, the precise composition of the military by the time of independence in many African countries carried all the potentialities of ethnic resurgence.

Some scholars have argued that colonialism did not simply create new potential national states; it also created the tribes themselves. Groups that never before considered themselves as a cohesive political community were converted into one such community by colonial methods of administration. Kabwegyere cites some examples, including that of the Acholi in Uganda who were later to be regarded as a particularly martial community and provided a disproportionate number of soldiers for the Uganda Army in the days of Apolo Milton Obote.

> "Present day Acholi is a result of an ordinance in 1937 which amalgamated both Chua to the East and Gulu to the West.... People in these two districts knew themselves more in terms of their clans, e.g. the Payira, Patiko, Padibe, etc. than in terms of a collective identity, the Acholi. The clans were the units for collective identity but not for collective action since clans were rarely occupants of a homogenous territory although they had a common culture.... It was Barrell the administrator in Gulu who finally gave the amalgamated District the name Acholi. 'I can think of no better name for the new District than the 'Acholi District'; there is no native name for the country as a whole...."[16]

Administrative convenience in the colonial period thus helped to bring together clans that previously never engaged in collective action, nor were they subject to the same collective administrative authority, into a pattern of relationships which now created ethnic-wide political consciousness. The Acholi began to see themselves as an amalgamated community, although tensions between clans continued, and divisions between east Acholi and west Acholi have persisted ever since. Field Marshal Idi Amin moved further towards dividing the east and the west once again, but what matters from the point of view of the

---

15   M. J. Dent, "The Military and Politics: A Study of the Relation between the Army and the Political Process in Nigeria," Robert Melson and Howard Wolpe (editors), *Nigeria: Modernization and the Politics of Communalism* (East Lansing: Michigan State University Press, 1971), p. 373.

16   *Ibid.*, pp. 43–45.

colonial genesis of "tribalism" is the simple fact that a broad new Acholi political consciousness became superimposed over the narrower parochialisms of the sub-units of the Acholi.

By the time Obote was overthrown, the Acholi constituted the largest single group within the Armed Forces of Uganda, although in relation to the rest of the population they were clearly one of the smaller groups of Uganda. Between a third and a half of the Ugandan army consisted of Acholi.

Their preponderance was partly an outcome of their categorization as a tribal unit in the colonial period, and partly the outcome of their presumed martial qualities.

Related to this second presumption was simply the issue of physical height. As an ethnic community the Acholi and other northern tribes of Uganda had produced a disproportionate number of tall people. Since recruitment into the Uganda armed forces gave preference to candidates who were 5'8" or over, the northern communities had a prior edge in physical anthropology. Among the northerners, the Acholi enlarged after a while this edge in terms of actual recruitment into the armed forces.

By the time Amin captured power from Obote, Amin was all too aware of the preponderance of the Acholi within the armed forces. Would these be loyal to the new regime under Amin or would they maintain a prior loyalty to Milton Obote? Amin's reasoning in terms of determining potential allies was again couched in ethnic terms. He himself is a Kakwa, from a relatively small group in Uganda, though it extends substantially across the border into the Sudan, with ethnic compatriots also across the border in Zaire.

In his early announcements as to why the coup took place, Amin asserted that the Acholi, in alliance with Obote's own tribe, the Langi, had plotted to disarm all other soldiers, and assert a complete ethnic monopoly of military power in Uganda. Thus tensions against these two communities started from the early days of Amin's assumption of power. Since then thousands of Acholi and Langi have perished in the wake of Amin's political and military insecurity.

Almost every year since he took over power in 1971, issues of ethnicity have been profoundly interlinked with issues of domestic balance of power. In July 1974, the Acholi and the Langi were once again singled out by spokesmen of the Amin regime as plotters against his government. It was asserted that they were waiting for an invasion of pro-Obote refugees from Tanzania. The domestic Acholi and Langi would provide internal support as the refugees from across the border sought to undermine and then overthrow the government of Idi Amin. Many Acholi and Langi in Uganda decided to flee the country in the wake of these renewed accusations. Ethnicity in Uganda had worn once again the ominous face of militarized revenge and brutality.

Among those Ugandans in exile in Tanzania, ethnic factors were also at play. Even when they plotted to invade the country and overthrow Idi Amin's government, the Ugandan exiles were sometimes torn by their own ethnic cleavages. The Langi were at times at variance with the Acholi. And even on the eve of the joint invasion of Uganda in September 1972, the internal strains were not entirely absent. Old traditions within each community affected their behaviour in exile. Just before they departed on their ill-starred adventure against Amin in September 1972, the old soldiers in exile in Tanzania invoked an Acholi war dance and song, a ceremony of consolidating courage and inspiring confidence. Some of those who were to be joint fighters in the attempted invasions were irritated by the Acholi traditional war ceremonies in preparation for this collective enterprise. But the war dance and song, the invocation of Acholi martial symbolism, captured both the tensions of ethnicity and the resilience of indigenous traditions.[17]

But is this kind of militarized situation more bedevilled by ethnic factors than a situation of civilian politics? The answer varies somewhat from one African country to another. But, to the extent that in most African countries recruitment into the armed forces was more ethnically specialized than participation in civilian politics, the military situation had graver ethnic risks than the civilian political system. Certainly in Uganda, politics in the first eight years of independence was a more ethnically representative phenomenon than access to military careers. Parliament, the Cabinet under Obote, and increasingly the civil service, provided more of a cross-section of the different communities of Uganda than the armed forces could ever claim. The process of political mobility, in the sense of different regions and tribes having some access to effective political participation and representation at some level or another, was more convincing when political power depended on the interplay of civilian pressures than when it came to depend upon the balance of ethnic factions within the armed forces.

In the latter situation, clearly there is a greater potential explosiveness of ethnic factors than in a situation of civilian contests of will. This is not to underestimate the tensions involved in politicized ethnicity. All that we are trying to demonstrate is that militarized ethnicity, partly because of the selective nature of recruitment into the armed forces, has a higher potential for "retribalization" than politicized ethnicity.

Those who blame both tribalism and the creation of nation-states on colonialism do have a point, but what they often overlook is that tribalism might be an outcome of the creation of the nation-state. Whether or not British colonial authorities explicitly began to categorize the Acholi as one community, those Acholi would have begun to think of themselves as such as soon as they saw themselves in competition with other groups for the limited resources of a new territorial entity called "Uganda". What is being claimed in this assertion is that it was the exercise of bringing together divergent linguistic and cultural

---

17   David Martin refers to the irritation of the younger exiles over the Acholi war dance and song in the preparation for the invasion of Uganda. Martin seems to suggest that it was the younger, modernized or westernized soldiers in exile, who were particularly unhappy about such a ceremony. In fact, in addition to the reservations of the more modernized or westernized of the exiles, there were also reservations on the part of those who belonged to other ethnic communities. For Martin's allusion to this episode consult his *General Amin, op. cit.*, pp. 189–190.

groups within the boundaries of a new state which generated new levels of ethnic consciousness. Even if the British had not explicitly bracketed the different clans into a new community called Acholi, the forces of competition within the national system of Uganda would have resulted in the discovery among the Acholi of a shared culture and language. This ethnic consciousness was almost bound to be sharpened in the scramble for a share of what independent Uganda as a new political community had to offer to its constituent parts.

The attainment of independence did not redraw the boundaries of the new nation-state. The persistence of ethnic consciousness and ethnic identity had therefore to be related directly to the continuation of the new national boundaries. In Uganda, as elsewhere in Africa, it was not simply a case of the new nation-state lacking a transethnic identity and legitimacy of its own. It was a case of the very presence of such a nation-state lending legitimacy to the ethnic sub-units and strengthening parochial loyalties.

In some African countries under military rule the extent of retribalization might for a while be disguised by the appearance of a firm political order with "iron discipline". But ethnic resurgence does take place as soon as the iron military grip begins to loosen, or even when civilian rule is restored after a period of military control. Ghana under Kofi Busia did witness a resurgence of ethnic particularism following the rule by the National Liberation Council. At best, a military regime succeeds in putting ethnic cleavages in a society in "cold storage". At worst, military rule, partly because of the pattern of recruitment into the armed forces and partly because of the nature of army rule itself, simply degenerates into eruptions of militarized ethnicity with periodic violent confrontations. This process of retribalization is indeed an aspect of retraditionalization, but with a heavy political cost.

Cattle-Raid Complex Under African Militarism

But why is the level of mutual brutalization in some African societies so high? Why does retribalization under military conditions carry such a heavy risk of killing and counter-killing? Again East Africa's experience falls considerably short of being unique. Evidence of mutual brutalization is already available elsewhere in the continent.

One part of the answer is simply that the different ethnic groups in an African country are not always ready to regard each other as anything more than rival "nations" next door. An African country becomes a kind of international system in miniature, with ethnic groups behaving in part as if they were autonomous little states in their own right competing for scarce resources. Unlike the broader international community, an African country does normally have a government in power; but even that power at the center is regarded as a scarce resource which the different contending parties seek to control or at least to share. Those who actually do possess the scarce resource of central political power find themselves strongly tempted not to share it except on the basis of special alliances. Favoritism, ethnic nepotism and ethnic

THE WARRIOR TRADITION IN MODERN AFRICA

competitiveness play their role in creating inequalities and disequilibrium in the distribution of political goals.

But the old warrior tradition also intrudes and conditions attitudes, especially in situations where soldiers attempt to monopolize the central institutions of power. In many East African societies the old warrior tradition was based not simply on the ambition to maintain collective security, but also on the ambition to foster collective prosperity. The warrior was not simply a person who waited until his cattle or his women were attacked before using his military skills for defensive purposes. On the contrary, the warrior was also a person who considered economic competition as being not primarily a rivalry between individuals or sub-groups within the same society, as competition is taken to be in western capitalist countries, but more a continuing dialectic of rivalry with alien or semi-alien societies nearby. Out of this concept emerged cattle-raiding and similar forms of militarized economic acquisitiveness as an aspect of the warrior ethos.

> "The experience of warriorhood during adolescence helped in transforming an Embu boy into an Embu man.... The tradition of raiding for live-stock was strong in the cluster of societies in the area, and the Embu trained their young men both to protect their own herds from enemies and also to raid the neighbouring peoples.... Raiding enemy tribes for live-stock (and women) and in the process achieving fame in fighting were dominant concerns of warriorhood in Embuland. The first raid was important for a young man, contributing to the legitimization of his new role."[18]

The idea by which members of a community found it legitimate, and indeed part of the duties of warriorhood, to take economic advantage over other ethnic communities was something which was bound to affect the behaviour of soldiers in uniform in the post-colonial era.

Many commentators on African behaviour have too readily assumed that the reference point for African soldiers was always and inevitably the imperial model. But is the behaviour of African privates in Nigeria or Uganda really like the behaviour of British privates, or does it bear closer affinity to the behaviour of traditional warriors? Is the soldier in Zaire more reminiscent of a Belgian soldier than of a pre-colonial Congo or Luba warrior?

Robert Price once invoked psychological categories to explain the apparent attempt by African soldiers to emulate the imperial military model. Price used reference group theory to explain what he called "the emulation paradox".

> "An individual's reference groups are those social groups to which he psychologically relates himself, with which he identifies. To become a member of the group in a psychological sense implies the internalization of its central norms and values—for to be a member implies certain modes of thought and behaviour."[19]

---

18 Satish Saberwal, *The Traditional Political System of the Embu of Central Kenya, op. cit.*, pp. 17, 29.
19 Robert M. Price, "A Theoretical Approach to Military Rule in New States: Reference-Group Theory and the Ghanaian Case," *World Politics*, Vol. XXIII, No. 3, 1971, pp. 403–404.

Applying the theory to the Ghanaian military especially, Price argued that the training process undergone by the officer corps was "such as to produce reference-group identifications with the officer corps of the ex-colonial power and the concomitant commitment to its sets of traditions, symbols and values."[20]

For a while it might have been true of the officer corps that the most immediate reference group was that of the former colonial power, but writers like Price may have underestimated the resilience of traditional norms among the great majority of African soldiers. Certainly many East African soldiers come from societies that still have initiation ceremonies based on ancestral warrior ideas, though currently no longer translated into actual practice. The socialization processes of many of these societies continue to emphasize particular primordial concepts of courage, masculinity, and attitudes to rival ethnic groups. There is comparable evidence elsewhere in Africa that among the categories that could be resurrected from the ancestral past is simply the "cattle-raiding complex" – the concept of militarized economic competition between collective social units.

> "The extensive participation of Habe (non-Fulani Hausa) and Fulani in slave-raiding and war was achieved by mobilizing contingents from the fiefs; and military action offered such troups rewards in the form of booty, appointments and promotion. The frequency and success of this military adventure may have persuaded many people to support the system of government. Since political and administrative office provided the principal means of enrichment and social mobility together, and had clear military commitments, the recruitment of officials for these expeditions presented no problems."[21]

In East Africa this "cattle-raiding complex" was exploited by the Europeans in the initial stages of their own conquest of the region. The British in Uganda, for example, economized on their own military expenses by recruiting African soldiers and letting them do some looting on the way for compensation.

> "It was important to capture cattle, goats, etc. from the conquered people; this was food for the soldiers.... The great number of soldiers with the few British officers, moving with goats, cows, etc. must have been spectacular and frightening. The few officers could not control the multitude of soldiers especially when they were hungry.... Thus the soldiers were not only top-dog on the power of the gun dimension, they also had economic power. It is difficult to measure the social disequilibrium that was caused by relative deprivation among the people by the presence of the rich gunmen."[22]

This phenomenon of "rich gunmen" late in the nineteenth century and early in the twentieth century anticipated a major trend in the Africa of the 1960's and 1970's upon the withdrawal of the European masters. The cattle-raid complex first had bedevilled relations between African ethnic groups, was later exploited by the imperial power, and has now begun to condition the appetites, acquisitiveness, and ethnic attitudes of African soldiers in power after independence.

---

20 *Ibid.*, p. 407.
21 M. G. Smith, *Government in Zazzu* (London: Oxford University Press, 1960), p. 100.
22 Kabwegyere, *The Politics of State Formation, op. cit.*, pp. 73–74.

What this means is that there are aspects of the re-Africanization of Africa which might not be specifically functional or beneficial. That these aspects are retrograde from the point of view of justice and inter-ethnic amity in African countries does not invalidate the proposition about the traditionalizing impact of the phenomenon of under-educated Africans wielding considerable political power in political communities much larger in size than their orginal ancestral societies.

Decolonization and Cultural Nationalism

But although certain aspects of re-Africanization are immensely costly in human terms in the short run, the process of retraditionalization in totality might well be a fundamental aspect of decolonization. Much of the previous literature on modernization in Africa too readily assumed that the road to political development was through westernization. Political development was envisaged in terms of building institutions comparable to those of western systems, and consolidating values and styles derived from western cultural experience.

But with the growth of a new rival literature based on the concept of *dependency* the whole concept of "development" has been either rejected or drastically redefined. Where it has been redefined, development is now conceived in terms of a progressive reduction of dependency, a commitment to practical decolonization not only politically but also economically and culturally.[23]

While some writers have emphasized economic decolonization, this writer regards cultural decolonization as more fundamental than many have assumed. Mental and intellectual dependency, a lack of readiness to break loose from the metropolitan power, a compulsive urge to imitate and emulate what the West has produced, are factors which have on the whole had grave economic and political consequences for societies which are still unwilling to take drastic decisions for their own transformation, but they are also phenomena with deep cultural causes. The lack of a political will for an economic transformation might in part be due to a state of mental and cultural dependency.

From this point of view then, trends towards retraditionalizing Africa become as aspect of decolonization. In reality, Africa is never likely to move to what it was before the European came. In hard assessment, it would be suicidal if Africa attempted such a leap backwards. But a partial retreat towards renewed respect for indigenous ways, and a conquest of cultural self-contempt, might be some of the minimal conditions for cultural decolonization.

---

23 Some of the works by Samir Amin, Johan Galtung, Walter Rodney and Colin Leys are among those which belong to this new genre of developmental literature. Perhaps the most sustained and most recent application of this radical perspective to an African country is Colin Leys' book *Underdevelopment in Kenya*, (London: Heinemann Educational Publishers, and Berkeley: University of California Press, 1975).

Again soldiers in power, sometimes naively, have often taken some of the most drastic decisions towards decolonization in this domain. Mobutu Sese Seko's drive to resurrect African authenticity in Zaire is one case in point. The General has had tense confrontations especially with the Catholic Church over aspects of the church's influence on the cultural ways of Zaireans.

Among the more dramatic symbolic moves made by Mobutu Sese Seko was the decision to compel all Zaireans to have indigenous names, rather than European or Jewish names adopted at baptism. The General argued that a religion which aspires to be universalistic must be ready to recognize cultural pluralism in the world. Why should Christian names necessarily be of European or Jewish extraction? Why could not indigenous African names qualify for baptismal status in their own right? Why did God have to despise every aspect of indigenous African cultures, down to the names which parents chose for their children?

An order went forth required all Zairean citizens to ensure that their passports had Zairean names. The President himself renounced his baptismal name of "Joseph". Many other Zaireans were deeply torn by this decree requiring them to give up European or Jewish names they had carried all their lives. Many understandably regarded this as an intrusion into a deeply personal affair. And yet the cultural nationalism which made Mobutu require his compatriots to respect indigenous names, and the Catholic Church to be more respectful of local cultures, was pregnant with the symbolism of cultural revival.

The authenticity drive in Gaddafy's Libya also included a preoccupation with passports. But in the case of Libya, the ambition was not simply to force the local citizens to do justice to their heritage, but also to demand reciprocity in cultural respect from the international community at large. Visitors to Libya were required to have passports which included the use of Arabic. Why after all should the language of passports all over the world be so disproportionately based on the linguistic heritage of western Europe? Why must Arabs and Africans have to use French or English as one of the languages of their travel documents, while the French and the English made no reciprocal linguistic concession to the customs officers at Arab or African ports?

There are of course a large number of practical reasons why the world has had to bow to English and French as the most widespread of the languages of mankind. But there are also important issues of cultural reciprocity involved in that simple gesture by Colonel Gaddafy in Libya to force visistors to Libya to have travel documents legible and intelligible to Libyan immigration officers in the national language of Libya itself.

In Uganda, some modifications in the marriage laws of the country, including greater recognition of polygamous relationships, have also been part of the stream of retraditionalization. So was the adoption by President Amin of Kiswahili as a national language of Uganda, in spite of the fact that the language is less well known that it is in either Tanzania or Kenya, and in spite of the immense educational difficulties which would be involved in implementing this linguistic decision.

Even the ruthless expulsion of influential foreigners, with all the lack of humaneness involved, could also be seen as part of the process of decolonization.

"Colonel Gaddafy, deeply concerned about foreign penetration of the culture and economy of the country, decreed a host of steps; seizure of Italian and Jewish property without compensation; announcement that all business concerns, save oil companies, must be owned entirely by Libyan nationals; nationalization of banks and public transport; emphasis on Islamic standards."[24]

Gaddafy's expulsion of the Italians was later followed by Idi Amin's expulsion of the Asians from Uganda. Both moves could only have been done under a military regime, with all the relative insensitivity to the diplomatic and humanitarian implications of those measures. Certainly the British fear of Idi Amin at the time of the expulsion of the Asians emanated from the very fact that he was a soldier in charge of a rather undisciplined army, and was capable of taking physical action against British Asians and even British Europeans in Uganda in a manner which would have been inconceivable under Milton Obote. Once again the rugged and semi-literate nature of the military regime was a factor behind the expulsion of those influential aliens, and that expulsion in turn could be seen as part of the ruthless and painful process of decolonization.

The total picture in Eastern Africa is still incomplete with regard to the retraditionalizing role of African soldiers. The concurrent process of modernization must always be taken into account in evaluating these issues.

But a convergence of four factors should alert us to the current or potential re-Africanizing role of the armed forces in Africa. These factors include the rural and parochial origins of most of the recruits into the armed forces, the minimal acculturation of the soldiers as compared with the better educated civilian populations, the ethnic patterns of military recruitment with the potentialities of retribalization, and the partial resurrection of the warrior tradition.[25]

Conclusion

On the whole the cultural influence of Europe is of longer duration in West Africa than it is in places like Uganda, Zaire and Kenya. In the field of both civilian and military education that has meant a longer tradition of college, university and Sandhurst training in Ghana and Nigeria than among Africans on the eastern seaboard.

---

24 Claude E. Welch Jr., "Radical and Conservative Military Regimes: A Typology and Analysis of Post-Coup Governments in Tropical Africa," paper prepared for delivery at the 1973 Annual Meeting of the American Political Science Association, New Orleans, Louisiana, September 4–8, pp. 13–14. Since, the oil has also become increasingly subject to state ownership and control.
25 Consult also Ali A. Mazrui, "The Resurrection of the Warrior Tradition in African Political Culture: From Shaka the Zulu to Amin the Kakwa," presented on the panel on "Terrorism and Politics in Africa," Sixteenth Annual Meeting of the African Studies Association of the U.S.A., held at Syracuse, October 31–November 3.

If there is a process of westernization still going on in Africa, one would expect West Africa to be further ahead than East. Political scientists in the 1950's were therefore taking a justifiable gamble when they regarded the growth of western-style nationalistic movements in West Africa as a harbinger of comparable movements elsewhere.

On the other hand, if there is now an inchoate but insistent reassertion of indigenous political values at the highest level of government, it is perhaps less likely to have started in sedate and highly anglicized Ghana than in tumultous Zaire, in the Central African Republic and among the Nilotic and Sudanic peoples of Uganda.

Let us now draw out the tentative hypotheses which lie in these observations. We may, in other words, hypothesize that everything else being equal the process of "modernization" in the western sense is likely to go fastest in those societies which have experienced the deepest western impact either in duration (Ghana and Southern Nigeria) or terms of proximity to white settlers (Kenya, Rhodesia and South Africa).

By contrast, the process of political retraditionalization is likely to start first in those societies which have had least time to adjust to the impact of the West. By "political retraditionalization" we mean here concrete attempts to formulate policies either under the influence of indigenous mores or in pursuit of ends defined according to indigenous criteria. Zaire and Uganda are cases in point.

The third compound hypothesis is that military rule in Africa has consequences which are *both* modernizing and traditionalizing. Built into this compound hypothesis is the expectation that military rule in a place like Ghana (high acculturation) would reveal its traditionalizing role more slowly than military rule in the hands of the Kakwa and Lugbara in Uganda (low acculturation). But since the bulk of the army of Ghana also consists of men of relatively low acculturation, each successive coup in a place like Ghana would bring up more of the less westernized Ghanaian soldiers into prominence. The first Ghanaian coup was more "Sandhurst and British" than the second. The third, should it take place, would be less "British" still. The difference between Ghanaian soldiers in power and Ugandan and Zairean soldiers in power will probably narrow, without necessarily ending.

Our fourth compound hypothesis concerns a comparison between civilian and military rulers in Africa. We agree that there is no evidence yet that soldiers are greater modernizers than the civilians they replaced. But the evidence from East Africa would seem to suggest that soldiers may be greater traditionalizers than the more westernized civilians they ousted. For better or for worse, this is certainly true of Idi Amin as compared with Milton Obote, and true of Mobutu Sese Seko as compared with such figures as Kasavubu and Moise Tshombe.

But how do these factors relate to the experience of a country like Ethiopia? The balance between the modernizing and the traditionalizing functions of soldiers has to be different in Ethiopia, partly because of the ancient ancestry of the traditional imperial system while it lasted, and partly because of the brevity of Ethiopia's colonial experience under Italian occupation. There were aspects of the traditional imperial system in Ethiopia which were so anachronistic that almost any major military challenge to it in the second half of the twentieth century was bound to have a conspicuously modernizing aspect.

Yet even in Ethiopia it would be surprising if the performance of the army did not gradually manifest once again a compulsive urge to retraditionalize aspects of Ethiopian life. Without being directly ruled by the West for any length of time, Ethiopia under Haile Selassie had been partly absorbed into the Western world's strategic empire. The literary presence of the United States in the country, and the increasing cultural orientation toward the West which the imperial elite manifested, had started a process of westernization at that level of Ethiopian society. If the Ethiopian soldiers were now to embark more earnestly on both decolonization and democratization, the former process might well include a theme of cultural nationalism and traditionalization. The latter process of democratization, on the other hand, would correlate closely with modernization in Ethiopia.

In this regard the experience of Libya would turn out to be a precedent for Ethiopia. The military overthrow of King Idris of Libya created a radical change in the country. Domestically the soldiers did inaugurate a process of at least structural and economic democratization, as educational opportunities were vastly expanded, foreign economic control was reduced, and the wealth of the country was used more extensively for the welfare of the masses and the development of the country.

But while the soldiers' impulse to *democratize* Libya after King Idris has initiated modernization, their urge to decolonize Libya has resulted in a new Islamic fundamentalism. Economic democratization in Libya has increased a consciousness of the future and the need to plan for it. Cultural decolonization, on the other hand, has awakened memories of the past and rekindled an interest in protecting its heritage. Both modernity and tradition have provided reasons and motivation for reform in Libya after the monarchy. Both might also instigate radical change in a post-imperial Ethiopia.

Behind both examples lies the partially disguised but sociologically fundamental tendency of soldiers in Africa to respond to their rural, social and cultural origins. Either wittingly or through the mysterious sense of direction of unconscious behavior, African soldiers are becoming media for the selective re-Africanization of the countries they rule.

NOTES ABOUT AUTHORS

Jonah Isawa Elaigwu is lecturer [assistant Professor] in the Department of Government at Ahmadu Bello University in Nigeria. His doctorate was from Stanford University in California. His research experience includes East Africa, as well as Nigeria and the United States. Among Dr. Elaigwu's interests are policy-makingin situations of institutional fluidity, the process of state-formation and problems of civil-military relations.

Judith Lynne Hanna is in the School of Arts and Humanities at the University of Texas at Dallas, where she teaches in the doctoral program and is developing an interdisciplinary graduate arts (graphic/plastic, music, dance) therapy program proposal incorporating an anthropological perspective. She received her Ph.D. in anthropology from Columbia University and M.A. in political science from Michigan State University. She has conducted research in East and West Africa. Dr. Hanna teaches African dances and writes on the nature and sociology of dance and ritual movement. For the past three years she has been an editor of *Dance Research Journal*. With W. J. Hanna, she wrote, *Urban Dynamics in Black Africa* (Chicago: 1971) and numerous articles on urban politics and African universities. She is currently completing a study of the anthropology of dance.

Ali A. Mazrui is professor of Political Science at the University of Michigan and a member of the faculty of the Center for Afro-American and African Studies at the same university. Born in Mombasa, Kenya, Dr. Mazrui was previously Dean of Social Sciences at Makerere University in Uganda. On the warrior tradition, his most pertinent book is *Soldiers and Kinsmen in Uganda: The Making of a Military Ethnocracy* (Beverly Hills and London: 1975). Related works include *Violence and Thought* (London, 1969) and *Protest and Power in Black Africa* (jointly edited with Robert I. Rotberg) (New York, 1970). What happens to African warriors when they die? Dr. Mazrui has attempted to answer the question imaginatively in his novel *The Trial of Christopher Okigbo* (London and New York, 1972).

Dent Ocaya-Lakidi was born in Acholi, Uganda, and educated in Uganda and Canada. On graduating from the University of Toronto he took an academic appointment in the Department of Political Science at Makerere University in Uganda. His intellectual interests have been wide. They have ranged from Plato's *Republic* to the war songs of the Acholi, from the role of parliament in contemporary Tanzania to problems of educational policy in colonial Africa. Professionally Mr. Ocaya-Lakidi also prefers versatility to specialization. He is experienced not only in university life but also in the commercial aspects of publishing and in journalism.

Louise Pirouet came to Kenya as a teacher in 1957, and in 1963 moved to Uganda where she became a research assistant in the Department of Religious Studies at Makerere University. In 1968 she completed work on the spread of Christianity in Uganda for a doctoral degree of the University of East Africa, remaining at Makerere until early in 1972 as a lecturer. After three years in Britain she returned to Kenya in 1975 to join the staff of the Department of Philosophy and Religious Studies at the University of Nairobi. She has published a number of articles and papers on Ugandan and East African history, and has also been involved in text book projects.

Aidan Southall is professor of Anthropology at the University of Wisconsin, Madison. Professor Southall has so far spent about twenty years in Africa. He was previously professor of Sociology at Makerere University in Uganda and Director of the Makerere Institute of Social Research. His field work over the years has included the Malagasy Republic as well as Uganda. His books include *Alur Society: A Study in Processes and Type of Domination* and *Townsmen in the Making: Kampala and Its Suburbs* (with P. C. W. Gutkind).

Victor C. Uchendu is professor of anthropology and director of African Studies at the University of Illinois at Urbana. Born in Nigeria, Dr. Uchendu's field research has included work among native Americans, as well as in West and East Africa. He was once Director of the Makerere Institute of Social Research in Uganda and has since also served as president of the African Studies Association of the United States. His work in anthropology has covered a wide spectrum – including economic anthropology, state-formation, rural change and political culture.

Godfrey N. Uzoigwe is professor of history at the University of Michigan and a member of the faculty of the Center for Afro-American and African Studies on the same campus. Dr. Uzoigwe obtained his doctorate in history from Oxford University in England, and later taught for a while at Makerere University in Uganda. His books include *Revolution and Revolt in Bunyoro-Kitara, Anatomy of an African Kingdom: A History of Bunyoro-Kitara*, and *Britain and the Conquest of Africa: The Age of Salisbury*. Dr. Uzoigwe is a Nigerian.

Warren Weinstein is associate professor of political science at the State University of New York, Oswego. He has travelled extensively in Africa, and has paid special attention to French speaking countries in the continent. He edited and co-authored *Chinese and Soviet Aid to Africa* and also co-authored *The Pattern of African Decolonization*. In his empirical research he has paid particular attention to Rwanda and Burundi when conditions have permitted. His other interests have included the political sociology of human rights in Third World countries.

Claude E. Welch Jr., Professor of Political Science at the State University of New York at Buffalo, has a long-standing academic interest in the political role of the military. Among his recent books on this subject are *Civilian Control of the Military* (State University of New York Press, 1976), *Military Role and Rule* (Duxbury Press, 1974), and *Soldier and State in Africa* (Northwestern University Press, 1970). Dr. Welch served for many years as the Chairman of the African Studies Committee at the State University of New York at Buffalo, and has been chosen to the Editorial Board of *African Studies Review*.